Boston Buddies

Boston Buddies

*Boston Marathon 2018:
Inspirational stories about
overcoming life's challenges
one mile at a time*

Vince Varallo

Foreword by Larry Rawson

Dedication

Dedicated to my wife Renee, for putting up with all my craziness over the past 9 years since I started running.

Acknowledgements

I would like to thank all the runners that contributed their stories for the book. You are what makes the "Boston Buddies" so special.   Also, thank you to Dave McGillivray for allowing me to interview him about his experience at the 2018 Boston Marathon, Larry Rawson for contributing the Foreword, and Katherine Switzer for all the encouraging words and contributions you have made to the Boston Buddies. Thank you also to Ian Eckersley for helping gather stories for the book in faraway Australia!

Table of Contents

Foreword

By Larry Rawson, two-time national and two-time regional Emmy award winner for track and field, and sports journalism commentary.

A summer marathon in the Antarctic came to Boston on April 16, 2018. The dichotomies that occurred in the race are truly hard to comprehend. Our international telecast went out to 175 countries in the world and they were spectators to the craziest Boston Marathon in at least 30 years, some say ever, and kept them riveted to their screens. As you read the stories of many of the runners in this book, the facts that occurred are hard to believe. The weather forecast for Boston and the vicinity issued just before the start of the race that day was the following:

1. Temperature 38 degrees.
2. Rain expected the entire morning varying from light to heavy all along the race course right in to Boston.
3. Wind between 15 to 25 mph with gusts to 40 mph from east to east south east, in other words a blustering head wind for the entire race

When the race started in Hopkinton the officials announced it was 38 degrees with the wind steady at about 21 mph. It was raining, and the wind chill put the real temperature at 28 degrees. Athletes from all 50 states, 109 countries, and 29,960 entries in assorted weather gear, headed to the starting line. Twenty-three athletes from the elite field did not finish the race including past champion Buzenesh Deba, American record holder Deena Kastor, and one of the early leaders Mamitu Daska. On the men's side, two-time Boston champion Lelisa Desisa and Galen Rupp tapped out during the race. Molly Huddle said she felt "frozen" at one point in the race. Shalane Flanagan felt it was the most brutal conditions she'd ever run in. Desi Linden, who won the race, said that as early as 2 to 4 miles into the race, she didn't think she would be able to finish! Tatianna McFadden put 2 layers of garbage bags under her uniform and wore plastic gloves in her victory. Her time was 31 minutes slower than what she has covered the course in her past victories. When she finished, her legs were purple from the cold. Marcel Hug, the men's wheelchair champion was 30 minutes slower than what he had accomplished in prior Boston's. I was struck watching his interview on our international telecast after the race, how difficult it was for him to coherently talk about the experience. In actuality, over 50% of the elite field did not finish the race.

For all my experience over the decades I've been honored to commentate on Boston, I can't remember 2 athletes being as aggressive as Geoffrey Kirui and Yuki Kawauchi were given the adverse conditions. Kirui led the parade of the royalty for much of the race, acting like he was impregnable to the viciousness of the day. I am amazed that he didn't tuck in behind those around him and let them break the wind for him and commented about that several times. The #2 ranked marathoner in the world almost defeated the elements. In the end however, the weather was the winner. His last few miles were really painful, and he faded badly but held on for 2nd place.

Yuki Kawauchi was from another planet. He surged away from the lead pack despite the strong headwinds, constant rain and wind chill throughout the race, which was right around freezing. He would fade back into the pack and 10 to 15 minutes later surge again. I kept wondering when he was going to crash and burn but it never happened. Boston was his third marathon in less than 2 months. Go figure. In February and March, he had run 2:11 and 2:14, winning both, then ran Boston! Stunning.

The epitaph of the 2018 Boston Marathon contains some startling anecdotes:

1. The Wellesley Carter Memorial United Methodist Church on the race course was so concerned with conditions that they opened their doors to the runners offering relief from the rain and freezing temperatures, providing hot coffee and food.
2. Eighty-one people were hospitalized.
3. 2,500 received medical attention.

I mentioned the dichotomy that existed in this race. Consider this after what you've just read. The 2018 Boston Marathon had more runners re-qualify for Boston than the 2017 marathon, which was dry but much hotter. The elites ran much slower than the middle of the pack runners in the 2018 race. I averaged the previous 5-year times and compared it to this year's finishing place and its corresponding time.

Place	1st	10th	100th	1,000	5,000	10,000
Women's slower by	-17:48	-16:24	-0:32	-0:32	-1:52	-12:32
Men's slower by	-5:45	-12:10	-3:18	-0:46	-2:42	-7:47

Note how well the middle of the pack and slower runners ran vs the elites.

A few last thoughts; running in hot weather debilitates the body much more than the cold. Larger packs of runners in the middle of the race may have saved people from the headwind. All in all, it was truly an amazing day in Boston.

Introduction

April 16, 2018, 26,948 runners huddled up in the little town of Hopkinton Massachusetts 26.2 miles away from the Boston Marathon finish line. The weather forecast called for 38-degree temperatures, two inches of rain, a sustained 15 to 25 miles per hour head wind, and a real feel temperature below freezing. But that was nothing compared to the challenges that many of these runners faced on their journey to the start line. Cancer, ALS, HIV, autism, and divorce are some of the challenges you'll read about that these runners had to overcome to be able to participate in one of the most  prestigious marathons in the world. No one was going to let the weather stand in their way of running a race that meant so much to them in their own unique way.

We weren't quite sure what was in store for us as we were about to trek through the famous course that has broken hearts and crowned heroes, but there was no way we weren't going to give it our best. Little did everyone know that this year a Japanese school administrator would win the men's race. A nurse anesthetist and a mom of three would place second and third in the women's race. The 2018 Boston Marathon was the year of the underdog. Regular people like you and me who keep showing up every time we get knocked down. It's amazing what you can accomplish when you don't give up.

I'm from Philadelphia and the movie Rocky was based here. There's a quote from Rocky that sums up my thoughts about the people who took on one of the toughest Boston Marathons in recent history.

"The world ain't all sunshine and rainbows. It's a very mean and nasty place and I don't care how tough you are it will beat you to your knees and keep you there permanently if you let it. You, me, or nobody is going to hit as hard as life. But it ain't about how hard ya hit. It's about how hard you can get hit and keep moving forward. How much you can take and keep moving forward. That's how winning is done.", Rocky Balboa

Keep reading and you'll see how winning was done, and hopefully find some inspiration from the grit and determination of the people who made the 2018 Boston Marathon the stuff that legends are made of.

Boston Buddies

Before jumping into everyone's story, let me explain the origin of the "Boston Buddies." When training for a marathon you tend to spend a lot of time alone. But when training for Boston, it is like being on a deserted island. Anyone that is the significant other of a marathon runner knows that we go into hibernation mode when we train. Training typically consists of 5, 6, or even 7 days a week of running for about 18 weeks. Some runners run 100 miles per week! You can pretty much forget about a social life because weekends are typically reserved for long runs of up to 22 miles or so. Early Friday and Saturday nights are common for marathon runners because they are either tired from running that day or need to get up early the next morning. Often, the spouses of marathon runners are considered a marathon widow or widower. In other words, both the marathon and the family of a marathoner sacrifice a lot to make it to the starting line of the Boston Marathon.

On November 21, 2016 I was goofing around on Facebook reading some posts on the official Boston Marathon Facebook page. I was looking for motivation and comradery as I was coming back from an injury and planning to start training for the 2017 Boston Marathon. I thought maybe I could find some fellow runners and we could encourage each other during our training as only we know what we are really going through. I posted a simple comment on the marathon's Facebook page. "Is there a Facebook group dedicated to those training for the 2017 race? If not, I'd like to start one, I could use the motivation." I immediately had three replies, Rob Fried, Duane Watts, and Ron Joseph. All were interested. I quickly created a group called "Boston Marathon Training" and invited these three guys that I didn't know.

Rob was the first to join and he invited a bunch of class A runners including John Hadcock, Tim Moley, Jim Murray, Yvonne Leippert, and Dolores Doman just to name a few. It was a small and intimate group in its infancy. However, the group had a different feel to it. I know runners are different, and those that qualify for Boston are unique. We sacrifice a lot to qualify and usually at the expense of our social lives, friends and family. But now we had a group that I felt instantly connected to and we all understood and respected each other for what we had accomplished. We all had a shared goal and there was something special growing in the group. We were small but posted a lot to motivate each other.

In early January of 2017 Tim Moley posted a video of himself on a treadmill. He was giving words of encouragement to everyone, talking about his knee surgery and how he was fighting to get back into shape to run in April. At the end of the video he put a challenge out there for everyone to post an "intro video" telling the group why they run. Personally, I really don't like posting videos of myself and didn't think people would do it. But he was persistent and kept posting videos. And you know what, other runners starting to do the same and I must admit, it really changed the group. It's one thing to see a picture of someone but when you hear them speak it changes your perspective on things. And then Mandy Becker posted her intro video and it was at that moment that I knew we weren't just a group of runners, we were a place people could go for support, comfort, and understanding. You'll read about Mandy's 2018 Boston Marathon experience soon, but her intro video was a tear-jerking story about her childhood and how she had such great memories with her dad and how he was her biggest cheerleader. He had since passed, and she saw running as a connection with her dad. There was true emotion in her video and she left it all out there. The group changed that day. Others started posting intro videos and they were emotional. I remember telling my wife that the group morphed into a much closer-knit family than I could have imagined.

What also started happening was people were realizing they had similar problems, whether it be a divorce, a disease, the loss of a loved one, etc. Someone else had a similar story and they could find strength in knowing that someone else had already gone through what they were experiencing but found a way to continue marching towards their dream. Although we were still only a handful of people, you could tell we were blossoming into something more than just a disconnected group of runners in a Facebook group.

Little by little, other people started posting intro videos. Some were funny, some were tear jerkers. But for whatever reason people were comfortable posting intimate details about their life to this group, and they found so much support from all the members encouraging them to never give up on their dream. There isn't much that you will go through in life that someone hasn't already experienced. This group seemed to be an outlet that connected people with similar goals, but equally similar problems, and it was great to see that people could rebound from whatever problems they were facing. Personally, I started running when I was going through my divorce. Well, turns out a lot of people started running when they were going through their divorce. It was helpful to hear other stories and see that people can still succeed in life after going through such uncertain times.

Since then we have added lots of members, and you'll read some of their stories in this book. Women who beat breast cancer, men with HIV, a non-verbal autistic runner, widows and widowers are just a few of the members that found their way to the start line of the 2018 Boston Marathon. My hope is you will find inspiration in what you read and realize that obtaining your goals, whether running related or anything else in life, takes hard work, persistence, and a never ever give up attitude. Oh, and remember Tim Moley who I mentioned earlier, he had to have full knee replacement surgery in March of 2018 and missed running Boston. But, in September of 2018, just six months after surgery, he defied all odds and ran the Erie marathon, and qualified by over 6 minutes. That is some real inspiring stuff right there! So sit back and enjoy their stories and I hope to see you in Boston.

Lori Riggles, Bib 29070

Ramer, AL, 50, 5:52:44

I did not expect to be struck by a truck while running on April 17, 2016. I was a lifelong runner who was training for my ultimate goal, to run the Boston Marathon. Instead, I was being taken by life flight to the nearest hospital. Running with thoughts of negative splits was preempted by seizures, and resuscitation was completed three times to save my life. Gasping for air at mile twenty was replaced by the inability to breath on my own. Unconscious for five days with little  hope for recovery, I suffered multiple fractures to my pelvis, vertebrae, and wrist. There were countless injuries on the right side of my body and a massive head wound, as it was split wide open from the impact. I was not expected to live, but miracles can take place in your life when you least expect it. Little did I know, exactly one year from that painful day, not only would I be running again, but I would be running the marathon of my dreams, the Boston Marathon.

After countless surgeries, I became conscious, and soon realized that I was incapable of any physical activity. The pain was excruciating and beyond anything I had ever experienced. Running had once been a coping mechanism that I had used daily to navigate the turmoil of a difficult childhood, along with the positive moments that had filled my life. Now, I was unable to walk, write my name, or even feed myself. As I endured physical, cognitive, and occupational therapy, I wondered if I would ever recover.

My prognosis was grim, but I had the support that I needed to undergo what was the most physically challenging year of my life. The medical staff that saved my life were beyond comparison. My daughters put their own lives on hold to take care of me. My brother talked to me about both of us running a marathon together as I lay dying. My son, who studied for his college finals by my hospital bed told me constantly that I "would get through this." As I lay in a coma, he raised the money for the best physical rehabilitation beyond what insurance would cover because he believed that I would be capable of running a marathon a year later.

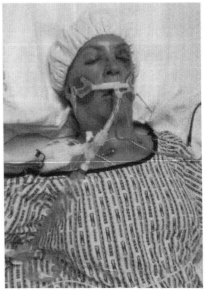

Therapy continued throughout the summer, as did additional surgeries. I had to relearn everything physically, and to retrain every muscle. I remember that tying my shoe was once an insurmountable goal. Due to the multiple injuries in my hand and right side, what I once took for granted as a simple task, was seemingly impossible. As tears filled my eyes, my therapist told me what I have said to my students over and over again- "there is more than one way to learn something." I was then taught to tie my shoes in a different way, that my injured, broken body was capable of.

Tears would fill my eyes, as I would try repeatedly to complete the latest endeavor. I would often fail, over and over again. I refused to let pain take over me. Although, at times, it was extremely challenging. In times of difficulty, when I fell flat on my face and realized that getting up was so much more difficult than remaining on the ground; those who were closest to me inspired me to lift myself up precariously again and again and again. After what seemed like an infinite number of attempts to lift my arm or to write a word, I would know that I could prevail.

I am a teacher. Three things that I teach my students helped me heal and grow stronger: perseverance, never giving up, and work ethic. I would have never guessed how important those principles would be in my own life. Persistence came into play, as I worked diligently on basic tasks with physical and occupational therapists. Every day was a victory in some manner, and I would make a list of things that I was grateful for. My focus was on the positive moments of each day, rather than the pain that I was enduring and how difficult my recovery was. I wanted to be an example to the children that I try to inspire to never give up until they reach their goals.

It was a special moment in my life when I learned to walk again. I knew if I was able to walk, I would eventually be able to run. The people who worked with me refused to let me give up and inspired me every step of the way. I looked up to other runners, believing that I would one day be capable of running again. Many times, it was tempting to give up on the different types of physical obstacles that I was going through. I felt if I pushed through those obstacles and saw those moments as something to overcome, it would be beneficial in my recovery, giving the physical aspects of my recovery my best effort, I felt, was important. I appreciate how far I've come.

I knew that the prayers and encouragement of so many people had gotten me to the life changing moment when I ran that first 200 meters. It took me an hour to complete, and it was a true, painful struggle as I was aware of my healing bones and muscles with each step. I have never been prouder in my life. Pace, which I once felt was important, no longer amounted to anything. I never looked back and have been on a running streak ever since that day: June 18, 2016. Why? Because I can run again!

Team for Kids gave me the extraordinary opportunity to run the Boston Marathon on the one-year anniversary of my accident. When I joined Boston Buddies in 2016; I was inspired by the amazing runners who never doubted that I would be able to run the iconic race or overcome all the difficulties that I have experienced from my accident. The positive support of those runners was a key element in my recovery and my refusal to give up.

When I was 13 years old, I had the impossible goal of running the Boston Marathon. Seeing a picture of Kathrine Switzer's iconic run in Boston changed my life. I decided right then and there that I wanted to run the race. On April 17, 2017, the one-year anniversary of my accident, I ran the Boston Marathon for the first time. Running the Boston Marathon on that day will always represent a triumph that I never would have believed possible. My journey from wheelchair to Boston Marathon shows that it is possible to overcome adversity, despite how overwhelming your circumstances.

As I stood on the Boston Marathon starting line in 2018, I reflected on the triumphs and the challenges that I had overcome. I remembered that I was not expected to be able to walk, yet I was running again. Little did I know that Boston 2018 would end up being the biggest challenge of my journey. The arthritis which had formed from my previous injuries was so flared up that I wondered how I was ever going to cross the finish line. These thoughts and other thoughts of pain were circulating through my head at the start line. How on earth was I going to run the Boston 2018 marathon when the pain was so intense that I felt like I was going to collapse? As I began my first mile, tears filled my eyes and I prayed to finish somehow, someway. Memories helped me reach the finish line. Thoughts of those who prayed for me. Reflecting on the students I wanted to inspire. A remembrance of my family who were with me every step of the way and therapists who worked endlessly with me. Lastly, I had my own goals for myself and encouragement from my Boston Buddies who believed in me before I believed in myself. Yes, the weather was something that I have never run in before. Yes, the pain was so intense, and I felt like I was going to collapse. None of that mattered. What truly mattered was that I was going to finish that race and I was going to cross the Boston Marathon 2018 finish line as part of my journey. Crossing that finish line will always be looked back on as one of the greatest moments of my life. No, it was not my fastest time or my greatest moment. The most important thing was that I finished the Boston Marathon 2018, and that in itself was a true triumph!

The Boston Marathon will always remind me of the beautiful journey in my life from a traumatic accident to running marathons. As a young child, dreaming of the Boston Marathon, I never would have imagined my journey to the finish line. Yet, on my unexpected path, I have obtained the strength, courage, and fulfillment that were needed to bring my life to the victorious moment of crossing that Boston Marathon finish line in 2018! Running the Boston Marathon in 2018 for Kathrine Switzer's Team Fearless was an amazing experience that always remain the most memorable marathon of my life.

Team Alie, Bib 1475

Great Neck, NY, 27, 2:56:54

"Team Alie", also known as #TeamSAlieBoyd; Alex (Alie) Schneider, Boyd Carrington, and Sal Nastasi represents three men drawn together by unselfish acts of kindness and a love of the sport of running.

Alie is 27 years old and has autism. Autism is a broad range of conditions characterized by challenges with social skills, repetitive behaviors, speech and nonverbal communication. Autism affects about 1 in 59 children. Both Alie and his identical twin brother Jamie have severe autism. The Schneider twins are both nonverbal. They do not communicate when thirsty, tired, hurt, or cold. Boyd Carrington and Sal Nastasi are Alie's coaches and running partners and were Alie's guides as they trekked through the Boston Marathon course in those historical conditions on April 16th. Guides who run the marathon with an athlete do not get a bib number or an official finish time. Both Boyd and Sal had devoted months training Alie, and this was Alie's race. From the early hours before the marathon and throughout the day, his guides assumed a huge responsibility taking care of Alie. While on the course, they needed to keep him on pace, hydrate him, be aware of his body temperature, and be prepared for any unforeseen events along the way.

Alie started running when he was 15 years old. His parents, Robyn and Allan, could tell he had a passion for running. When he ran, they saw a transformation; almost Zen-like from the very beginning. It was a look of euphoria. Both boys started running in special needs running clubs, where they were paired with seasoned volunteer runners. They ran in a few local races, but Jamie started having some behaviors, so Allan thought, "Let me try running with Jamie; I can keep up with him and I can gauge his behaviors better than anyone." Allan has MS, so running has helped him cope with the effects of the disease. Soon after, Robyn laced up her shoes for the first time and found running therapeutic to lessen the detrimental effects of chemotherapy from breast cancer. Robyn and Allan would alternate running and racing with Jamie. Aside from local races, Jamie ran 8 marathons, including 4 Boston, all with his dad. Running became the focal point of their lives and has been a source of strength as they face the challenges of day-to-day life.

They soon met Kevin McDermott, a USATF certified trainer who took on the challenge to coach Alie, and he remained his coach for 11 years. Kevin set the foundation that has shaped Alie into the runner he is today. When Kevin first started training him, he realized the first major hurdle was pacing. Alie would take off like a rocket each and every time he ran. and stayed on that pace regardless of how far they were running. Sometimes that pace was a 6- or 7-minute mile. Kevin tried various ways to slow him down. At first, he tried holding out a branch while they ran so Alie wouldn't go past it. He also tried holding onto his shirt and would pull on it to get him to ease up. Eventually he discovered that running diagonally in front of Alie was the most effective and safest option for both of them. Kevin trained and ran with Alie in close to 200 races. However, about a year before the 2018 Boston Marathon, Kevin moved with his family to Costa Rica. Robyn and Allan needed to find a new coach that had the heart and commitment to take over so that Alie could pursue his passion to run Boston again.

Boyd frequently "ran" into Alie and Kevin when they would train together. Like Kevin, Boyd is also a USATF Certified coach. Occasionally he would run with them, and on one occasion, while seeing them during his out and back running routine, he told Kevin that he would be willing to help as a pacer if he ever needed someone to run a marathon with Alie. Kevin then mentioned this to Robyn, and in May of 2017 Boyd decided to help coach Alie. Boyd is a competitive guy and didn't quite know what to expect when he first started running with Alie, but he thought he would give it a shot. At first, he admits, he didn't really enjoy it because it was unstructured, as he was co-coaching Alie with another runner. He contemplated quitting, but his girlfriend Tara Wilson suggested that he read Robyn's book about her boys, *"Silent Running-Our Family's Journey to the Finish Line with Autism"*. Boyd remembers reading about total strangers helping the twins have a beautiful and meaningful life and he realized the truth in an old saying, "It takes a village to raise a child." Reading her book changed his perspective about coaching Alie and he wanted to do something rewarding and beneficial for the Schneider family. So he took control and slowly started adding some structure around Alie's training. He asked Robyn to buy Alie a Garmin watch with a heart rate monitor. When Boyd trains a runner he'll ask how they feel, because obviously, you can't ask someone to do something without knowing how they feel. But in Alie's case, he cannot verbalize how he feels, so the heart rate monitor was one indication of Alie's fitness level. "Alie never questions what he is instructed to do, so as a coach you really need to pay attention so as not to exert Alie and cause an injury. Alie gives 200% every day and his natural instinct is to go out, wind up, and run fast without thinking how far he has to go". Boyd wanted to make sure that he didn't burn him out.

Sal met Robyn 10 years ago when she started a race for autism awareness for her sons. Sal is the lead singer and plays guitar in his band, "Ready in 10". His band played at the race that day. Later, he would often see Robyn, Alie and Kevin on the Bethpage bike path. Sal would run in the middle of the day, the same time she would run on her own, while Alie was running with Kevin.

When Alie was training for the 2017 NYC Marathon, Boyd asked Sal if he would run the second half with them. He agreed, and they ran an amazing race, pacing Alie to the finish line in 2:50:05! He was so excited and energized about Alie's performance, but he couldn't commit the time to train him on a regular basis. Then he read Robyn's book. He called her up and said, "Your book changed my life. I want to run with Alie and help with his training. What do you need?" They started running three times a week in every weather condition. Sal thought, "When you train, you need to train in all conditions because you never know what the conditions will be on race day." In March 2018, Sal ran a 25k race with Alie in the snow, finishing in a time of 1:35:03 which in hindsight really helped them prepare for what they were about to embark on in Boston.

Alie is no rookie when it comes to running marathons. This was his 6th Boston marathon and 18th marathon overall. His PR is the 2017 New York City Marathon in a time of 2:50:05. Obviously, he's one tough runner like the rest of the people in this book. Boyd and Sal are both incredible runners as well. Sal ran Boston in 2013 in a time of 2:35:26 and Boyd's PR, in 2014 is 2:36:26. The goal for Boston was to run sub 2:50, but given the weather conditions, that goal was thrown out the window and finishing safely was Boyd and Sal's number one concern.

Heading into the weekend, Boyd was hoping the weather wasn't going to be as predicted. Saturday was nice, Sunday was misty and chilly, so he was hoping marathon Monday would be the same. If it were they would be fine. But as we all know, Mother Nature had other plans for these three! Sal was stalking the forecast and realized Monday would be the worst-case scenario. He admitted that if he wasn't running with Alie he might not have run at all. As they rode to Hopkinton the morning of the marathon, he remembers looking out the window at the freezing rain and snow and thought, "What are we doing?!" He understood the toughest part was that it wasn't about him, it was about protecting Alie and making sure he is safe and comfortable. "Alie will just follow what you do; he doesn't react to the rain or any weather conditions for that matter." Sal just planned to make him as happy and content as possible. Robyn and Allan had been checking the weather starting from ten days out. They were prepared; with ponchos, rain jackets, throwaway clothes, gloves, hand warmers, hats, you name it. Robyn knew that Alie didn't pay much attention to the weather, so she was hoping his love for running would carry him through.

Robyn remembers being worried about the new Nike Vapor Fly 4% shoes they just bought Alie for the marathon. They were so thin and light, and she was concerned they would fall apart. After consulting with Boyd and Sal, and given the conditions, they all agreed it was best to stick with what they felt would be best and chose the Saucony Kinvara for Alie's race day shoes. Team Alie had decided to race in matching clothing. Boyd thought it would be best to wear shorts, so they decided that black shorts, an orange tank top with "Team Alie" across the front, a long sleeve black running shirt for under the tank, black running hat, black gloves, and black compression leg sleeves would be their uniform.

Race morning was finally here! Robyn and Allan were excited but very worried, as Alie had never experienced such harsh weather conditions quite like this. They can distinctly remember hearing the hotel windows rattling that morning and realized the weather people may have actually gotten it right. It was going to be miserable. Robyn rented a limo to drive Alie, Boyd and Sal to Boston Common where she took pictures; tearfully kissed him good-bye and watched as he boarded the bus for the long journey to the starting line in Hopkinton. Boyd remembers riding to Hopkinton and seeing all the trees that had fallen or snapped from the previous storm. He knew the conditions would be bad. But when they arrived at the Athlete's Village it wasn't anything remotely close to what he was expecting. It was like Woodstock. There was just mud everywhere. People were walking around with plastic bags; there was so much rain, and the village was a complete and utter mess. His feet were frozen before the race even started, and he remembers trying to walk and how difficult it was to move around in ankle deep mud. Most people were just standing around under the tent. Boyd had run Boston 3 other years, and these were by far the most miserable conditions he had ever experienced. Team Alie found a place in the tent to huddle up and stay close to each other for warmth. Boyd remembers he couldn't put anything down because it would just get ruined.

Alie qualified on his own for the marathon with his NYC time, but he also runs in the Mobility Impaired division, so it was a relief when they were finally able to leave Athlete's village and start heading to the start corrals even before Wave 1. Alie never really knows how far he will be running at the beginning of a race. Whether a 5K or a marathon, he just gets on the start line ready to run. He is completely dependent on his coaches for pacing him based on the distance he will be running. Robyn and Allan believed he knew this was a special race and a long one, having run the marathon several times before. And once they saw the twinkle in his eye and the calmness in his demeanor, they knew he was excited. Boyd believes, "Although Alie doesn't speak, he is very intelligent. He can sense from other people's behavior. He picks up on their energy and excitement." On marathon day they could all tell he wanted to run.

They all walked/jogged to the start, found some port-a-potties and were able to get Alie to go to the bathroom. Sal thought, "Thumbs up, good day, one less thing to worry about." They finally arrived in their corral just after the National Anthem. Sal was not nervous about the race. He knew it would be a challenge, but "Once you get running you're just running. You're doing the same stuff, it just sucks a little more."

Boyd remembers thinking they trained all winter for this and felt confident they were prepared. The announcer finally released their wave and now it was showtime. Just as they started, a funny thing happened. In first 800 meters Boyd spotted a $20 bill and quickly stopped to pick it up. He caused a bottleneck, and a bunch of runners started yelling. Boyd later read a blog about a guy who saw the $20 bill but didn't pick it up. But Boyd couldn't resist! Sal thought he was crazy. Alie stops on a dime, so if Boyd stops he stops. And he did. Boyd and Sal knew they needed to get moving again before someone stumbled on them and knocked them down. So they took off again together, and in the first mile, running through sleet and fierce winds, suddenly Alie did something they never saw before. There was a steep downhill and Alie grabbed on to both of them and locked arms. They ran like that for about a half mile. Sal was talking him down saying, "It's all right". When they finally got him to a flat area they separated, and Sal was telling Alie, "You'll be OK." This was an emotional moment for Sal, realizing that Alie grabbed onto them because he trusted them to keep him safe. Now that they were separated, Team Alie got into their arrowhead formation where Alie would run in the middle. Their plan was for Alie to tuck in behind them while they blocked the elements. Boyd thought, "Alie always wants to run fast. The challenge is holding him back. He doesn't understand that these conditions are grueling, and we'll have to take it easy."

Keeping Alie at an appropriate pace throughout the marathon exerts a great deal of energy. Even in the arrowhead formation, he invariably tries to pass them. So while one of them reins him back to the appropriate pace, the other zigzags to the water stops, grabs one for themselves and one for Alie. This enables Alie not to exert himself zigzagging past runners to the water stops. This tag-team approach allows them to stay on course to maintain their pace. If one gets a cramp, the other keeps Alie on pace while the other stretches. Keeping Alie safe and with them the entire race is a number one major concern because he could run off at any time.

People were cheering for them and a few runners moved closer and ran with them. Alie was pumped and kept pushing the pace. But Sal and Boyd both thought, "Around mile 11 or 12 we knew conditions wouldn't allow for a PR and it took a lot for us to slow him down." They were passing a lot of runners. Alie doesn't understand pace, he just gives it all. They were running based on feel and the signs for a fast race just weren't there.

When they got to Wellesley, the girls were screaming his name, and he was smiling. They could tell he was happy. Gusts of wind and rain were pelting them in the face and they were just laughing. Boyd and Sal kept thinking that their number one priority was to take care of Alie as best as they could. At mile 13 Boyd knew it wasn't going to be a PR day, but he knew Alie would never give up. He knew he had to try and rein him in.

The next big milestone was getting to the Newton Hills. Sal remembers turning the corner at the fire station just at the start of entering Newton and approaching the first hill thinking they are good to go. Then came that second hill and Boyd said, "Is this Heartbreak?" Sal was thinking "Uh oh", because there were two more hills before Heartbreak. Just before getting to Heartbreak, Sal turned to Alie and said, "Come on buddy, we got this, WE GOT THIS!" Just at that moment, Boyd needed the bathroom, so he jumped over a fence and left the team. He told them to keep going and he would catch back up. So then it was just Sal and Alie. Sal did everything he could to motivate Alie saying, "Alright buddy, it's me and you. After this last hill it's all downhill from here. Come on buddy, COME ON BUDDY!" Alie was actually pushing the pace as they ran up Heartbreak Hill. But at mile 22 Sal could tell Alie was starting to slow down. Around mile 23, Sal kept talking to him and encouraging him. Usually he must hold him back to maintain their pace, but at that moment he was encouraging him to go faster. He looked at his watch and when he saw that they were running 6:50s, he decided to run Alie's pace, as he could tell he was feeling fatigued. By then Boyd caught up to them and Team Alie was intact. They were both thinking the same thing, "Let's just get him to the finish safely."

Team Alie ran the last four miles at a 7, 8, then 9-minute pace. For most people that is still incredibly fast. As they ventured through Boston and made the right on Hereford and left on Boylston, the crowd was cheering loudly. Alie ran a brave and very strong race. Team Alie finished in 2:56:54!

Once they crossed the finish line however, Sal remembers the next hour as one of the worst hours of the day. Boyd was in a daze. Once you stop moving if you weren't covered up immediately your core temperature drops. Boyd was fine as soon as they finished but as they were walking

around the finish area he became weak. The medics put him in a wheelchair, but he was craving a Starbucks, so he hopped out of the wheelchair, jumped a fence, and was going to use his lucky $20 to buy coffee. His hands were shaking so badly he couldn't get the money out of his pocket. He gave the barista his jacket and the woman said, "Take it, it's free." Meanwhile, back at the finish line, Sal was alone with Alie. He had his arm around him waiting to get his clothes, trying to warm him up. He just wanted to get him to his parents. They stood there for 30-40 minutes. The medical volunteers eventually came up to them and asked if they needed medical attention. Sal said, "This is an autistic runner and I need to get his clothes." "They hurried us along and we finally got our dry clothes and made our way to the changing area." Alie was freezing. Sal couldn't bend his fingers and said it was torture getting clothes on Alie. He couldn't even get his phone out of his bag to call Robyn because his hands were so frozen. Luckily Robyn called, and he was able to say, "Hey Siri, pick up the phone." He told Robyn they were OK and getting their clothes. Once she knew where they were she made her way to meet up with them.

Allan was with Jamie waiting back at the hotel while Robyn and Tara worked their way through the streets to find them. It was chaos. The gusty rain hadn't let up and the wind was howling. The streets had barricades blocking them from where they had to go, creating more of a delay to get to Alie. At one point Robyn pleaded with the security guards to let them through. It was a nightmare. When they finally met up with them, Alie couldn't move and was frozen to the bone. Luckily, they were right in front of the medic tent and they brought him in to warm up. The medics laid him down, wrapped him in warming blankets, gave him fluids, and did whatever they could to keep him warm. As Robyn stood next to Alie who was covered in layers of blankets from head to toe, with only his face peering through, all she could see was Alie smiling! He had that special twinkle in his eye, the one that confirms his love of running. She couldn't stop kissing him. Robyn held onto him tightly, steadying him as they walked back to their hotel. Robyn and Allan were bursting with pride. His performance was indeed impressive, and a true testament to his unwavering endurance and passion for running.

Oh, and by the way, Alie finished first in his division!

Some final thoughts from Team Alie:

Robyn: "Each time Alie or Jamie cross the finish line of a race, my heart is full and bursting with pride. When they run, I know that they are fulfilling their passion. Boyd, Sal, and Kevin have selflessly devoted themselves to enriching Alie's life by training him to reach his goals, and I'm grateful."

Allan: "When Alie and Jamie are running on the course alongside all the other runners, they are no longer defined by their autism. They are just two runners fulfilling their love for running. Their story has inspired people all over the world and that is so gratifying."

Boyd: "When coaching an athlete, be sure to understand the athlete. With Alie, I can read his body language. That has helped me immensely to structure his training and increase his level of performance. He is strong and determined to finish fast, and that's why coaching him is so rewarding."

Sal: "You can never be as proud of yourself as you can be for someone that you're helping. It's amazing to watch Alie as he progresses. Though the day was tough, it was great to soak in the end of the race with Alie and Boyd...well worth the suffering!!"

To read more about Alie and Jamie Schneider, go to: www.autismrunners.com

Marty Clark, Bib 9264

Portland, ME, 55, 3:23:50

Normally, I travel to Boston for the marathon with my friends, my run squad. I always stay at the Sheraton. This year was different because I went by myself. I saw the weather forecasts and wasn't worried about the rain, I knew I just needed to focus on the task. If I listened to the communications from the BAA about how to prepare I would be fine. I dressed in layers for race day. I wore throw away track pants, rain gear, and a rain jacket. I bought two $1 ponchos from advice on the Boston Buddies page and figured I would wear one to the bus and one to the start. I wore vinyl gloves over the top of my cotton running gloves, a baseball hat, and spare sneakers I could throw away. Even with all this preparedness I was still soaked before I even loaded on to the bus to Hopkinton.

Once I boarded the bus, I sat next to a woman from Japan who now lived in New York. She had run the NY Marathon three times and we struck up a conversation. She told me in broken English that she thought some guy named Yuki would win. "Yuki will win! Yuki!" she repeated. I must be honest, I had no idea who he was. She was confident he was going to win, and he did!

When I boarded the bus and found my seat, I accidentally put my spare shoes, the ones I planned on running in, on the floor. I forgot that school busses have their heaters on the floor. When we reached Hopkinton, my shoes were scalding hot, and all I could think was, "I hope I didn't just ruin them or cause my feet to feel too hot once I put them on for the race." Oh well, I needed to move on.

Heading to the start I could see the headquarters of Outside Interactive. Their office is smack in the middle of the start line around corral 4. The Boston Buddies held a contest to raise money for the Second Step and twelve lucky runners won the VIP treatment at their headquarters. The VIP  treatment included a warm place out of the storm, hot coffee, and breakfast foods. Who knew how valuable that would be this year! I remember being a bit envious, thinking about my buddies in the confines of a warm office as I trekked down to Athlete's Village in freezing wind and rain. But there I went. Once I got into the village, it was awful. It was pouring, mud was everywhere. There wasn't a dry patch anywhere to be found. I went to the tent where everyone else was gathering. I went out into the freezing rain to find a port-a-potty. I could see people were going in but weren't coming out. I was looking at social media and saw that people were posting photos of themselves inside the port-a-potty and saying this was their home for the next hour. WTF, this is why I was in line for so long.

I finally heard the call for wave 2 and started heading to my corral. I got to my corral and as they were counting down I heard someone calling my name. It was Hollie Corbet, a local runner from Maine. Finally finding someone I knew pepped me up and got me excited to race.

The announcer said "2 minutes" so I started taking off my layers. I peeled off my poncho, but my arms were still protected from makeshift arm warmers made form leggings at the dollar store. They whisk water better than normal arm warmers. I had on my USA singlet that I usually wear, shorts, and a double Bondi band around my head. Being from the Northeast, I'm used to running in the winter, so I felt I was plenty equipped to run in this weather. The announcer sent us out and off I went. I had nutrition and hydration positioned at two point on the course waiting for me. One was at mile 14 with my Maine Track Club. I prefer not to drink from the cups on the course for various reasons and like having my own hydration. I was very much looking forward to getting to mile 14 and 21 to refuel and see familiar faces.

Somewhere around mile 7 or 8 I had to stop and pee. I remember taking a little extra time to gather myself to turn on my music and get some gum. I was on a BQ pace and was still feeling good. I normally don't stop but for whatever reason, this time I did. I started back on to the course and was running again. Around mile 9 I started running on the right side of the road. Up ahead, I saw runners diverting around something. I couldn't tell why but I noticed that people were running around someone as she floated back and forth. I saw about 20 runners go around her. As I came upon her I thought her tattoos looked familiar, although I never met her in person, once I saw her face I recognized her as Mandy from the Boston Buddies.

I said, "Mandy, it's me Marty from the Boston Buddies. Are you okay?" She just shook her head no. She couldn't talk and tears where pouring down her cheeks. I said, "Do you need medical attention." And she shook her head. It freaked me out that she couldn't talk and all she could do was look at me and cry. I was horrified so many runners knew she was in distress and passed her by. I said, "Mandy, I'm going to get you to the medical tent." I grabbed her arm and threw it over my shoulder and started running with her. She could barely walk let alone run. I wasn't at all concerned that this was going to cost me time, this was just what I had to do right now. I don't know what was keeping her going, it was scary, and her strides weren't even a foot apart. We didn't even talk because the effort was that great. Another runner came up and asked, "Do you need help?" I said, "yes." He grabbed Mandy's other arm and put it around his shoulder and we ran together. We ran until we saw a fire woman and brought Mandy to her. We told her she needed medical attention and the fire woman took it from there. I didn't want to leave her, but she was in good hands now. When I passed her to medical personal I felt Mandy was fearful I was letting her go. I knew she was in good hands because the medical professionals on the course are top notch and they could do more for her than I could. I look back now and keep thinking that if I hadn't made that stop our paths would not have collided and I would have missed Mandy.

I headed back on to the course a bit shaken but continued to focus on the task at hand. Once I reached the Newton hills I saw another Boston Buddy, Heather Lane, with whom I met at a training run on the course three weeks

24

prior. We stuck together to get each other through the hills but then I lost track of her. I then saw two Boston Buddies running together, Paulo Benefico Correia and Sarah Bachand. One of my race photos shows Sarah and I giving a fist pump as we ran together. I ran into a few more from our group including Vince, Kelley Batton Duel, and Carlos Jose Soto Tock. At around mile 24 I met up with my brother David, who lives just off the course. I stopped to see my family, told them that I loved them and got some much-needed hugs. I got back on the course and headed for Boylston St. I finished in 3:23:50, well under my BQ time, so I was pumped.

I crossed the finish line and I didn't see anyone else I knew. Everyone had their hood up on their heat shields, so I couldn't see anyone's face. It took me a long time to pick up my dry clothes at gear pick up. Once I finally picked up my bag, I couldn't move my arms to take off my shirt. One of the awesome volunteers peeled off my soaking wet shirt and helped put on my dry shirt. I was crying not because I couldn't move my hands, but because of the humanity of this your person. They took my rubber gloves off and my hands were dry, but they were so cold, and I couldn't move my fingers. I finally gathered my things and headed to the subway to get to my hotel only 0.4 miles away. Once I got to my hotel I went straight to my room but couldn't get my hotel key out of my bag. The woman in the room next door heard me struggling and came out into the hall. She was expecting her husband. She unzipped my bag, found my wallet, got my key out and opened the door for me. She said she was expecting her husband to return in similar condition. Only in Boston! I then took a scalding hot shower, ate some food, then went to meet my Boston Buddies at Cheers.

Once I got to Cheers, I messaged Mandy's boyfriend Patrick asking how Mandy was doing and let him know who I was. He was so grateful. I'm not a religious guy, but I believe something brought us together that day. I'm just happy that something put me there with Mandy in that moment and I'm sure we'll be lifelong friends.

Mandy Becker, Bib 8660

Clayton, NC, 39

I qualified for the Boston 2018 Marathon by running a 3:11:42 in the 2017 Boston Marathon. I had only run one marathon prior to my BQ and that was the Rock N Roll Raleigh Marathon. I've been running since I was 14 years old and ran in college at UNC Ashville. It's quite  difficult finding time to do the necessary training for Boston being a single mom and full-time aide at a nursing home. I try to follow Hal Higdon's Advanced Marathon plan but must adjust it depending on my schedule or my daughter's schedule. Training typically was done between 5:40 and 6:40 in the morning before I had to get my daughter on the bus and then head to work. I also work every other weekend, so the normal long weekend run can't happen on a regular basis. I did whatever I could to fit training in between all the other responsibilities I have to take care of in my life.

Going into race weekend I was confident I was going to have a great performance. I had a great 24-mile training run at a 7 minute per mile pace. I had a few injuries that I knew would be painful, but nothing I couldn't overcome on race day. I stayed in Framingham and was going to meet up with some fellow runners to car pool to athlete's village. As we were driving to the car pool I remember thinking I just didn't want to get out of the car and my teeth were already chattering. I asked Patrick to just drive me to the start rather than go with the car pool. Driving through the backroads I was looking out the window and saw snow and ice along the roads and I was actually scared. All I could think about was how bad this was going to suck, but I'm the toughest person I know besides my dad. I'm just going to do this just like I do everything in life. I'm going to tough it out. Patrick dropped me off at Hopkinton State Park where yellow school buses were taking runners to athlete's village. Before getting out of the car I put on my make shift poncho made of trash bags, took a quick stop in the port a potty, kissed Patrick good-bye, and boarded the bus.

I can remember sitting on the bus and my teeth where chattering uncontrollably. I had plenty of clothing on to keep me warm, I just couldn't seem to raise my body temperature. I was wearing running shorts, a sports bra, tank top, long sleeve shirt, my trash bag poncho, as well as a Walmart poncho, sweatpants, sweatshirt, and rubber gloves. Once we arrived at athlete's village I got off the bus and trenched my way to the awaiting mud puddles in the middle school field. From the time it took to get off the bus, to the time I got to the field my feet were drenched. I quickly found a port-a-potty and took off my shoes and my toes were blue. It didn't help that I have Raynaud's syndrome, so my fingers and toes were going numb. I put my shoes back on and ventured under the tent to try to escape the rain, but I couldn't escape the water. I was standing against a pole for 2 hours, with my teeth chattering, and my feet completely submerged in water. For 2 hours all I could think about was how horrible this was going to be. The hypothermic process started, and I knew I had it. My arms were folded under the trash bag and by the time they called my wave to leave athlete's village I could barely move my arms. Once I finally made my way to my corral I started saying the Lord's prayer. I was waiting until the last minute possible to start unpeeling my layers and I started to cry as I thought about what the next few hours were going to take out of me. I was so wet and drained that when I felt the urge to pee in the corral, I just went. I was wet anyway so why waste the energy leaving the corral.

When the race started I remember taking off my last layer thinking, "This sucks." As I started running the rain was soaking my shirt and I was being pelted with ice balls. My chest felt like it was collapsing, and it was becoming hard to breathe. Once I got moving on the course I actually did okay running the first few miles. I started out 7:10, 7:15, and 7:20 per mile. But I was absolutely freezing, and my vision was becoming blurry. I really thought I was having a heart attack because I didn't know what was going on with my body. At mile five I knew something was wrong and felt like an elephant was standing on my chest. I kept on running despite it all, thinking I'll warm up. I was still at a 7:30 pace at mile 6, but at mile 7 I didn't know where I was going, and I was just running with the other runners. Once I got to 8 miles I couldn't see my watch or my feet. I thought I was dying, and my chest felt like it was collapsing in on me. By mile 9 my feet were wobbly, and I was bouncing back and forth from the left side to the ride side of the road and I couldn't catch my breathe. I just kept saying to myself I'm not going to quit, I'm not stopping.

At around the 9.5-mile mark I remember looking down thinking I was going to die but someone will find me, so I figured I'd just keep running until I collapse. I felt a hand on top of my shoulder and the voice said "Mandy?" I couldn't see and couldn't focus on anything. I remember hearing, "it's me Marty from Boston Buddies. Are you alright?" I shook my head no. He then asked, "do you need help?" and I shook my head yes. He put my arm around his shoulder and started running with me to get help. Another runner saw us and offered to help and put my other arm over his shoulder. They carried me off the course to the Natick fire department where a woman fire person took me into the fire house. I had a baker cyst on the back of my knee and it had also burst. The firemen immediately took off my long sleeve shirt and put me under three blankets. Marty said, "I don't want to leave you" but I was in good hands and wanted him to continue. He hugged and kissed me and headed back into the race. He saved my life that day even though I had never met him before.

I sat in the fire department for an hour and half. The firemen couldn't get an IV in me because my blood was so cold. I was hyperventilating, I couldn't get warm, and I still couldn't stop shaking. I remember the firemen asking if there was someone to call and at first I said my mom, but no, that's not right she was back home. I then told them 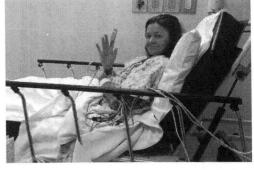 Patrick's number. They called Patrick to let him know I needed help. He drove his car as close to the fire department as possible and walked the rest in the rain and wind. Once he arrived they let him know I needed to get to a hospital. I remember thinking I didn't want to go because Medicaid wouldn't cover me because I was in another state, but I was in no condition to argue. Patrick went in the ambulance with me and they took me to the Framingham hospital.

We arrived at the hospital around 1:00. The ambulance was able to get an IV in me with warm fluids and the hospital covered me with more blankets. At around 5:00 I started feeling better. I remember thinking the race was over and looking at my phone seeing all the texts from people asking if I was okay. Patrick went back to Natick to get his car and by the time he was back I was feeling much better. He asked what I wanted to do and of course I said, "Let's go to Cheers to meet with the Boston Buddies!" I would be sad but what else would I do?

I remember getting to Cheers and seeing Marty thinking this man will forever be my angel and he saved my life. He is an uber nice, wonderful guy. I couldn't wait to just give him a hug for saving my life. If Marty hadn't run by me and stopped to help me I really don't know what would have happened to me. I think it was my dad, coming down watching over me and asking Marty to watch over me. He probably said, "Mandy is going to need some help, send Marty."

We still stay in touch today and I hope we always will. As for Boston, I will go back one day!

Yuki Kawauchi, Bib 11

Kuki, Saitama, JPN, 31, 2:15:58

We all knew it was going to be a cold and rainy race, and I felt a lot more confident about being able to handle it having the experience of the frigid Marshfield Road Runners New Year's Day Marathon behind me. That was very important for my preparation for Boston 2018. As the Patriots Day race went on, I would say they were the toughest and harshest conditions I've ever run in – but in another sense, I told myself that these were the best conditions possible for me. Having run other marathons in other tough conditions that helped me.

In the last part of the race I was telling myself that if I didn't give in to my own weakness I'd finish 2ⁿᵈ, that it would be enough just to earn a medal in the legendary Boston Marathon. But what my agent Brett Larner said to me right before the race kept coming back to me: "This is the day you were born for." I kept pushing forward, making an ally of the bitterly cold Boston rain and headwinds as I ran, my motivation and emotions running high as I told myself, "You were born to run Boston!"

I knew I was in the top two towards the end of the race, but I didn't know if I was second or first. I never gave up. I knew he was up there. I could see him. I ran my own race and I ran him down. When I passed the leader (Kenya's

Geoffrey Kirui) I didn't look to see who it was, and I just kept focus on going forward, forward, forward, running my race and keep going.

Breaking the finish line tape and the flag-raising ceremony afterward were something I will never forget my entire life.

Before the race, I think there was probably not a single person in Boston who thought I would win today. When they played the Japanese national anthem after the marathon it touched me very deeply.

The day after the race I walked by the finish line and runners from all different countries stopped me to say hi and take pictures together. It felt like a dream and I was very, very happy. When I landed back in Japan there was an incredible number of journalists waiting at the airport. When I got to work (in the admin office of a Japanese high school) my boss and colleagues greeted me with an ovation and gave me a cake and a bouquet of flowers. My family, friends and fans all seemed to be surprised and overjoyed. I felt the same way they did. Winning a World Marathon Majors race was a wonderful thing, and the joy I've experienced as a result has been the greatest in my life as an athlete. Becoming the Boston Marathon champion means the greatest recognition among my rivals and fans and among amateur marathon runners worldwide. I've come to realize that this means I must work harder to become a stronger, faster marathoner runner to live up to that recognition.

I think it has been decades since someone who was working a full-time job that had nothing to do with running won the Boston Marathon. I think it means something special that someone just like any other marathon-loving amateur who runs dozens of marathons only because they love doing them was able to earn this victory. I hope that I've given some courage and hope to amateurs around the world who are working hard both at their desks and on the roads.

It was very special to become the first Japanese runner to win here since Toshihiko Seko in 1987 - the same year I was born. I can't help but feel the hand of fate in this.

I will never forget the 2018 Boston Marathon. It was the best crowd support I've had anywhere in the world. Thank you, Boston.

Sarah Sellers, Bib F42

Tucson, AZ, 26, 2:44:04, Women's Second Place Finisher 2018 Boston Marathon.

April 16, 2018 is a day that changed my life forever. I entered the Boston Marathon as a complete unknown - even to myself – but it proved to be the most unforgettable day ever. My brother, Ryan Callister had told me he wanted to run the Boston Marathon, so at the last minute I decided to sign up as I thought it would be fun to run in the historic Boston event at the same time as him.

My training had gone really well heading into the race. My average before Boston was about 90 miles a week. I hit 100 miles a few weeks in a row. It was basically the first good training block I had put together since college in 2013. On the one hand I was excited about what I could do, but I didn't want to set unrealistic expectations and then be disappointed with what happened.

Going into the race my number one goal was the 2020 Olympic Trials 'A' Standard of 2:37. I thought that a stretch goal would have been low 2:30s. Then with the forecast being what it was those goals went out the window. The new goals were just to compete and to push myself and the absolute dream was a Top 15 finish.

I was super nervous a week out from the race as it was only my second marathon. Heading out to Hopkinton on the bus on Patriots Day, I transformed with my nerves going from 'out of control' to being almost completely calm. There were a few other girls on the bus with me from the Boston Athletic Association Elite Team and we agreed to help each other out and work together – a 'Team America' collective agreement.

Early on, it was weird as the pace was slow. I think we went through the first mile in around 6:20 and with the net downhill it felt super slow. I'm used to running a faster pace, so my leg turnover felt different. The conditions were tough for everyone and I wasn't comfortable in that kind of headwind as I never felt like I hit a real rhythm. I could never settle in and relax. I was trying to conserve energy while aiming to maintain my forward momentum.

I tried to make moves slowly and tuck in with groups. So, I felt pretty comfortable. The first ten miles of the race I was with groups of other women for most of the time. But there were several sections where I was kind of running by myself. I had been with a pack, then the pack had kind of slowed, so I had broken off and was trying to catch up to another pack of runners. There were several miles where I was fighting the elements.

Mentally I prepared myself before it by thinking that at some stage in the race, 'the demons are going to come, and I need to be prepared for it', so I was ready for them when things got tough. It was a case of playing mind games and just focusing on small achievable goals and then at other points I just tried to turn my brain off and just think about getting to the next drink station. As the race unfolded, I had no idea of my place. I started out really conservatively and then some time before halfway, around miles 10 to 12, there is a section where I was off by myself again. I was very worried because I felt that the headwind was really affecting me, my pace was struggling, and I was getting fatigued at an early point. I looked over my shoulder and there was a pack of women behind me who were catching up to me. I actually slowed down to 7:30 or 8:00 minute pace for 30 seconds and let them catch me. I tucked in and ran with them for several miles. Rachel Hyland, who ended up fourth, made a move off the pack. I was pretty comfortable, covered her move and went with her and ran with her for several miles. Then I kind of waited until after Heartbreak Hill to make any other moves. Going into the race I was nervous for the hills, but I felt pretty good and I realized that was probably my strongest point in the race.

Things seemed to get really crazy through the back end of the race. Some of the women I was passing, I was in complete disbelief – women who I have the utmost respect for who they are as athletes and as people - like Shalane Flanagan and Molly Huddle. That was probably the point where I felt like it was a dream. I had tried to visualize the race beforehand and to be mentally prepared. It wasn't what I had anticipated. It was honestly equivalent to walking outside and seeing a dinosaur — it was that unreal! I kept having to remind myself [that] 'I'm feeling the wind and the rain, I'm feeling discomfort, so it must be real.'

I feel like the last five percent of any distance race you are just hanging on for dear life. That's definitely the point in the last stretch - coming down the last mile it was actually a crazy feeling. I felt like it was just this screaming tunnel. It was so loud. I could see the finish coming down Boylston Street and I was just fighting to get to the finish and hoping that no one was making up ground on me. I was kind of out of it and not thinking super clearly at the end of the marathon. I was thinking that the crowd was just going crazy, so I figured I must be doing really well. Then Yuki Kawauchi, who won the men's race, passed me with maybe 150 meters to go. When he passed me, I thought that maybe they were cheering for him and not cheering for me.

I crossed the finish line and I stopped my watch out of habit. I honestly had no idea what place I was. If you had asked me at that moment I would have said hopefully top 10. Then I asked a female official who was standing there, 'What place am I? What place am I?' She said, 'Oh, you're second.' I said, 'No, what place?' And she kept repeating several times, 'You're second.' It was a surreal feeling. I was cold and hurting and it was raining, and these were all the feelings and stimuli that told me this was real.

So how did it happen? I'm still not quite sure — a combination of great preparation, a perfectly-executed race and the perfect collision of circumstances on that one day.

Am I mentally tougher than the other elite women like Shalane Flanagan? No - but Boston has proven to me that I can match it with the best on my day. There were ten women who had run sub-2:23 in the field, so they have the mental toughness. I think there is a physiological aspect to it where some of those incredibly tough runners, for whatever reasons, the weather affected them in a way that they weren't able to mentally push through.

My mental toughness started at a young age when I would be out on the snowy trails with my dad. We would go on night hikes in the snow and find unconventional ways of having fun. I think another factor is that because of my work as a nurse anesthetist I am doing hard workouts after a long day when I'm often mentally exhausted. My day to day work also gives me some perspective

away from the road. I see what patients and families go through every day and it really gives a lot of meaning and perspective for me to realize that I love the sport and there really is a lot of bigger things out there.

The Boston success has brought all sorts of exciting opportunities for me – a sponsorship with Altra, entry into New York Marathon and a clear pathway to the Olympic trials for Tokyo 2020. I don't know what the limit is of my potential. It's daunting, yet exciting to be mentioned alongside the other top US women marathoners, especially with our country going through a golden period of women's running. It's going to take a ton of work to consistently compete at a high level, but Boston has given me the confidence to permit me to think that I belong up there and that I can compete with those women.

Katherine Switzer

What can I say? It was epic! It reminded me of the cold weather of my first Boston run in 1967, except there was so much more rain throughout the entire course this year. So I no longer can say Boston 1967 was the worst, because 2018 was like being inside a washing machine on the cold rinse cycle for the entire race.

The 2018 Boston Marathon is history, but what remains are amazing memories from doing my 40th Boston TV broadcast, the 3rd year of the BAA's celebration of 50 years of women at Boston, and best of all, our 261 Fearless Charity Team weekend. Many of our Charity Team members are also Boston Buddies! I even met a few Boston Buddies at the Expo, at the AT&T store on Boylston Street where we were having a book signing, and also at adidas RunBase for many Adidas/261 activations.

Our 261 Fearless Charity Team had runners from six countries, and it is so cool to connect through the magic of running. I look back to a very successful weekend and am so proud of our Charity Team who managed to raise $350K. Thank you so much! Another amazing result: All of our 47 Charity Runners made it to the finish line, despite the tough

conditions. Several on our team were injured and said they would start the race but had no anticipation of finishing. But plenty of people on our team helped each other; and by golly, running, walking, limping, they all made it. I told them the next day they were like the soldiers in Shakespeare's famous St. Crispin's day speech, when King Henry told them that for the rest of their lives they would remember this day and have bragging rights forever that they did it. I can imagine these runners 50 years from now, as little old ladies around the fire, telling their grandkids how tough Grandma was! Don't you love it?

The days before the actual race were full of events with the team and our amazing 261 Fearless partners. If you want to relive the experience of our runners check out the video we posted on the 261 Fearless Facebook page on April 16, 2018.

I was so pleased to have a Charity Team at the start line of the Boston Marathon – where the 261 Fearless story all started. The 45 women and 2 men from around the world were running and supporting our non-profit organization by raising money to make our mission and goals happen! They braved the tough weather conditions and managed to accomplish something amazing for themselves as well as for 261 Fearless. For 261 supporters who could not be at Boston, a huge thank you goes to many 261 local clubs who joined us in spirit by organizing special "261 runs Boston" virtual events with their members.

As for me, I was on the photo bridge of the finish line for WBZ-TV doing race commentary with Lisa Hughes and Toni Reavis. We were freezing our backsides as the water poured off the overhead canopy and down our backs for five hours.

And, as we all know, it was one of the most astonishing races in history, as most of the top guns succumbed to the cold, making way for the tough-as-old-boots runners to come through, including everyone's heroine, Determined Desi!!! A whole new cohort of 'unknowns' gutted it out and became overnight heroes. On those long, dark and lonely training nights, we have all dreamed of starring in Boston...and these people did! Bravo to them!

Thank you, Boston Buddies! You are making the Boston Marathon even more special by sharing your stories with us all!

Dave McGillivray

The Boston Marathon Race Director Dave McGillivray was kind enough to allow me to interview him about his 2018 Boston Marathon experience and his opinion about the events, and the courage of the runners that showed up that day.

Were these the worst weather conditions you've seen as the Boston Marathon race director?

"It depends on your interpretation of "worst". I didn't consider it a real dangerous day. I felt it was uncomfortable, miserable, and challenging. However, it wasn't 2012 when it reached 89 degrees, and we all know what heat can do to runners under stress. In one sense, there really is no such thing as bad weather, just bad gear.

There are 30,000 runners and handful of us. They may feel they can run in any conditions, but can we safely manage in any and all conditions. Runners must take personal responsibility of themselves. If someone showed up in shorts and a t-shirt they would be in trouble. We can only deal with so many of them. Just remember, there were people that ran their personal best this year so certain people perform better in these conditions. But I will admit, going in I was extremely concerned.

When the event is under unusual stress it can expose weaknesses and that is where we can look back and assess what happened and improve our operations next time. Nothing was catastrophic, and the silver lining was that we learned a lot from that experience. Believe it or not, the number transported to medical facilities wasn't significantly greater than the average we've had on other days.

The conditions were uncomfortable but if you dress properly you can still run comfortably.

A funny scene that happened on its own was on Hereford Street. So many runners had layers with a poncho or a plastic bag thinking they would shed them after a few miles. But the conditions never let up. Runners continued to wear the extra gear throughout the race but once they made the turn on Hereford Street they discarded it. Clothes were all over, curb to curb. Even some of elite athletes kept their jackets on the entire race. Something we learned for next time is maybe we line streets with barrels with signage for clothing just to try to keep the roads clean.

Another interesting observation - normally, the elite athletes get two bibs. One bib on front with their name, and a bib on back with their number. But when there is bad weather they get a third bib for the front with their name. If they wear something over their singlet they put this third bib on that. They can then throw away that top with the third bib. A lot used their third bib and pinned it to their jacket. Shalane slit it, so it was on each side of the zipper. She ran the whole way with the 3rd bib. Desi pinned the bib vertically and put it on one side of her jacket. Look at finish line photos, she has her bib on one side."

What was your favorite part of the day?

"The day before the marathon, I was on the phone with a lot of people, meeting with many committees, trying to stay ahead of the curve. There was a lot of pressure to be prepared and get our message out to all the participants, volunteers, and medical staff. I consider that pressure a privilege. It's all about preparation.

I manage a lot of races all over country throughout the year, however, the people that organize this marathon are the most experienced. People will rise to the occasion and get the job done.

Again, a lot of people say runners can run through anything. But can we manage through anything? We have to consider all possibilities when preparing for the race. Will all 10,000 volunteers show up? Will structures stand up? What if something happened in one of the smaller towns that we run through. The spectators are ours and their responsibility if something were to go down. The residents of the town may need resources and the race is out of luck.

As it turned out, everybody stepped up. The heroic volunteers were out there for hours and hours and we had a lot of volunteers that were hypothermic. Remember, the runners generate heat as they run, but the volunteers are standing and handing out water and it was extremely cold and windy.

Considering everything that could have gone wrong, I'd say the race went off extremely well."

How close were you, if at all, to canceling the race?

"I don't believe we ever seriously considered cancelling the race. We tried to focus on what we could do to minimize the uncomfortable conditions. One thing we did that was unplanned was to let wave 4 go with wave 3. We didn't want the runners to have to wait around in the cold, wind, and rain and risk hypothermia. We wanted to minimize risk as much as possible.

The conditions did take their toll however, and the attrition in the AWD (Athletes With Disabilities) division and elites was higher than that in previous years. Usually there is 1 or 2 that drop out but there were 15 to 20 this year."

What were your thoughts at Athletes' village and the start of the race?

"An unfortunate part of the history of the race is the fact that we have very little space to work with. There are no massive parking lots or buildings for shelter. There isn't any more real estate now then there was 100 years ago. We have the same space for 30,000 runners that they had for 200. This is not an easy thing to manage. We also have significantly more security, and security personnel, too. We have to work around security rather than security working around us.

As for Athletes' village, we would love to say don't go there, go here, but we don't have that luxury. That's where personal responsibility comes in. For instance, at the beginning of the day I took off my shoes, put plastic bags over my feet, then put my shoes back on, so my feet never got wet. Those who took care of themselves did fine, those that didn't, didn't fare as well.

In 2007, there was a nor'easter. We learned that year that the drainage at the school fields can force the water under the tents in Athletes' village. What can you do when you have huge 80' x 200' tents and they are in a flooded area? We didn't know until that morning and by then it's too late.

At the time of year the race is run you never know what you are going to get weather wise. It's tough to respond because of limited resources and space.

It's like diving into a pool for the first time, you're nervous before, but once you dive in you have bragging rights. More bravado, or even a badge of honor because you are now able to say you've done it. Those that ran the 2018 Boston Marathon now have bragging rights."

In 2015 you ran the marathon at night like you normally do, and I read you said it was some of the worst weather you ran in. How was your night time run this year?

"A lot of people say my conditions were easier than theirs. But after being in the rain, wind, and cold for 12 hours first, I must admit that when I went to Hopkinton I had some serious doubts about running this year. I was thinking "why should I keep doing this?" But then I thought, "I have done this 45 times, how could I not do it." I must admit, it was a rough go, one of the toughest ever. But I did finish.

In my opinion, it definitely was worse this year than in 2015. This year I was fatigued going in, probably 50% on the starting line. I was tired mentally, emotionally, and physically. It was tough to get into it this year but once you start running and get into your grove, and do what you normally do, you figure it out and keep going."

Do you have words of encouragement for anyone that had a DNF that day?

"There's always tomorrow. The idea is sometimes it's not your day. In many regards it more courageous to leave the event and avoid getting seriously injured rather than fight it out on a really bad day. There's no disgrace in a DNF especially in conditions like that. There's no such thing as failure. The only way to truly fail is to not try. Just lining up was admirable. I know it was disappointing for those that had to stop but take it in as part of the experience. Let it go, but I know that is easier said than done.

Galen Rupp, who was a favorite to be in top 10, even dropped. He thought why punish himself, it's not his day. Then 3 weeks later he ran the Prague Marathon in 2:06. Just consider the marathon a long training run.

A DNF can sting. When I ran my first Boston, I was 17 and didn't have an official entry because you needed to be 18 to run. I ran it but dropped out in the hills. So I dropped out of my first marathon but have run 155 marathons since. After that first marathon, I felt I didn't earn the right to run that day. I took a much more serious attitude to make sure I could toe the line and be prepared whenever I showed up to run a race."

There were a lot of people who beat the odds and ran that day. There are blind runners, people with a prosthetic leg, wheelchair racers. Is there one that stands out that you said "wow, that is what this marathon is all about?"

"All of them. 30,000 human interest stories. I don't think 26.2 is easier or harder for anyone. Everyone has their own challenge. Headwind was a major challenge.

I was on the lead vehicle. I can remember passing athletes with disabilities and being inspired by their determination. However, what they had to do to get there was way more challenging than 26.2 miles. The optics can be very different than reality."

What are your final thoughts about the day?

"People say what separates Boston from all the other races is the experience of all those involved. Many of the people that work in this organization have done this for 20-30 years. They are experts at what they do. I often say I'm not a director, I'm a conductor. They know what they need to do. 90% of the course is also residential. Residents can step out of their front doors to see, cheer on and help the runners and it is a tradition that has been handed down from generation to generation. It's this experience that brings people back year after year."

Jacob Flaws, Bib 2500

Thornton, CO, 31, 2:58:29

When I got the call that her cancer was back, my heart sank into my stomach and I knew it was bad. She had battled breast cancer for 3 years, beating it the first two times, but this time felt different. I hoped she would beat it again just like she had when it first showed up in her breast and then a year later in her brain. After all, the scans had been clean for a year after each of those successful battles. This time it was in her spine, and the doctor's said it spread too quickly for them to get at it. A week later, my parents told me I needed to come home if I wanted to see her one last time. It didn't seem real.

My aunt Colleen fought in the hospital for 26 days before the cancer took her life. It was devastating, she was only 56. This is the same woman who raised me as a child, my daycare provider from when I was three months old until I was in my early teens. She was the wife to my dad's twin brother, and mother to three of my best friends in this world. It didn't seem right. She was the one who always cared for us, cheering us on in everything we did. She never sought recognition and instead, she made sure we shined. She spent her life caring for children, not only her own, but as a daycare provider, she gave love and care for strangers who quickly became like family. Then one day she was gone.

Running has always been my outlet. It gives me the space I need to regroup my thoughts and purify my soul. Two weeks after Colleen passed, I wanted to honor her memory in some way. As I was halfway into the training cycle for my second Boston Marathon, I decided to set up a GoFundMe page dedicated to running Boston in her honor. The proceeds I raised would be donated to her husband, my uncle, Jay. After one day, I had raised almost $1000. The community around my family was showing their support and their love and it was overwhelming and amazing.

Although I was battling injuries myself, I wanted to get to the start line and finish Boston, just to make the tribute complete. After a decent mileage buildup and many rounds of physical therapy on my torn abdominal muscle, I felt like I was ready to give it a shot.

I got into Boston on Saturday afternoon, the 14th. I generally get nervous before races, especially marathons, but this one was bigger, and I was really feeling the anxious energy during my travels. This one meant something more. Saturday night, my dad who had met me out in Boston, persuaded me to go check out the "Cheers" bar in Boston, from the TV show. I thought it was weird, since neither of us drink and I don't recall him ever watching it as I was growing up, but I obliged. Once we arrived and walked in, I saw my cousin, Jordan, sitting at the bar. One of Colleen's sons, and one of my closest friends, Jordan had snuck into Boston to surprise me because he wanted to watch me run in his mom's honor. I was floored. Love and family are sometimes all you need in life.

Monday morning dawned raw – the wind was already up, the rain was steady, and there was snow on the ground. I had maybe slept three hours the night before, my mind just wouldn't shut off. I knew that with the money raised in the GoFundMe page and the massive amounts of support and well-wishes I'd received, the tribute to my aunt was already a phenomenal success – regardless of how I ran. But in my own heart, I felt like I had to run well to truly honor her. I wanted to do something special in the race as a way of completing the tribute. Yet, with the weather, I was concerned about even finishing, lest my body shut down on me from hypothermia. Right then, it dawned on me that I could do all I could and still possibly not reach the finish line – a troubling thought.

I tried to stay as dry as possible in the Athlete's Village, but the Woodstock-esque mud pit that greeted us challenged everyone's preparation. The steady gusts of wind threatening to topple the tents and port-a-potties were also a reminder of the powers of nature that we were all up against.

Waiting in the starting corral, soaking wet, freezing cold, I felt the surge of energy go through the crowd of runners when the gun went off. Everything else faded away, and it was time to do what we came here to do – despite the weather – we had to get from Hopkinton to Boston by foot or by canoe or by any means possible.

Last year, my first Boston, I ran along the edges of the road, giving out a large volume of high fives to the numerous spectators lining the course. I was hamming it up and playing off the crowd's energy. This year – I was tucked in. I wanted to conserve as much as possible, and to stay behind the wall of runners in front of me.

The first four miles felt like I was running in ski boots, my toes were numb, and all could feel was the main "stump" of my foot. This slowly went away as I started moving, but as my toes reattached themselves to my body, my hands and fingers started to lose touch. The wind, rain, and cold were penetrating, and there wasn't much I could do.

The first ten miles or so were pretty uninspiring. I was so busy concentrating on conserving my strength and staying out of the headwind, that I really just battened down the hatches and ran on autopilot. About half a mile out of Wellesley, however, I began to hear a deafening roar of human voices. As I neared, it clicked in my brain, the Wellesley College scream tunnel ladies were out in this monsoon in full force, ready to guide us to the half-marathon mark and on to Boston. I had to fight back my emotion as something awoke in me at this moment. Hearing the Wellesley ladies sparked me, and this is where my race started. I stuck my arm out and gave all the high fives I could as I sped through the rows of roaring ladies. It was incredible!

I hit the half-marathon in 1:28:43. Although I had some signs of life, this half marathon split didn't bode well for Boston, since runners almost always give a lot back on the second half of the course, and that's on a good day. But I didn't give up hope. Though I did have to start opening my gels with my teeth as my hands were now useless, frozen bricks!

Right after the 15-mile mark, I found what I was looking for – my dad and Jordan were waiting on the side of the road for me. I pumped my chest and yelled "Let's go baby! Let's do this!" They were screaming their support right back at me. I gave them two high fives and ran past. Something in my brain clicked, I was going to get to Boylston Street no matter what – even if I had to drag myself. What a powerful boost!

Something else happened right after I passed my family. Despite the tempest raging around me, the driving rain, the blustery winds, the pervasive cold, I developed this strange sensation of calm. I was at peace. I felt Colleen's presence all around me. At that moment, I looked up to her and said aloud, "This is for you, Co!" And I took off.

I attacked the Newton Hills with a vengeance. I gritted my teeth and broke away from the pack I had been running with. I was going to destroy Heartbreak Hill if it was the last thing I ever did. I kept reeling off really strong miles, right around 6:45. I went up Heartbreak in 6:54. I barely even slowed. At the top, through my still gritted teeth, I talked to Colleen again, and again out loud. I said, "You watch what I'm about to do. Just watch what I'm going to do now." I don't know why this mantra came out, but it did, and I kept repeating it. I flew through mile 22 in 6:31, my fastest of the entire race. I had my game-face on and I was fighting to keep my emotions in check. I felt so close to Colleen in these last miles that I wanted to start crying, but I kept telling myself to channel that energy and to hold off on using it all up.

I flew down into Brookline, then into Boston. I couldn't feel the pain, I couldn't feel the weather, all I could feel was the effort and the indescribable joy that was in my soul.

As I turned from Hereford left onto Boylston, the sound of thousands of screaming voices reached a crescendo. I burst into tears. This was the moment I had been waiting for not only the whole race, but I soon realized, it was the moment I had been waiting for since Colleen died. I hadn't dealt with the emotions yet, with all the pain of losing her. But there on Boylston Street, with 600 meters to go, it all came flooding out. I sped up and my stride lengthened. I was almost home.

At the finish line, I lifted up my homemade "Colleen Strong" shirt and pointed up to Colleen in heaven. My tribute was complete. Not only had I finished the race, but I came across in 2:58:29. In some of the worst Boston Marathon conditions in recent memory, I had managed to run almost even splits. My second half was 1:29:46 and several of my fastest miles of the race came after the halfway point. In horrible conditions, I had managed to run a full minute and a half faster than my first Boston a year previous. The numbers didn't seem to make sense to me. I didn't think you were supposed to be able to run that way at Boston. But I did. I was proud. I was bawling. Most off, though, for the first time in two months since we lost Colleen, I was complete even if for a fleeting moment.

It wasn't a world record. It wasn't a "podium" finish. Heck, it wasn't even a PR. But what I did in the pouring rain, driving headwind, and icy temperatures at the 2018 Boston Marathon is my proudest running achievement. I got tough,

I battled, and I persevered. I could have not fought. I could have made excuses – after all, they don't get much easier than when presented with those conditions. In that weather, excuses are already built in. But I took the tougher road. I gave it everything I had in spite of the weather and in spite of my injury. I looked into my soul and saw exactly who I was. That's what the Boston Marathon, or any marathon for that matter, is all about.

My shirt said "Colleen Strong" because in her battle in the hospital, beyond what even the doctor's predicted she was capable of, Colleen fought on. She showed a level of strength that inspired my entire family and proved not only the depth of her courage but the power of her wonderful heart. I paid attention, Colleen. I learned from your example. It may have only been in a cold, rainy race of 26 miles and not in a hospital bed fighting cancer for 26 days, but for me, this was the most meaningful way I could possibly honor such an amazing person. I'll always remember that feeling of catharsis on Boylston Street and the bittersweet moment where I finished a race not simply to complete a marathon, but to somehow bring a glimmer of hope to my hurting family. Never underestimate the power of the human spirit.

Alberto Encarnacion, Bib 5399

Tepic, MEX, 39, 3:54:44

The idea was to just get to 25 kilometers. This started seven years ago while walking beside her because she was feeling agitated while talking, she was feeling overweight, we walked slowly, no rush, I was just enjoying talking with her.

I ran my first kilometer as a warmup before playing squash with my kids, this is how it started, without the goal of hanging medals around my neck, just because I wanted her to feel loved and accompanied. It all became chaos when we knew the reason for her agitation, in the following three months she went down, she could walk no more and when she slept I continued running.

Helpless despair kept me adding kilometers one by one, each one praying the Lord to make things right. Four months later she wasn't with us anymore and I had only reached 21 kilometers. I had promised 25 kilometers one day, but she wasn't able to hold on and see me do it.

I spent my days running, there were many moments of despair, running was my cure because I couldn't spend my time at home crying. I quit my bad habits, no more TV, no more wine, no more meat, I realized my example was being closely followed by my three beautiful children. Three years passed and running became a means to control my thoughts and to become an example. I joined a local running club, but it didn't work because I was undisciplined, and I didn't follow the order of things to be done. I told them I could not follow a methodology, I wasn't there for the pictures, I just wanted to run so I started to break the mold.

I signed up for my first marathon, which in fact was a celebration with a special dedication to my angel. I didn't focus on time because I knew my suffering and pain would never compare to the one she suffered, so I didn't complain and enjoyed it.

After the first, I promised just three more, one for each of my children, I wasn't true to my word and in my fourth marathon the prize came! My Boston qualifier! I really didn't know what it meant, in fact I didn't imagine myself running in another country and I couldn't even imagine the meaning of running Boston!

And there I was on my road to Boston, without a coach, just filled with the desire to run. Injuries and other setbacks as plantar fasciitis came, but the trip was already paid for, so I focused on enjoying the moment without hesitation. I didn't have time to cry and my mind held its ground when the day came, when you do what you love, the weather or circumstances are not going to stop you from enjoying and being grateful. I didn't run with my feet but with my heart, that splash made me believe in myself and believe we are capable of anything as long as we focus on being happy.

Training continued, marathons became something special. After Boston I focused on running Chicago where the weather was again the factor that made it difficult to lower my time but anyway I enjoyed a lot.

I wish the anger of impotence for not being able to save my wife forged a better human being in me; I am grateful for the good friends running has given me, I am grateful to each and every one of my Boston Buddies because the bond within us is for a greater goal, the goal of helping and encouraging others to run the best marathon in the world, the Boston Marathon! To which I will someday be back

Gene Dykes, Bib 7648

Bala Cynwyd, PA, 70, 3:16:20

In 2006 I ran the NYC Marathon. At age 58, it was my first marathon as a runner. I ran one nine years earlier when I was a jogger, but I'm trying to forget that experience! At NYC I qualified for Boston, which I also ran, so my career as a marathoner was given a kick start. By the fall of 2013 I had completed 25 marathons and 13 ultras. I was a decent marathoner, having won my age group in a few small ones, but I was nowhere near the big time, and my improvement seemed to be stalling out. Up until that point, the only goal that seemed reasonable was to win a marathon in a major city. I knew that I had no prayer to win at NYC, Boston, or Chicago, so I made attempts at Philadelphia, Miami, Honolulu, and Toronto, but I came up short.

I decided to hire a coach to see if that could improve my chances. What followed was a success story that surpassed my wildest imaginings. In just five months my marathon time dropped from a 3:29 at Toronto to a 3:09 at Boston, good for a third-place finish. To make a long story short, I am still working with my coach, and I have substantially improved every year since that 2nd Boston. I have gone on to win my age group at Boston three times, set a world record for age 70 (2:57:43) at the Rotterdam Marathon, and in the ultra-world I have done crazy things like running three 200-mile races in three months. All because I decided to take a chance on hiring a coach.

There are several possible takeaways from this story. 1) If you are not achieving the success you've hoped for, maybe you'll be a late bloomer like I was. 2) If you are really serious about discovering what the best is that you are capable of, hire a coach! 3) Try lots of different styles of running - road, trail, 5K's and ultras, fixed time races, and stage races. It's all good!

As for this year's Boston, guess what? It wasn't a whole lot of fun! I worried about what clothes to wear right up to race day morning, and I really felt that I nailed it. Unfortunately, my rain pants were chafing me something awful, and I had to ditch them at mile 6. After that, my legs got so cold that I couldn't feel them. Most of the race I ran with my head down so that I could barely see the runners ahead of me, and then I tried to hide my consciousness in some deep recess of my mind where I could ignore what was going on. Something as simple as reaching for my water bottle would jolt me back to reality, and since the finish line was not yet in sight, I retreated again. Normally, I relish all the sights and sounds of a race, but all I wanted to do was zone out. My legs weren't listening to my brain, so there was no use trying to set a pace. On the flip side, my legs were probably telling my brain to slow the #$%@ down, but I couldn't receive that message. Better luck next year! I've had three hot ones and two cold, windy ones now, so I'm due for a break.

Judy Neufeld, Bib 29198

Somerville, MA, 34, 5:27:34

People say running a marathon changes your life. I didn't believe them until my life changed when I ran the Boston Marathon on April 16, 2018.

I started running after the Boston Marathon bombings in 2013 to connect to a city I truly loved and felt most like home. I ran my first mile just 5 days after the 2013 terrorist attack to grieve and honor those whose lives were forever changed, including my own friends. It was a way for me to process all those emotions. But I never knew that first run and first mile would change my life. I started training for my first 5k and ran it that summer. I knew that running the 2018 Boston Marathon was the perfect  way to celebrate my 5-year running anniversary and I wouldn't want to cross my first marathon finish line in any other city than Boston.

I ran the 2018 Boston Marathon with 261 Fearless and couldn't imagine running with any other charity team. My whole life's mission has always been about empowering women and 261 Fearless does just that through connecting women runners across the globe. I am so inspired by Kathrine Switzer and was honored and humbled to have been chosen for the team.

I have so many amazing memories from just the training runs over the brutal winter. But nothing compares to the day of the race. I had, of course, been hearing about the weather conditions for days but tried not to let it get to me too much. But once I walked outside for the first time and the wind whipped through my bright yellow poncho, I knew it was going to be an adventurous day.

People asked me after the race how I did it. How I got through 26.2 miles in that weather for my first marathon. I told them that when I stepped onto that start line in Hopkinton, I thought about everything I had been through to get there. When I thought about all the races, training runs, self-doubt, anxiety, pride, excitement, blood, sweat, and tears, I knew wanted this more than anything. I wasn't going down without a fight. Like Kathrine Switzer said, I had to finish this race, even if it was on my hands and knees. And so, with her words ringing in my ears, I was off.

The real heroes of the day were the volunteers and spectators. I was so lucky to have my family in town and friends out on the course, so I knew I could look forward to seeing them at different intervals. It allowed me to break down the race into smaller segments and it turned out that seeing them became a part of my survival tactic. My fingers had frozen numb from the cold and rain and I couldn't open my fuel packets, so my friends and family did every time I saw them!

The rain was constant, and the wind would come through and blow through the poncho every so often. Not long after I crossed over the halfway point in Wellesley did it start hailing, ever so briefly. I remember feeling the pellets of hail on my head and hoping my poncho wouldn't rip. Every part of my body was soaked, and I could feel the water sloshing around in my shoes. After I turned onto Beacon Street in Brookline and ran through a major puddle around mile 24, I really hit the wall. I remember seeing the Green Line sitting there and thinking if only I brought my Charlie card, I could get on the T. It was a pretty hilarious thought at the time, but I was so desperate to be out of wet clothes and in a warm room. That is what motivated me the most at the end of the race!

My absolute favorite moment of the race was turning left onto Boylston from Hereford Street. Like all the other runners, I ripped off my poncho and tossed it to the side, so I can run down Boylston and cross the finish line without looking like a banana in my yellow poncho. When I finally made that turn, I was overcome with such emotion that I had to stop and cry and catch my breath. I held my head as I cried and cried, and when I finally came up for air and started running again, the crowd around me went wild! They gave me that needed boost to run as fast as my numb legs would take me. And then just 25 or so yards from the finish line, I got to see my family one last time where we gave each other big, wet hugs, and they sent me off to finish the race. I crossed with the biggest, wettest, smile on my face. I had finally done it! I was a marathoner! I had run and finished the Boston Marathon during some of the craziest weather conditions we had ever seen.

I ran to honor my city. To honor the survivors and victims of the 2013 attack. This race was a thank you letter to Boston. For giving me the strength and resilience I have today. For making me a runner. For allowing me to understand what "Boston Strong" truly means.

Love that dirty water. Boston, you're my home.

Craig Williams, Bib 18641

Windermere, FL, 55, 3:39:04

One of my earliest childhood memories is crossing the finish line of a 100-yard dash at my school's annual sport's day. I must have been 8 or 9 years of age at the time. The field was the town's Australian Rules football field and during the offseason sheep were allowed on the field to help keep the grass under control. The running track that day was a rutty mix of hard soil with small hoof prints, clumps of dry grass and of course, sheep poop. The running lanes were marked with white marking chalk that puffed up like flour when you stepped on them.

The finish line was a length of hay bailing twine and it hurt if it was held too tight and you had the thrill of finishing first. That day I did finish first in several races and discovered that I had a talent to run fast and win. I liked the feeling of running, winning and the challenge of improving my running efforts. And so, it was then that my love of running began, and I have been running ever since.

Fast-forward 40 or so years; married, two children, a dog, mortgage a career and running is still present in my life. During this time an annual event I always looked forward to was to watch the New York City Marathon the first Sunday of November. It was the 2009 New York City Marathon when I watched my soon to be running hero, Meb Keflezighi win. I watched that day and thought back on all the running I had done and that I had never ran a race of any considerable distance. I then began to dream about running a marathon.

Earlier that same year my brother Paul was diagnosed with ALS and during my efforts to find a way into New York for 2010 I discovered that you could enter through a charity. Coincidentally and fortunately the ALS Association - Greater New York Chapter was putting together their first New York City Marathon team. They had 5 charity spots. I signed up immediately with a commitment to raise $3,000. I was in. All I needed to do was Run & Raise, as I called it back then.

We lost my brother Paul to ALS in June of 2010. Running my first marathon, the 2010 New York City Marathon for TEAM ALS, was a very emotional and personal event for me. I have gone on to run all the subsequent New York City Marathon's through 2018 in Paul's memory for TEAM ALS and raising over $20,000 in donations.

My running had now taken on a new purpose and meaning. I started running with some motivation from that time on. I entered local 5K's and set running a local half marathon on the Jersey Shore as a goal during my marathon training. One of my best memories of those days was running a half marathon and half marathon relay with my son. He ran the half marathon totally untrained and beat me be a few seconds. He had enough in the tank to finish strong with a 1:54:32. We also took first place in a half marathon family relay that same year. My passion for distance running was growing and I loved the personal challenge and commitment it presented me.

Fast-forward again a few years to some very unfortunate events and incidents that led my very isolated running world to collide with the running community at large and set me on my journey to Boston 2018; 2012's Hurricane Sandy and the Boston Marathon bombings of 2013. Prior to these two events I liked to run alone and focused on trail running, and didn't really run with others, except for race day. All would change after getting involved with relief and charitable efforts related to both these tragic incidents.

Hurricane Sandy: Preparation and training for the 2012 New York City Marathon was well underway when I learned of an additional opening on TEAM ALS. I immediately thought of my friend, Lance Sven, who, unknown to me at the time had dreams of running a marathon to honor his Uncle Roy. Without hesitation Lance volunteered for the open spot on the team. We were both excited about the prospects of running a marathon together. This wasn't to be as the 2012 New York City Marathon was canceled due to Hurricane Sandy's impact on the greater New York area. This cancellation led to our idea of running the marathon anyway. With a lot of last minute and frantic organizing and support from Lance, his family and friends we began organizing to run a marathon anyway. New York City was full of runners that had committed to themselves and charities to run a marathon. Lance and the supporting team quickly organized via social media an ad hoc race (the original New York City marathon course) in Central Park with the requirement that each runner come with a donation for Hurricane Sandy relief efforts.

The day was a huge success. Truckloads of donations were collected, and runners got to experience one of the best marathon courses in the World in an atmosphere of genuine comradery and a spirit of giving back to the community. Out of this event the Run Anyway organization was born and that connected me with Boston and many new running friends and adventures. I could write more about that magical Sunday in November 2012, but it would be better if you were to read Lance's book, "Run Anyway" as it includes more on this and his 2013 Boston Marathon experience.

Boston Bombings: Run Anyway's next mission was to secure a spot in the 2013 Boston Marathon and raise money for a local Boston charity. Lance contacted a charity that needed runners and he went to work raising donations and training. You all know the outcome of that sad Monday in April 2013. Lance had just cleared the finish line when the bombings occurred. He was safe and reunited with his family later that day. It was from this day and Run Anyway's charity efforts that we learned about a relay that had been organized by 3 British runners and adventurers that was going to carry a baton (Miles) from California to Boston in efforts to raise donations for the Boston Marathon bombing victims. The "One Run for Boston Relay" connected me with many new running friends that eventually led to friendships with Vince Varallo and Jackie Smith, along with many more running friends. The initial connections and events spurned by Run Anyway and The One Run for Boston Relay have generated so many running adventures I can't even begin to write about them all. Vince and I went on to finally meet in person at a relay baton exchange for the Run 2 Respond relay at the 911 Memorial in New York City a couple of years later. This relay is sponsored by the Fire Fighter Five Foundation and managed by Steve Bender.

My new-found running community exposure and friendships exposed the prestige of the Boston Marathon to me. I was in awe of Boston and never thought in my wildest dreams that I would run or qualify for the Boston Marathon.

It was at this time I turned my attention to the Boston Marathon and qualifying to earn my spot and be able to say I had qualified and run in the World's oldest and most prestigious marathon. One friend in particular, Jackie Smith (we met at the Ragnar Adirondacks through connections from the One Run for Boston Relay) shared a similar passion and we became running buddies with a mission, "BQ or Die Trying." Jackie and I became regular running buddies taking on 60K's, 50 Milers, Ragnar's and more when she ventured down from Boston to New Jersey.

For me to BQ required a 10+ minute improvement on my then current marathon PR. I needed a 3:30:00 or better (much better as we know) to qualify. My initial attempts were feeble at best. I really didn't have a good understanding of what it felt like and what was required to raise my running effort and commitment to a level that would give me a BQ. It took me a few attempts to figure this out and I guess that is the lure and mystic of qualifying for Boston. You have to go to a place physically and mentally you haven't been before.

Beginning in 2014 I attempted to qualify by running local marathons; New Jersey Marathon, Rhinebeck Marathon, New York City, Marine Corps Marathon (twice), Philadelphia, Lehigh Valley and Steamtown. As my race times improved and I understood what it took to train for and run a smart race I also moved up an age bracket in the Boston qualifying times. The stars had aligned for me late in 2016 with two BQ's. Marine Corps and Steamtown and the upcoming birthday age-group bonus. This would allow me to apply for Boston 2018 with a 5+ minute cushion. This year, 2018 I qualified at the Utah Valley Marathon with a 3:26:51 for Boston 2019, a 13+ minute cushion. Coincidentally, my very first marathon time was 4:26:49. I have improved my time 1 hour over my first marathon 9 years ago.

I recall the Lehigh Valley attempt in 2015 as the race I learned the lesson of going out too fast, too soon. I had a blistering first half and a very humbling second half. Robert Santamaria, whom I met through the One Run for Boston relay joined me for this one and we both fell short of our BQ goals. We both finished but well beyond our qualifying times. Jackie was there as well to cheer us on.

Boston 2018, despite the weather was all I expected from Boston. To toe the line in a corral of similar paced, like minded and worthy runners was a dream come true. I ran a disciplined race that day and it was the last 2 miles that got me. While I did BQ at Boston, by 56 seconds (another dream) I had one of those runner experiences you can only get in a race like this. The last couple of miles along Commonwealth Ave. were tough. I was cold, very cold and my legs, lips and hands were numb, and I knew I was becoming a little disoriented. I knew enough at the moment to realize that I may be borderline hypothermic but with about 2 more miles to go I needed to finish and finish strong. There is a little dip on Commonwealth Ave. that takes you under an overpass just before you turn right onto Hereford. I saw the small decline and incline and said to myself that I was going to allow myself to walk up that small incline. You couldn't even call it a hill. This would be my one luxury and give back to the course. I wanted to enjoy the walk and brief reprieve it would provide my numb legs. I could see that I was close to my BQ time too, but walking sounded better at the time. I had slowed down to walk and had taken maybe 3-4 steps when a runner came up beside me and shouted "Go, Go," and I did. That was all I needed to get moving again. I met that runner, Natty Lou back at about mile 6. Natty and Ali were running together, and they recognized my TEAM ALS shirt from posts in a Facebook running group we belong to, Runderful. We ran a couple of miles together and chatted. I didn't see them again until mile 26 when I needed their verbal push. I turned right onto Hereford and left onto Boylston and finished with a BQ. I didn't even see or hear my wife, Carolyn who was at the corner of Boylston and Hereford. She said she was shouting at me. She later said you looked out of it. I have never missed seeing her on the course. A shout out to her as well. She was at mile 17 and again at the finish in those conditions. I had tunnel vision while running down Boylston. All I could see was the finish line and that's what I ran towards. My mind was fuzzy to say the least when I crossed the finish line. I was a little disoriented and welcomed the volunteers and allowed them to wrap me up in a race poncho and I shuffled with the masses out of the finish area. I really didn't know where I was going. I was looking around and saw a familiar landmark and knew I was heading in the right direction to meet up with Carolyn.

Carolyn spotted me in the wave of silver race ponchos by looking at my shoes. I had taped my new Nike Vaporfly 4% with white duct tape over the toes to help keep the water out. That didn't work, and I lost the tape on one shoe after about 8 miles. One shoe still had the tape on it though and that's how Carolyn spotted me. She walked up beside me and started talking to me. I initially thought she was a spectator asking questions about the finish area. It took me a little time to figure out that it was her. She knew I was "out of it." We decided to forgo our plans of a beer and food and went right back to the  hotel. I took a long warm shower and hopped into bed to warm up. I continued to shake and shiver uncontrollably for about 2 hours.

After resting up we decided to catch up with the Boston Buddies at Cheers and finally Jackie, who had volunteered at her favorite water station, Mile 18 and weathered the same conditions we did as runners. Listening to all the stories and catching up with friends was a great way wrap up what was a Boston for the books.

I'm already in for 2019. Registration is complete and accepted and the hotel and flights are booked. I will never forget Boston 2018 and all that we went through together.

Colleen Clark, Bib 20222

Manahawkin, NJ, 44, 4:02:25

My road to Boston started the same as my road to marathoning. I was never going to run Boston. It was elitist. Exclusionary. Discriminatory. Not for me. And while I believed these to be true, the runner in me liked a challenge. Boston would be a challenge for me. My required qualifying time was not my current pace. So when a very good friend asked me if I wanted to get a coach with her, I struggled. Running Boston had been a goal of hers for quite a while. We had run a marathon together before and had a great time. I wanted to support her, and I wanted to run another marathon with her, but it did feel a bit hypocritical though. In the end, I declined. I had just started a new

job and I wasn't sure I could commit to serious training and the new firm at the same time. So I passed on trying to qualify for Boston. That was October of 2016.

Fast forward to April 2017. A couple of friends were running Boston and very excited. They told me I should try to qualify. They were sure I could do it. (Aren't friends great? Especially running friends. They believe in you even when you don't entirely believe in yourself). I had trained to run the Coastal Delaware Marathon with my friend. Two weeks out I injured my Achilles. In disbelief, I rested. A week later I still could not run at all. My friend with the coach ran it though. We tracked her progress and cheered her on. We were so ecstatic when she got her BQ! Her first! We decorated her house with blue and yellow balloons and streamers. She did it. I came back to running stronger than I left it. I had this quiet, persistent thought that I wanted to run Boston with my friend. Another friend had also qualified, but only had a two-minute cushion. On long runs she would talk about running another marathon before the cut off to improve her time. She had run Boston five times and told me amazing stories.

Without telling anyone, I signed up for the Chasing the Unicorn marathon, which was the last weekend before the qualifying cut-off date. I asked my friend for her plan but would not admit I was trying to BQ. It felt like too much pressure. What if I couldn't do it? I ran hard all summer, early in the morning before work. I learned about cumulative fatigue. I read the book "How Bad Do You Want It?" I was exhausted. And I got faster. Finally, a week before the race, I admitted to my friends and family that I was trying to BQ. My friend who got her BQ said she would come to the race, over an hour away, to cheer me on. My other friend with the two-minute cushion ran another marathon the same day to improve her time. I did it. I qualified! With a five-minute cushion. My boys were there, and my friend cheered me on. It was a great day. My other friend qualified the same day with a BQ that got her into the race. The long hard week of selection, however, we learned that my friend who got her first BQ missed the time cut off by 13 seconds.

It was an unbearably cold, dark, snowy winter in New Jersey for spring marathon training. Layers and wool socks and hand warmers were the norm. My yak trax got some running time. Getting up early to run in sub twenty-degree weather in the dark before work was mentally tough. I didn't want to, and I really didn't want to do any kind of speed work. So I didn't. I put in all the miles. The training cycle became about checking off my distance boxes and keeping track of weekly totals. I did two 22 milers – a first for me. I heard the course at Boston was seriously challenging, which made me nervous. I wanted a good finishing time, something I would be proud of. I just couldn't seem to motivate to train for speed. I joined a Facebook group dedicated to Boston Marathon training. My new Boston Buddies were inspiring. Dedicated and fast. I learned a lot about the course. We supported each other's training and commiserated about the tough winter weather. Boston celebrities were in the group and posted from time to time (Katherine Switzer commented on one of my posts!). I loved hearing stories about Athlete's Village and the Expo and how amazing the crowds were. I was so excited to get there. It still seemed a little unreal that I was actually going to run Boston.

Two weeks before the race Boston Buddies started posting about the weather forecast. At first it looked good! Tailwind, not too hot. We were all optimistic. Then the predictions changed. Partial tailwind and the probability of some rain. We posted about what to wear on race day and how to pack. The sage advice of Boston alumni was "Bring everything, Boston is unpredictable." We went from disappointedly hoping the forecast would change (while checking every half hour to be sure), to trying to optimistically tell ourselves that we have run in worse, to finally resigning that the day was not going to be what we hoped and dreamed. But Boston did not disappoint! It is a five-star race experience, to be sure. The expo had top notch vendors, lectures from authors and celebrities and a detailed run down of the course, among other things. The city welcomed 30,000 runners, their friends and families with enthusiasm and excitement.

Race morning weather was exactly as predicted. It was raining sideways as I got on the shuttle from my hotel to Boston Commons. Runners were dressed in odd layers topped off with rain gear or plastic bags. There were so many theme park ponchos that day! The comradery and excitement that usually comes before a race was missing. We got off the shuttle to drop our clear bags at bag check and walk to the school buses that would take us to Athlete's Village and the starting line. We were immediately soaked, and I silently thanked the BAA for suggesting that we bring extra throw away shoes. By the time I got in line to board the school buses, I couldn't feel my hands because they were so cold. The 45-minute bus ride was somber. The wind was howling, the rain pouring and the windows inside the school bus were fogged over. But wait! This was not the experience I saw in video clips from prior years. People were talking and laughing in those videos. The sun was shining. The atmosphere on this bus reminded me a bit of a natural disaster. We were in survival mode. We were bracing ourselves. I gave the gentleman next to me, an older man from Italy, one of my hand warmers. He didn't have any and he couldn't feel his hands either. The gal across the aisle from me gave me her extra grocery store bags to tie around my dry shoes. We were not excited. We were not happy.

Let's just be honest here. Athlete's Village was awful. It was a mud pit with a few tents over top. People were huddled together vying for a spot where their shoes would not sink in the mud. It was very cold. I didn't even get in line for the port-a-potty. I just couldn't make myself go out in the rain. Time came to walk to the starting line. Masses of runners filed out along the path and then the road. There were no spectators waiting to cheer for us there. I followed waiting to see the corrals and hear the air horn announce our start. It was freezing and wet. Course officials were telling us to keep going. Suddenly I realized I walked over the starting mat! Then I heard the officials announce: "Just go! It doesn't matter what corral you are in. Due to the weather we are not using corrals." How terribly anti-climactic. I was sad.

Things got better once I started running, as they always do. I felt better and tried to be grateful that I was running the Boston Marathon. There were spectators! I could hardly believe it. I was thankful to them and worried about them at the same time. It started to hail in my first three miles. I laughed out loud and turned to the girl next to me. She was looking down. I decided to make the most of it. I was going to enjoy this experience as much as I could. I gave up on achieving any certain time. I stopped at the bathroom after the 5k point! I would never do that. I thought about so many things while running, as usual. I was thankful for the experience. I was glad my boys were home with my parents instead of out in this weather. I wished my friend was with me. I thought about my family and friends at home tracking me at every timing mat I crossed, feeling their support from a distance. I promised myself I would never have to run again after I finished. People watching was a crazy distraction during the race. Runners ran with plastic bags on their feet! I steered clear of them, certain that they were going to slide to the ground at any moment. Shower caps on heads, black garbage bags trapping runners' arm swings. It was surreal. And an obstacle course! Discarded rain gear littered way too much of the course. I really didn't want to fall on it. So I ran around it (ending the marathon at 27.5 miles according to my Garmin!).

The spectators were wonderful. I have no idea how they withstood the weather. They offered dry socks, gloves, food and most importantly, support. I ran with music, but I could not hear it at all during the race. What I heard were the crowds cheering for us and the rain and wind. The spectator support played a really large part in getting us through this race. I hope they know that. The course was as hard as I imagined. The Newton hills were killer. Heartbreak almost made me walk. I was so incredibly thankful to the spectator with the sign announcing, "You just finished Heartbreak Hill!" This was my first go at the course and I felt betrayed that there were more hills beyond heartbreak, even if they were much smaller. In truth, I kept my eyes on the ground most of the race, under the brim of my hat. I did not take in the views like I thought I would.

The worst for me was, "Right on Hereford, Left on Boylston." Expectations can be a tricky thing. I was excited for this iconic finish. When I turned right and saw almost every inch of the street covered in discarded rain gear, I was angry. I wanted to cry a bit. I felt like I could hardly lift my legs high enough to get over the plastic. Relief came when I saw the finish line. I ran faster. I did it.

I FINISHED THE 2018 BOSTON MARATHON!

Then the best thing of the day happened. Soon after I crossed the finish line my son texted me. He asked me how it was. Then my friends started texting. I was so happy to hear from them! It was all I could do to walk the additional mile or so, shivering so hard I couldn't carry my gear. I couldn't feel my hands. I had to wait to respond to my friends. Thankfully the mylar warming blankets had a Velcro closure. I found an Uber and went back to my hotel for a hot shower.

I said I would never run a marathon. Then I said I would never run Boston. Then I said I would only run Boston once. But Boston, we are not done.

This is my 2018 Boston Story. Thank you to my boys and my parents for your support. Thank you to my friends for believing I could do it. Thank you, Boston Buddies, for your knowledge and comradery. Thank you to the spectators for getting us through it. And thank you to the B.A.A. for putting on this amazing, iconic race.

Yvonne Leippert, Bib18486

Coram, NY, 50, 3:50:12

Boston 2018, my 6th Boston and 25th marathon, and I finally had time to absorb it all in! By far the toughest marathon I've done. Got there on Friday and did the expo thing and Saturday was a beautiful day. Did the 5k at a modest effort saving something for Monday of course. Doing the B.A.A. medley this year I needed to get that in and I loved it! My friend Tara Wilson won the masters with a huge PR and I was so proud of her! Then Monday came and all everyone was talking about leading up to it was how bad the weather was going to be. The  worst Boston ever blah blah blah, but hey my thought was, "Well it can only get better", so that's awesome!!

Dolores and I were driven to the start by Gary and Jane and the traffic was so bad we missed our 10:50 start time by over 15 minutes but that was a blessing actually. We stayed warm and dry in Gary's car and basically just walked to the start bypassing the trash and muddy athletes' village. We made a quick stop at the port-a-potties and went to the start with the wave 4 runners. I lost Dolores somehow in the crowds and all I remember was another runner saying, "Is this the start?" I said, "Yup start running!" The race officials wanted the runners to just go at this point because the rain was torrential and 20-30-mile winds were of course a headwind. Overdressed for fear of having a relapse of the hypothermia I had in 2015, I wore a compression long sleeved top rain coat, a singlet over that, and a poncho that acted like a sail in the wind (not in a good way lol) for the next 26.2 miles. I donned a skull hat, my new Boston Buddies hat that my bestie Timothy Moley had given me, and a shower cap from the hotel, then my rain hood over that. Who cares, no one could see who I was, you would never recognize me! Oh and of course compression pants and my new Vapor Flys that I wore on Saturday at the B.A.A. 5k. They proved to be the best piece of equipment I had that day not for their speed, because that was out the door due to the weather and winds, but every time my feet got soaked due to stepped in unavoidable puddles which was constant, those shoes immediately drew the water away from my feet keeping them warm, dry and no blisters or anything! My feet are pristine, and I have all my toes nails (at least all nine that I had before the race LOL)!

Well back to starting in Hopkinton. What amazed me most was the sheer number of supportive spectators that were there cheering on all the runners for the next 26.2 miles. It made me smile the whole way. I couldn't really see any of them clearly through the rain, but I felt bad for them, but their enthusiasm was certainly appreciated. I didn't see anyone I knew the entire way, not that I would recognize anyone, or they would recognize me. Before coming into Wellesley, I heard the scream tunnel clearly! It was so welcoming, those girls and their genuine spirit! The oranges and water stops were endless, and I took advantage of that. Another memorable moment was coming up Heartbreak Hill and hearing someone on the loudspeaker saying that there was a warming station at the bottom of the hill. I was grateful that I did not need that this year I was dressed appropriately and never really got cold. Then coming into Commonwealth Ave, I saw people discarding their ponchos and I saw the blue lines signifying the last mile. I discarded my poncho making a right onto Hereford and left onto Boylston. I know it was selfish, but I wanted at least one picture for my memories of this year's Boston. I never took my phone out because I didn't want to ruin it.

Ok, I'm done, I'm smiling and the wonderful volunteers put a medal around my neck and wrapped me in a warm thermal blanket and I walked through the rest of the corral to meet my besties James Murray and Moley at the Church on the Corner of Arlington and Charles soon after my girl Dolores Doman and I were reunited. We warmed up in a furniture store next door (thank you to that really nice salesgirl in there) and then we jumped on the T and went back to Dolores' hotel and got cleaned up! Then, last but not least, was an awesome celebration at Cheers where everyone knows your name and I was reunited with all my Boston Buddies!

It was a great weekend and I wouldn't trade it for anything! I will always remember this Boston for sure and will be back next year for sure. BQ'd this one by 10 min but it didn't matter that's not what it was about. This year was about "Together Forward" and mental grit, that's what all these Boston Buddies have got! Thanks to all my family and friends for all your support this day and leading up to it! It's a lot of work but worth it! Next up Berlin! Gimme some a 'dat nice weather and a tailwind tho! Xxxxooo

Angelia Finnegan, Bib 24810

Garland, TX, 61, 5:05:39

This is only a small part of what the whole Boston 2018 experience was like - but I didn't want to write a book with just my story! First of all, the fact that I was even running in the Boston Marathon was so unbelievable. I started running at the age of 55 and ran my first marathon in 2014. Boston was my 13th road marathon. We planned our trip right after I knew I was in. I had a 7:15 cushion so thought I was OK, but it seemed crazy to me that I would actually be accepted. It wasn't on my radar until about two months before I decided to go for it.

We decided to fly in on Sunday because the hotels were so expensive, and I figured I wouldn't be able to do a lot before the marathon anyway. That all changed the week of the marathon. Also, being a part of Boston Buddies made me realize how much I was missing! Who knew? The week of the marathon someone posted that they had received a notice from their airline that their flight may be delayed or cancelled. I never even thought about that. So of course I started checking the weather and there was this huge storm moving through the U.S. I was so stressed out that I wouldn't be able to get there in time to pick up my bib!

We had two other couples who weren't running that were also coming with us. We ended up cancelling our flight there and taking one on Saturday instead and hopefully our friends would have no problems. I was still concerned but it gave us more time to figure something out if we had to. All went well, and we stayed at a hotel near the airport the first night. I'm so glad we did because on Sunday we were able to go to the finish line and take pictures and then drive to Hopkinton and take more pictures and drive most of the route for the first time. Plus, I was so tired after Saturday and it gave me more time to rest!

Like everyone else, trying to decide what to wear with the weather forecast was hard - but I decided to dress warm and had a rain jacket I had found online that I wore the entire time that actually kept me dry. I wore my biking tights because they are warm, gloves, two shirts, visor plus the jacket had a hood. My feet were the coldest with water in them from the start, but the numbness came and went throughout the race. The worst part for me was pre-race and the Athletes Village. I should have listened to others and brought my shoes and wore old ones to leave behind.

Instead I had an extra cheap poncho that I tore in half on the bus and tried to wrap around my feet. That didn't really help in that mud pit! It was very crowded, wet and confusing. The start was just run up there and go. I never saw any drinks or food. It was so cold, and I just stood under the tent and shivered until it was time to go.

Even though the weather was crazy, I loved it up until the half. I saw my husband and friends at the 10k mark and again at the half. I was a different person at the half! I was feeling the cold and rain and it was pouring. The volunteers were so amazing. I kept telling them thank you and I couldn't believe they were just standing out in the rain and wind. Whenever I would start to struggle there would be someone yelling "Hey, it's the Boston Marathon!" I would perk up and say, "That's right!" It gave me the boost I needed!

At mile 22 I saw my friends again but this time I was cruising by them waving and felt pretty good! This was when it started getting emotional for me. I just couldn't believe I was going to finish the marathon that I never thought I would even be running in - let alone in these crazy conditions. I planned on taking my jacket off near the end but all I could do was take the hood off my head. When I finished I walked to the family area and had to go in the building for a few minutes because I was feeling sort of dizzy.

But I soon recovered and came out and found my friends and went back to our hotel for a shower and to go out to meet the Boston Buddies group at

Cheers. We had such a blast there. When we walked in there was this huge cheer and clapping! Haha, I said it was better than the finish line! But that's the way the Boston Buddies are. Encouraging, helpful and an amazing group of people. I'm so glad I found them and learned so much. I plan to qualify again for next year. I wasn't sure I would want to go do it all again, but after this experience, I definitely want to experience it all over again!

Annie Braddon, Bib 22595

Adelaide, Australia, 58, 4:15:10

I've been a runner forever. I turned 59 a week after Boston. This was my ninth Marathon. In 2014 I ran a 3:45 at the Melbourne Marathon and qualified to run NYC in 2015. This was going to be my first international marathon. I ran a 3:46 in NYC and had a BQ for 2017. On returning home, a niggling foot issue had worsened, and an MRI revealed a stress fracture. It was nearly nine months before I was running again. I decided I would not be able to run another marathon, so did not try to get into Boston in 2107 - a decision I regretted. So in July 2017 I went to Queensland to run a BQ time of 3:50:37 which gave me a buffer of over 19 minutes, and I got into Boston 2018.

The excitement was dampened when after my BQ race, a hip issue turned out to be a tear, so I endured another forced break from running between July and December 2017. I watched the Instagram countdown go down, 300 days till Boston, 250, 200. Finally, in mid-December I started running. I had to do a 20-week program based on quality not quantity, and only did four long runs. All of the rest of my training was under an hour, 3-4 runs per week, plus a cross training session, strength & core workouts.

Joining the Boston Marathon Training FB group was the best thing ever. In a short time, I felt connected to the members of the group, and their knowledge of Boston and the marathon was fantastic. The people in this group became friends and they were always there to support and to help in any way they could. I am sorry I didn't get to meet more of the members but am now connected to them either on FB or Instagram, we are bonded by the fact that we ran the 2018 Boston Marathon in the worst conditions since 1970 (maybe ever!)

My goal time for Boston was 4:00, hopefully sub-4. I thought even if I just ran at my long run training pace, I would do 4:15. My official finishing time was 4:15:10. At first I was disappointed with my time, but as I heard the stories coming out how hard the run was under the conditions, and that so many people had heartbreakingly had to pull out, I was at peace with my time, I had finished, and ran strong although slower than I had hoped.

Before leaving Adelaide there was rain predicted for race day, the veterans on the group were giving helpful hints on what to bring for a wet weather marathon. The day before my flight I went to the $2 store and grabbed a clear plastic poncho, a pair of $2 fingerless gloves, packed 2 garbage bags to sit on in Athletes' village (which I ended up wearing on each leg to try to keep dry), rubber gloves, a hoodie and track pants to throw away at the start.

On the morning of race day, 7:30 am, we stuck our heads out of our hotel door after breakfast, and it hit us that we were no longer in Adelaide, Australia - the driest state, on the driest continent. It was bucketing down, the wind was blowing sideways, it was freezing cold. We stepped outside to walk the five minutes to the bag drop, and were instantly saturated, the poncho flapping in the wind, feet soaked.

Bag drop was a very well organized and quick process, time to go to buses for the trip to the start line (still no let-up in the weather!). We would have loved to have taken photos of the buses all lined up, but it would have meant taking off rubber gloves, and another two pair of gloves, not to mention trying to get my phone out of my pocket. The trip to the start was quiet, and the bus was nice and warm. I think the weather was on everyone's mind. On arrival at the Athletes' village the rain and wind were still relentless, and we could see that there were piles of hail stones, all along the sides of the road, and lots of mud, mud that was ankle deep.

So now our wet soaked feet, were muddy, wet, soaked feet. The line to the toilets wasn't too bad, but we were standing in ankle deep mud. We then made our way to try for shelter under the big tents, but the wind was just blowing through, and because of the amount of rain, it was a big wet, mud area. The blue wave was asked to start moving to the start corral, and a woman asked us if we would like our poncho taped around the waist to stop it from blowing. Just another way that all the athletes banded together, to help anyone they could. I think this is the one thing that saved me. That poncho was the only thing I had to help keep me warm.

We started to move to the corral, when I noticed my shoelace was undone. There was nowhere to stop to try and retie it, so I kept moving with the group. We soon found that the PA system was down, and there was to be no official start, so everyone was unsure of what was happening, and started running. I decided to go to the side of the road and tie my shoelace, which meant taking off three pairs of gloves, and my hands were still freezing. I couldn't tie the lace tight enough, so I had to just start running and hope for the best. I went over the start line, had to ditch my rubber gloves and another pair, leaving me with my $2 fingerless investment.

The wind and rain were relentless, and it was so freezing cold, a cold I had never experienced in my life. I ran with my zip hoody for 9km, but it was so soaking wet and heavy, I made the decision to throw it away. Heck, I had on a t-shirt, arm warmers and a plastic poncho and gloves. I would surely be okay, the weather would warm up, and the rain would stop. She'll be alright mate! How wrong was I? Not in Australia now! The crowds were amazing, the volunteers were amazing, all smiling all cheering everyone on.

Someone had said not to use music if you run with it, and I was so glad I didn't bother with mine. I could hear and feel the electric crowd. I didn't seem to be warming up very much, and every time I thought the rain was easing up, there would be another torrential downpour. It was hard to look up, with the wind and rain in your face, I was trying to take in as much of the atmosphere as I could, but it was hard, it was just so freezing cold. I made the decision early on not to look at my Garmin, and as I crossed the timing mats I just kept thinking of home, knowing my husband was staying awake to track me. So all that was in my mind was to get to the next timing mat. At halfway I looked at my Garmin to see I had crossed in 1:57:30 and I still felt that 4 hours was doable especially when the weather cleared up (yeah right).

I felt good, and strong, so kept running by feel. The crowd was still fantastic, I was trying to high five as many people as I could to take my mind off the cold - taking in all the moments that the group had said to look for - Santa, the scream tunnel, Heartbreak Hill. I found it hard to deal with the cold - little things annoyed me - my zipper on the flip belt was stuck; I couldn't get my gels out and my hands were so frozen that I couldn't find the gels at the rear of the belt. My hands weren't working so I decided to walk a bit and get them out. But the crowds are yelling my name, telling me not to stop, so I kept running. My Garmin buzzed, so I looked down, 32km, I'm now feeling better, 10km to go, I felt a lift in my spirits. I can do 10km.

I looked at the time, I'm trying to do the math. I'm actually in for a change at 4 hours, I just can't drop my pace, can't slow too much. But then I looked up and see a 30km marker. What? This can't be so? I looked at my Garmin again, 32km! (by the end of the race, my Garmin had me at 44.7km?!) My spirit was now crushed. I felt colder than ever, the rain was pouring, I started to walk a bit. I needed a gel, but the crowds were yelling not to stop, and in a split-second decision, I saw a port-a-loo and headed to it to try get my flip belt zipper undone, get a gel, and try to tie my shoelaces. I have no idea why I made this decision - it wasted time. I still couldn't get my zipper to open, and my hands wouldn't move. I seemed to have lost some gels from my back pocket which I found was open.

I got my mind back on track and started taking gels from aid stations. The crowds were building over the final 8km, and my pace had dropped to about 6:00 - 6:30min per km, but I now felt like it didn't matter, I just had to get to that finish line. I hadn't travelled all this way and worked so damned hard to get to Boston and go home without a medal. I was so freezing I couldn't feel anything, yet at the same time, everywhere was hurting from the cold. Finally, I saw mile 25, 1800 meters between me and my medal. My teeth were chattering, I was crying, but somehow everyone's spirits had lifted. I took off my poncho and dropped it on the ground with thousands and thousands of other pieces of discarded gear. I was trying to not trip over any, I was trying to look up, and take it all in. The rain and wind were still hitting my face.

But suddenly I'm on Boylston Street and I can see the finish line. I can hear the person on the PA system, I hear the crowds cheering louder and louder. Then, finally I stepped over that finish line. I have done the Boston Marathon! My entire body is now shaking with the cold, I'm being told to keep moving but I was crying, I got my poncho to keep me warm, and I got that sweet medal. I kept moving and was trying to get my phone out to call my friend, but it takes ages. My hands were frozen solid, and I was walking around in a daze. I made my way to gear pick up and got my bag, but I was too cold, too wet, too freezing to try to get my jacket out. My phone seemed to be frozen. My friend and I didn't have a meeting spot. I know she would have finished before me. I'm wandering around crying with joy, happiness and because I'm so freaking freezing. Then I saw a message "I'm waiting at Starbucks until you come." I found her, and we were both crying, both frozen. We both can't speak because we are so cold, we just hugged each other and cried. We started to head to our hotel but were a bit disorientated. But like everything else, the BAA has a volunteer on the street corner, with a map, to help direct you back to your hotel. We had been out in the weather since 7:30am, and it's now near 4pm. We warmed up and can't bear the thought of going outside again that evening.

Two small town girls from the Adelaide Hills, in faraway Australia have just done the Boston Marathon in conditions that we couldn't have ever imagined. I'll never think running in our winter time is cold again. The disappointment with my time didn't last very long, I feel stronger for getting through that day, connected to everyone who beat the weather, and for not giving into it. I feel sad for those who had to pull out - they would be devastated. April 16, 2018 once again showed me how strong we can become when things get tough. Would I change the weather that day? Not now. I'm happy to be a part of history.

Bruce Lee, Bib 7087

Markham, Ontario, 45, 3:24:14

There are two factors which make Boston a very tough race. First, tough course, with a steady downhill first half, then killer hills on the second half. Second, unpredictable, uncooperative New England weather.

Overall, that was by far the hardest race I have ever run in my entire life. Not only did I witness firsthand how technically challenging this course really was, but I also managed to see that famous New England weather. They said this was the worst race day weather in more than 30 years – maybe in its 122-year history. 25,000 participants needed medical attention. 25 elites did not participate. Surprisingly, I had a decent sleep the night before the race. I believe it was because I was relaxed from abandoning my PR goal and knowing I was going to run "just for fun" (which for me meant running a BQ but not a PR). Aside from the decent sleep, the morning was a disaster from the start. The Inn didn't have the food out by 5 am as was promised the night before. A few participants from Montreal were already scrounging up bananas from their rooms. I poured myself a bowl of Special K and ate it dry. Being in Corral 1 allowed us to board the bus which takes us to Hopkinton at 6am sharp. But with the pouring rain, none of us wanted to leave early and be stuck in the Athlete's Village, freezing and wet. Finally, the innkeeper showed up with a cart of breakfast food and apologized to all of us. Peanut butter sandwich, banana, water and I'm all set. I packed another sandwich and banana in my start area bag, filled up my water bottle and was ready to go. After kissing goodbye to T, I donned my $2 Canadian maple leaf disposable poncho and ran 0.3 miles to the closest subway stop. A few runners were already sitting at track level, waiting for the inbound train. "This is soooo shitty," one of the runners looked at me and said. 'It is really shitty,' I agreed, 'but you know, lots of runners would kill to be in our position right now. This is Boston.'

One of the runners handed me fluorescent green duct tape. "Tape your shoes. Keeps the rain out." Another runner told me about this hack at the Marathon Sports store on Boylston the previous day. What an ugly looking but brilliant idea. Just like how I saw other runners in shower caps and others wearing latex gloves. The uglier you appear, the drier you are.

Thanks to a local female runner on our train, I knew which way to go. We followed her and transferred to the proper train which took us right to our baggage check. We had both decided to listen to the constant warnings regarding the port-a-potties: the washrooms are limited in Hopkinton (use the ones before loading onto the bus). By the time we entered the secure bus loading area, I had lost track of my green duct tape friend. I lined up for a bus without him. I was still carrying his duct tape. On the bus, I sat with a lady from New Hampshire. She introduced herself as Jenny (funny, because she reminded me of my running friend Jenny Avila, who had just written minutes before on my timeline wishing me luck). I turned on my phone and T immediately reminded me that we had forgotten to check if our kids' school buses were canceled. In regard to the sudden bad weather back at home, before we had left for Boston, Paul (friend from our Running Room clinic) had rebooked his flight due to freezing rain. We followed his advice and did the same. This was the right move as freezing rain hit the Toronto area and our original flight was cancelled. I checked the status of the school buses with my phone, and sure enough the weather at home was still terrible and all buses were cancelled, I called my mom and suggested that the kids have a snow day today. Once that was settled, I was back in race mode.

Jenny said she was an ultra-runner, qualifying for Boston on her first marathon while two months pregnant with her son. She said she had a goal of running sub three hours, but she had abandoned that goal due to the weather. Suddenly, I started doubting myself. I handed that duct tape to the runners behind me. I ate my sandwich and slowly ate the banana. Beneath the duct tape pulling and ripping sounds, the chatter between the runners, and the normal sounds of a driving school bus, I pondered. I felt like a fake. I felt like I had no business being here. I just let that self-doubt hang there for a moment and then started to shut my eyes. The two of us drifted off and slept for a few minutes.

When we finally reached Hopkinton just before 9am, we got off the bus and Jenny and I parted ways. The rain did not let up at all. All of our ponchos, garbage bags, and raincoats were prolonging the inevitable. We are going to be soaked. Not soaked, and then dry, but soaked and freezing for hours. When they called the 10am start time for our wave, the rain let us know it is not giving us any breaks. Then the wind came. The announcer did all he could to keep our spirits up. "This IS the Boston Marathon! The most prestigious race in the world! You will be part of history! Red Bibs, let's get you to the start area!"

In the start area, I noticed a guy wearing a "Running Free" shirt. I asked if he was from Markham (because of the local Running Free store), and he corrected me saying, "No, from Orangeville." While we were hemmed into our corrals, another guy beside me rubbed Vaseline on his face. I said, "Damn, I forgot mine." He then offered me some. "Normally, I wouldn't accept Vaseline from another guy, but sure I'll have some." Everyone around me laughed.

One experienced runner described the course. Some of the tips I had heard many times before. "Don't bank time on this course." "Watch for the hills." "There are four of them." One tip was very useful. Water and Gatorade stations are aplenty, but they are staggered on each side of the road. Don't cross over to the right, if you are on the left, and vice-versa. Just stay on the side you are on, and the water stations will be staggered on both sides. Don't try to cross over or you will get run down by other runners. This was a great tip. I dumped my Canadian-themed poncho as we started to move. This ended up being a bad decision. As we walked to the start line from the start area, there were many more port-a-potties. The last chance. Of course they all had massive lineups. So what do boys do? They act like boys. There was a shorter line of guys urinating onto the temporary orange safety fence blocking a narrow creek onto someone's yard. I mentioned to the other guys, "Not only is this an asshole thing to do, but all it takes is someone in those houses with a zoom lens, and this shit is going to be posted online everywhere."

When that business was done, we were at the "real" start line. Soaking wet, and wishing I still had my poncho, I noticed the duct tape on my shoes was no longer sticking. The shoes were already wet from walking to the subway and bus. Tape does not stick to wet things. Next time tape your shoes when dry, I told myself. Another futile effort.

The race started. Forget about going out too fast. The pack determined the speed. I was forced to run the first kilometer in 4:30 (7:10 mile), which was fine. I pulled over to remove the duct tape now hanging from my shoe. The first 10k passed by uneventfully. According to my Garmin, I hit it at 45:30 in Framingham. Bit slow, but perfectly fine. I felt relaxed knowing I didn't bank any time and just played it by feel. The rain poured. I was having fun. I waved to the spectators and tipped my hat to the military servicemen whenever I could. I saw my first race dropout. A man shouted how he blew out his hamstring and asked for medical attention. It scared the hell out of me. When I took my first gel, I noticed my race bib was bunched up. This was because the magnetic Race Dots (bought at the expo, used for the first time) had managed to touch corners and my bib was folded. I stopped to fix it, thinking I lost one of the magnets. Luckily, I didn't.

But after that struggle, I realized the first Clif Energy Zone was up ahead. I struggled to take a gel, and all for naught. It took a good 30 seconds off my time. As I approached Wellesley, a man ran up beside me. We started hearing the screams from the infamous Scream Tunnel. "Are you Canadian?" He asked. "Your Running Room hat gave it away"

"Yah, from Markham, Ontario. You?"

"Nova Scotia. Halifax."

"I could hear the east coast accent on you. Do you know the famous reporter from your city, John Tattrie?"

"Yes, of course."

"Well he wrote a really good novel, Black Snow. It's a historical fiction novel based on the Halifax Explosion. It's like a buck on Amazon. Seriously, buy it, read it."

"Sure, I'll check it."

The screams started to get louder as we descended into the tunnel. "Let's go have some fun!" I beckoned. I high-fived the Wellesley students, as many as I could and blew kisses to them. I was elated. I picked up my pace as soon as I high-fived the last one. This is such a blast! I hit my half at 1:35:30, according to my watch. This was the perfect pace. At around 14 miles, the rain started coming down hard. A guy beside me yelled "Yeah man!" I shouted like a madman, "Yeah man! Bring it on, assholes!" The rain continued to punish us. We fought back against the adversity. It was a steady downpour for the next couple of miles. As we turned the corner at the 17-mile mark approaching Newton, "More than a Feeling" by Boston played on loudspeakers.

"... When I'm tired and thinking cold, I hide in my music, forget the day…"

This was the start of the famous four hills. My pace had already slowed down at this point, and it was apparent I was going to not match my 3:15 Scotiabank Toronto (debut marathon) time. I began to take the hills a little slower. My friend Rachel was a spectator at the 19-mile mark. This offered great relief for me, as an excuse to look and make eye contact with anyone who remotely looked like her. Anyone who I glared at, smiled back and gave their encouragements. No sign of Rachel, however. I learned later that this was where the elite American, Rupp, stopped for medical attention. I was bracing for Heartbreak Hill. Heartbreak Hill always had place in my heart (so to speak). The song "Marathon" by my favorite band, Rush mentions it in a punning way as a "test of ultimate will, the heartbreak climb uphill." But when I looked at my watch, I saw I had just passed 32k. I slowed down and asked a spectator, "Was that Heartbreak?"

"Yeah, you did it man! That was it!"

"Really? Shit, seriously?"

Heartbreak broke my heart in a different way. It just came and went in a heartbeat. I picked it up, hoping to salvage a good finishing time. The final rolling hills during this stretch really wore me out. Of course, the rain came steadily again. The spectators were more abundant now as we headed into the city. The roads were uneven, and the streetcar tracks added a little extra challenge. I spotted the Citgo sign. I was warned many times that there was still a long way to go. In my official race photo, I looked calm, poised and relaxed with the Citgo sign behind me. The truth was, I was starting to blackout. Two more kilometers in this state, was a really tall order. The last thing I needed to do was push the pace or panic. I looked at my watch: 3:10, with 2.2k left. If I slowed down now, my BQ time would be in jeopardy. Heading down the underpass into the downtown core. Where is the turn to Boylston? I was starting to feel very lightheaded. Blackouts began again…

Two days earlier during the expo, my friend Toussaint had insisted we watch a movie in the makeshift enclosed theatre area just outside of the shirt exchange. They were showing a video run through of the course, and it was very well presented. It turned out to be very valuable information. The video was filmed by someone driving the course from Ashland to Boylston. Below the video, the elevation graph moved with the drive. On the top right corner, previous runners described the course.

"...as you turn the corner onto Boylston, brace yourself. You will hear a deafening roar. You will realize what your dreams are, and how hard you've worked. Crossing the Boston Marathon finish line will change you forever"

The video slowed toward the finish area and suddenly they added the soundtrack of the crowd and they blended in the footage of a previous year's race, sun shining, focusing in on a female finisher crying as she crossed. I held back my tears. T wiped her eyes. The audience was silent in anticipation of what was to come when it was their turn to cross that finish line in a couple of days.

As I turned the corner onto Boylston, I saw the finish line. The rain pelted us. I had plans to salute the crowd, but I didn't even hear their cheers. I wanted this nightmare to be over. One final glance at my watch and I was minutes away from losing my BQ time of 3:25. I kept my head down as I crossed. I gave a light fist pump and was afraid to change my stride, worrying that I would stumble. I stopped my watch. 3:24:20. In the words of Shalane Flanagan, "F*ck yes!" The volunteers handed out silver robes and put them on us. They offered some relief from the rain and the cold (more than the conventional heat blanket). You could still see the shivers and hear your own teeth chatter. Next, came the medals. Volunteers kept pushing us along. If you moved any slower, the volunteers offered to push you in a wheelchair. When they put the medal around my neck I shouted, "Yeah, that's what I'm talking about!" This was the very same thing I said in the last few marathons when they were placed around my neck. As I was being herded along, it hit me. It hit me hard. I went off to the side, rested on a barrier and I cried. The volunteers who stood behind the barrier just let me have a moment. The hood concealed my face. From their view, there would be a crowd of silver hoods moving along like a herd of sheep. Then there is one sheep off to the side, head down. The lone sheep who just realized he grinded it out to earn a small dream. In less than a minute, I rejoined the herd of 2018 Boston Marathon Finishers. As we crowded in front of the gear check-in tent, what came next seemed like a marathon itself. The rain came down hard. We were all shivering, and even though the volunteers were working as hard as they could, they could not retrieve the bags fast enough. The crowd was getting restless as they shivered. "Motherfucker!" One guy yelled. His outburst was in sync with the sudden heavy wind and the relentless torrential rain. There was a short, dark haired lady beside me shivering and chattering her teeth loudly. Larger men started pushing her off to the side and she began to shiver, harder and unable to fight the crowd moving in front of her. I reached out my hand and beckoned to her. "Come." She took it and I pulled her in front of me and eventually pushed her to the front, reminiscent of my mosh pit days. The crowd sheltered her from the rain and provided her temporary warmth. The volunteers gave the lady her bag and my tiny good deed allowed her to be on her way. Finally, more volunteers came in the tent to help. Bag #7087 was handed to me and my next challenge was to fight the crowd, the rain, and the road closures in order to find "T" in the Family Area.

As I walked as fast as I could, asking directions to whomever I could, I headed down Arlington Street, I noticed another road closure, but the police were directing us inside a building. I read the address, 75 Arlington. Runners were changing, stripping down to their underwear right in the lobby. I took the opportunity to change into some dry clothes. One runner asked to borrow my phone. Before checking the hundreds of notices on all my social media and texting platforms, I took a selfie and thanked Boston. I thanked Boston for the amazing people, the amazing city, and the amazing volunteers who stood for hours in this weather to make the race a success. To every Bostoner who took the time to salute me in my red Boston Finisher Jacket. To the MBTA staff who let me on the train for free after the race. To all the runners who grinded out the storm with me, I thank you all. To the ones who babysat our kids, Georgia, Sabrina, and my parents so I could earn a dream. To Markham Running Room, and the veteran marathoners who trained me. To T, the best one-woman crew and the best coach one could ever have. Thank you.

Boston.

Thank you.

Now to find my one-woman crew. The brave one who braved hours standing in the cold rain <3.

Pila Cadena, Bib 24223

St. Petersburgh, FL, 61, 4:22:01

I am a runner. Running has always been my medicine; not just for my body, but my soul as well. It has always been my constant. Thru the years I have experienced the agony of living with cancer; not once but 3 times. I, however feel very blessed that I've survived and have been able to continue living a great life, thru my running!

I run because every time I step out the door I am Celebrating Life one mile at a time. Thru the years of treatment and setbacks, running has always been my way of clearing my mind and keeping my body going forward. I have run many, many races but long distance has always been my favorite; it's my time with God, myself and Nature! I love coaching and sharing my experiences with others for inspiration and strength. If I can inspire one person every day I feel I'm doing my job at giving back. I am a very strong person and believe that I can be a great example to others. I set my standards very high.

Surviving cancer has taught me to be resilient, determined and not give in. Just like running, it can get tough out there but if you put your heart into it, those dreams can, and will, become a reality!

I am a Runner...I Celebrate Life!

Chris Russell, Bib 18051

Littleton, MA, 55, 3:49:48

We are near the 'one-mile-to-go' marker. Eric says something about one more hill.

The crowds are thicker and more enthusiastic than they should be, but this is Boston. The spectators take it as seriously as the runners. A multi-colored sea of umbrellas lines the road and the encouragement is loud enough to rise above the storm. Because it is the Boston Marathon, and this is *our* race.

I am slowed but not walking. Eric has those ultra-marathon legs and is pulling me. If he wasn't there I might, I just might, take a walk break. But I don't. And we grind on.

This race has ground me down but has not beaten me. The rain continues to come in sheets and stand-you-up blasts of cold wind. It is a din of squishing footfalls and the wet-plastic scrunching

of ponchos, trash bags and rain coats. All cadenced by the constant buffet and roar of wind-driven rain smashing into humans. That one more hill Eric is talking about is not really a hill. But I know what he means. It's Eric's 10thBoston and he has decided to run it in with me even though my pace has deteriorated in these last 2 miles as my legs lose the battle to this Boston course.

I will not stop.

It's my 20th Boston so I remember when they added this underpass to avoid a road crossing many years ago. I remember the old days of looking ahead and wishing with all my heart to see the runners disappearing to the right onto Hereford Street. Now we looked ahead to see the moving tide of storm shattered humans jog left and dip under and out the other side. We don't walk or slow our grimly purposed grind through the storm. We rise out of the underpass. Shifting to avoid the walkers or stumblers, or just having to jostle through yet another weaving, wet, exhausted, human-trash-bag blasted into our personal space by the gusty rain. There is not much antipathy left for these wayward castaways. An elbow, a shoulder, a tired shove and we all keep moving. It's like being inside a washing machine filled with ponchos and rain gear with a cold firehose turned on you at the same time.

We all just want to finish.

Ironically, I felt a tail wind slap me on the back as we grinded up Hereford. The only tail wind on the course. Maybe a bit insulting. Too little, too late. Eric says his family is in the crowd somewhere up by the turn onto Bolyston and I grudgingly grind a wide tangent as he searches the crowd. Nothing against his family but I don't think I'd stop here to see God if he were behind the barrier. The pull of that finish line is too strong, and I'm exhausted from 3-plus hours of pummeling rain and wind and cold. Typically, in a rainy race people will strip out of their protective clothing in the first few miles as they warm up. Not today. They never warmed up. But now, as they approach the finish line and the anticipated succor of hotel rooms and hot showers they begin to shed their rain carapaces en masse. For the last 10 miles I have been looking out the 6-inch circle of my found poncho's hood. Now as I pull it back and look down Bolyston it is an apocalyptic scene. Usually in high wind situations the discarded rain ponchos and trash bags will blow across the course like dangerous plastic tumbleweeds to tangle the runners' legs or lodge in the fencing. Not today. The cold rain is so heavy that it plasters the detritus to the pavement like so many giant spit balls. Through this apocalyptic landscape we grind out the last ¼ mile of this storied course. There is not much of a sprint in my stride as we push through the timing mats. I pull up the found poncho so the timers can see my number. I'm still clutching my bottle in one cold-cramped claw. I never finished my drink. I'm not sure I could let go of it if I wanted to. My hands ceased to function as hands more than an hour ago.

Grimacing we finish. Around us runners throw their arms up in celebration. The look on their faces is a combination of triumph, relief and disbelief. They have survived the worst weather that Boston has ever offered up. They got it done on a day that was at once horrible and at the same time the most epic journey in a marathon most will ever experience. And not just any marathon. The Boston Marathon. They lived to tell the tales, and this one will be talked about for decades.

I was wrong. I thought I had seen everything and raced in every type of weather. I have never seen anything like this. The closest I have come was the last leg of the Hood to Coast Relay in 2016. I had the same 30 mph head wind with the same driving rain. But the difference that day in Oregon was that the rain was a few degrees warmer and I wasn't going 26.2 miles on one of the hardest marathon courses. I have experience. I ran my Boston PR in '98 in a cold drizzle. I rather enjoyed the Nor'easter of '07. I had a fine day in the rain of 2015. Friday, as the race was approaching, when we knew what the weather was shaping up to be I wrote a blog post to calm people down. In that post I said not to worry too much, it's never as bad on the course as the hype makes it out to be. I said that the cooler temps were good for racing if you could stay out of the wind. I mollified the nervous by noting that in the mid-pack there are thousands of people to draft with. I cautioned against wearing too much rain gear as it would catch the wind and slow you down. Instead, I recommended, wear a few layers to trap the heat. I was wrong. I have never seen anything like this.

Most races would have canceled or delayed in the face of this type of weather. Not Boston. This type of weather at Chicago would have resulted in a humanitarian crisis on the scale of an ill-timed tsunami rising out of Lake Michigan. This weather at New York would have driven the runners and spectators into emergency shelters. Not the Boston Marathon. This old dame of a foot race has been continuously pitting the best runners in the world against each other for 122 years. This race is part of our cultural fabric. It's special. We don't stop for weather. It's too important to us to stop for anything. I remember emailing Dave McGillivray from a business trip in the days before the 2007 race as the Nor'easter bore down on New England. I asked him if the reports were true, that they were considering canceling the race? He responded matter of factly that he didn't know about anybody else, but he was going to be there. It's not bravado or false courage. It's a mindset that we are part of something bigger than ourselves. The organization, the athletes, the cities and towns and the spectators are all in it together. Together, on Monday, we all screwed up our grit and ran our race despite what wrath nature decided to unpack for us. The athletes who run Boston are not the type to give up. They have earned the right to be there. Either by qualifying or working to raise thousands of dollars. This is not the one-and-done bucket list crowd. This is a cohort of seasoned endurance athletes who have trained hard and long over many years to get here. If they skipped runs for bad weather, they would never have made it to the start in Hopkinton.

For the first time ever I decided to skip the Athlete's village in Hopkinton. From past experience I knew it was going to be a mess. Based on the reports I have from other runners it was like a medieval battlefield scene. The athletic fields turned into ankle deep mud under the marching of 30,000 runners. Athletes struggled to find shelter under the tents. Some crawled under vehicles in the parking lot in an attempt to get out of the elements. It was already raining and blowing hard as the day broke in Hopkinton. The temperatures struggled to find 40 degrees. There was no good place to be. It was a mess. There was no way to stay dry. Waiting around to be called to the corrals, runners started to accumulate a core temperature loss that would haunt them throughout the race. The organization did the best they could, but it was miserable and chaotic. I avoided it. My youngest daughter offered to drop me off in Hopkinton and I took the spectator bus downtown (instead of the athlete bus to the Village). Seeing what the conditions would be, I took Eric's offer of safe harbor at Betty's place.

It's a long story, a Boston story, and it goes like this... A long time ago, a family from St. Louis owned a home in Hopkinton. They started a tradition of hosting the visiting Missouri runners in that home. Eventually that family from St. Louis sold the home to Betty's Family. They continued the tradition, and this is where Eric, one of my running buddies, who is from St. Louis, has been sheltering before his Boston Marathons. This year, Betty has sold the house and moved into a senior center, right next to the start. She arranged to have the center's hall open to the Missouri runners. I joined a dozen or so gathered there in the warmth, replete with food and drink and good nature to wait for the start. We didn't know how lucky we were to have this safe harbor. Around 10:30 Eric, another runner and I made our goodbyes and started walking to the corrals. We walked out into the storm. We were ostensibly in wave 3 corral 3 but were soon to find out that much of the rigorous Boston starting procedure had been blown out the window. I made them stop at the big porta-potty farm on Main Street.

I took my dry race shoes, socks and hat out of their bag and wiggled into them in the cramped plastic box. Ready to race. I tossed the sweat pants, old shoes and ski hat to the volunteer who was stuffing soggy cast offs frantically into a rattling plastic bag. I have raced and run in all kinds of weather. I generally know what to do and how to dress. Monday, I dressed for racing in a 35-40-degree rainy day. I had trained in much colder weather. I wasn't expecting this day to be too cold, especially once we started racing and warmed up. The only real risk was at the end of the race. If we were forced to walk or slow down, we might get chilled. I dressed based on my experience from 19 previous Boston Marathons and 60+ marathons over the last 25 years. And I was wrong. I wore a new pair of high-cut race shorts that I bought at the expo. I have a rule of thumb, especially after a winter training campaign, 35 and above is shorts weather. We were close to but above that line. I slipped on a thin pair of calf sleeves in deference to possible wind chill and rain. Calf sleeves are good compromise between shorts and tights if the weather is on the line and add additional protection against cramping on cold days. For the top I added a layer to what I would usually wear. I had a thin tech tee shirt that I had made into a tank by cutting off the sleeves as my base layer. On top of that I wore a high-quality long sleeve tech tee I got from Asics for the 2014 NYC race and on top of that my Squannacook singlet with the bib number. People forget that the bib number is waterproof and wind proof and helps keep your core warm. Three layers plus the oversized bib should keep the core warm. I wore a pair of tech gloves that were designed for this in-between type weather. You wouldn't want to wear these when the temps got below freezing but they usually work well in the in-between temps. I topped it off with a simple Boston race hat from 2017. That's the same scheme I've used in countless 35-40-degree rainy runs.

I was wrong.

Mentally I was prepared. I've been doing this too long to worry about things I can't change. I was happy to not have another hot year. I had had a decent training cycle and my fitness was good. I had avoided injury except for a minor niggle in my high left hamstring. I was ready to race. I slept well. I was ready to respect Boston. I was wrong. This was a different thing. This was different than anything I had ever raced in. 65 seconds. That's how long Eric said it took me to poop at mile 9. I knew those porta-potties were there in the parking lot across from the reservoir. I have used them in previous years. I told Eric I wanted to stop. We had concluded that today wasn't the best racing weather by that point. We had been holding race pace fairly consistently up to that point down out of Hopkinton and into the flats of Ashland and Natick. I didn't feel horrible, but I didn't feel great either. I was worried about spending too much and getting caught at the end. My effort level was good, but a little high. My heart rate was good. But I weirdly felt like I was burning energy faster than normal. I could feel the energy I was expending fighting the storm. Our ability to draft had been minimalized. With the gusting wind and driving rain runners were having trouble staying in their lanes. Even if you could get on someone's shoulder that just meant you were in the wettest part of the road. The runners you were trying to draft stuck to the dry crown of the road and in order to get into their shadow you had to run in the water filled wheel paths. Even a veteran like me, who knows the course, couldn't make good tangent decisions as runners weaved and wobbled in the storm. My watch says I ran an extra ¼ mile. People were running in all kinds of rain gear in an attempt to stay the effect of the tempest. Shoes wrapped in bags tied at the ankles, runners clutching space blanket fragments, trash bags, ponchos and even shower caps that they had stolen from their hotels. All bets were off. I wanted to slow down and drop off of race pace to conserve energy I knew a forced break was a good psychological way of doing this. Anyone who has raced with me knows that I will keep repeating things like "we have to back it off" but for some reason struggle to put this sentiment into execution. A potty break would be a good reset.

Once we had the race monkey off our backs Eric and I settled into a reasonable pace and looked up ahead to anticipate the girls and the hills. I wasn't feeling great, but it wasn't critical. I didn't really know if I needed to be drinking more or how nutrition should work in this weather. I told Eric it was now a fun run and he said, "Anything under four hours is good". We ran on through Natick and Framingham. Eric turned to me and asked, was that the ½? I said I think it was. They hadn't put up the arch that has been there in recent years due to the wind and we almost missed it. Eric kept marveling at the spectators. He kept repeating 'these people are the real story'. He was amazed that they were still out in force lining the course and cheering. The spectators at Boston take it as seriously as the runners. If I could turn my head in the final miles I would see the incongruent, multi-colored sea of umbrellas lining the route. The spectators at Boston are not spectators, they are partners, or rather part owners, with the athletes.

Coming down the hill out of Hopkinton there were a couple of kids in bathing suits frolicking in a front yard. One guy was wearing a mask and snorkel. There are countless stories of spectators tying shoes and helping runners with food and nutrition when the athlete's hands were too cold to work anymore. One out of town runner, in a fit of hypothermia went to the crowd looking for a spare rain poncho and got the nice LL Bean rain coat freely off a man's back so he could finish the race. In some ways it reminded me of 2013 when the people of Boston came together to help each other overcome adversity. It's been five years, but our spirit is still Boston Strong. We ran on through to Wellesley staying on a good pace but trying to recover enough for the hills. Other years you can hear the girls at Wellesley College screaming from a mile away. This year the hard rain damped the sound until we were almost on top pf them. They were out there. They were hanging over their fence imploring the shivering runners with kisses and high-fives. Eric and I ran through smiling as always. Even though my energy was low I drifted over and slapped as many wet hands as I could.

Coming into mile 15 some combination of our slower pace and the increasing ferocity of the storm started to get the better of me. I could feel my core temperature dropping. I was working but I couldn't keep up. How did this happen? How could someone with my experience get it wrong? Why was this different from any other cold rain run? It was, in a sense, the perfect storm. The perfect combination of physics, fluid dynamics and temperature conspired to create a near perfect heat sink for the runners. The wind, on its own, was just a strong wind. The rain on its own was just a hard rain. The temperature on its own was just another spring day. But the combination pulled heat out of your body faster than you could make more. The volume of rain driven by the winds penetrated through my hat and washed the heat from my head. The same cold rain drove through the three layers of my shirts and washed the heat from my core. My gloves filled with cold water and my hands went numb. When I made a fist water would pour out like squeezing a wet sponge. The rain and wind were constant but would also come in big waves. We'd be running along and a surge in the storm would knock us sideways or backwards like being surprised by a maniac with a water cannon. I would stumble and lean into it and mutter "Holy shit storm!" or "Holy Cow Bells!" Really just to recognize and put words on the abuse. The wind was directly in our faces. The rain was directly in our faces. The whole time. We never got out of it. There would be lulls but then it would return with one of those smack-you-in-the-face hose downs. My shoulder and back muscles were sore from leaning into it. I was having difficulty drinking from my bottle because I couldn't squeeze my hand hard enough. I resorted to holding it between two hands and pushing together between them. People reported not having the hand strength to take their nutrition or even pull their shorts up after a potty stop. I was starting to go hypothermic and my mind searched for a plan. Eric knew I was struggling.

I started scanning the road for discarded gear I could use. The entire length of the course was strewn with gear. I saw expensive gloves and hats and coats of all descriptions. We passed by an expensive fuel belt at one point that someone had given up on. Eric knew I was suffering, and I told him I was going to grab a discarded poncho if I could find one. As if on cue a crumpled orange poncho came into view on the sidewalk to our left and I stopped to retrieve it. Eric helped me wriggle into it. It was rather tight, and that was a good thing. It was probably a woman's. It clung tightly to my torso and had a small hood that captured my head and hat without much luffing in the wind. It's at this point that Eric says I was a new man. I may not have been a new man, but the poncho trapped enough heat to reverse the hypothermia and we got back to work. By now we were running down into Newton Lower Falls and looking up, over the highway at the Hills. Eric said, "We're not walking the hills." I said, "OK" and we were all business. We slowed down but we kept moving through the first hill. I focused not on running but on falling. Falling forward and catching myself with my feet. Hips forward. Lift and place the foot. Not running just falling.

The hood of the poncho was narrow. I had an enforced tunnel vision, but it was somehow comforting, like blinders on a race horse. I could see Eric's blue shoes appear now and then on my right, or on my left. I settled into my own, little, six-inch oval of reality and worked through the hills. Other runners would cross my field of vision and I'd bump through them. I was in the groove. I don't know why but people's pacing was all over the place during the race. It might have been the wind or the hypothermia, but they were weaving all over the road. I had to slam on my brakes for random stoppages the entire race. Eventually I just ran through them as best I could. I didn't have the energy to stop. This kind of behavior is unusual at Boston in the seeded corrals, but the whole day was unusual. I think the relative chaos of the start may have had something to do with it.

When we got to the corrals they had ceased worrying about protocol and were just waving runners through. If you wanted to bandit Boston this year or cheat, Monday would have been the day to do it. But you also might have died in the process, so there's that. We got through the chutes and over the start mats without any formal starting ceremony. The flood gates were open, so to speak. Because of this I think the pacing was a bit strange at the start and we passed a lot of people. I was racing, and Eric was doing his best to hold me back. We chewed through the downhill section of the course with gusto. Given the conditions we were probably too fast, but not suicidal. Both of us have run Boston enough times to be smart every once in a while. We were holding a qualifying pace fairly well and trying to draft where we could. Eric had to pull off and have someone tie his shoe, but I stayed in my lane and he caught up. We rolled through the storm this way until I realized this was not a day to race and we had to conserve our energy if we wanted to finish. We metered our efforts and this budgeting process culminated in the voluntary pit stop at mile 9.

In Newton between the hills we'd focus on pulling back and recovering enough for the next one. Eric had a friend volunteering at mile 19 who we stopped to say 'hi' to. We were slow, but we were moving forward. We reached a point of stasis. Every now and then Eric would pull out his video camera and try to capture the moment. I was thinking sarcastically to myself how wonderful it would be to have video of my tired, wet self, hunched inside the poncho like a soggy Quasimodo. I had brought a bottle of a new electrolyte drink called F2C with me. It was ok but because of the cold I wasn't drinking much. I knew my hands couldn't get to the Endurolytes in my shorts pocket. I had enough sense to worry about keeping the cramps away. I managed to choke down a few of the Clif Gels they had on the course just to get some calories, and hopefully some electrolytes. Eric and I continued to drive through the hills. I miss-counted and thought we'd missed Heartbreak in the Bedlam. With the thinner crowds I could see the contours of the course and knew we had one more big one before the ride down into Boston. We successfully navigated through the rain up Heartbreak and Eric made a joke about there being no inspirational chalk drawings on the road this year. Eric was happy. He had wrecked himself on the hills in previous races and my slow, steady progress had helped him meter himself. With those ultra-marathon trained legs he was now ready to celebrate and took off down the hill. I tried my best to stay with him but the hamstring pull in my left leg constrained my leg extension and it hurt a bit. I was happy to jog it in, but he still had juice. I told him to run his race, I'd be ok, secretly wishing he'd go so I could take some walk breaks without a witness, but he refused. He said, "We started this together and we're going to finish together." OK Buddy, but I'm not running any faster. I watched his tall yellow frame pull ahead a few meters through the last 10K, but he would always pull up and wait for me to grind on through. And so we ground out against the storm and into the rain and wind blasts through the final miles.

In my mind I never once thought, "This is terrible!" or "This bad weather is ruining my race!" All I was thinking is how great it was to get to be a part of something so epic that we would be talking about for years to come. The glory points we notched for running this one, for surviving it and for doing decently well considering – that far outweighed any whining about the weather. This type of thing brings out the best in people. It brought out the grit in me and the other finishers. It brought out the challenges for those 2700 or so people who were forced to seek medical treatment. That's about 10% of those who started.

It brought out the best in Desi Linden who gutted out a 2:39 to be the first American winner 33 years. In fact, it brought out the best in the next 5 female finishers, all of whom were relative unknowns. The top 7 women were 6 Americans and one 41-year old Canadian who came in 3rd. No East Africans to be seen. The day brought out the best in Yuki Kawauchi from Japan who ground past Kenyan champ Geoffrey Kirui in the final miles. It was an epic day for epic athletes and I am glad to have been a part of it. I am grateful that this sport continues to surprise me and teach me and humble me. I am full of gratitude to be part of this race that pushes us so hard to be better athletes, to earn the right to join our heroes on this course. I am humbled to have friends in this community, like Eric, who can be my wing men (and wing-ladies) when the storms come. I am thankful for that day in 1997 when a high school buddy said, "Hey, why don't we run the marathon?" Those 524 miles of Boston over the last 20 years hold a lot of memories. This race has changed me for the better and I'm thankful for the opportunity.

Courtney Pragel, Bib 17947

Murfreesboro, TN, 36, 3:32:43

It was a symphony. The opening movement in Hopkinton. An allegro of strides pounding the pavement. The roaring crescendo reached with a left turn on Boylston Street. Every mile in between a blessing. 26,948 of us started the race Monday morning. 25,746 of us crossed the finish line. We all heard the symphony. This is what it sounded like to me.

8:05 a.m.: After riding the subway from the house we where we were staying, I said goodbye to Jonathan and Camden in the lobby of the Hyatt Regency Downtown Boston. Miles Tate and I would both be catching the bus from Boston to Hopkinton for the start of the race. It was a long trip. It would have been simple to have perilously considered how the only option for return was my own two feet. Miles and I chatted happily for the trek. The conversation kept the nerves far away. Thanks Miles.

9:00 a.m.: Runners poured out of busses by the hundreds. I followed the crowd because everyone seemed to know where they were going. The weather was simply terrible. 36 degrees, pouring rain, winds gusting to nearly 40 mph. We were all in this together, but we didn't exactly order these conditions. I had been a nervous wreck about this weather situation for two days. Finally, I told myself, "Well Court, you're going to PR (Personal Record) Boston regardless. It's the first time you've done it. Think happy thoughts." I had trained so hard for this race. I made a quiet goal of getting a second Boston Qualifying time this race, but in this moment, that seemed impossible. I had made myself come to terms with this. I was going to run my best race and enjoy the experience.

"If you're wearing a blue bib time to line up in your corral. Blue bibs only." I was wearing a blue bib. It was time.

10:50 a.m.: POP. The gun fired, and a sea of runners took flight. No words spoken. Thunderous strides pounded the pavement. The symphony had begun. Rare is the run that I cannot predict my outcome within the first mile. I kept turning my wrist to make my watch visible and see my time. I was sub-8:00 minute mile, and I felt good. I no longer knew the actual time. What mattered now was keeping that pace in the 8:00 minute/mile window and getting myself to Boston. A quiet voice whispered within me, "Today may just be better than previously expected."

Miles 1-19: The weather was wretched. At mile seven, I could not feel my fingers. I have never been that deep in a run and experienced this. But my pace was still sub 8:00. Given what was raging all around me, I felt spectacular. It was impossible to not feed off the energy of my fellow runners. But the spectators were something else completely. I know the weather kept many inside. I stared longingly as I passed local coffee shops and saw people sipping that sweet, hot drink while buckets of cold rain pelted my body from head to toe. Anytime that happened, though, I would hear the crowds just up ahead roar, and my face would stretch into a smile from ear to ear.

"Look at you with that smile right there! You are doing great!"

"You go 17947! You keep smiling!"

Go I did. Occasionally, the weather would give a brief reprieve. It was heaven. The girls of Wellesley climbed the rails and pushed us onward near the half marathon mark. I was maintaining my pace and feeling excellent. The inward voice whispered again quietly, "This day may bring something great." The symphony played on.

Miles 20-25: Entering Newton. Newton means hills. Crowd support was strong when I arrived at this section of the course. Thank goodness for that, because here you begin to ascend Heartbreak Hill. If it were run at Mile 5, it would be a warm up. If it were run at Mile 15, it would be an irritation. Running it at Mile 20.5? Akin to scaling Everest. My quads were screaming at me. Get up this hill. Get up this hill. It's all downhill from here. GET. UP. THIS. HILL. My pace took a hit. But I got up Heartbreak Hill. "You just scaled Heartbreak Hill and you are still smiling?" Yeah, I was smiling. I was running the Boston Marathon. And I was on pace to PR.

Miles 25 and 26: The Citgo Sign. One mile to go. My watch died. I had no clue what my pace was anymore. It did not matter. I knew I only had about 10-12 minutes left to run in Boston, and I was going to savor them.

Right on Hereford, left on Boylston: The Boston Marathon is a point to point race. We run 26 miles directly. Then, we approach the two most iconic turns in all of running. Right on Hereford. The symphony swells. Left on Boylston. The crescendo. I did not even think about the weather anymore. The music of the crowd played so loudly, so beautifully, it carried me home and across the finish line. Finishing Time, 3:32:43. A Personal Record by 14 seconds. A qualifying time for the 2019 Boston Marathon.

The finish line: Elation. I turned to my right and congratulated my neighboring runner. "Thank you!" she said. "We have to be the stupidest people alive." I laughed. And then my body began to tremble. I could not stop it. A fellow runner put her hand on the small of my back and thrust me to the front of the pack. "Somebody get her a blanket!" The next thing I knew, a race official is directing me to a bus. "You okay? We gotta get you warmed up." "I can't stop shaking" I couldn't. Even now, as I try to recall the feeling, I cannot mimic it. The official took me to a bus and sat me down. "You stay here as long as you need. Get warm, and do not go anywhere until you are ready." Other volunteers eyed me carefully. "You okay?" After a few minutes, I was. Many, many athletes were unable to complete the race due to the conditions. I was blessed and held in God's Hands. Prayer and love covered and carried me. Overwhelming.

Gratitude: No one completes a race alone. Jonathan worked so hard to make this trip special for our family. It was a dream come true. I was surrounded by the love in Boston. To say I am overwhelmed by to outpouring of support and encouragement I received is an immense understatement. Every single word spoken to me lifted my heart. For the prayers. For the love. For the care. Thank you. Let's do it again next year.

September 12, 2018 Boston Marathon Registration Week: On Wednesday, September 12, my grandmother passed away. Years ago, Alzheimer's ravaged her mind. Only this week did her body give up the fight. My Granny thought my running was simply nuts (and maybe she was right). She never quite understood it, but she would always ask how it was going. Mentally, she was gone when I ran this year's Boston Marathon. My first time participating. But she was with me. My Granny never got to visit Boston in her life. So today, when I submit my 3:32:43 (BQ 3:40) in hopes of returning in 2019, I'll do it for her. Yes, she would have thought we were all crazy running those streets. But man, I think she would have loved Patriots' Day.

Rob Fried

Great Neck, NY, 57, 1983 Boston Marathon, 2:35:11

My infatuation with the Boston Marathon.

I started running from a fluke injury playing soccer in high school. I tore my MCL and was told that running, after I came out of the cast, would help strengthen my legs muscles. So I followed my doctor's orders. In no time I was hooked. I started in June 1980 and within 3 weeks I ran my first race, a 10k in 45 min. I was thrilled as I continued and by year's end that time went down to 39 in 10k. As I was running I read everything on the subject and saw the story of Rosie Ruiz and the 1980 Boston Marathon. I knew then I wanted to try to run a marathon.

The criteria to run Boston was to have a previous time of 2:50 to be allowed to run. I was now already a college runner as a walk on at Adelphi University. I learned more about the sport and in a short time on the team my 39 10k went to 34 min! I said to my coach, "I'll run Penn Relay's Marathon." The year was 1982 and it was a hot day in Philadelphia. I was on 2:40 pace at 24 miles and something called "the wall" hit me. I could not take another step past 24 miles. I walked\ran to Franklin field with a 2:57:21 to show for it. My dream of Boston shattered I said, "Never again do I walk." I attempted the 1982 NYC Marathon and this time I carried Lifesavers with me for a sugar boost, no gels. The Lifesavers were timed properly and now I finished my marathon sub 2:40 so Boston was a go for 1983.

I trained very hard that winter for Boston and knew I was in the biggest race of my life. I was 22 years old and one of the youngest runners at the start in Hopkinton. At 9 am we pulled into the gym and sat on the floor waiting till Jock Semple yelled at us to walk to the start. It was a noon race then. I went into my coral up front and only a few rows back from the front. I felt I did not belong. Everyone was good because 2:50 was the BQ.

The gun went off and I took off. I remember the downhills and the small rural towns and thought, "This is Boston?" Actually, it's a race of small towns until the end when you arrive in Boston. At 17 miles I asked a fellow runner, "Are we in the hills yet?" He said, "You bet your ass we are." Funny how things stay in your mind 35 years later. I imagined Heartbreak Hill as a barren wasteland

of skeletons of runners who died getting to the top and their ghosts wandered forever in torment never reaching their goal. The reality is Newton is a wealthy, pretty town and nothing like I envisioned. I climbed the hill, ran the last 10k, turned right on Hereford, long looping left to the old finish at Prudential Center in 2:35:11. I was put in the garage for an IV to get back to life. I had 3 more Boston's in 1985, '86, and '87 and called it quits.

I started medical school and had enough. Funny thing, I never missed it. In 2013 I decided to get back in shape and start running again 26 years later. I ran the Philadelphia Marathon on 35 miles a week and hit my BQ and back to Boston 29 years after my last in 1987. I met Vince Varallo online and he approached me about starting a running group to train together. I said sure. This small gathering of running friends grew fast. It exploded to what it is now 4500 members. I returned to Boston now a 55-year-old man and saw the changes. It was a 3000-

runner race in my era, but now had 30 thousand. I ran the race and cried as I saw the course return in my mind like I never took off any time. I finished in 3:25 and now I was a Boston Marathon finisher again. The race can leave you humbled as well as make you a local hero. I love the race, the city, and this event changed my life in 1983. I got a profession after it and now a second chance to be young again. It's my fountain of youth.

David Fanfan, Bib 7625

Valley Stream, NY, 41, 3:28:44

It's difficult to put into words what happened on Monday, April 16, 2018 in the Commonwealth of Massachusetts. A place I once called home for a brief year. Before that, a place I often visited to see family, go on class field trips, or just explore. On Patriot's Day, I saw Boston from a whole new perspective. The way I've come to love touring towns: through marathon running.

Those who closely follow my social media have come to learn that I spent a year in Boston studying international business. It was my first leap towards my interests to international affairs. An accelerated leap that abruptly changed the trajectory of my life, to say the least. One of the best life decisions I ever made back, in the face of an economic downturn. This life change coincidentally aligns with the time I decided to pursue marathon running.

I was already familiar with Boston. My beloved uncle laid down roots here and I loved visiting my extended family growing up. It was a hop, skip and a jump from southeastern Connecticut, where I lived when my father was stationed at the New London Naval Submarine Base. So, there was no magical moment for me, nor nostalgic admiration for those small New England towns that the Boston Marathon course passes through.

Then what made getting here so special for me? Why did I work so hard for years to finally run the Boston Marathon? Was it to remember some of my favorite moments in Boston? My first visit to the Omni Theater, The Museum of Science, the Salem Witch Trials exhibit in Salem, MA, or biking and running along the Charles River. All these memories are part of my experience with Boston and were in my thoughts as I ran from Hopkinton to Boylston.

I can't talk about my Boston Marathon experience without shedding some light on my training. I decided to switch my training regimen up from my 2017 marathon. I needed a whole new perspective on my training. I hired a coach, one who formulated an insightful plan that focused on my marathon weaknesses. It was risky for me to change my methods for the Boston Marathon as I was hoping for it to be my best marathon yet.

The dreaded hamstring!! I have had a hate-hate relationship with my hamstring screwing up my marathon potential. The good news is I was slowly gaining core strength with each marathon training cycle, so those left hamstring strains were less and less a factor in slowing down my marathon times. Coach prescribed more strength training. In the months leading up to the Boston marathon, I was religious about getting those strength workouts in. It was a significant change in how I trained in the past. Bulgarian lunges, balance toe touches, step-ups with weights over my shoulders: just to name a few of the exercises. Combine that with an increase in mileage, running more weekly 20+ milers than ever at marathon goal pace.

"Keep your long runs at or as close to 7 min/mile as possible and all of your shorter distance paces would come down." Coach emphasized as I slowly saw my long run paces come down. He also introduced me to the mid-week long run, where I would run 12 to 14 miles every Wednesday, also at marathon goal or faster pace. My legs were exhausted hitting 76 miles peak, the week before the United Airlines New York City Half. It was great, and my legs were feeling strong. I looked forward to strength training, twice a week. I loved running longer distances.

"Cut back on the speed work to limit strain on your hip." That was hard to do. I was so used to those track workouts that helped develop some speed so that I can have that kick for late race surges. I complied and left the track alone. I made limited appearances at the Armory in Washington Heights, which ended up being a pleasant advantage to my wallet saving that $20 per track workout. I ended up doing speed work only 4 times this whole cycle besides my strides during taper. I was becoming a true distance runner: Steady pacing and consistent running. I didn't feel sore nor my hamstring didn't feel tender after each distance training run.

When I changed my training methods, I knew going in improvements weren't going to happen overnight. It would take a couple cycles to get used to this style of training. I kept up with my biweekly massage regimen and introduced my legs to the Air Relax recovery boot. I also religiously did a recovery run before my strength training, at about 2 minutes less than marathon goal pace to lock in any gains from my long runs. It was great! Running or strength training just about every day.

I remember the race day weather for the 2016 and 2017 Boston Marathons. Both instances saw hot days that made it difficult for runners to perform their best after mile 20. The heat got the best out of plenty of great runners, and I knew I had to prepare. "If race day Boston in mid-April is usually hot, let me make sure that my muscles can get used to warming up quickly, like it would in the summer" I concluded. The treadmill became a welcome addition to my regimen. Now I always hated the treadmill. The mind-numbing routine of running in place while a conveyer belt moves under your feet. I just can't! This is driving me nuts! I run 25 minutes, then break for a stretch. Another 20 to 30 minutes, then break for some water and another stretch. By the time it is over, I logged in 12 or 15 or even 18 miles some workouts – all at marathon goal pace or faster. I soon figured out that I should allow the machine to randomly change the incline, to prevent overuse injuries to your muscles. By the time taper came around, I was used to it. I can go the whole 60 minutes if I have to. The treadmill is my friend. An excellent alternative to running outdoors, where mother nature had a great time in the Northeast United States. Every week in March, there was a Nor'easter to throw off my training. An extended period of sub-freezing temperatures in January to make matters complicated. Almost a quarter of my miles were on the treadmill (before strength training, on cold days, or at least once a week), and I believe I'm a better runner because of it.

There is something about running for charity that allows me to have more focus and gives my runs a sense of purpose. After 13 marathons (well really after my 12th in London), I knew if I wanted to run my best Boston, I would have to channel some of that focused energy from charity fundraising that has allowed me to succeed in the past. So I signed on for the American Cancer Society's Team DetermiNation Mini-Series. They let me choose my race and I run to benefit their cause. I signed up through the Illinois Chapter again, and the reconnected me with the New York City Chapter where I was made an Assistant Coach.

This was by far, the highlight of my training. I was there Tuesday nights in Central Park, and Saturday mornings in Brooklyn's Prospect Park, helping runners run train for their first half marathon. All were motivated to raise money for cancer research in the process. That energy was amazing. To see their consistent dedication was truly inspirational and put my marathon life into perspective. I was once a first-time half marathoner, training while raising money for charity. Who would have thought 9 years later I would be running the Boston Marathon? I knew there would be some future Boston Marathoners from among this group. And it was great to see them lay down their roots for their journey to come.

What was special about making it to the starting line was being among the best. It's amazing how a place you are familiar with can transform based solely on the energy of the people there. I was around some amazing people. People who also worked very hard for months or years to get there. Three days before the Boston Marathon, I weighed in at 178 lbs, 13 lbs over my Chicago Marathon BQ performance, and 6 lbs over my last marathon in New York City this past Fall.

"It'll be fine," I thought. I may be carrying a little extra this time around but I'm a stronger runner, I'll muscle through if I have to.

"Stay off the bike! The leg muscles work in the opposite direction that will counter any improvement in your running!" These words from my coach were on repeat in my mind throughout my Boston Marathon training cycle. This would finally be the year I was going to work on my bike training and finally conquer the 100-mile ride. Instead, I had to make sacrifices. Sacrifices to run my best Boston Marathon.

Here I was in Hopkinton, a town not unlike any other familiar New England town. There was nothing special here. It was just cold, windy, rain that would start and stop in torrential downpours. The last-minute adjustments were a major help. I've done everything I could to get here, listened to my coach attentively, and ready to give my best effort yet. "Wear a light jacket, wear shorts, cover your ears, and wear gloves. The weather is going to be bad out there." Coach said during our previous day's phone pep-talk as I was stood in line to meet Marathon Champion, Meb Keflezighi. "I don't have a light jacket, but I was going to wear a singlet and my half tights. I figure once I get running, I should be fine." "No! Get at least a shirt to cover your shoulders! Wear the shorts instead of the half tights! Your legs are going to be heavy with the half tights in the rain!" Well here's some extra stress I wasn't anticipating. I wasn't planning on buying anything extra besides my celebration jacket and souvenir glass for my collection. I packed light, choosing to only bring things that can fit in a backpack for the Amtrak ride from Penn Station to South Station.

At the top of Heartbreak Hill my calves were burning. The last time I felt this much strain in my calves was mile 23 of my San Francisco Marathon, June 2013. It had cramped up on me then, and I was worried it would cramp up on me in now. Were my legs heavy as Coach said it would be? I didn't spring for the shorts as suggested. I bought the shirt to cover my shoulders and managed to find a free neck scarf from Janji on Seaport Blvd, just a 5-minute walk from the expo. But it was too late for any extra, out-of-budget spending.

It was probably the extra weight I was carrying. My calves weren't used to carrying as much in a marathon. All of my strength training focus was on my quads and hips. I did everything I could to strengthen the area around my weak left hamstring. One can say I was successful in that regard. No hamstring pain throughout the entire marathon; not even the burning warning signals.

"Maintain a 7:15 pace until you reach mile 18, then make your move." Coach drilled this into my head before we ended the call. "If you find yourself going too fast in any particular mile, make up for it on the next by slowing down, and vice versa." Coach knew exactly where I was at and how I did in my training. My original plan was to do what I always do: stay as close as possible to 7 or 7:10, and then see where I was at after Mile 20. I could either try to run my best in the final 10k or hold back to prevent injury if I had enough of a cushion. His adjustments weren't that far off from what my original intentions were, but it was clear he wanted me to make it through Boston injury free.

The weather had a different plan for my pacing. There would be no best marathon yet. As I arrived at Boston Commons via Uber (my first time ever using Uber on my own) by 6:30 A.M, I knew this wasn't going to be pretty. I made sure to keep my throw away gear on to the start gun, Wave 1 Corral 8. That first run jacket I bought in my Team In Training days was finally gone. So many sacrifices to make it to Boston and I was confident I can run my best Boston, regardless of the weather. The winds were blowing in the opposite direction of my path to the finish. A battle indeed but I was holding the coach's pace. Thirty mile per hour winds were not enough to discourage me. Especially in the net downhill first half. The torrential downpour came intermittently. The rain combined with the wind made it difficult for my legs to get warm. I've run enough of these to know when I can effortlessly adjust speed, kick when I needed to, and settle in to my desired pace. Instead it was cold, brittle strides with every foot strike. As long as I followed the coach's wisdom and if my legs could warm up by mile 18, this could still be my best marathon yet.

My first pee stop was immediately after the start gun in Hopkinton. I found my usual rhythm. Quick grab and go at every water stop: Gatorade – sip – water – sip – water – overhead if I was hot, or sip otherwise. It became an art for me. "You grab water like a pro", a runner directly behind me complimented. Immediately after I hear those words, I can hear the screams of Coach Ramon Bermo, whom I assisted during those American Cancer Society workouts, "Go David!! You got this (maybe something in Spanish because he was so loud) Great job!" or something along those lines. This man was at mile 6 cheering with his windbreaker hood on by himself in the pouring rain. Incredible!!

This is going to be a great race! I'm finally feeling good. The weather can't deter me. My bladder can, though. My pace began to uncontrollably slow, that sensation came at the 15K mark. It's not like me to have to go again so badly so soon. I had been running for an hour and I thought, "OK… another 30 seconds won't hurt." The next two available port-a-potties were occupied so I stopped went on the nearby pavement sidewalk.

The sensation returned as I ran through the Scream Tunnel. "So these are the Wellesley girls that offer kisses to the runners! They look really young. Thank you, but no thank you," as my thoughts briefly moved away from my urge to go. "If I ever saw my little sister out there, trying to kiss sweaty (on a drier day) strangers running by man…." That soon left my head as I knew that would never happen. And then came my 3rd bathroom break of the race. With the rains and the winds continuing, I started thinking about my health. It was very unusual for me to have to go this often. "Maybe I need to see a doctor when I return to New York."

One hour thirty-seven minutes at the halfway mark. My race was slower than usual, but I knew I could still salvage this thing for my best marathon yet. My legs were still strong. All I needed was that one good kick and settle into a dominant race pace that could get me to an amazing finish. Each foot strike was still brittle and cold that would just linger in my lower legs. Freezing and wet, my legs soon became numb as another sensation came just before the last downhill leading to the Newton Hills

"Not today!" I shouted to Roland as we met by chance at yet another marathon. "Where's Delgado?" as I gave him an Obama fist bump. "He's way ahead." Roland replied before I sped up along level ground to hit the next port-a-potty for my 5th bathroom stop, right before the 2nd stretch of the Newton hills.

"Good for him!" I yelled as I sped off. At least someone was having a good day. By then I was miserable. I could have paced the rest of the race with Roland, but somewhere in the back of my mind, I still felt I had a shot to make this thing great. If only my legs would get warm already. After 18 miles, all these pee breaks had taken away about 3 minutes off my time. Pee stop number 6 at mile 18, and I thought, "I should be making my move!" But I knew Christine and the rest of the Brooklyn Tri Club were about half a mile away. Keeping my eyes peeled, I see the big sign they had made for me. I quickly ran to it and tap on it several times. This was my second brief moment of joy as I gave Christine a hug and was feeling so grateful for their cheers. This was the first time anyone held a sign with my name on it during a marathon.

Again, misery returned as I started Heartbreak Hill. The extra stride length with every step of the first 16 miles stretched my leg muscles. It brought a new kind of leg pain during this ascension. I can feel myself running slower with every step. Anger started to settle in the below freezing weather, and I had to pee yet again. I focused on the port-a-potty at the top of what I now know was the end of Heartbreak Hill.

"Your Heartbreak is over!" The guy holding those words in a sign made eye contact as I came to a complete stop in front of the bathroom. "It's over!" I told him. That last mile took me 10 minutes. I relieved myself for the 7[th]and final time, realizing my legs had no kick for a late race surge. I was angry that I allowed myself to be in such a vulnerable position. The wind was blowing fierce, the rain would precipitate in surges that made the nearby wheel chair athlete struggle to make it to the top of the same hill. It was a rough day for many. A PR or anything close was far from my mind. I just wanted to survive this thing and go home.

I had a 5:30 PM train to catch at South Station. Any delay would risk me not being able to make it into work tomorrow. Thus, walking was out of the question. I jogged. Mad at myself for running through this terrible weather. No marathon was worth this. But then I thought as I approached mile 24, this was the Boston Marathon. I worked so hard to get here. It was more than just this race.

"Great! Just what we needed!" a runner to the side of me sighed as another torrential downpour mixed with hail started poking at our face. The brim of my CPTC cap had blocked the drops giving me a visible path forward. It was a slow and steady jog to the finish. Salvaging my legs for the next race, while the next race was far from my mind. Rather the 13 previous marathons, the training runs, the different run clubs, the charity fundraising campaigns, the amazing friends I met, the travel, the health benefits, clogged my brain, all at once, as my legs kept moving. Each little hill on the net downhill of the last 5 miles, gave my legs Heartbreak Hill flashbacks.

'ONE MILE TO GO" That huge yellow unicorn painted on the road in Kenmore Square came before my eyes as my head remained down while hail drops hit my brim. "Run with dignity!" a wise coach at Central Park Track Club once said. I did just that as I locked into form like it was the Weekly Form Run with the North Brooklyn Runners. My survival instincts carried me through those last miles, in the face of horrific weather trying to blow me off course. One last mile soon became a right turn on Hereford Street, from Commonwealth Avenue. Then another left turn to Boylston Street and the street wide John Hancock signs above the finish line was 600 meters away. The crowds were roaring and emotion overwhelming me. Another World Marathon Major with two to go! And this one was about survival. "It was only two days ago, I was running in 70-degree weather! But today, this is what I get for my first Boston Marathon! Lucky me!" I declared to the unknown runner while waiting for the start in the mud drenched Athlete's Village in Hopkinton. "Lucky us, my friend!" he replied. "We are going to get through this together!"

Thank you:

- Coach John Henwood for his consistent guidance, meaningful advice, and steady patience, with an occasional kick in the butt.

- Coach Ramon Bermo, of Team DetermiNation for cheering in the horrible Boston Marathon weather. Just another example continued selflessness towards the running community.

- The NYC Muscle Whisperer, Ria Magtoto, for helping to keep me injury-free throughout my 800-mile training winter.

- And my teammates at the Central Park Track Club - New Balance for the continued inspiration.

- The Brooklyn Tri Club for the cheers and those open water swims that have made me a stronger runner.

- The Illinois Chapter of the American Cancer Society's Team DetermiNation for setting up my latest fundraising campaign.

David Scott, Bib 14409

Jacksonville Beach, Fl, 57, 3:47:53

The marathon is always a fickle beast and even when well trained, you never know what you are going to get. April 16th, we expected, and got, some pretty extreme weather, yet it was worse than I and almost everyone imagined. I saw well trained athletes dropping at all stages of the race, some due to the normal injury attrition, but many due to hypothermia.

As the day wore on the weather worsened and the temps kept dropping with wind chills most likely in low 20's if not into the teens. I started in Wave 2 at 10:32 am and it wasn't horrible. Yet.

I wore shorts, long sleeved dri-fit shirt, race singlet, rubber gloves under running gloves, a dri-fit beanie hat, and clear plastic hooded poncho. By mile 6 (1st 8 are downhill miles) my left calf which I have been nursing the past 30 days decided it didn't like going downhill and really tightened up. I've grown used to it, so it really didn't slow me down, but did change my stride. That led to the right calf joining the tight calf party about mile 10.

As I was deciding if my calves were going to let me finish, the gait change and leaning into the cold heavy winds got my lower back into the pain party.

Just about then I hit the halfway point still on goal pace but knowing the Newton Hills loomed 4 miles ahead. I had to adjust everything as my quads were getting cold and numb. Then the hills started. Only 4 up-hills but by mile 17 even on a good day they are challenging for us Florida flatlanders.

With the wheels rapidly not wanting to turn over it turned into a death march to the finish. I suffered through heartbreak hill at mile 21 but still had 5+ miles left. I just wanted to finish knowing I'd miss my goal time, but I didn't want to drop out even though my mind said, "@&!?# it, let's hit the med tent and get out of here." The miles passed way too slowly, and I kept getting slower. Right before mile 25 I decided to stand more upright for the upcoming small hill and my lower back said Nay-Nay and I had a shooting pain. I stopped to try and stretch it but when I tried to start running again the shooting pain struck again. I walked the quarter mile or so up the hill (more of just an incline) then once at the top I started to run again. I lost 3-4 mins by stopping and then waking that hill, but I knew I'd finish now. About 3/4 of a mile ahead was the famous 'right on Hereford (street)' then 'left on Boylston' which brings you to the final long straightaway to the finish line. You can see the finish line but it's much farther away than it appears. I got a bit emotional seeing the finish line approaching as I was going to be a Boston Marathon Finisher and I teared up a bit.

I crossed the finish line exhausted but ecstatic and thought I'd be warm soon. Boy was I wrong. You first got a bottle of water, then a bit further down you got in line to get your medal, then another walk to get your bag of food. Then came the post-race foil blanket which by the time you had it placed around your shoulders you were really freezing! Now you go another 100' to the bag drop area to get your warm dry clothes.

The volunteers weren't ready for the crush of freezing athletes that got there at that time. (Not their fault. All the volunteers endured the conditions and were totally amazing!) It took 30-40 mins to get our bags and everyone was visibly shivering, some uncontrollably. It was scary seeing some people that appeared to be getting hypothermic right in front of our eyes. Finally, I got my bag but with only one small tent for all of us to change in the line was endless. I found another tent and used my post-race foil blanket to change under. With the concrete soaked and being extremely cold it took about 10 minutes to change. Finally, I was dry and warm. The guy behind me was sitting on the cold wet concrete and was too cold to stand to change. I kept trying to help him, but he kept refusing, most likely due to hypothermia. I got the volunteers to get him a medic and hope they took good care of him. I then went back out into the cold rain once again to find somewhere warm for food and a well-deserved beer. It was a half mile walk in the rain.

I have vacillated between "I suck" and "At least I didn't quit" the past 24+ hours as I felt I should have run faster. The weather was so brutal the top 7 elite athletes based on their personal best times did not finish the race. A few due to hypothermia.

I do know many people who had amazing races, but they were fewer than normal. I know personally quite a few people who had to drop out due to hypothermia and it's scary. Moral of the story here. All who started the race regardless of their finish (or not) are amazingly strong bad-asses! Just getting off the bus sucked!

To all those who ran I tip my cap to you. We will always be remembered for the race of 2018 and possibly one the worst race conditions ever. To the volunteers! Holy hell you're amazing! To put up with cold exhausted cranky runners while enduring crappy conditions and taking care of us as you did is something you should be proud of. Without you there is no race. To the hordes of fans lining the entire 26.2 miles standing out in the rain. Y'all ROCK! The energy you infused into the runners kept us going! Thank you!

To all my family and friends who stalked, err tracked me, and sent me your great vibes and post-race congrats. I love you guys!

I am a Boston Marathon Finisher! It still hasn't sunk in.

Abdullah Ahmad AL-basha, Bib 489

Amman, Jordan, 24, 3:25:28

I started running in December 2013 just to make my body stronger and healthy. I ran my first half marathon in the end of the same month and finished in 1:23, good enough for tenth place. I started to think I wanted to run every single race in my country. The next race was an ultra-marathon, 50km, and I came in 7th place in 3:35:45. I met a girl from Florida in 2016 and she told me about the Boston Marathon. I learned you have to qualify for it so my first marathon after learning about Boston I qualified with a 2:39:54 at the Amman International Marathon in October. It is a really hard course with a lot of hills and five laps around down town, so it's really tough and boring. I tried to register for the Boston Marathon in 2017 but it was too late, but I still followed

every news article about Boston and was finally able to register for the 2018 marathon. When they sent me the confirmation I told all of my friends. My friend, the girl that told me about Boston, was running it too with charity so it was really exciting because it was her first Marathon. I arrived at 7 pm on Thursday after 26 hours of travelling and I stayed with my friend's mom. My host's neighbor ran the Boston Marathon 9 times, so she gave me a lot of information about the course. On race day I had a lot of the clothes. It was the first time I was really nervous before a race. My target was 2:30. When I started the race I was in the first wave of the first corral. I ran my target pace until mile 14 and then I got cold, and slowed because my legs were freezing, and I couldn't hold anything in my hands. I was cheeky, but I wouldn't give up, so I threw the target out and changed my mindset to just finish the marathon.

After the finish I was complaining about my time because it's my worst time ever 3:25 and its was 55 minutes off my target but everyone there just told me that you just finished the Boston Marathon, you must be proud of yourself, we're proud of you and people don't look for your time in Boston Marathon. But I kept thinking the course is really easy and there are a lot of people cheering for me so it's a shame of me to do that bad. Now I must get back to run the Boston Marathon again and do it well.

Denise Roderick, Bib 22978

Keene, NH, 50, 3:53:40

Back in my early years I was always a runner, nothing of great length, kept it to the short and quick. Years of motherhood behind me, I was always into my fitness but running became a thing of the past. Marriage and motherhood kind of got in the way, no regrets of course. My beautiful daughter Lindsay at the age of 23 invited me to run the Beach 2 Beacon in beautiful Cape Elizabeth Maine. Of course, I said yes, I'm fit, so why not? She told me I had to train, for a 10K, I don't think so, like I said I'm fit. Days went by and she insisted that I train. I realized there was this awesome run club in town and well maybe if I join it would help me prepare. I'm kind of shy and hate showing up for things that make me uncomfortable, but damn it, I need some help. It's a Monday night, I showed up for this Run Club thing to hear we're doing hill repeats! What the heck are those I asked myself? Here we go, a nice easy mile warm up to the hill. The coach said, "we'll run 3 minutes up, mark your  spot, easy run back down, and repeat 6x's". Holy hell I thought! Off we went. I passed everyone, I marked the furthest spot, who am I? The coach on my 4th time down is trying to chat on her way up. "How old are you, how long have you been running?" I can't really answer, I'm focusing on hill repeats, damn it! We get back to the starting point and I have this amazing conversation with this remarkable woman. "You could win some local races, you're fast, you're a natural, you're my project she says".

My summer is filled with various races and lots of training. I run the Beach 2 Beacon, I trained well (or so I thought), my daughter blew my doors off! She is fast, no way I could keep up! I finished, and it wasn't too bad. I've now been bitten. Training for a half marathon is next. What better one to do than the one in my hometown, The Clarence DeMar! A summer of training and a successful race, 2nd in my age division, what? Hmmmm... maybe a marathon is next!

Yup, I've been bitten! My daughter and I ran the Vermont City Marathon on the hottest day of the year, temperatures were so dangerous, the race was closed down! Fortunately for me, I finished with an official time. Not the time I trained for, but hey it was official. My daughter, not so lucky, the heat got her at mile 18. It wasn't the marathon we wanted so what the heck let's do it again. The following year, a beautiful day, a little warmer than we wanted. We lined up at the start and Lindsay was off like a shot, she is 25 years my junior, so I let her go. I had a plan, to qualify for Boston and I was going to stick to my plan and remain focused. It was a hot marathon, a successful marathon for me, I finished, I qualified with minutes to spare. As I met my family and gathered the embraces of my support team I saw my daughter, tears in her eyes, she missed qualifying by 4 minutes! It broke my heart, she worked so hard and missed by such a small window and here I am a qualifier. It was a rough few days getting her to come around and understand the great competition in her age group.

Boston, my girl, Lindsay, my biggest fan, my biggest supporter, the girl who weathered the storm to be the first to greet me at the finish line! She is my heart, my soul! All because of her, I'm One Happy Runner.

Pat Winiecki, Bib 28974

Paramount, CA, 66, 6:04:46

On a dreary December day, I was leaving Whole Foods when my phone rang. I ignored it, thinking it was spam. When I arrived at my car, I noticed I had a voice mail. It was from Fearless Deb. I almost dropped the phone and could barely hit the return call button. Fearless 261 was going to take a chance on me! I recognized I had the opportunity of a lifetime. I was launched on a journey beyond my wildest imagination.

I needed to set up a Facebook account, CrowdRise account, Skype account, participate in international team calls, write/edit and continually publish and distribute my press release, train for a marathon, work full-time, avoid catching the flu - one of the worst we've had in Los Angeles, and nonstop spread the story of 261 Runs Boston 2018 by word of mouth. This in itself was life-changing and beyond what I, at 66 years old, had on my to do list!

The build-up on social media over the months and final days through 4 channels, 261 Fearless Team Boston 2018, CharityTeams.com, 261 Fearless Friends and WhatsApp was FUN, gripping and empowering. It was a lifeline I could never have imagined possible.

I flew into Boston from Los Angeles on Thursday, April 12, 2018. It was cold and beginning to rain. I again went to Whole Foods for milk to take down with my array of vitamins. I noticed a little card on a rack that said, "This is the best day of your life.' I stared at it and thought it over with more than just a little reservation. The weather forecast continually worsened over the days until we knew for sure we were in for a tough ride.

The events of race week breathed even more grit into me. They were timed perfectly, giving me everything I needed, in the right amount, at the right time. The virtual friendships we had developed over the months through social media fully bloomed when we were finally able to meet face-to-face.

On April 16, 2018, our Dream Team boarded the team bus in Boston under ominous, dreadful conditions. We exited the bus in Hopkinton under worse conditions. But a bright and cozy house with Fearless Deb, our supporters and our soulmate teammates were there at the start line. The fire was well and truly lit.

261 Fearless Team Boston 2018 took that menacing start line together, donning our 261 Fearless trash bags, shower caps and bright, crazy smiles. The mile markers began to pass, and I continued to be amazed I was still moving forward. In this marathon, I never had the feeling that I "had this one." No one was joking, no signs saying, "You're almost there" at the two-mile marker. The few amazing people on the sidelines were looking on in disbelief. Their signs were soaked or had flown away.

I continually checked myself - temperature, posture, fueling, attitude, having fun, best day of my life? I thought of my team, Kathrine, Deb, Susan Hurley, Lingzi Lu (memento pinned to my shirt, courtesy of Susan Hurley), our supporters, my family, my new, one-day old nephew, and how they mean the world to me. I listened to the other runners saying, "It could always be worse." I felt like I was alternating between the sets of the Deadliest Catch, Titanic and the Perfect Storm. I saw the dog, Spencer, with his flags and a man clearly saying and looking directly at me with amazement in his eyes, "Go 261 Fearless!"

I was aware of slipping into hypothermia somewhere within the last mile and a half. I played mental math games to keep myself alert and focused. If I could calculate the time to the finish line, minutes per mile, estimated overall time, I was reassured. At the turn onto Boylston, I lovingly recall a woman who somehow knew me and yelled, "Pat!" I heard my name announced in the finish chute. And then it was over. I crossed that Finish Line. The volunteer who placed the medal around my neck said, "Congratulations! You are a Boston Marathoner." Oh, sweet heaven! Done for 261 Fearless, my loves everywhere, and myself.

At our post-race team breakfast, wise-beyond-belief Kathrine said, "So, was it the best day of your life?" Without thinking, I said, "Yes." And it was.

My Love to All

Eric Carpenter, Bib 11757

Savannah, GA, 47, 3:24:03

A few years ago, I looked at myself at work and thought, "I'm the fattest person in this room!" Without knowing it at the time, that moment began my journey to Boston.

I'm 47 years old and have run, on and off, all my adult life. However, I didn't begin taking it seriously until a few years ago. After my fat self-diagnosis in 2015, I realized that I needed a tangible goal to motivate me to begin eating right and exercising. I decided to register for the Rock 'n' Roll Marathon in my home city of Savannah, GA. Over the next ten months I lost fifty pounds and got into some of the best shape of my life. Unfortunately, when race day arrived, so did the heat and humidity (in November no less!). I had no specific time goal; I just wanted to complete the marathon. When I was at about mile 21 I learned that the race had been stopped due to the heat. We all had

to run straight to the finish line no matter where on the course we were. I ended up running around 24 miles, but what a major disappointment!

I'm happy to say that I used this situation as further motivation. I trained throughout 2016 to do much better in that year's Rock 'n' Roll. At some point in 2016 my nephew, who has run Boston a couple of times, told me that since I had turned 45 years old I had a better chance of qualifying for the Boston Marathon. Before he told me this I had never thought about it. Of course I had heard about the Boston Marathon and had even watched it a few times. However, I had never dreamed of running in it. I'm not sure why, but my nephew's email lit a spark. I decided to go for a BQ in Savannah. To my amazement, I not only hit a BQ, but did so by enough to get into this year's Boston (by one minute, four seconds to be exact).

Like many of you, after I qualified I began training harder than ever. Although I ran in numerous other races, Boston was what was always on my mind. Everything led up to that. Thanks in part to the Boston Buddies Facebook group, the marathon was just about all I could think of for a couple of months leading up to the race. I'm sure we all have amazing stories about April 16th. Like you I will never forget the incredible weather. Now that I look back on it, I'm glad it was exactly the way it was. It made the day even more unforgettable than it would have been otherwise!

Somewhere early in the race near Ashland a simple yet profound thought hit me, "I'm actually running in the Boston Marathon!" Several times along the course I was nearly moved to tears as I thought about all those who had come before me on those very roads. At other times the fabulous crowds made me want to cry (and I'm not generally the crying type).

Thank you so much to the Boston College students! I couldn't have made it to the top of Heartbreak Hill without you! Now I'm in the middle of trying to figure out how to get back to Boston next year. Because of the weather, specifically the headwind, I feel like I have some unfinished business on that course. I keep looking at various marathons for hitting a sub five-minute BQ. I've almost chosen one. It will soon be time to begin training like a madman to get back to Boston. I can't wait!

Iain Hook, Bib 27966

Spalding, GBR, 65, 5:41:16

I am starting this piece with these words from a New York Times correspondent the day after the race "It was an unspeakably miserable; I can wait to tell you about it". This was my twelfth Abbott World Marathon Major and my second Boston. The race conditions were the complete opposite to 2016 when I ran. The training and preparation for this year would not have prepared me for what was going to challenge me on "Patriots Day", not even my time on Mount Everest years ago.

I was mentally and physically ready after the BAA 5K on the Saturday and alongside meeting the elite runners (some who didn't finish the course) and learning to stay off one's legs. The day before I started to watch the TV and weather reports. That's when I came to the realization that I would be running in unprecedented weather conditions. I slept well prior to race day - waking I did all the pre-race rituals and got ready. I had already taken the precaution of asking the hotel manager the day before if I could have an old bath robe to keep me warm. I wonder what all 30,000 plus runners must have looked like on that Monday morning!

Making my way to the bus with friends I felt ready. But then I had a nose bleed which caused me issues throughout the race. I was lucky to be in the gym at the start which gave some of us extra protection from the snow and driving rain. My focus was on finishing, not on getting a good time especially at my age of 65.

My memories of the race are constant rain and wind. I just ran with the thought "I can do this." The spectators, staff, volunteers and emergency services were all doing a great job. I can remember prior to turning left onto Boylston street, the road was full of runners' ponchos. I was now in sight of the finish line and thought "I've done it." I kept thinking of receiving the Boston medal and the main reason was to receive my second six Abbott World Marathon Majors Medal!

As a Director of the London Marathon for the last 18 years it's been a privilege to run Boston and the memories it holds for me in so many ways. I honestly believe that in years to come that those who ran in 2018 will have a very special bond due to the extraordinary weather conditions and the friendships made.

In Conclusion when people ask me what it was like to run this year's Boston Marathon, I respond simply "Imagine running through an icy car wash for 26.2 miles"

Esther Arviso, Bib 22135

Farmington, MA, 49, 4:19:05

It has almost been two weeks since I ran the 2018 Boston Marathon. I'm finally able to sit down and type what I have been noting in my journal. This is one experience I want to remember forever. I learned a lot about myself on Patriots Day, April 16, 2018. My goal was to finish the Boston Marathon in under 4 hours. That didn't happen, instead my faith and hope endured, and I learned that I am a lot tougher than I thought I was! Thousands of runners including myself, watched the weather hoping for a change in forecast, the Saturday and Sunday before marathon day. Unfortunately, that never happened in fact the weather only got worse. The evening before the race I was very nervous because of the weather. Regardless, I was already determined to be at the starting line the next morning.

Race morning: I'm not sure how much sleep I got but I know it wasn't enough, but I felt good. Matt helped me get ready by wrapping my running shoes with shower caps and duct tape. As soon as we walked out of the hotel the wind was strong and it was cold and raining. The shuttle and subway ride to the bus area were filled with runners so that was good knowing that I wasn't the only one doing this run. By the time we got to the bus area the rain was pouring.

The long bus ride to Hopkinton seemed like the longest bus ride ever. There was snow along the way and it kept raining and raining. I was still in good spirits and actually felt excited. I kept telling myself, "you're not the only one that's running in this insane weather, there are thousands of runners", that was motivating.

Athletes village was a mess, mud, water puddles everywhere, I even saw someone fall in the mud. It was so cold and windy and of course still raining. I didn't wait too long before my wave was called. I stripped off my top layers and threw them in the trash. My plan was to throw the shower caps and rain poncho away before I started my run, but I opted to keep them on. Matt did such a good job covering my shoes that it didn't really bother me.

From the athletes' village to the starting line was another long walk. There were so many people that the crowd was moving so slow. While taking a quick potty break I missed my wave call and didn't realize I did! I started freaking out. I don't know what I was thinking or doing because I missed my wave by an entire 10 minutes or so. I started running before the start line and finally crossed the start line after my wave was long gone. What is wrong with me? And there I was with my shower cap shoes and my blue rain poncho; my first Boston and I miss my wave start! Now that I think about it, I feel like that's where my run plan went the wrong way. It was a mess at the start line, you could barely hear the announcer and people were in crowds everywhere. I wasn't the only one that missed the wave. I saw several of us trying to weave our way through the crowd.

The first 5k: The course was all downhill but I wanted to keep it slow and not go out too fast but that wasn't hard to do because my legs were feeling weird already. Around mile three I noticed my right quad was very tight almost like it was ready to cramp up. I got scared, "I may not finish this race!" I ignored that fear as best as I could and kept going. This was not how I wanted to feel at mile 3, with 23 miles to go and not feeling confident at all. My legs felt numb and heavy. I knew then that I just needed to keep going and not worry about my pace anymore, so I kept myself behind and with other runners.

The rain was still pouring, relentlessly, sometimes slapping me from the side or right in my face. Around mile 7 the guy running a few steps ahead of me abruptly stopped, bent over, and I believe his stomach had turned on him. He was sick, and I felt bad and only hoped that he got better enough to finish the race. I don't know if it was the thought of my sub 4 goal slipping away or if I was just cold that I wanted to just stop, quit, call Matt and tell him I can't do this, but deep down I knew I was not going to quit. I knew there was more in me than the elements of weather trying to defeat my Boston dream. I could hear Matt telling me, keep going don't stop!

My hands were frozen, and I couldn't get to my energy gel, so I stopped at a water station and a volunteer had to help me. I remember my sister Cheryl telling me, be a blessing to someone else, get your mind off yourself. I decided if I'm not going to reach my sub 4 goal maybe I can help someone else finish the marathon the best way I can. I started thanking the spectators and giving them high fives. The dog with the flag was so cute. The little kids along the route were standing in the rain cheering us on. I tried my best to enjoy the company of other runners and sent nothing but good encouraging thoughts to those that were walking on the sides.

When I reached 13 miles I was half way and I told myself, you can do this, but I was cold, and the rain kept coming down and getting worse. When I run I like to be at peace and in rhythm, so around mile 13, I was struggling to find that peace and that rhythm. It was tough, it was difficult, I needed to dig deeper to keep moving forward. I knew I still had a long way to go. My legs felt like they were going to cramp up, so I had to keep moving. I saw people on the sides walking or going into the medical tents. Sometime after mile 13 I saw someone walking sideways across the road as if she was about to fall over, I quickly ran up to her and grabbed her before she fell. Another gentleman and I walked her to the water station which was not too far, and the volunteers took her from there. I stopped there for a while. I asked a volunteer to dump the water that had accumulated in my poncho hood. I could feel that sack of water on my back when I was running.

Some miles seemed forever, and I remember looking at my watch and I would see 17.8 or 18.2 and I would round off the numbers to the nearest tens, forget the tenths and hundredths (yeah that engineering head tends to stick with you no matter where you are, I even thought of better road drainage designs coming into Boston area, ha-ha. Despite how tired and cold I was feeling I was looking forward to the Newton hills. The hills were not as bad as I thought. I think it was the second hill a lady was barely walking. I stopped and told her that she is more than halfway done and to keep going. I told her I can jog with her and so we did but only for a few yards. She started crying and said her hip hurts and told me to keep going. I hope she finished.

I didn't realize I reached Heartbreak Hill until someone told me. I ditched the rain poncho and the shower cap (they were wearing away by now) somewhere after mile 20. There were a few more little hills that seemed harder than the Newton hills after the Heartbreak Hill. At 21 miles I told myself only 5 miles to go! But where is the damn CITGO sign! The iconic Boston Marathon sign that supposedly tells you you're a mile to the finish line. It seemed almost forever before I saw the sign. I knew my family was tracking my run, so I didn't want to let them down and I wanted them to know I was still moving forward and that I did. I was also feeling good and at the time I thought I picked up my pace but after looking at my splits the next day, I wasn't going any faster. Ha-ha. I guess my body was so cold that that I couldn't get my legs moving faster than I thought I was.

"Right on Hereford, left on Boylston!" I'm there turning corners and I see my family to the left! I wanted to stop and hug them but there were rain ponchos and plastic all over the road and I had to watch my step plus stopping felt like my legs would lock in place and not move. So I had to keep moving. I waved at them as they were drenched in the rain. I still regret not stopping to hug them. Once I turned on Boylston I was emotional. I finished the 2018 Boston Marathon! Priscilla was at finish line and I cried. This woman has always believed in me from day one when I started pursuing the Boston dream. She knew my ups and downs and now she was right there to see me cross the finish line. I have been blessed with a great running pal.

The finish line to pick up gear bags was another long freezing walk. It was still raining and by now I was freezing and shivering. I couldn't even use my phone. Another volunteer had to call my family for me. My reunion with Matt and my boys was another emotional moment. My youngest son was looking at me with the biggest smile (with his dimples) and that made me cry even more. The night before when I couldn't sleep he told me that when something bad happens something good always comes out of it. They were also wet and cold. I'm so proud of them for enduring the weather to see me finish. They were so proud of me.

As I type this I still can't believe I have the Boston Marathon finisher's medal! 2018 Boston was truly a historic marathon: it was the coldest Boston Marathon in 30 years and my favorite elite runner Des Linden became the first American woman to win in 33 years, and I'm so proud that I am now part of this history! This is one that I will forever remember. "Keep showing up!"

Last but not least, I know it was all God's grace that got me from the beginning to the end. He has never failed me, and He will never fail me. I felt my mom, sisters', brothers', and friends' prayers all along the way. I almost gave up but the thought of all the encouragements from family and friends kept me going. It was by far the hardest race I've ever ran in my life, yet I was smiling when I finished. All for God and all His grace! I have achieved goals in life and they were not easy, I have learned to leave no room for fear or defeat but to be filled with hope and faith. I have the capacity to endure every challenge and I know that even in my weakest moments God gives me strength to keep moving forward. You don't know what you can achieve, what you can accomplish, how far you can push yourself, how to dig deep, unless you actually do it and you keep doing it over and over. It's all inside of you. You are a lot tougher than you think you are!

I am forever grateful for my husband Matt and my boys for all their love and patience. Thank you to each of my family members and my friends. "Courage is the fear that has said it's prayers and decided to go forward anyway." ~Joyce Meyer. Until next time Boston!

George Leary, Bib 14434

Keyport, NJ, 54, 3:51:55

My name is George Leary, 54 years old from a small shore town in New Jersey. I have been running consistently for the past 6-7 years after a 25-year layoff. I ran cross country and track in HS and my idol was Alberto Salazar. In 1982 he won the Boston Marathon in an epic race with Dick Beardsley in 80 plus degree weather and that is when my dream of running Boston was born.

I have tried to qualify since 2015 and have come close a couple of times. In 2016 I ran a 3:29 in the New Jersey Marathon and finally got a chance to apply to Boston, but I knew my time was not fast enough. I finally got my BQ in April 2017 at the Coastal Delaware Marathon with a 3:26. I can still remember the pure joy I felt when I received the acceptance email from the BAA. I booked a hotel room that night for my wife and daughter, both of them have been to every marathon and stood in cheered for me during the good ones and the 4-hour plus ones. My other two children are just as supportive during my whole training and second job of running. There is a joke in my family that "dad has a second family that he goes to visit when he says he is out running for hours at a time ".

I started training for Boston in December using the BAA level 4 plan. I enjoyed the plan very much and had no issues up until the last 3 weeks and I developed a bad case of shin splints in my left leg. I was so stressed out with the thought of not be able to run. I was driving my family crazy. I didn't do any running the last two weeks leading up to the race and rehabbed my leg like it was my job.

I had no idea if I was capable of running 3 miles or let alone even finish the race, I told my wife and daughter it could take me 4 to 6 hours, but I will finish. There is nothing for me to add about the weather, for me personally I think it was a blessing. It forced me to relax and just enjoy the race and not worry about time or performance. I have a major problem in all my races of putting too much pressure on myself and going out too fast.

I was at the starting line in the pouring rain, cold and shriving with the biggest smile I have ever had. "This is the Boston Marathon." I repeated to myself! I ran by how I felt, and barley looked at my watch. I just kept saying to myself, "Get to the next mile. This is the Boston Marathon". I hit mile marker 12 and I could hear the Scream Tunnel, I watched YouTube videos of this portion of the race and couldn't wait to experience it. It lived up to all the hype and even more. I stopped and kissed the girls, high fived them, hugged them. I was living a dream that so few people get to do!

The next couple of miles, my mantra was, "Get to the Newton Hills, this is The Boston Marathon". I felt good going into the hills but after Heartbreak I started to cramp up a bit. I previously had to walk in a couple of my past marathons when hitting the wall, but, "This is The Boston Marathon", and I wasn't going to disrespect it by walking!

Onto the last couple of miles and I kept thinking, "Just get to the next mile. This is The Boston Marathon!" I told my wife and daughter before I left to just stay in the hotel, but if you want to watch try to get a spot on the corner of Hereford and Boylston. I made the left onto Boylston and started to look for them, I couldn't find them or hear anyone calling out my name. I was looking into the crowds when I saw my wife out of the corner of my eye, I stopped turned around and yelled her name. She saw me, and I ran over to her and my daughter who was filming on her phone. I cannot express the feeling I had when I saw them, other than I started to cry, I kissed them, and my wife said, "You are doing it". I know nothing about making people's dreams come true, because I'm probably too selfish. My wife for 30 plus years, has made all my dreams come true, for her to stand with my daughter for 4 plus hours in that weather with no guarantee of even seeing me is truly amazing.

I crossed the finish line, wept like everyone else, shivered like everyone else and shuffled along like everyone else, however when the volunteer put the medal around my neck, I closed my eyes and said, "This is The Boston Marathon."

Kaisa Nuttall, Bib 18198

Santa Rosa, CA, 38, 3:31:49

Like so many first timers, I thought my venture to Boston in 2012 would be my only. At that point in my life it had been a bucket list item - a "one and done," so to speak. It would be my fourth marathon, and one where I had put in the time and work and was confident in my ability to race well. This was much unlike my home life at the time, which was crumbling due to an abusive marriage. I had a beautiful 5-year old son that was growing up in a dangerous environment, and I had to protect us both. I still remember exactly where I was on the trail when I realized I had to leave.

When we arrived in Boston in 2012 it was already hot, and I knew that my chances to PR (and break 3:30) were gone. I decided to enjoy the race, soak in the environment, and enjoy the crowds. It was a marvelous experience that made recovery easy, and I would need it. Four days after I ran Boston 2012, I left my abusive marriage. I didn't have a plan, I just knew that I couldn't stay any longer. Running had been not just my physical strength, but my inner strength as well. It gave me the clarity and time alone to know that I had to leave, and the strength to rise above all of the challenges that would come as a result.

While I never stopped running entirely, I did stop competing - for five years. During that time my divorce would be finalized, and I would spend the next few years focusing on my son and improving myself in every way I could think of. I would become a volunteer coach for a local youth running club, go back to school, and continue to work full time while juggling single parenthood.

Life was busy but progressing. 3 years after my divorce I would meet Chris, a transplant from the East Coast who came out to work for Lucas Films designing toys. He would bring the strength of a positive partnership I hadn't known before. And then a string of events would test this strength, as well as my resolve: my dad had a near fatal injury that left him permanently disabled, I would change jobs, and I would find myself in the ER without warning, due to a sudden onset of pain so severe I was vomiting and passing out - all within 5 weeks. When the ER didn't take me seriously - accusing me of just seeking narcotics, I checked myself out against medical recommendation, and told Chris I would rather die at home. Four hours later they had MRI results, and told him to bring me back immediately. I would be diagnosed with colitis and resulting abdominal adhesions (from appendicitis, when I was 6yo!) creating a full intestinal blockage. I was rushed into emergency exploratory surgery, where they would find roughly two feet of necrotic bowel, which was removed. Chris slept in a chair next to my bed; it is an image that is burned into my memory despite being completely loaded on painkillers.

The day after my surgery I was refusing painkillers and was working on a plan to get out of the hospital, which included walking laps around the Med/Surg unit. At one point one of my doctors stopped me and said, "Next time a marathoner tells us they are in pain, we will believe them!" I had Chris bring my Garmin from home, and I walked two miles of hospital wing circles, while dragging my IV behind me. It was the first time I thought about racing again. I was released 3 days after my surgery and started running 6 weeks later - once I had been medically cleared.

With 8 weeks of training I ran the half and placed 2nd in my age group. The memories of racing fell over me, and I knew that I wanted to go back to Boston, but I sincerely doubted my body at that point. It was worth the entry fee for a hometown race - the same one I had qualified at before, to find out. I had 12 weeks to train on a familiar course that runs alongside vineyards, farms and a creek bustling of critters. Not long after I started training for my BQ race I started a new career in, which allows me the flexibility to juggle running and parenting. My boss knows how important running is to me; he is my co-coach for the youth running club. In August 2017 I BQ'd with a 6:28 buffer in my hometown race in front of my sister, Chris, and my boss (and co-coach) Mark. It was a moment of strength that brought me to tears, much like my first BQ.

When I toed the line for Boston 2018, I believe I pulled my strength from so many experiences I have gone through to get me to the finish line, as my mantra for that race was, "I am stronger than this- I'm a survivor!"

Greg Zinner, Bib 6660

Carolina Beach, NC, 44, 3:04:18

I fell in love with the Boston Marathon the moment I BQ'd, November of 2016 at the Richmond, VA marathon. Tears overwhelmed me as I slowly walked thru the finisher's chute, knowing that all the hard work from the past several months had paid off, and I had earned my spot into the world's most prestigious race. I spent the next year as far away from anything marathon related as I could; focusing on improving my 5k times, and coaching kids in Track and XC. But come December of 2017, it was time to embark on an 18-week plan to get me to that start line in Hopkinton in the best possible shape. I met up a few times with members of my hometown running club, the Wilmington NC Road Runners; we talked about training plans, travel, how to simulate the hills here in the 'flatlands" along the coast. I listened with rapt ears to those who had run the fabled race before.

It was the hardest 18 weeks of my life run wise; I was catapulted physically, mentally, and spiritually into new dimensions. I gritted my teeth, I bore down, I counted off miles, and I loved every minute of it, and felt so grateful and blessed to be one of the lucky ones who had a bib waiting for them in Boston. I barely survived the toil, as just about every run the past few weeks included some sort of aches and pains in my legs. I didn't get sick (until a few days after the race). I was ready, prepared, I knew I could smash thru that big 3-hour mark, then we all saw the weather forecast. I scrambled for gear that last weekend in Boston, I frantically called my girlfriend back home, convinced that we are all doomed to pedestrian times, and all that hard work? But the shakeout run the day before with some of my Wilmington Road running friends buoyed my spirits. After all, we were all in this together. So, I bundled up for the start, and walked through a freezing downpour from Athlete's Village to the start line. I paused shedding layers for the National Anthem. I walked, then trotted to that start line and then I was off. After 17 months, I was finally running in the Boston Marathon. Instincts took over, I didn't have time for excuses. I adjusted my goals and expectations only slightly and ran my guts out for 26.2 miles. Because that's what you do when you possess one of those coveted bibs. That's what you do when the whole world is watching. That's how I honor all the messages, well wishes, thoughts, prayers from so many wonderful friends and family members. Seeing the Boston Strong painted on the overpass during mile 25, turning right on Hereford, left on Boylston made all the freezing cold, rain, wind worth every minute of enduring. Hearing my name on the PA system, I managed to wave to the crowd. Crossing the finish line, completing the hardest race I had ever run in brought tears to my eyes once again. I fought with just about everything I had, and was rewarded with a 3:04, which was a new PR, and earned me another trip next year.

I'll never forget being a small part in such an epic adventure, and the lifetime worth of thrills of being able to share in the journey with so many wonderful people. Hats off to all who ran, and especially to all those who volunteered, and supported runners on the course. We are all Boston Strong. See many of you again in 2019.

Ian Eckersley, Bib 16096

Brisbane, AUS, 57, 4:11:31

"Boston Strong: I'm Boston Strong: I'm Strong".

That simple, personal mantra has twice carried me through a 15-year aspirational journey to the Mount Everest of marathons, Boston. It culminated in the toughest physical challenge of my life – Boston 2018. While my knowledge and awareness of Boston was rudimentary in my first two decades of running, I had an athletic awakening at Honolulu Marathon in 2003 when I met the legendary Bill Rodgers, with whom I've maintained a friendship. "Ian, you've got to come and run Boston." And so I did in 2016, finishing in an unsatisfying 3:20.57, a long way off my 2:26 PB. While I thought scaling Mt. Everest once might satisfy me, by mid-2016, I was plotting, scheming and running down my next BQ. Despite being a former elite runner – experienced, yet

injury-prone –getting to the starting line in "great shape" was still a massive challenge – and the road to Boston 2018 was littered with injury potholes: osteoarthritis in one knee and, simultaneously, chronic Achilles Tendinopathy, which deteriorated into a 2cm (1-inch) tear three months before race day which necessitated a massively reduced running load and a creative cross-training regime of pool running and training on a Bionic Runner. With just three runs over 30km since January 1 and no hill running, just getting to Boston was a heroic achievement laden with dedication, discipline and countless hours of painful medical and physical therapy.

I had a welcome distraction from pre-race nerves once I landed in Boston (after a 26-hour flight) with my media and publicity work for the Indigenous Marathon Foundation (the brainchild and passion of 1986 Boston winner, Australia's Rob "Deek" de Castella) and his 2018 Boston entrant Zibeon Fielding – a 24 year old proud Indigenous man from Mimili in remote South Australia, who's running in just his second marathon at Boston. There are welcome social catch-ups with old Boston friends and with Zibeon and fellow Aussie runners.

The novelty of light race eve snow is tempered by the deteriorating race day forecast which has us Down Under runners on edge. Scoring a VIP pass, enables me to fill the three hours before my Wave Three start in warmer and more comfortable environs of Hopkinton school gym, making dozens of "new friends" which leaves me more relaxed than I've ever been before a marathon. For me the early km's of a race are just about settling into a solid, strategic pace ("Go out at 4:40/km and just see what happens") and I'm highly cognizant of my internal dialogue which mostly revolves around my heightened emotional state and a cocktail of enormous pride, joy and exhilaration. Friends had questioned why I even bothered travelling to Boston when I was injured and in sub-optimal shape "Hey, it's Boston – you don't qualify and not start – and you don't start and not finish! One day you'll understand".

I tried to stay on my pragmatic race pace although the raw emotion and energy is truly uplifting. Then around 14km everything goes "pear-shaped". My dodgy Achilles tightens, prompting me to adjust my foot strike. Less than five minutes of compensatory modified running passes when 'bang' my right calf muscle grabs fiercely. Sharp pain grips my lower leg bringing my stride to an immediate and shuddering halt. I know I've torn my calf muscle (later diagnosed as a partial tear) and survival instincts kick in. While trying to suppress the mild panic, the gritty and fiercely proud competitor kicks in: "This is bad but it's not the end of my race. I've worked too damned hard and sacrificed too much not to finish, even if it takes six hours." I began walking and am consumed by hordes of runners. My head and heart were caught in an emotional swirl – humiliation that I've been reduced to a walk with still 27km to go and that thousands of runners were passing me. Pain, disappointment and frustration are in the mix, but I quickly accepted my fate and just got down to business, drawing on the Deek motto of just putting "one foot in front of the other." Somehow. I would find a way to cautiously convert the walk into an awkward stiff-legged running shuffle. The pain is excruciating but the shuffle is quicker than walking and doesn't aggravate the tear. I set a target of running to Wellesley – a motivating and inspiring landmark for all Boston runners. When I reached it, I accepted the energizing offers of a few female student kisses, then resigned myself to the sobering fact that I've still got half of the race to go.

The road to the foot of Heartbreak Hill was a blur of feet slopping through mini-lakes, a body in survival mode as it fights an external battle with the horrendous weather and the course, and an internal war with raw emotion, intensifying pain, mounting fatigue and a mind that ebbs and flows between strength and vulnerability. I'm thankful I've written my name on my singlet – it's the spark for endless and personal crowd support: "Good job Ian, "You got this Ian", "Boston loves you Ian. I love you Ian" shouted a sports jock.

"Boston Strong: I'm Strong. Boston Strong: I'm Strong". My mantra became more vocal as if the louder my voice, the more empowered and faster I would become. Heartbreak summit appeared, and the downpour became a torrent. The heavier it rained, the louder the crowd cheered as if to say to the weather gods: "Is that the best you can do!" Relief and satisfaction engulfed me as I passed Boston College. The final 8km was torture but finally, joyfully I turned into Boylston Street. Euphoria griped me, and a larger-than-life smile dominated my face. It was my slowest marathon time by 45 minutes. Pride, satisfaction and relief overwhelmed me. I didn't surrender to adversity, the weather gods or the marathon gods. "Boston Strong, I'm Strong. Boston Strong, I'm Strong."

Jessica Jones, Bib 9498

Dauphin Island, AL, 40, 3:25:49

This race epitomized what I've said dozens of time about running having its ups and downs. The women's champion, Desi Linden, in a post-race interview, said her plan was to "ride the wave". The first American woman to win the Boston Marathon in 33 years! Her plan was to ride the wave. She thought about dropping out. Seriously, sort of planned on dropping out. That gives some perspective to my race. I wrote much of this Monday after the race. Well after the race, a shower, some food, and relaxation. But, I didn't want to post until I'd really thought about it and had a little time to objectively think about the experience. But not too much time to dull the raw emotion of it.

It was really cold, really wet, and really windy. I wore layers to Athlete Village. For those who are not familiar, this is where all the non-elite runners hang out until the walk to the corrals. A couple of fields outside of a school with tents, port-a-potties, and tens of thousands of runners. Layering included a trash bag and a poncho. Grocery bags over my shoes. Anything I could do to stay as warm and dry as possible before the start. I stripped down on the walk to the starting corrals to shorts, tank, arm sleeves, gloves, and hat. Opted to keep the poncho. It seemed to help to not have the cold rain directly on my skin. On the walk, I thought about my goals again. The A goal of 3:10 was unrealistic. The wind gusts could stop you in your tracks. The B goal of a PR, maybe, but unlikely. The C goal of 3:20. Doable.

I made it to the corral with only two minutes before the start of the wave. Fine with me. Less standing around. Off we go! Wave 2 of the 122nd Boston Marathon is headed to Boston! The first bit is all downhill. My poncho was long, so it kept getting wrapped up around my legs. Easy fix. Bunched up the end and tied a knot. 80s t-shirt style. My splits were 7:46 and 7:38 for the first two miles. This is usually the too fast part of the course. That throws A and B goals out the window. And, C goal is teetering on the edge. The conditions were harder than I gave them credit for. I decided then to just go with it and run by feel.

That decision was really weird for me. I've never not had a time goal in a marathon. Even if it is an "easy" time for me. I kept the C goal of 3:20 in my head. Sort of. I didn't check my splits. I planned on simply enjoying the experience of another Boston Marathon. That, also, turned out to be a tall order. The weather was brutal. Relentless rain. Sometimes light, sometimes hard. Sometimes pelting rain straight in my face. Steady wind. Strong gusts. Cold. Really cold. It felt like temps in the low 30s. The saving grace really was the crowd! The folks who stood for hours in those miserable conditions just to cheer on strangers! The girls in Wellesley are always entertaining. A guy in front of me stopped for more than one kiss. Brought a smile to my face. I kept that poncho on. Every time I thought about taking it off, the rain would pick up or a strong gust come across. Nope. Not losing it. I checked my watch again at the halfway point. I was on pace for 3:18 or so.

The hard part was yet to come with more frequent bands of heavy rain. By the time I got to the Newton Hills my hands had gone numb. Without being committed to a time goal, I lost focus. It made this the most mentally difficult marathon I've ever run. A few awesome patches of spectators picked me up. I gave high fives to a bunch of kids. Then, I had to pee. I seriously considering just letting it fly, so to speak. But, without commitment to a time goal, what's a 20-30 second detour? No worries. Easy stop. Enter into Newton Hills. This is a tough mental and physical part of the course on a good day. Medical tents started to look inviting. But I stuck it out. Desi Linden said she kept taking it "just one more mile". I didn't know at the time that was the winner's mindset, but I was doing a similar thing. Just an hour plus behind her. And, without the media coverage. Then, I needed to go number 2. (As a side note, it makes me feel a little better that Shalane Flanagan, American elite, NYC 2017 Marathon Champion, needed a potty break.) Only once before has this happened during a race. And, then, I sucked it up and survived the final 4 miles because I didn't want to lose the time. Today, why suffer? Make the stop. Oh, that was more difficult than anticipated. Dealing with a poncho (yes, I still had it on), soaking wet tank and spandex shorts with mostly numb, gloved fingers. Not easy. Not quick. That mile split was 9:06 (I checked after the race). Good thing I had conceded any time goal.

I was back on course a little before mile 20. Just in time for Heartbreak Hill. Mentally, I had found some resolve. Owning my decision to run by feel. Living the moment. Let's do this final 10K. It got mentally easier each mile, but not physically. I hurt from the cold, I was freezing from head to toe. Things hurt. My hands. My arms. My legs. Not the normal I just ran 20 miles hurt. A different hurt. My splits slowed, as did my spirits. And then, the Citgo sign. One mile to go. Only one more mile. Under the overpass, and up the other side. I could see the right-hand turn onto Hereford. I finally ditched my poncho. I needed to have my bib showing for those race photos. I did pre-order, after all. Right on Hereford, left on Boylston. I slowed down to soak it in. The struggle of the past 3 hours was worth it. No matter how miserable I felt. The crowd did not disappoint! I teared up. I've never teared up in a marathon. Ever. I savored every step on Boylston. Listening to the cheers, seeing the finish line inch closer, I didn't care about the clock. I'd only glanced at my watch once since halfway. I knew I had slowed, but I was finishing. I was persevering through the toughest race conditions, physically and mentally, I'd ever experienced. On one of the most challenging courses. I crossed the finish line, arms raised. Then I cried. Relief. Accomplishment. Appreciation. Owning it. Living it. Being it. A Boston Marathon finisher.

Peg Hoffman, Bib 20577

Fort Wayne, IN, 40, 4:13:25

"Boston or Boobs?" This is the dilemma I pondered as I drove away from my plastic surgeon's office on a snowy day in January 2018. Running the Boston Marathon was not a dream I had all my life. I did not run my first 26.2 until 2013. With a time of 4:40 I was in a category far from Boston qualifiers and the attempt to qualify never crossed my mind. I viewed the marathon as a bucket list item – planning to be "one and done". And that was how it was until I moved from Virginia to Indiana and continued to run as stress relief. Running also became a social outlet – I moved to Indiana not knowing a soul but after joining the local Fleet Feet training group, I quickly had a family of friends.

In 2015 I decided another marathon could be fun and I knew I could do better than my first where I made rookie mistakes such as seeding myself too far back and then weaving to get around slower runners as well as poor (oops – no!) nutrition. I ran the Bayshore Marathon in Traverse City, Michigan in 4:12 and felt great the whole way. My usually much faster friend, Jamie, ran with me as he was coming off an injury. He encouraged me that next I could run a sub-4 and after a while, not only did I believe him, but by early 2016 I looked up what I would need to BQ (3:40) and started to think that although it was a long shot, it was a possibility.

Thus I signed up to run Bayshore again in 2016. My training was spot on for a 3:37 and I couldn't wait to race. Unfortunately, after a cold winter of training, race day was warm and humid. I did not adjust my goal time – it was BQ or bust. Unfortunately, the latter came true as I began to fall off pace at mile 16 and even walked water stations later in the race, clocking in at 3:51. I was heartbroken and angry that after all that great training the weather did not cooperate. I decided I would wait at least a year to run another marathon – I needed a break.

But then I did the math – even though I was only 38, I would be 40 for the 2018 Boston Marathon. For a fall marathon, I only needed a 3:45 to BQ. So in November 2016 I ran the Indianapolis Monumental Marathon. The weather was perfect; the course was flat; and I had my friend Jamie to pace and encourage me. I ran the race nearly perfectly according to my negative split plan. With a 3:41 I was pretty sure I would get into the 2018 Boston Marathon.

It was still far away but I kept up with my running, completing another marathon and half marathon, and felt unstoppable. That is until I went in for my annual gynecology exam and suddenly the following weeks were filled with mammograms, ultrasounds, MRIs and appointments with surgeons, radiologists and oncologists. I had breast cancer. Due to a family history of the disease, it was in the back of my mind that sometime in my life I would probably receive the diagnosis, but I did not expect it at age 39 when I was in what I thought was the best health of my life.

There was a month of uncertainty between my initial diagnosis and surgery – had the cancer spread? Who were the best doctors? Should a single or double mastectomy be performed? During this time I used running as a stress relief as well as time to mull over these questions. I knew I would have to take time off from running to deal with the cancer, so I tried to appreciate each and every step while I could.

On July 21st I had a double mastectomy with immediate reconstruction. Two days later I received the blessed news that the cancer had not spread and because of the early detection and aggressive surgery, I would not need radiation or chemo. Despite this wonderful news, I still found myself bed bound, with fever, in terrible pain and unable to even sit up or lay down without help. Although it was far from top of mind, running Boston 9 months later seemed impossible.

Unfortunately, I was plagued with one complication after another and had to have three unplanned surgeries. The last one was the day I was originally scheduled to complete a half iron distance triathlon. This last surgery was because the doctors had to remove the reconstructive implants my body was rejecting. I was left flat with many scars and deformities – not the "new boobs"

I had expected. I was told to take time to heal and then I could try reconstruction again.

By mid-September I was no longer bed ridden but walking to the mailbox was a challenge. My children would cheer for me to make it up the stairs to tuck them in at night – it was painful but worth it. I began physical therapy and I put the same dedication I usually put to tempo runs and mile repeats into just trying to lift my arms. I spent countless hours each day doing exercises that the average person could do with ease. The day I could finally lift my arms enough to put on deodorant was a huge triumph.

My healing sped up and in October I ran my first mile. By November I was up to 5 miles and starting to feel like a runner again – albeit a new runner. I certainly didn't have the speed or stamina I used to but going for a short run felt good. In December I graduated from physical therapy and started loosely following the BAA level 2 training program; I started to believe if I put in the effort I could get to Boston.

But then I met with my plastic surgeon in January who said I was now healed enough to attempt reconstruction next month. It would be a number of surgeries over a 10-month time frame if things went according to plan. While I would not be bed ridden the whole time, after each surgery there would be at least 6 weeks of no running. If I wanted boobs, there would be no Boston. While for some runners this would seem like an easy decision – breasts just get in the way, right? – it was not so simple. Where I once had a voluptuous womanly chest, I now had scars and deformities. My clothes and especially bathing suits did not fit the same. I avoided the mirror and did not change in front of my husband – and certainly not in the women's locker room as I used to. I wish I could say they didn't matter, but when it came down to it, I did not feel the same without breasts. And thus the dilemma, Boston or Boobs?

Of course the best place to solve dilemmas are on runs. As I ran, I thought about how good my body felt as a whole and how good it felt to be out of bed and not in pain. Did I really want to go through a long process of surgeries and down time for aesthetics? What kind of example would this be setting for my children?

My decision was made. Boston > Boobs! I had a race shirt made saying just this on the back with my name on the front. And on the morning of April 16, 2018, I headed for the start line of the Boston Marathon.

The morning was frigid, rainy and blustery. I wore quite an unusual race outfit with numerous layers, rain poncho and bright yellow dish gloves over thinner gloves. My friend Jamie that ran with me in 3 previous marathons said he would be honored to run with me once again, so we met at my hotel before heading to the buses. I wore an old pair of running shoes and carried my racing shoes in Ziploc bags. On the way to the buses a huge gust came and blew one of my shoes under a police car. It was so far under I could not reach it. I panicked thinking, "How am I going to run without my shoe?!" Fortunately, a kind, tall, fellow runner saw my predicament and crawled under the car to retrieve it for me. He sacrificed his own warmth as he had to submerge himself in a puddle to get it.

The line to the buses was extensive but eventually I found myself out of the rain and on my way to Hopkinton with other Wave 3 runners. Once we arrived, Jamie and I decided to hit the first set of porta potties. We slugged through the mud pit to wait in the long line. Wave 2 was called while we waited. When we finally made it though, wave 3 (my wave) was called. I thought this was perfect timing at first. We were on the path to the starting line but again, the line was moving slowly. While we were still not even past the first tent, wave 4 was called. Now many wave-4 runners were in front of us! There was not much to do except go with it and be thankful for chip timing. As we got closer to the start line I changed into my dry socks and shoes. This helped but my feet still felt frozen and it was a very awkward feeling. I had already missed the start of wave 3 so when Jamie wanted to use the porta potties close to the start line, I didn't mind. We finally crossed the start line about 30 minutes later than planned.

Although I did not have a time goal and always intended to run by feel, I had trained to run an 8:45 pace on a perfect condition day. Since the conditions were far from ideal, I thought a 9:00 pace seemed reasonable to start. Having started with Wave 4, there were many slower runners in front of me and I tried not to weave too much. My first mile was 9:28. Despite the pelting rain and chilling wind, after a few miles my feet had thawed, and I felt in a good rhythm. I ran miles 2-16 at a steady 9:00 pace. I loved not having a finish time goal and being able to focus on the crowd and scenery. I read the homemade signs, high-fived the kids and searched for my family that I was able to see twice along the course.

Before the Newton hills began, I took off my rain poncho because I wanted the spectators to be able to see my shirt. This was temporarily a great move because I was cheered by name up Heartbreak Hill and along the rest of the course. However, I was getting wetter and colder every minute. My pace slowed starting at mile 17 and my legs began to freeze up. I did not feel drained cardio wise, but my legs were not working like usual. Nevertheless, I was smiling and thinking about how fortunate I was to be out there running this epic course. As I ran the infamous last stretch down Bolyston I thought about how far I'd come since being unable to get out of bed by myself or brush my own hair.

Marathoners often like to say the first 20 miles are a warm up for a 10k race. On this particular day, the marathon was my warm up for my trek back to my hotel. This journey was the toughest of the day. As soon as I stopped running my hip flexors and other muscles froze and I could barely hobble. Worse yet, I began to shake as my body temperature dropped. I remember walking to get my medal and eyeing a wheel chair, thinking about how nice it would be to sit down. There were also medical helpers eyeing me as I looked like I might need the medical tent – however I was set on getting back to my hotel where my family was waiting for me, so I faked my best "I'm all right" smile. My hotel was one of the closest to the finish line and I thought I could make it. However, I was moving at a snail's pace and I became a bit disoriented as to how to get back as there were so many people, tents and roads blocked off. I began to shake severely and hyperventilate. A worker at the back entrance of another hotel saw me and rushed me in to warm up. He even offered me a hot shower at that hotel, though another worker gave him a look and said, "I'm not sure we are allowed to do that." By this point I knew I was only a block away from my own hotel, so I forged on. Finally, I was to my hotel room where my sister was waiting. Upon seeing my condition, she quickly called my mom, an ex-RN, to help her. I was trembling and breathing too heavily to talk. They helped me out of my shoes and then put me fully clothed in the warm shower. It was a flashback to when I needed help showering after my surgeries. Luckily after some hot tea to warm my insides (first time drinking tea in the shower) and 30 minutes under the hot shower stream, I was mostly recovered.

I do not think I will ever regret my decision of Boston over Boobs. It was an epic, memorable journey – not just the race itself but every step of my recovery, training, Hopkinton to Boston and hypothermic trudge back to the hotel. I will forever hold in my heart the encouragement from friends, family and race day spectators. I will forever be proud of myself for the grit it took me to get to the starting line and to cross the finish line.

Jillian Hillman, Bib 28637

Lunenburg, MA, 35, 4:29:49

Marathon Monday, it rained, it was cold, and the winds, well they were not at my back. It was the most perfect storm and truthfully, I expected nothing less with the luck I've had since the end of February. My training got derailed with an IT band injury that turned into a knee injury that kept me sidelined for most of March, which yes made me 50 shades of crazy! When you go from running 150 miles a month to 20 you feel like a complete mental case and you overanalyze every single detail. Prior to being sidelined my training was on point. Hitting paces, getting stronger and faster, running hill repeats and actually secretly liking them, I was certain Boston was going to be my marathon. I had memorized every single pace I needed to be at to break that 4-hour barrier as I was chasing that "sub4 marathon" finish I could almost taste it. Yes, I'm terrible at math but let me tell you, I was getting damn good at number crunching paces.

So most of March was spent at physical therapy, the chiropractors, getting laser, having manual manipulation done, visiting the orthopedic, doing exercises that would "make me a better runner" Please doc, I'll be a better runner if I can actually run (yeah, I said that to him) riding a bike that took me nowhere, and swimming which yes, is great exercise but man the thoughts I had while swimming was something else, remember you can't exactly talk to anyone while your swimming!

I was doing everything, and I mean everything to get back out on those open roads and just pound the pavement. Running for me is therapeutic and relieves stress, and well let's just say that I needed a run. Life is sometimes not perfect, and things get unexpectedly thrown at you and how you deal, and figure things out says a lot about the type of person you are! Let's just say I thought about quitting my journey to Boston on more than 1 occasion because life was getting tough and I couldn't run because well I was injured. I've gotta say, "Thank you", to everyone who wouldn't let me quit, you all know who you are.

April 16 was quickly approaching, I was 10 days out and hadn't run more than 5 miles at a time, I found myself at the orthopedic surgeon office waiting for my first cortisone injection. This was it, the miracle shot everyone told me about. I was ecstatic I'll be able to go out get a few miles in and feel confident showing up in Hopkinton. Hahhaha WRONG! I was told absolutely no running until marathon Monday. That gave me the most upset stomach ever. I said, "OK so how do I know if this will work? Show up and hope the running God's answer my prayers?" Docs response, "Yes".

And well folks that's what I did, I showed up. I arrived in Hopkinton undertrained not undermotivated! Boston was still going to be "My Marathon" I didn't care when I finished, I just needed to finish. I needed that unicorn that I had been chasing and I wanted to wear that jacket so bad. I ran that race Monday through the wind, rain, and cold and looking back it sucked but let me tell you something, it's a day I will never forget, I felt like a little girl running in the rain with an ear to ear smile. I was doing something I told myself back in 2016 I would do, I dreamed big and did It! My finish time was 4:29:49 and it wasn't that dream time I envisioned but crossing that iconic finish line was everything I thought it would be if not more.

Thanks for All of Your Love & Support... stay tuned you never know what I've got planned next.

Bunroth So, Bib 29033

Lynn, MA, 56, 4:56:15

Monday, April 16th. 4:30 am. My phone's alarm is going off. I wake up and take a shower, amazement and disbelief coursing through me as it begins to sink in, I am running the Boston Marathon today. A feeling that continued even as my daughter Evalynn drove me to the Boston Common, where I would be boarding a bus to Hopkinton along with many other 2018 Boston Marathon Runners.

"Geez, what a day to run a marathon, huh? You ready for this, Dad?" she asks as she navigates through the congested roads of Boston, rain pelting the windows so ferociously at this point that even with the wipers on high, visibility was limited.

A nervous laugh escapes me, "I am," I pause. "I just want to finish. That's all."

"You'll finish," she says with certainty. "Walking, or running, you'll finish it."

She drops me off at the corner near the State House approximately 7:30 am. As I'm exiting the car, she yells out, "You got this, Dad! We'll see you at mile 10!" As I walk towards the security check area, I feel my jacket is already getting soaked through

153

and I know that since my wave isn't scheduled to start until after 11, our shuttle won't pick us up for at least another two hours. Yet in spite of the cold dampness of my jacket being soaked, I'm still excited to get this experience started.

We arrive at the village around 9:40 am which means we have another hour and a half to wait. The rain and wind at this point is horrendous, creating two inches of mud in the field. Standing under one of the tents, excitement gearing me up, I think about all the races and training I've done to prepare me for this marathon. Just before Thanksgiving of 2012, I began running. My first race was a 5K Fitness Challenge at the Susan B. Anthony School in Revere, MA and since then I have participated in 123 races to date, ranging from 5K, 10K, 15K, 3M, 4M, 5M, 7M, 10M, 20M, Half Marathon.

Unfortunately, our wave wasn't able to start at 11:15 as scheduled due to technical difficulties with the speakers. At 11:30 I hear the announcement, "wave 4 with all corals please make your way to the starting line". I proceeded to leave the tent with the others to join the crowd that was already waiting on the path towards the starting line. I felt a lightness in my stomach from the buzz of everyone around me. By the time I get to the starting line and begin my race, it is 11:43 am – at this point, I am drenched from the pouring rain. It's around mile seven that I begin to see runners sitting on the sidewalk waiting for Emergency Aid Volunteers to pick them up, the torrential downpour only adding to the fatigue of running: splashing through large puddles; dealing with the weight of the rain on your back; the stinging sensation of rain hitting your limbs, nonstop; the threat of muscles cramping up on you as you push on – it's taking everything I have, both physically and mentally, to keep running. I have run through all four seasons, but today, this weather is beyond any training I've done. But still, I keep going.

As I approach mile ten in Newton, I'm scouring the faces of supporters on either side of the road, hoping to catch a glimpse of my daughters and nieces. I tell myself that it's possible I might have missed them already or will miss them with the poor weather conditions and sheer amount of people cheering everyone on. But soon enough, I hear them as I run through puddles of water: "Jackie! Jackie Chan! Over here! JACKIE!" – Jackie Chan was a nickname my daughters came up with years ago because they believed I bore a striking resemblance to the talented martial artist and actor. A smile erupts over my face as I see my two daughters, Evalynn and Barbara, with my nieces, Buntha and Analisa. They're all bundled up in soaked through jackets, wind whipping their faces. I hug them all, already memorizing this moment for years to come. I take this opportunity to finally take a quick break to hastily ingest some Gu Gel. I can feel that my hands are becoming numb and that my toes are frozen. But still, I can't stop smiling because I'm so happy from seeing my family. It was just the motivation I needed to continue. I hugged them once more and continued my journey towards Copley.

As I continued on, images blurred past me: more runners were being transported to medical tents; diehard marathon fans still standing in the rain to cheer for runners, their outerwear drenched; the Wellesley college students giving out high-fives to the runners along the course, which I avoided only because I knew it would take more energy out of me and I needed to invest all the energy I had to finishing this race.

With the rain beating down on me, I reflected on my marathon training: it did not go as planned. I had done four long training runs with the Melrose Club in Melrose, MA. I ran one half marathon, two 20 milers, and sprinkled 5k, 10k, 15k races in between. It's safe to say that I did not have nearly enough mileage from my training to prepare me for the marathon. Exhaustion coursed through me, my feet were stiff, and my hands were so numb that I couldn't take out my reserve of Gu Gel from my waist pouch. Luckily for me, and I'm sure other runners, Gu and Cliff gels were handed out all along the course, allowing me to restore my energy as I pushed on.

It was after Heartbreak Hill that I began to walk more just to keep myself going. I had gone into this experience knowing I might need to do some bit of walking, and although I did more walking than I had intended, I refused to stop. It was important that I keep moving the entire time, even if it meant at a slower pace. I knew what stopping would do, my body would betray my resolve and determination and force me to stop entirely and not just for a few moments. I distracted my mind from the soreness settling into my muscles by scouring the blurred skyline for the Citgo sign. Seeing that meant I wasn't too far off from the finish line.

Finally, the Citgo sign was in my sight. I looked up into the air, the rain falling on my face and I visualized myself at the finish line already. Everyone kept cheering us on as other runners and myself ran by them and I yelled out, "Boston Strong" with both my hands up in the air. As I made a left turn, I saw the finish line approximately a fourth of a mile away. It was then that I realized that in a matter of minutes, I can officially call myself a Boston Marathon Runner. After I cross the finish line, I knelt and kissed the ground. I finished! The moment I got up my two legs stiffen up and I dragged myself over to receive the finisher's medal; excitement, pride, and accomplishment etched in my heart.

I'd like to thank my family: my children, my siblings, my friends, and most importantly the MYSTIC Running Club of Wakefield for believing in me and supporting me and giving me a chance to run my first marathon, the 122nd Annual Boston Marathon 2018. Coming from Cambodia, a country where running is the least favorite sport, participating and completing one of the most renowned marathons in the nation, the Boston Marathon, has been one of the best experiences I've ever had.

Jo Franklin, Bib 11362

Erskineville, AUS, 40, 3:28:58

Running the Boston Marathon had been a dream of mine for about, errr, 18 months. To be honest, I'd never even considered Boston until my friend Jen suggested it to me in September 2016. Still, the idea didn't really take off until 12 months later when, after BQing at Gold Coast Marathon, I was informed that I had successfully qualified for Boston 2018.

Unfortunately, the road to Boston was a bumpy one for me: at the start of my training, I found out that cancer had returned in my neck. This meant a major 6-hour operation at the end of November, as well as taking a full month off running. When the hospital physio visited me on the day after my operation, she visibly winced as I told her I was doing Boston. But, as they say, "never tell a marathon runner they can't do a marathon" (especially Boston!); and come January I kicked off my training.

After living in the UK for more than a decade, I was not accustomed to training over a Sydney summer, but I thought I could use this "heat training" to my advantage when I got to a much cooler Boston. In my mind, the day of the marathon would be dry and sunny with a top of 14 degrees Celsius. Perfect conditions to roll down the mostly downhill course, I thought. While I wasn't aiming for a PB, my goal time was 3.25.00 (secretly 3.20.00) and I felt confident I could achieve that — especially in those conditions!

Just under a week out, I received an email from the marathon organizers with a weather warning and guidance to help runners "run efficiently, to maintain a healthy body temperature, and keep yourself safe." Safe from what, I thought? Hypothermia is what! This meant a complete outfit change. Luckily, I had my winter compression gear that I'd worn during the previous week in New York and I'd also bought some cheap clothes to layer up in before the race. These included a poncho, a beanie, a scarf, my cap and gloves and, very importantly, a cheap pair of shoes so I could wear these to the race and change into my dry running shoes and socks just before the start. The night before the race I also decided to wear my black running jacket, thinking I would discard it part way through the run. (Because surely, I would warm up by then!)

Come race day I met my colleague Simon — also doing the marathon — at Boston Common and we were bussed out to the start line in Hopkinton 26 miles away. The bus was super warm, and we could thaw out from our short time being outside. On the way, Simon calmed me down after I had a little stress about the gear bag drop (don't ask!), and soon we started to get excited for the race. That excitement quickly disappeared once we arrived at the athlete's village where we were simultaneously hit with freezing winds, horizontal rain, and arctic temperatures. And then we saw the mud right by the portaloos (or porta-potties as they're called in the US). We had no choice: we had to queue up for them, as is customary before any big race. After that, we huddled in a tent, also full of mud, but thankfully the lovely organizers had provided us with fruit, bagels, tea and coffee. So, I grabbed a coffee (my third that morning) to warm myself up.

After removing the extra layers and changing my shoes and socks (but keeping the poncho on), I shivered my way to the start line (losing Simon in the crowd). And then, before I knew it, we were off! I was actually running the Boston Marathon! I quickly discarded the poncho, although many runners kept theirs on, and the weather was soon forgotten. It was a lovely downward slope and felt great. The course was so scenic, taking us through some charming New England towns; and the crowds were already out, cheering us on and ringing their cow bells. I ran past a man playing drums on his front porch, another man singing Hound Dog on the back of his pick-up truck, college students drinking beer at 11am, and loads of kids offering up their hands for a high five. About 5 km in I had a quick loo stop and noticed my heart was beating quite fast — a combination of excitement, the cold, and too much coffee. I needed to calm myself down, so I did what I often do in a long race: broke it down into 5 km chunks.

The first half went by really quickly and I noticed I was paying less attention to my pace and focusing more on the distance I was covering. The weather was worsening but I kept going, getting water or Gatorade at almost all the drink stations — despite never getting hot or feeling sweaty. Mile 13 soon approached, which meant the Wellesley Scream Tunnel was close. I naively thought this would be an actual tunnel and I looked forward to a brief respite from the rain. But it was not to be, as the actual tunnel consists of the ladies from Wellesley College screaming out "Kiss me!" and pointing to their cheek. Well, "when in Rome" I thought, and I kissed one of the students on the cheek, which was met with more screams — and gave me a little boost.

I knew the set of hills was approaching at mile 16, meaning an up-and-down course for the next 5 miles. The hills themselves aren't that steep; but by that stage of the marathon, my legs were getting tired and heavy, and I was feeling weighed down by all the wet layers. At mile 18, I was on the lookout for a sea of red supporters from the Prospect Park Track Club (AKA PPTC, our sister club in Brooklyn). I'd run with PPTC in New York just the week before, and I knew they were in Boston to support some of their club runners. I was absolutely thrilled when the first thing I saw was a "Go Jo!" sign and I knew it was them. So there was a lot of screaming and high fiving, which gave me a *huge*, much-needed boost (such legends, those PPTC guys!) knowing there was just over 10 km to go. And before I knew it, I was on Heartbreak Hill and, while it's not a patch on our one in Sydney, it's still pretty tough — especially by mile 21. But as a I reached the top, I saw a huge sign that read "Heartbreak is over!" And it was largely downhill from there.

The last 7 kilometers of a marathon have typically always been the most enjoyable for me. Not so for this race. I was tired, I was cold, I was drenched. And I just wanted to get out of those wet clothes! But with the constant chants of "You got this!" from the supporters, I kept on running. Thank God for that crowd! I saw the CITGO sign at mile 24 and knew I was almost there. I unzipped my running jacket at mile 25 so I could display my number and KR singlet, hoping the cameras would capture that last stretch. And then I reached Boylston Street and the crowd were going wild. I felt like a rock star. It was *incredible*! I threw my hands up in the air and cheered along with them as I crossed the line. I did it! I COMPLETED THE BOSTON MARATHON!

The high of completing the marathon quickly turned to focusing on not getting hypothermia. I read later that over 2,500 runners had suffered from the medical emergency — including a number of the elites. After crossing the line, we received our medals and silver blankets and we all huddled together as we queued for our gear bags. My teeth chattered incessantly. Once I had my gear, I headed for the women's changing rooms and got into my dry clothes as quickly as possible (including my Boston runner's jacket). I then found my friend Nancy (a welcome sight!) who noticed my lips were turning blue; she led me out of the rain to the train and we headed straight for a celebratory burger and cider in Harvard. As I took off my coat at the restaurant, the table next to us saw my medal and runner's jacket and congratulated me. Love the Bostonians!

That was definitely the toughest race I've ever done. The temperature never got above 7 degrees Celsius, the headwinds blew at up to 40 miles per hour, and the rain was torrential. Full credit to the amazing volunteers and supporters who braved such horrendous conditions to keep us runners going — I couldn't have done it without them! I'm still on a high from the marathon and I feel so proud to have finished with a time of 3.28.58. It's not *quite* the goal time but *who cares*! I'll save my PB attempt for Blackmore's in September!

Joanne Willcox, Bib 22085

Utica, NY, 55, 4:11:10

Wouldn't you think after 26 marathons, a runner would be able to simply relax and get to sleep? Even after 7 previous Boston Marathons, this was still a big deal. I'm not fast by Boston standards but I am able to qualify. So yeah, it's still a big deal to me and sleep won't come easy Sunday night. I want to hold my own in my age group, my division. Trying to justify the anxiety is typically how the hours before race day is spent. Was it the discomfort that lie ahead based on the weather conditions, wind, cold, rain, all together in one day? All those elements in one day was new even to this experienced marathoner. What should be worn to keep my core temperature up and my hands, feet warm?

The nutrition aspect of the marathon doesn't bother me anymore. I have a routine. Get up at 5:45 and eat ½ a raisin bagel with honey at 6 am. Take a 5 Hour Energy at 6:50 am to get my system moving. *This works every time so there is no bathroom worries on the course as I can't drink coffee before a run. At 7:40 am, a Clif Bar. Morning snacking would end with ¾ of a banana at 9:15 am as the bus pulled into Athletes Village.

Ted and I were in the hotel room tuned into the local station watching news live at Hopkinton. The weather didn't look bad but when we left the room at 8:05 am, it was a different story.

My final outfit for the conditions ahead was as follows. Vaseline and Glide under sports bra and on toes, feet and legs. Compression capri with high knee compression toe socks. I put plastic baggies over my socks. I had an old pair of sneakers to wear to Athletes Village and wrapped my race shoes (Hoka's) in a plastic bag. A sports bra with a tank top. My outer layer was simply a red EMS rain resistant coat (the hood folded up, so it wouldn't act as a parachute in the wind), a fuel belt, a water proof baseball cap and water proof gloves purchased at North Face the Friday we arrived. The bib number was pinned chest level over the zipper on the red rain coat. There was no way that coat was coming off. I covered the baseball cap with a cheap blue wool hat for extra warmth.

To keep warm before the race, a sweat shirt, pants, old sneakers, a clear plastic garbage bag, and a yellow Marathon Tours rain cape, a thick leaf bag to sit on.

Ted walked with me to the buses at Boston Common. The wind and rain beating at us every step of the way. My pants got so wet, they were heavy on the bottom and began falling down. One porto stop before getting on the bus. I had an enjoyable conversation with a lady sitting next to me from Chicago. She was apprehensive how her day would go as she had been injured, only exercising on an elliptical trainer for the last 3 weeks. It seemed all runners had the same worries about whether their training would get them to the finish line in these conditions. When exiting the bus at Athletes Village, cold, wind and rain hit. The mud couldn't be avoided. Tip toeing across the mud to the end line of port-a-potties and standing in wet grass made me grateful I had a change of sneakers. The announcer said 20 minutes until Wave 3 could leave.

I made my way behind the tents, on leaves, trying to avoid as much mud as possible. In a corner where two buildings came together there were 3 runners standing with a skid in front of them, acting as a shelf. I inched up and was welcomed in. I put my bags down, laid out the heavy garbage bag and changed my shoes, took off my wet pants. The plastic baggies were left on my feet in hopes they would keep my feet dry until they warmed up once running. Wave three was called.

I went to the potties close to the starting corrals to take off my sweatshirt. The clear garbage bag and yellow cape stayed with me as I still had 10 minutes to go. While waiting for us to start running, I was looking at what everyone was wearing. The variation in attire went from full out winter jackets to simple tanks, shorts and arm warmers. I toyed with keeping my garbage bag on until my body heated up but chose to trust my jacket would work well enough once warmed up. *I should have wrapped my hands in the plastic and run with it for as long as possible.

Within the first 5 miles my hands were soaking wet. Those water proof gloves were not so water proof. I tried to get my gel and chomps out of my fuel belt, but the phone had trapped them at the bottom. The glove had to come off in order for me to get my gels. Got the glove off but couldn't get it back on. Ate 3 chomps and put the rest plus one gel in my rain jacket pocket. My fingers were numb, and the gloves were soaked. I started to panic and thought "What if I couldn't get any more gels? My hands are frozen now, how will I ever make it 21 more miles? Just calm down. You won't make it if you panic. All these other folks are as uncomfortable as you are. There will be Clif gels at mile 11 ½ and 17. Take deep breaths, there is nothing that can be done except to keep moving forward and try to relax. KEEP GOING! "

It was no good looking at my pace because I didn't care. The goal was just to finish. At mile 10, another attempt to get a gel out of my pocket. I stopped at a port-a-potty to get out of the elements. Struggled to get my wet capris pulled back up, took ½ of the gel but there was no way one glove was going back on my hand, it had to hang off my fingers. On occasion, I thought I felt the baggy over my sock bunch up, but it didn't. I kept them on throughout the entire race and they didn't cause any discomfort. Not sure they helped but I am glad they stayed on. I looked longingly at the medical tent wanting to stop so badly but thinking that everyone around me is running and I'm just cold, not hurt, not sick, just keep running. At mile 11 1/2, the Clif Gels were being handed out. I took two, trying to hold onto them, dropping one after about a mile. My teeth proved unsuccessful in opening the gel and I was only able to squeeze a little bit out of the small slit. It was just going to be a carb-depletion run, trying to console myself with the thought that when marathons were first run, there was no such thing as gels.

Sights and sounds: There was a barefoot runner. There was a man in just shorts, no shirt. There were skinny runners in nothing but arm sleeves, tank tops and short race shorts. Runners with no socks and bleeding ankles. How could they not feel the cold when my body was shutting down? It was so cold that a guy in a Santa Claus suit sat along the course cheering us on (I think he is there every year?!). There were kids braving the cold, cheering us on with hands held high. The Wellesley screamers were out in full force. It was around Boston College where there was a noticeable lack of spectators from all previous years.

The rain and wind came in biting waves. It let up then down poured. Gusting wind, then let up. I truly believed it had to get better, but it didn't, the rain got heavier and the winds never died. I tried to look forward to conquering the hills as usual, but my conquest resulted in only the first two. I was beaten and gave into a walk. Once I stopped to walk, I wondered if I would be able to run again being so stiff with cold. Somehow, I was able to jog along, trying to focus on getting to Cleveland Circle. The joy of dropping into Cleveland Circle wasn't the same as previous years. It offered no relief only large unavoidable puddles of water. Although there were only 4 miles to go, the effort was hard, and the motivation gone. By mile 23 there was a strong urge to quit. My jaw was tight and aching. Hamstrings hurt, legs stiff and heavy with cold. Hereford was thickly littered with plastic bags, coats, gloves, all items that runners had used to block the elements. This was the very first Boston Marathon that I walked on Boylston street toward the finish line. It felt awful not having the desire nor strength to run to that finish line. Walk. Jog. Walk. Jog. I was done. Crossing that finish line never felt so good and so bad at the same time. I didn't need water, just the heat sheet. The volunteer wrapped me in it so tight it was perfect, but it didn't stop the shivering.

Ted and I were supposed to meet at the church on the corner before Boston Common, but I couldn't make it. Instead, I cut right to the family meet and greet area, tempted to stop in the med tent as my body was shaking badly. Instead, I fumbled to get my phone and was only able to call Ted once I got into a tall glass building (200 Clarendon) where other runners were entering, seeking warmth. I was crying, shaking, feeling so cold. I wasn't alone. Once Ted found me, we sat for 10 minutes before heading back outside towards the hotel.

After getting help peeling off wet clothes and getting into a very hot bath, I felt great. In fact, feeling that good after running a marathon makes you feel rotten like you didn't give it all you had. It isn't long before depression sets in as you begin to forget the discomfort and wonder it you'll ever achieve your goal again. No doubt the weather factored into the results but was there a way to run this year in those conditions that would have enabled me to meet my goal?

Final result: 4:11:10. Finished 7307 out of all 11604 women. Finished 241 out of 669 in my age group.

Thoughts for future races if ever in these conditions again: Base layer should be sports tank with long sleeve shirt on top. Thick running tights with long

Injinji toe socks (cover legs and feet with Vaseline/Glide) and a waterproof sock over the top. Bring dry sneakers to change into before the race. Plastic gloves over the top of a large mitten to keep hands dry and enable me to get a wet mitten on and off with ease. Waterproof baseball cap with head band and hat. Waterproof rain jacket on top. Keep clear garbage bag on as long as possible. Try to put gels in a place that is accessible even with cold hands.

After the race, I thought never again will I run in those conditions but now I've had a week to think about it, I WOULD do it again but with better preparation.

Tommy Collins, Bib 26292

Farmingham, MA, 42, 5:11:11

I was born and raised in East Boston, MA - otherwise known as "Eastie." I've always excelled in sports but running never interested me. In fact, I only "ran" if my coaches made me.

Funny thing is my dad was a runner. He ran Boston and New York several times as well as competed in Iron Mans and Triathlons. From time to time he'd ask if I wanted to go for a run and it couldn't have been further from my interests.

Fast forward to June 1st, 2006. My night from hell that turned into my night from heaven. My ball game got called because of the weather. It was pitch black out, thunder and lightning everywhere and just pouring buckets and buckets of rain. I left the game to head home and got t-boned by a young girl. Turns out the traffic lights were out on the main road I was on, so she must not have realized it was a major intersection when she crossed through. Aside from the trees 6 feet apart that my car somehow managed to sneak through at 30+ mph, I'll spare the details. Except that my wife was 3 months pregnant and my back was ruined. But I was alive.

My activity pretty much stopped after that. By the time my daughter was born that December, I'm guessing I gained 30 lbs. from the crappy diet I had been used to. I was out of work for a while and ordered food in a lot. Over the next

10 years my back never really got better. Neither did my diet. At the start of 2016 is when I needed to make some serious changes.

I'd slowly gained weight to the point I was about 60 lbs. heavier in 2016 and probably 70 heavier than I ever wanted to be. My doctor recommended I go for a 15 minute walk each day to help with stress and to get my body moving. Because I've always been a competitor, once I got into a habit of walking I started to track my times. My goal was to "beat my last time" each day. My walks grew to about a half hour and I'll never forget the day, when I was halfway through my walk, I realized I couldn't beat my last time simply just by walking faster. I had to run!! NOOOOOO!!!!

I remember the exact corner I was on and the exact 20 feet I ran when I felt I was going to die. I walked a lot and ran (a little) but guess what? I beat my last time! The more I did this, the more I ran which was still not a lot, but I continued to better my last times. Soon it was "run a light pole and walk 5 light poles" and by the end of '16 I knew what I had to do. My 2017 resolution was to run a 5k every single month of the year!!!!

After I ran my 4th 5k (Sandy Hook in April 2017), I wanted more. Forget the 5k's, give me a 10k! Something inside me said it had to be something in Boston because all of my "firsts" were there. So I trained myself for the B.A.A. 10k in June. Then of course after that, I had to go bigger. "I'm signing up for the Half in October!!!" I trained for the half, got injured 4 miles in, jacked my back up (stepping into a pot hole of all things) but I finished.

A recent addition to the Boston Buddies, Troy Moran, had been a mentor through these Boston runs and asked if I'd considered running Boston. This is a guy who had run 22 or 23 Bostons in a row. I knew I had to do it. How could I not?? My first breath was in Boston, first 5k, 10k and half had been in Boston. Hell yeah, I'll run Boston!!!

So then that became my next journey. Training was awesome. The "Last Long Run" was incredible but I wouldn't change anything in the world for the experience I had on April 16th, 2018. It's so hard to explain. So many family and friends who helped and supported me along the way also showed up. This includes all my Boston Buddies. Without you I'd be lost!!

Huge shout out to my girls!! My wife Debbie and daughter Ava have put up with me as I've gone through all of this. The early morning noise I create, the late evening crankiness I've displayed, and they've done nothing but support me the entire time! They are why I get up every day and why I am who I am today.

I will forever be Boston born and bred. Thankfully there's no changing that. And I can now say that with the help, guidance as support of the greatest group in running, I will also forever be a Boston Buddy! Thank you!

John Burke, Bib 8779

Gorham, ME, 48, 3:05:57

Written by Isabelle Burke, John's daughter.

As my father was getting ready to run his first Boston marathon, I was able to see all of the different components that goes into the training. From eating the right fuel, getting down to the lightest possible body weight, and just running like crazy. My dad was running up to 65 miles per week to train for this. I don't think I would have the dedication and drive that it takes to completely change up my whole life dynamic. I saw my dad training through all the blood, sweat, and tears. And to be able to see such a positive outcome after the race is just so priceless to me. My dad inspires me every day to try new things,

he is always encouraging us to be the best we can be while striving for success.

As he began his competitive running career back in 2016, he proved to my sisters and I that no matter what it's always good to try new things. He taught us that if you believe in something, you can achieve it. He is a firm believer in and always preaches Positive Discontent and Competitive to us in sports and in life. It didn't matter that this was new territory for him, as soon as he got started it would be something he took very seriously. "If it's worth doing, it's worth doing to the best of your abilities" he often says. I think other people could learn a few things from my dad. First, no matter how hard things seem to get; there's always light at the end of the tunnel and you can never ever quit. He always says things like this to help encourage us to never give up. Second, just because something is new to you, doesn't make it impossible. My dad began running for fun at the age of 43 and competitively at 46. Most people take their whole lives to achieve all that he has in the running world. At this stage in his life, he could have offered many reasons (excuses as he calls them) as to why he would not or should not be successful at running. Lastly, I hope people can take something from his never fading positivity. Rain, snow, or shine my dad is out running with a huge smile on his face. He doesn't let the negative self- image, or the harsh words of others falter him from doing what he loves to do most. No matter how physically and emotionally exhausted the sport makes him, no matter how many messed up toes, lost or black toe nails, agonizing shin splints, or torn tendons in his feet, he gets he still gets out there every day and runs.

I seriously admire everything my dad has been able to accomplish. I reached out to the Gorham Times to write this because it makes me so immensely proud that my dad has had the opportunity to fulfill his dream of running in The Boston Marathon. All I have heard him talk about these last few years getting ready and running like crazy is how much it means to him to have his children be so proud of him. Well I can confidently say I have never been prouder of my dad. I have never been prouder of anyone in my life than I am at his major accomplishments in such a short amount of time. Even though the weather didn't cooperate, the rain, wind, and sleet that day made me even more proud of the incredible man who is my father. With all of the obstacles in his way he still managed to run the marathon in 3 hours and 5 minutes, his best marathon time yet but not the best he will ever run! I can only imagine how much faster he would have run if the sun was shining that day. All in all, I could not be prouder of my dad, I look up to him in everything he does, and I strive to be just like him some day.

Written by John himself.

Running the Boston Marathon was a dream of mine since I was a kid. Life however went on and the dream dissipated. I ran a lot as a kid and won many local races in my age group. I ran track in Westbrook where I grew up and I was pretty fast. I went into the Marine Corps as an officer and had to be very fit. As the leader, you must lead from the front. In order to do so, I had to stay fast. I got out of the USMC and got away from running. I gained weight and 7 years ago, I found myself weighing over 200lbs for the first time in my life. I hated this.

I started working out (weight lifting) and doing a bit of cardio. This helped a bit but not a ton and my love for food, wine and fun with friends was still there. Five years ago, I figured I would give running a shot. This seemed to work. Not only was I losing weight, but my mind was becoming surprisingly clearer with each and every mile. I was feeling less stress and pressure. Around this time (April 15th, 2013) the Boston Marathon was changed forever with the bombing. It was this precise moment that I knew that I had to resurrect this dream. The problem was I was way too slow to qualify. I kept running and I kept getting faster, then on my birthday in March of 2015, I turned 45 and the qualifying time, though still far away, seemed much more manageable by dropping from 3:15:00 to 3:25:00. At his point, it became a focus.

I tried my luck at my first marathon in May of 2016 in Ottawa, ON. I ran a 3:39:15 on a very hot and humid day. I was happy to have completed my first but dejected over missing the qualifying time by almost 25 minutes. This set back frustrated me but drove me harder and then on Christmas night of 2016, I watch a documentary on the Boston Marathon Bombing and it moved me beyond measure. It cut deep, and I felt so much anger and sadness and emotion that I was now driven by not just my own desires to run a race, but by others suffering and a desire to become a part of their healing by helping this great race in this great city move forward. I watched in awe as these victims picked the pieces of their lives back up and I wanted to be a part of that so badly. The very next day, I signed up for the Sugarloaf Marathon in Maine. The race was in 4.5 months and it was winter, and I had to get training and training hard. I had prepared for Ottawa on my own and it was not enough. I had used a marathon training plan out of a book, but the plan was not flexible, and I kept dealing with common over-use injuries from running. It just wasn't working so for Sugarloaf, I hired a professional coach- PBM Coaching (Kurt Perham) out of Brunswick, ME. "KP" had a full schedule and no room to take on another athlete but I wrote him a lengthy email with my story and he agreed to a phone chat. At the end, he agreed to coach me and only ask that I was serious about this, that I give him 100% ALWAYS. The journey began, and I ran many many long hard miles that winter around Gorham, Westbrook, Standish, Buxton, and Portland. I even hit Falmouth a time or 2. By April, I was averaging 55-65 miles per week and very few of those on a treadmill.

When The Sugarloaf Marathon came around on May 15th, 2017, I felt ready. I had a big gap to bridge with my last 26.2 time and my time need to qualify but I was hungry. I took to the start line on a very cool May day (45 degrees- perfect for running) in the Carabassett Valley and I ran. I ran hard and I it felt so amazing. I finished with not only a PR (personal record) but also with that coveted BQ9 Boston Qualifier). I ran a 3:12:15.

I was now in. I had 11 months to train for my very first Boston. I just had to train hard and stay injury free which was a challenge. I had many set-backs along the way including a few surgeries over the past 3 years that I had to be patient through and rehab. I stuck with Kurt and hired on a Nutritionist (Leslie Meyer) in late January as the final piece to making a strong showing at Boston. In running, physics trumps all. Weight matters. The lighter the runner, the faster the pace at the same effort. For me, every pound meant approximately 2 seconds per mile faster. Leslie came very highly recommended. Like KP, Les handles the nutrition for many professional Tri-athletes and runners. Between the workouts and the shift in eating, I was able to show up to the cold-wet starting line last Monday in the best shape of my life and 15lbs lighter than I was in February.

Being a runner, especially a distance runner is hard on the family. We tend to get obsessive. Lol. I have incredible friends and co-workers who followed this journey while supporting it along the way. My Parents flew in from Florida for the race and were AMAZING!!!! They are definitely my biggest fans. They were beside themselves happy when I told them back in February that I wanted them there with me.

I made a very long weekend of this race. It is my first Boston, so I wanted to take it ALL in. I arrived in Boston on Friday am. I stayed in the Seaport next to the Expo Friday and Sat night. I moved hotel to the start line on Sunday night. I attended several speaking series from past winners and elite athletes and I got to hang out with the Women's winner Desi Linden on Saturday night. I have met Des on three other occasions racing different races across America. She always offers amazing advice and direction. It was particularly great prior to this race. She told me "scrap your plan and just run to enjoy the Boston Marathon". The 1968 Winner Amby Burfoot had told me the exact same thing earlier in the day. After so much preparation and training, this was tough to hear but certainly needed to be entertained as it was coming from champions. Coincidently, Sheri Peirs (Elite runner from Maine- Westbrook High Grad) told me the same exact thing on Saturday at 6pm. She even said in a message to get a trash bag and wear it to the start. With all these pros echoing the same message, I went into the race understanding that my goal had to be adjusted and that it was going to be brutal. I adjusted my race-plan that night and decided to run 10 seconds per mile slower for at least the first 16 miles of the race. In hind-sight, I am so thankful that I did this as that extra effort may have cost me a TON of time if not a DNF in the end. This race came down to the ability to hold back early on and stay as warm as possible while doing so in order to make it to the Newton Hills in good shape. Then after completing Heartbreak Hill and passing Boston College at mile 21, being able to summons whatever you had left of mental fortitude, strength, and courage and pushing through the pain of the last 5 miles and 385 yards. This race took Grit!

I wavered 20x on what to wear. I packed almost every running item that I owned. I checked into the Courtyard by Marriott in Milford Mass at around 9:30pm on Sunday night and while checking in, I saw a roll of large trash bags behind the desk, remembering what Sheri had told me, I asked if I could have one and borrow a pair of scissors. I made a makeshift poncho by cutting a tight neck hole and 2 well placed arm holes. This item became what I feel was the key to my success. Sheri said wear it to the start, I wore the damn thing most of the race. It kept my core warmer. It did not keep out all the water, but it certainly helped. Despite the extra drag it certainly had, the benefits far outweighed the negatives. I tore it off between mile 23 and 24 and "embraced the suck" for the remaining 2-3 miles.

Additionally, I was being told by many that I was making a mistake wearing runners-tights and a fitted thermal shirt under my singlet. I also opted for hat and gloves. All this clothing was definitely heavy (especially after being 100% soaked before the gun even sounded) but again, maintaining as high core body temperature as possible was key. This all allowed me to do that. I did not feel the effects of hypothermia as so many did. It wasn't until 15 mins after the finish that I was paralyzed by the cold. I found myself delirious in the bathroom of a Boston Hotel that I basically snuck into as I waited for my family to meet up and deliver dry clothes. Approx. 45 mins had gone by since the finish at this point. I could not think straight or use my hands/fingers. It was rough.

I stayed in Boston Downtown on Monday night and met up with 50+ members of the FB Group (Boston Buddies as we call ourselves). We met at Cheers and had an absolute blast. We all drank beer and ate cheese burgers, French fries, nachos, etc. All the things that we pushed out of our lives while training for the BM. It was my first beer in over a month. I needed to drop weight to run faster so February and March were about cutting back on everything. I dropped 16 lbs. but as a celebration, I can't wait to put a few of those back on with all the food and drinks that I have missed.

On a serious note, I have also spent these past 2 days reflecting as a form of celebration. Reflecting on the experience of running and finishing the most challenging Boston Marathon in history. Not just that though, I didn't just run and didn't just finish Boston, I Raced Boston. There is a big difference. I competed. I fought hard and I never gave up. These past 2 days have been a celebration of that but in the end, the 2018 Boston Marathon will not be remembered for that. It was not about racing or even running, it was about personal growth and about building character. It was about becoming a better and stronger Human Being. I would not change the conditions that we had to endure for anything. The brutal and unrelenting weather gave us this amazing opportunity to grow. We all suffered and so many of us came out the other end stronger than we were when we woke up and laced-up on the morning of Monday April 16th.

Kam Jandu, Bib 29905

Hungary, 49, 4:51:53

I started running after an amateur soccer career came to its natural end. I completed my first marathon in 2005 in Cologne, Germany and to this date that time of 4:25 remains a PB. Having suffered from a heart attack at the ripe old age of 39 in 2008, I sought to find some answers as to why, and then lost my brother a few months later aged 42 also from a sudden cardiac arrest, the medics were able to quickly determine that I had a genetic issue. My brother did not get the second chance afforded to me, so I wanted to keep on running (under medical support) in his honor. I ran Berlin in 2010 and then Budapest in 2011 whilst I waited patiently to secure a place in the New York Marathon via lottery. At the third time of asking, I won a place in 2012 and got myself into the best shape possible by September. To my horror and shock, I suffered yet another heart attack, aged 44 – WTF, right? This time, the cardiologist placed a stent into the rogue artery and said I should be ok provided I took the prescribed medication for the rest of my life. Clearly, I could not run in 2012 which as most of you know was cancelled anyway due to Hurricane Sandy. It took a whole year of focus and training to get ready for 2013. With a well-managed heart, robust training and bags of enthusiasm, my family and I flew to the NYC at the end of October. But simply lifting our suitcase tweaked a back muscle and triggered severe sciatica which rendered me in agony on marathon Friday. I had already collected the race pack, was walking with a heavy limp, yet I was still determined to run. I even had a Facebook page set up to support my cause in honor of my late brother. With a crazy twist of irony and a heavy heart, I withdrew from the race 24 hours before so that my deferral could be carried forward to 2014 – there was no way I could run, and I was literally heartbroken.

Fast forward 12 months and undeterred I had unfinished business to run NYCM, and this time I would succeed in what turned out to be one of the coldest and windiest marathons in their history, but I got the job done. My World Marathon Major journey was well and truly underway having already run Berlin earlier.

It was another 12 months for my next WMM with Chicago in 2015 and that was a great experience overall and I got a reasonable time. I have always loved Chi-town, so this made the experience even better. At this point, I thought that I would aim to complete the majors by the time I became 50 with the last one being my hometown race of London. I had just turned 46 so was in good shape to meet this goal!!

2016 proved to be a fruitless year in terms of new races though having secured a lottery place in New York again, I set about training for it in the European summer because by August, I knew I had secured a place in Tokyo Feb 2017 so dare I say it, NYCM 2016 was going be a long training run. I'm not sure why, but it did not meet the same adrenaline rush as 2014 but no doubt it is and was still a great race, certainly the weather was a lot better than two years earlier. Literally a few days before the NYCM, I heard that I had secured a charity spot for London 2017 which meant that I was on track for majors four and five in just a few weeks time after NYCM. I worked it out that in 26 weeks, I would be running 3 WMM. Lots of winter training but it was great fun. Tokyo was an incredible journey because I had been there a few times on business but this time I was there to run, and the Japanese make this race what it is – truly amazing so arigato!

London 2017 – OMG. Having heard so much about the incredible atmosphere and charitable causes which makes this major in my opinion, the best race I have ever run, it certainly lived up to everything I expected. If anyone gets the chance to run just one major, this would win, hands down and yes, I am biased, but many of my runner mates from around the world who have also run it echo this sentiment. Major 5 completed! This left Boston so that was my destiny sealed.

In summer 2017 and whilst on holiday in Bali with my family, my friend Karen Selby (also a WMM six-star medalist) referred me to a UK sports agency who had slots for Boston 2018. She was on the priority list having secured a bib with a BQ time, she let me know and I managed to secure a bib within hours which was great news!

I was determined to be as fit as possible because this would be my last major. I drew on a Hanson plan which a few friends had done, and it had worked out for them. Despite very painful plantar fasciitis, I managed to follow the plan well and was delighted to join the various FB groups, especially the Boston Marathon Training group. We exchanged many tips, ideas and stories about experiences and it was probably one of the best running groups I have been a member of. Getting insights about the course, the history and the city's passion for this race proved very useful. Leading up to race day, a few members were talking about the weather forecast. Whilst others said not to worry too much about the weather so far out, it became evident that we were going to be faced with some freaky conditions – flashback to NYCM 2014, this time with shed loads of heavy rain and a mostly headwind. Whilst in Boston, my friends and I really got in to the pre-race experience like book signings with legends such as Kathrine Switzer, watching the Boston documentary at the ICON theatre and of course attending the blessing in the church on marathon Sunday. I had watched the Boston bombing movie – patriots day with my family a few weeks earlier so I was very aware of being in a city which had witnessed a horrific tragedy 5 years earlier but moreover that the spirit of the runners and the city itself were and will continue to go a long way to demonstrate that no-one, nor anything could break the resolve of this great city. The day before race day, we went to the Red sox game at Fenway park where it was freezing cold and even snowing at some point!

Marathon eve, we had a pasta evening at a local Italian restaurant in a group of around 16, most of whom were running the following day and five of whom were 6-star chasers, including myself. You could sense and note that the weather was not far from our thoughts so last-minute tips were being exchanged. Earlyish to bed and the alarm was set. I do not pray, nor am I religious but I did manage a few reflective thoughts that evening before bed. Tomorrow would be my one opportunity to run Boston and I knew I had to do it, not just to get the

AWMM 6th star but because everyone knows about the Boston marathon yet not everyone will get the chance to run it.

I slept well and managed to arise early for breakfast in the hotel with the numerous other runners. It was already raining outside, and earlier wave runners were passing by, wrapped up with many layers undeterred. After breakfast, I went to my room to put the layers on which had been prepared earlier in the absence of neck warmer/buff, I managed to wear a pair of my boxers around my neck which did the trick all day. Next and like 26000 others, we made our way to the bus pick up around Boston common. It was around a 15-minute walk and the rain was heavy, many people were trying to avoid the puddles without success, we were all soaked through even before getting on the bus. Having dropped my bag, the journey back to the bus was equally wet but we made it. Wave 4 is one of the last ones so there was certainly no stampede however, the relentless rain meant people wanted to get on a bus fast! We took our seats on the bus and tried to dry off, chatted with fellow runners and tried to relax on the 50 minutes journey to Hopkinton. Upon arrival and when the bus door opened, the heat simply shot out and we were met with what felt like a massive cold tornado – at this point I contemplated getting back on the bus, but my resolve was strong. We made our way around the building to the rear and at that point saw the muddy path down to the tents. Boy, many people had walked it already so the downside of being at the rear meant that we had the thick stuff to contend with. The wait here was an hour and included yet one more wait in the freezing cold, outside the muddy porta loo. I drank a coffee and picked up more layers which others had left behind. The best part about this was that everyone remaining were in the same boat – if you pardon the pun, we knew we were cold, but we were together and in just around 5 hours or under, we were going to be just fine.

Setting off an hour or so later in soaked through clothes, we battled to the start line and the runners were fairly sparse at this point, but we set off and it rained, rained some more and continued to rain. Complemented with a bitch of a headwind, the challenge ahead was set. From here on in, it is hard to remember but running alongside several thousand embattled heroes, we took on the greatest marathon of all.

We went up, then down and back up again and my many layers which were meant to come off as the run unfolded stayed on throughout. The rain was pounding my body and my shoes were simply full of water throughout because they could not drain faster than the rain was falling. Still, I managed to get to halfway in around 2:10 hours which was ok given the conditions, but the weather was relentless. There were a couple of occasions when I contemplated quitting before mile 16 but then when I saw the other runners, the fans who had come out, the security services and medics and volunteers, I could not stop, I did not want to stop. This became more profound as I thought about the church blessing the day before and how we were all made welcome to this wonderful city, I had to finish, I needed to finish, and I was going to finish.

The Wellesley tunnel sounds, Heartbreak Hill and the Citgo sign were all that I had hoped for and more. When the heavens opened harder and faster, I recall looking up and shouting – "Is that all you got?" I think I said this three times at least.

At mile 23, I knew that I needed to de-layer and lose my poncho, but I was still so cold, but the plan was set. Having negotiated the underpass, and seeing the crowds thicken, I knew that the end was in sight, then I experienced what very people ever will – I turned right on Hereford but before turning left on Boylston I shed my poncho – seems like I was not the first, nor the last either because there was a gaggle of outer layers on Hereford. I then turned left and ran the blue line towards the finish. I have very few photos from this point and very few overall because I guess the photographers had become sodden by now. My time was around 4:51 and slow, but my majors journey had flashed through my mind as I ran towards the finish. Not for long though because I wanted to savor everything about Boston 2018. It demanded my respect which is why when many asked me about my sixth star earned, I talk about Boston first because I owed the greatest and oldest marathon at least that much. I crossed the finish line and looked up to the skies, collected my Boston medal, then my six-star medal at the abbot tent. I then proceeded to get my bag and change as quickly as possible which was difficult because my body was shaking. I had no energy to find a changing room so the volunteers at a tent let me take shelter there. I will probably never meet them again but if they ever read this, thank you so much!

Unknown to me, my wife who was tracking me from our home in Budapest lost me at the halfway mark as did my friends around the world. Thinking that I dropped out or worse, I had a medical problem I managed to message my wife when getting back to the hotel. It seemed that my chip had become so wet, the tracker had stopped. Luckily there were cameras which enabled BAA to give me a finish time of 4:51 which was my slowest ever marathon out of 9. The time does not matter, what is most important is that just under 26000 people became brothers and sisters that day because we were badass enough to start, endure and finish this great race. I will not be back because the memory is too precious to tarnish but thank you to my Boston Buddies – keep on moving forward!

Ron Romano, Bib 6941

Weehawken, NJ, 57, 3:19:47

10 days before Boston, on an easy taper run, I felt a searing pain in my calf. For days it was painful to walk, and it looked pretty bleak for me to run. Aggressive Graston, atomic balm, rock tape and prayers got me to the starting line. Running in "The Perfect Storm" took my mind completely off my calf; I was so thankful to be part of this historic day. Felt fine till I came down the hill at BC, when I got really dizzy. Took my glasses off, hoping that might help, but I can't see without them! My faculties clearly weren't all there. Thank God I've run Boston so many times, I was able to put it on auto-pilot and get across the finish line. Ended up in medical tent with 93-degree body temperature. Amazing volunteers warmed me up and I happily joined my Boston Buddies at Cheers to celebrate our life changing experience!

Kati Toivanen, Bib 23061

Kansas City, MO, 54, 3:52:23

2018 was my first Boston Marathon and I felt honored and excited. Like everyone else, I had been obsessively staring at the weather reports, downloading new apps as if different sites were going to offer better news. I typically excel in the face of adversity, so while the race conditions were not exactly enjoyable, they played to my strengths: mental toughness, perseverance, stubbornness, and my ability to choose denial at will.

My first running bout took place in 1981, when I arrived in America for the first time as an AFS exchange student from Finland hosted by a wonderful, loving family in Williston, Vt. In an effort to connect with other students at the high school, I joined the cross-country team. I was not very good but worked hard and improved. It started my life-long fondness of running. I returned to the US to attend college and graduate school, eventually building an art career and a family of my own here. I never raced again until my son's elementary school had a fundraising 5K in 2013. That, and my elliptical breaking, got me started on a path to losing 30 pounds and lacing up for regular running.

In 2015 I ran my first marathon and my second one gave me a qualifying time for Boston, only to be cut due to field size. The Wicked Marathon in Wamego,

KS, my third, got me in for 2018. My previous training had been somewhat haphazard, so I felt the need for a real plan since I was going to the big league. I settled on the Hanson's Marathon Method, because it fit my lifestyle and the science behind it made sense. Kansas City, where I live, is surprisingly hilly, so I hit hills in every run, and I sprinkled hill-specific sessions into my schedule from the BAA plan. The training was challenging. During the week I ran after work, so I bought a head lamp and a vest with fancy, blinking (and obnoxious) lights. Most nights I would pick my son up from school, complete my workout, shower, eat dinner and then settle on the couch, making a sincere attempt to watch Netflix shows with Chris, my partner, but failing every time.

Saturday mornings I ran my long runs with a running group and enjoyed their unfailing support. My friend Martin had run Boston twice and his celebration jacket always gave me jacket-envy. My run group listened to my cranky comments early Saturday mornings - most days I had just completed 8 miles at 8 PM the night before. I called the combo a "marathon with a nap". Wednesdays I would do tempo runs with Run 816, a local running store. When they switched to the track in early March I talked Jeff from the group to continue tempo sessions with me and I dedicate miles 6-16 of my first Boston to him. He was there every week as we crushed those tempo runs in increasing distance, week after week. Mondays I would run hills and speed on my own. I have never trained as hard as I did for this marathon. I was methodical and dedicated. Nothing stopped me. I did not miss a single session. The winter was cold, windy and long. I ran in ice, rain, sleet, sub-zero weather and wind. I carried my training log in my purse everywhere I went.

The journey in April to Boston was so much more than running the race as I made it a trip down memory lane. A graduate from Clark University in Worcester, MA, I visited my photography professor Stephen DiRado on Thursday before the race. On Friday I took the train to Beverly Farms in the North Shore to visit a dear friend Kate Hackman. I explored the Institute of Contemporary Art, right next door to the Expo. Artist friends Chantal Zakari and Mike Mandel had a piece in the exhibition about the 2013 Boston Bombing and the subsequent search for bombers. They had experienced the events from their Watertown, MA, home.

My former sister-in-law Heather Wells opened up her home and heart to me for the race days. She dropped me off and picked me up from the race. She washed my soaking clothes and listened to my endorphin-induced chatter. Mike, my exchange family brother, and his son Sean had both qualified for the race and nine family members came from Vermont, upstate New York and Portland, Oregon, to cheer us on. We had a blast getting ready, scheming the spectating plan, previewing the course, eating and laughing.

The weather and concerns about what to wear found their way into every conversation. I had decided to wear the exact same set of clothes I had for my qualifying race in Kansas, which had been windy, rainy and 40 degrees. Seemed like a decent guess. I had no idea what I was in for. In Kansas I had rain. In Boston I faced sheets and buckets of icy rain delivered with gusts of freezing headwind. As we were on our race course reconnaissance trip the day before the race, Mike and I stopped at the Heartbreak Hill Running Company for last minute gear search. Our mental note of it signaling "one last hill coming up" was golden in the race.

Riding on the bus to Hopkinton took so long. I had brought an extra pair of old shoes and socks to Hopkinton, which I was grateful for. Also, my mylar heat sheet and an extra jacket came in handy. I felt for the two women from Australia I talked in the overcrowded tent. They seemed to be in a total daze and said they had never seen anything like it. I tried to joke around, but humor did not go over too well. Fear, shock and shivering took over people's minds and bodies. Walking over to the starting line was slow and chaotic. The rain ponchos and trash bags drove rain right into our legs and shoes. Once we started to move things improved and it was a relief to get the show on the road. The start was so unassuming I had to ask if we had started.

Despite the conditions, I had decided to run my best and an honest race, because I wanted to see the results of the new training method, honor my hard work and definitely I did not want to run another marathon before September to BQ. I was willing to make adjustments as necessary, but I was going to run my plan. (6 easy to warm up, 10 steady tempo, pushing through the Newton hills and cruising home – for average pace of 8:35). I was pretty much on track with my pace at halfway point, but the freezing rain and tripping over deep puddles and random clothing/plastic/mylar sheets just added a challenge I had not expected. I oscillated between engaging with the spectators and retrieving into the dark place of my own mind. My left cheek felt funny the next day, and I realized I had probably run the entire race with my left eye closed, my right somewhat protected by my hat and tilted head. The wonderful smells coming from the little restaurants in the towns along the way were torture as my stomach was growling. But I also felt nauseous and could not take in too many fluids. I busted some dance moves to the delight of the spectators. I high fived the entire lineup of the Wellesley girls. My right calf suddenly cramped with 1.5 miles to go and I had to dig deep to ignore it. I was determined to BQ. At age 54 I did not think I had another full marathon in me before September. This was it. I was going to get it done.

On Hereford I heard my name and saw the sign with my name on it. My Vermont crew was there, and I was excited, and touched. And then, the last stretch on Boylston was by far the longest 0.3 miles I have ever run. I crossed the finish line at 2:49 PM on Monday to the announcement of a moment of silence to honor the victims of the bombing in 2013. Five years prior I would have been just a few feet away from the two explosions. When I hugged my Mom in the family meeting area, I cried and laughed, so tightly I was afraid I was going to crush her. The day's events only hit me then.

With my 3:52.23 finish time I missed my time goal, but only by 7:23 minutes. At first disappointed, I later realized it was actually a victory over the elements. I got a new PR, if only by a minute, and qualified for 2019 with a 17+ minute cushion. The run was challenging, the spectators were heroes, and volunteers made of magic. The confidence and resilience of my training program along with my family, friends and running tribes – both physical and online - carried me through the DELUGE. And now I belong to another special tribe, the survivors of the 2018 Boston Monsoon-athon.

Jodi Wilding, Bib 24579

Brigham City, UT, 56, 4:30:01

This was my second time to run this magnificent race. One thing for certain is you can't take for granted the opportunity to be part of this iconic event. I know I never will. It has taken a lot of years of hard work, determination, and not giving up for me to get to that coveted starting line. And even though this year's race was less than ideal, there is nothing short of maybe being in a wheelchair that would have kept me from running it. Maybe even then I would have found a way! That being said — I heard someone say Boston race conditions this year were perfect, for a salmon. If you want to get an idea what it was like to run it this year, put a treadmill in a car wash and turn the temperature to 30 degrees. That about sums up this year's conditions.

So... how was it for me???

It was tough. It was incredible. It was cold. It was brutal. It was definitely the most challenging race I've ever run. It was miserably amazing! I'll never ever forget it or regret it as long as I live. I was in awe of the volunteers, the police (out in huge numbers), the spectators standing in torrential rain, the courage, the determination, and the sheer grit of the runners. It will forever be remembered as one of the greatest experiences of my life.

I checked the forecast for weeks on out in great fear of a cold rainy day and as race day drew near, it only got worse each day. Yep, a cold, rainy, and to top it all off, windy day! I don't mind the rain. Or the cold. Not even so much the wind. But all three together is where I draw the line. I was already in fear of running it in the New England cold and rain after hearing my friend's reports from 2015 when it rained. For some reason, it seems I always "get" the opportunity to experience the things I fear the most. Last year, it was the unrelenting heat. But this year, it was my greatest fear on steroids. 2018's conditions made history as the worst and coldest in the past 30 years. (I want to know what it was 30 years ago that could top this!) Temps in the 30's before wind chill, pouring rain (2"), and 30-40 mph headwind with gusts at 50 mph. I was trembling (more out of fear than cold) just thinking about it.

Trying to decide what to wear was one of the biggest challenges of all. You don't want to overdress, but you really don't want to under-dress either. When I knew it was going to be a freezing monsoon, I decided to opt on the side of overdressing and I am glad I did. Many runners were under-dressed and paid dearly for it. I wore several thin layers — and my new Saucony very thin waterproof jacket I found while in Boston, and a thin poncho. I had a throw away jacket and a thick hoody underneath my poncho to stay dry in the athlete's village that I bought the night before when I heard the temps were predicted to be 28° at the start. On my legs, I wore compression tights as well as another pair of tights on top and a pair of throw away sweats. I had on one pair of merino wool socks and then duct taped the toes of my shoes to help keep the toes dry and wore surgical booties over them in the AV (Athlete's Village). I wore surgical gloves over my regular gloves. I wore a headband with a hat and a shower cap over that. I had plastic bags over my shoes to help as well while waiting in the AV. I was prepared to literally soak it all in. It was nice to know we were all in the same boat. Actually, a boat would have been nice!

When I got in the car to head to the bus, it was pouring, and the wind nearly blew me down. I just looked to the heavens and had to laugh because it was almost comical to me that it really was going to be this bad. I thought to myself how crazy that I was really going to do this, but after working so hard to qualify and then make the cutoff and training hard for four months, I was not NOT going to do this!

I dedicated this race to the memory of my son Tyson who passed away 12 years ago at the age of 17 from Cystic Fibrosis. His death was my catalyst to begin running at the age of 45. It became great therapy for me and I really attribute my running to getting me through the grief at that difficult time in my life. I often feel him near especially during marathons when it starts to get hard. I am inspired by his encouraging spirit which I believe has nudged me onto many a finish line. When it gets hard I remember his life and struggles and the fact that he could have never run a marathon. It pushes me on to run for those who can't.

My husband dropped me off at the Commons and it was still coming down hard and the wind was ruthless. Everyone was geared up in ponchos or waterproof suits. It was quite the sight. On the bus, I sat by an incredible man from Singapore. He trained in 80° temps and was a little nervous about the conditions.

As we got off the bus, the wind was blowing so hard many people were running for hats or gloves that blew away from them. As we crossed into the Athlete's Village (AV), the heavens opened, and the rain just pelted us hard. The AV was a muddy swampy mess. I couldn't figure out why there was no one in line at the porta potties and then I saw why. You had to traverse a large mud pond to get there, which I did. Since no one was waiting in line, I hid out in a porta potty to keep dry while I tried to organize all my stuff that I was either taking or leaving. There was icy slush and snow around the tents from the night's precipitation. It was a crazy messy sight! People were shivering and muddy and already wet with no possible way of warming up. Definitely not ideal conditions for the start of a marathon.

When I came out of the porta potty everyone was making their way to the start. I was in Corral One but didn't hear them call it. I felt ready to get this show on the road until I dropped my glove in a puddle and had to wear it wet, but my hands were already frozen anyway. I then lost one of my surgical gloves on the way to the start due to the chaos. I frantically searched for one that someone had dropped and luckily found one. I drained out the water and put it on top of my other wet glove hoping the insulation would help. A sweet volunteer helped me get the bags off my feet as well as my throw away pants, jacket, and hoody. It was quite the feat to do alone when you can't feel your hands. The road from the AV to the start was scattered with shoes, socks, gloves, hats, jackets, and poncho's the runners had cast aside. My dream of a PR was also cast aside as the reality of what I was about to undertake sank in. The gun had already gone off before I arrived. It was much different than last year's ceremonial start when we lined up in our corrals and stood there waiting for 20-25 minutes for the gun to go off. This year you just took off as soon as you arrived at the start. No lining up, no music, no announcing, just chaos of people taking off their throwaways. Some of those throwaways included crazy things such as hazmat suits, painter overalls, complete plastic body suits, you name it! The smart ones kept their jackets, ponchos, hats, and extra layers on.

There was no time to contemplate what I was about to do, no time to think, just run. I took off and noticed even in those conditions, the excitement level was high. There was a good number of spectators at the start as if it were a nice warm day. Several runners were woefully under-dressed for the conditions. I even saw a man running barefoot. I so wish I could have gotten a photo of his bare feet splashing in the three-inch puddles. What a photo to remember. I know his feet had to be frozen numb because mine almost were and I had on socks and shoes!

The first four miles it continued to pour, and the wind gusts were brutal. At times the rain would come down in buckets harder than anything I have ever seen in my life. But, wet is wet. Once you're wet you can't get any wetter. So bring it on. It was kind of fun to run in big puddles and not even notice a difference. I heard someone say the puddles had white caps! I was feeling great with the exception of the miserable conditions.

At mile five I found three pennies! Straight from heaven no doubt, because I could still bend down to get them. However, with gloves on and frozen fingers, it was a little tricky. It took me several tries, but I eventually got them. In my mind, I kept hearing the words, *"You Got This Mom!"* in Tyson's sweet voice and I knew I was going to be okay. This one's for you bud!

I also found a quarter a little before the pennies and had to fight another runner for it. I don't remember what mile. So much of the race this year is a blur. I'm not sure if it's because I had my head down so much to avoid the sting of the sideways rain and wind or if it was hypothermia trying to set in or if I was just simply in survival mode. I remember last year's race so much clearer.

I kept my throwaway jacket on until about mile six or seven when it became too waterlogged to keep wearing so I tossed it. I noticed many runners who were wearing shorts, not only looked very cold but their legs were bright red. By mile nine, my feet had joined my hands and were also numb. I was looking forward to Wellesley College and the Scream Tunnel about mile 12-13. It was LOUD even though there were only maybe 1/3 as many as last year. You can usually hear them from a mile away but today the sounds of plastic ponchos and the hard rain coming down dampened their volume until about a half mile away. A little after that I ran past an older man holding a poster that said, *"Go Jodi*

Wilding!" When I saw it, I thought it couldn't be me. But, I slowed down a bit and yelled to him, *"That is my name!"*. He kind of nodded and off I ran. After going another 200 yards or so, the curiosity was getting the best of me and I had to run back and figure out the mystery even at the expense of costing me some time, so I headed back to him and told him that was my name. He told me he was a senior missionary from Brigham City and saw my name in the paper and wanted to cheer me on! What!??? Wow! I was amazed! Especially in those weather conditions! I had to have a photo with him and the poster, but my fingers were too frozen, so I asked someone by him to take one and send it to me, but no one could get their phones to work (thanks to the rain) as the clock kept ticking. Thankfully, one finally did. I lost about 7-8 minutes for that little pit stop (and added some distance), but it was so worth it. I would do it again in a heartbeat.

Around mile 14-15, I was starting to feel my calves cramp up. I knew that wasn't a good sign that early on and that the cold was starting to take its toll. But I soldiered on and kept pushing through. My clothes were getting very waterlogged. I was basically soaked to the bone, and by mile 16, it was becoming difficult to make my legs fire how I wanted them to. I began having thoughts of quitting especially knowing the Newton Hills were upon me and every time I looked at my pace I was becoming even more discouraged because my time was slowing. However, when I saw my pace band that I had printed with a photo of Tyson on it, his cute smiling face looking back at me gave me the inspiration I needed to keep slogging forward. I knew he was alongside me helping me through. About that time I decided to quit worrying about my pace and time. My goal became to just survive and finish. I had my name bib on the outside of my jacket, but my poncho had been covering it most of the way. I decided I needed some encouragement and so I tucked part of my poncho into the bib so the spectators could see it. It was a trade off because my legs were much colder with the poncho no longer on them but I felt hearing my name would more than make up for it. It was amazing to hear the spectators cheer me on by name! The lift that gives you is very real.

Then, just when I needed it most, I saw my family at mile 17 waiting for me with big smiles, huge hugs, some much needed encouragement, as well as my fuel, and warm dry gloves! I ran over towards them and my son Bryce gave me one of the biggest hugs I have ever had in my life. He wouldn't let go and I was grateful because it warmed me up some!

They were all soaked. We began to switch out my wet gloves for warm dry ones, but they had to take off both pair of gloves because I couldn't move my fingers. Their hands were pretty frozen too and so it was kind of a circus with all of us trying to make the change. My surgical gloves had water pooled inside the fingers and looked like a water balloon at the fingertip. I guess the rain had ran down my wrists into the gloves. It took a while to get the wet ones off and my wet fingers inside another pair of dry ones. But, once they were on, it was heaven. Dave said I looked like I had been dipped in a pool. I told him he looked the same. We took some photos and after a 7-8 minute pit stop, I was off again with renewed determination and strength to tackle the hills. That was the boost I needed.

I drank my fuel for the next couple of miles while on the hills which was a good distraction as was the most unbelievable and heaviest downpour I've ever seen in my life that just wouldn't let up. The hills just kept going and going but I was expecting that. I wouldn't allow myself to walk and I felt I crushed them considering it all. I think my fuel was kicking in and at the top of Heartbreak I was even feeling pretty strong. Exhausted as all get out, but strong. Better yet, I knew there was some downhill ahead and only five more miles to go! I forced myself to take some water or Gatorade at every aid station even though I didn't think I was going to be getting dehydrated, but I did anyway "just in case" because I didn't need dehydration thrown into the mix. The water was ice cold. Hot chocolate would have been a better option! hah I must have given hundreds of high fives along the way even though I barely had energy to do it. Last year doing it gave me energy, but this year it felt like it drained me instead. However, I was so in awe that so many spectators would come out to cheer us on in those conditions that I felt I owed it to them.

While still on the hills I started to feel intense pain in my upper back. This was new to me in a race. I am sure it was from tensing up due to the cold. About mile 22, my legs started to feel like heavy blocks of ice. The strength I was feeling earlier had left me and I had to fight every step of the way from then on. My goal was to smile the entire 26.2 miles (no matter what) because I believe smiling helps me mentally. I think it tricks my mind into believing I am actually having a good time. At that point, even when I heard my name, the best I could do was a thumbs up to acknowledge their kindness, but I couldn't make eye contact because it just took too much energy with the wind and rain blowing sideways into my face. I just smiled straight ahead and gave a thumbs up.

As I ran past Fenway, I was surprised to see so many Red Sox fans cheering us on because they had cancelled the game due to the storm for the first time on Patriot's Day since 1984. I saw many posters that said, "Just keep swimming!" I was not amused. There were moments when the rain slowed, and the wind quieted, though it never stopped the entire 26.2. Several times all *'you know what'* broke loose and it was like being in the middle of a monsoon. I just had to laugh. It truly was almost comical. It was as if the marathon was determined we were not going to triumph her today.

I took my poncho and shower cap off about mile 23, not because it had stopped raining, but because I didn't want to be wearing them in my final photos. Bad fashion mojo even though I was rockin' that shower cap! When I saw the Citgo sign, I felt relief but also frustration because even one more mile was going to take everything I had. Those last few miles I kept saying to myself, *"You are running the Boston Marathon!"* That, coupled with thoughts of how blessed I am to be able to do this when so many will never get to, pulled me towards that finish line. *"Do it for those who can't."*, became my mantra for those last few miles. I also kept telling myself (you talk to yourself a lot those last delirious miles!), *"You trained hard for this, you're prepared, and you've got this!"*

I have never been so happy when we came up out of the underpass and made our way onto Hereford Street. *"Right on Hereford, left on Boylston"*. Hereford was littered with ponchos that runners had discarded, I'm assuming so they wouldn't be in their finish line photos. It was like a mine field and you had to hopscotch over them.

As I approached Boylston, I was blown away (literally) by the crowds standing out there in that horrible weather every bit as enthusiastic as last year. As I made that last famous turn, I could already hear the roar of the crowd and I knew those last final steps were going to be a celebration with the world's most amazing, ear piercing spectators cheering all the runners on to that finish line. It's at that point you realize you are living your dream and the tears start to flow. That left turn onto Boylston gets you emotional. The feeling is indescribable. This year the celebration felt more like a victory over a hard-fought battle that you weren't sure you were going to win. The feeling was more of a sense of relief that you survived and came out alive when so many others fell along the way due to the weather conditions. The history in what those final steps represent always gets to me. I thought of all the people that have run this stretch in the past 122 years and all the struggles it took for many of them to get there. I also think of all the people who aspire to run it and never get a chance due to the strict qualifying times, injury, or something else in their life preventing them from being there. As I ran past the bombing site, the emotions took a hold of me again. You can't help but feel it and the emotions peak. Remembering what happened right at that spot only five short years ago silences out the roaring spectators for a moment and a deep sense of reverence washes over you.

But oh, what a sight that finish line is! It was beckoning to me and I to it. I was exhausted and ready to get out of the carwash I'd be in for far too long. As I approached it, so many emotions surfaced, and tears fell right along with the raindrops as I raised my arms in victory for conquering this year's epic race. That's all that mattered to me. That, and getting warm! I conquered and survived the Boston Monsoon-athon of 2018 with possibly the worst weather Boston has ever offered up. This race will be the one that every future race is compared to. It will no doubt go down in history and be talked about every year from here on out. It was not exactly what I expected but yet it exceeded my every expectation. It was definitely a once in a lifetime race. It tested my determination, my strength, my grit, my training and my will power every step along the way. Boston has always felt like a hallowed race to me but after running it in this year's conditions, it does even more so. It was a hard-fought battle, but it was worth every cold soggy mile, every gust of wind, and every frozen body part. I didn't reach my goal time, but I am okay with that. Survival and staying out of the medical tent soon became my only goals this year. What a race!

The looks I saw on the finishers' faces said it all. It was a combination of relief, disbelief, and gratitude. There were more tears than smiles this year. It wasn't the usual finish line celebration. It was much more quiet, somber and almost a slow-motion rush to get out of wet clothes and warmed up.

I must add I was in absolute awe of all the volunteers who braved that raw environment cheering us on and smiling. And though there were only about 20% of last year's spectators, those who did come out, will have my admiration forever. Brutal, nasty conditions, yet there they were still out there cheering perfect strangers on. There are no words for the appreciation I have for them all. And that includes my family. Absolute awe. I will never be able to erase the picture of all those people standing out there in the torrential rain just for us!

Boston 2018 was the worst marathon I've ever ran, and it was the best one I've ever ran...all wrapped into one. It was also the most inspiring, watching all those runners (each who has a story to tell) pushing through with all they had even though Mother Nature was pushing right back. I don't think it was possible to ever be prepared for what happened no matter what kind of weather you trained in.

Boston Strong took on new meaning this year. Crossing that finish line made you feel that if you could conquer that, there are no limits in what you can do in life. It made me reach deeper and realize a new depth to my own personal strength. It took all I had to keep running and it made me tougher. I was so inspired by all those who started and especially those who finished. Boston marathoners are unique in that they have earned the right to be there either by qualifying after training hard for years or by raising thousands for charities. Making it to the start says more than making it to the finish.

My medal this year means so much more to me than all my others combined. It will always represent the tears, triumph, discouragement, determination, persistence, anguish, pain, courage, fortitude, discomfort, endurance, grit, the list goes on and on. I wish I could hear the story of every medal recipient and what it took to earn it this year. I, for one, will treasure this medal for the rest of my life knowing all that went into obtaining it. It will always remind me that I was beyond fortunate to be able to qualify for this monumental race, then make the cut-off, then stay healthy enough to get to the starting line, and most of all to finish it in such abysmal conditions. The medal I earned this year will always represent to me that we CAN *"run the race that is set before us." (Hebrews 12:1)*

We walked a long way to get to the car but it was kind of fun because so many people would stop to congratulate me. Bostonians make us marathoners feel like Rock Stars! Even with all the other big sporting events going on the city rolls out the red carpet for the marathon runners. The energy in the city is electric! It's one of my favorite parts of running Boston. I didn't get a standing ovation on the subway this year like I did last year, but if I had been on it more, I most likely would have again. The Bostonians are some of the most incredible people I have ever met.

When we finally got in the car, I started to shiver, and my teeth started to chatter. We cranked up the heater and headed to our hotel. There was not a stitch on me that was dry. I had to literally peel the clothes off. I am sure if I had weighed my wet clothes and shoes, they would have been 10-15 lbs.! After we were all warmed up we went to dinner. I wore my race shirt and medal...

proudly. I saw a few other marathoners with their medals on as well. When we made eye contact we had an instant bond as if we had been in a war together and the look of, *"Good job! Way to survive!"*

This year's running and finishing the Boston Marathon has changed me. Before, during and after, the scripture kept coming to my mind, *"You must run with endurance the race that is set before you...."* (Hebrews 12:1). I have always said running teaches me many life lessons, but none more so than this particular race. I did not want to run this race in the conditions that were set before me. Not at all. But, it *was* the race that was set before me. I wasn't given the choice to run it in with mild temps accompanied by glorious sunshine and partial cloud coverage. The race set before me on April 16, 2018 was the last choice on my list of what conditions I would hope for. In fact, they were the *exact* conditions I feared the most. Actually, the conditions I feared the most were even milder than what I got. I had told myself so many times that if I ever had to run in those conditions, I could not do it. I would fail. When I learned the race set before me for the Boston Marathon was going to be so difficult, my doubts continued to grow. However, deep down inside me I knew I was strong enough, resilient enough and determined enough to endure it. Or maybe just stubborn enough! Whatever it is, I am not one to easily give up. Most runners at the Boston Marathon starting line wouldn't have made it there if they gave up easily. And even though it wasn't the race I hoped for, I did run the race that was set before me. With endurance. A lot of endurance. Endurance that came from a power not of my own.

So it is with life. Often, we are given the very trials and adversities we would not choose and definitely not hope for. Sometimes trials rain down upon us all at once with no break in between. Sometimes we are given the very thing we fear the most. Almost always we doubt our abilities to endure those trials and sometimes we even wish they would be taken away. But in most cases, we do not have the choice to reject or evict them from our lives. We must endure them. We must run the race that is set before us. And when we finish that race, we are often surprised at the strength we find deep inside ourselves that we didn't even know we possessed. We also recognize that we were given power beyond our own to complete the race.

The race of life that is set before us is a challenging marathon that requires endurance if we expect to cross that finish line with our hands held high. No, we don't get to choose our trials. We only get to choose how we will respond to them. And in the end, we discover that no matter what race we get, we are capable of running it so much better than we ever believed we could.

Alison Cunningham, Bib 28654

Stoneham, MA, 48, 5:54:29

In the mid-80's, I started running track in high school and was a mediocre sprinter at best. At that time, I had never run anything over a mile. In fact, I strongly disliked running distance. Fast forward to the late 2000's and I was now 39 with 3 kids and going through a tough time in my marriage. I decided to join a running club as it became a way for me to escape from my life a bit, while also getting in shape and making some new friends. It was so cathartic and a great way to work through all that was going on in my head at the time. I did my first 5k in 2009 and slowly worked my way up until I found myself completing my first half marathon in 2010 at age 40. It felt amazing to accomplish that goal! After that I went through getting

divorced and kind of took a break from running for a few years, except for the occasional 5k.

Then came the 2013 Boston Marathon and the bombing at the finish line. Two brothers from my hometown (9 miles North of Boston) wound up each losing their right legs as a result. As my town and the city of Boston worked on rebuilding, I realized that I had a strong desire inside to run the Boston Marathon myself and wanted to give back, I wanted to prove that I too was "Boston Strong". In 2017 that opportunity appeared as I applied for and was accepted onto a charity team called "A Leg Forever". This foundation was established by the mom of the two brothers mentioned above. It was designed to raise money for prosthetic legs for other people in need, just as others had helped them when they were in need. Most people don't know that prosthetics need to be replaced every 3-5 years for life. This charity makes this possible from the money the charity team raises each year in exchange for a bib to wear in this coveted Marathon. Over the next 6 months or so I worked hard at training and raising money for the cause, $6,000 was the minimum amount I needed to run.

During this time, I also discovered a private Facebook group started by Vince Varallo, for those training for the Boston Marathon 2018, I joined and immediately felt welcomed into the runner's fold. It was filled with people who all had the same goal: many were very fast, highly skilled, experienced runners. They had run several marathons, they had qualified for the Boston Marathon by running another marathon in a very fast time for their age except even faster as Boston has become increasingly limited with their acceptance times. There were also some people like me, where it was their first marathon and their first Boston, more often than not, these were the charity runners. I had heard over the years that some runners are upset with the charity runners as they're "taking a spot away" from a more qualified runner, so didn't know what to expect with this group. I experienced none of that animosity, only amazing support. I would post about my runs, the good, the bad, the ugly and receive encouragement and advice. I would post about an injury and receive the same. I truly felt we were all in it together and friendships started to flourish. We lived all over the world, but we quickly started bonding over this common goal. We dubbed ourselves "Boston Buddies" and became a running team of thousands!

There is an annual tradition of runners starting in Hopkinton at the starting line and traversing the first 21-22 miles of the course about a month before the Marathon (many local runners refer to this as the "Hop 22" and wear bunny ears). An idea formed that we should get as many Boston Buddies together as possible and finally meet in person for this unofficial event. Organizers stepped up and plans started flying, before long we had busses arranged and people were making their travel plans. It wound up being a nice, cold day and we all started off together and many finally met in person after many months of being internet only friends. It was great way to check out the course while also connecting with my new friends!

Then all the sudden, the night before the big event arrived. My ankle tendon injury that had plagued me for the last few months as my mileage had increased was feeling pretty good, all of my money for the charity had been raised, my charity running singlet had my name on it, so the crowds could cheer me on. I was pretty good to go! Then came the forecast: it had looked pretty bad for over a week, but we were all remaining hopeful that it would change. It didn't change and if anything, it grew worse, very cold temperatures, great winds and pouring rain at the exact time of the race. I was so nervous, my first marathon, my injury, the weather, but also extremely excited and eager. I was armed with lots of advice for running in bad weather and before I knew it I was on a charter bus with friends from my running club and heading to the starting line.

What unfolded over the next several hours, is hard to truly explain, it was unlike anything I had ever seen. Thousands of runners wearing throw away clothes to stay warm at the start (they get collected and donated), garbage bags, ponchos, hazmat suits, plastic bags over sneakers, mine were also covered in duct tape so they would hopefully stay dry. I had hand warmers and latex gloves over regular gloves, a rain coat with hood, a hat, and running leggings. I was basically dressed all in black and pretty much unrecognizable. My friends and I wound up at the very end of the runners starting (charity teams start at the end) and we started running the Boston Marathon! It was very windy, rainy, cold, and it was hard to see. There were some spectators, but not nearly as many as on a nice day (plus we were starting a good couple of hours after the elites). Along the way, I saw many other runners struggling, going into med tents and just plain stopping alongside the course. I was determined to finish what I had set out to do, for my charity, for the honor of being able to run this infamous race, for my kids, for myself. In order to have this race counted by the Boston Athletic Association you need to finish the marathon in under 6 hours. I knew it would be close for me. The last 5 miles I felt like I was on the set of the "Walking Dead", so many people had stopped running and were slowly walking to the finish, I knew I couldn't join them and dug extremely deep and kept running as much as I could.

I so wanted to finish within regulation time, but knew it was going to be close for me. I was doing math in my head at every race clock along the way, calculating as best I could my mile times. All the sudden I was turning right on Hereford and left on Boylston and towards the finish line! I couldn't see my family, but a few friends recognized me and cheered me on, crossing that line was so incredible. A friend texted me that I had finished with 5 minutes and 31 seconds to spare under the 6 hours. I had succeeded, I was a first-time Marathoner at age 48, with a time of 5:54:29! I had run in the worst conditions that course had seen in over 30 years, I had done what many friends and even elites hadn't been able to do, I had crossed that finish line on that crazy day! I was so grateful to everyone who had supported me along the way, not just that day but for the good 6 months prior as well. It would go down in infamy as one of my greatest achievements on a most epic day! Best of all I had raised over $8,000 for my charity and had made some lifelong "Boston Buddy" friendships!

Lauren Carnahan, Bib 14312

Latham, NY, 35, 3:42:51

When I ran my first marathon in 2015, I never realized how big of a deal qualifying for Boston was. I was just shy of a few seconds, not that I would have gotten in, but it was the accomplishment. It was in 2016, I ran my second marathon, the Mohawk Hudson River in Albany, NY. I secretly wanted to qualify and ran my heart out. I crossed the finish line, bawled my eyes out, and my friends didn't know why. "How old is Lauren? Did she qualify?" They didn't ask until we went out to celebrate. I didn't want to boast about it all, let alone on social media, but my one friend did. That is how my journey to Boston 2018 began.

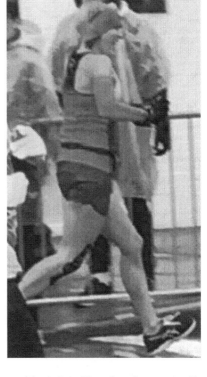

So I qualified in the fall of 2016 and had to wait until the spring of 2018 to run. The waiting is the hardest part! As registration and planning approached I had no idea what I was getting into. I reached out to friends that had made the journey to Boston and they were so helpful! I stumbled upon the Boston Marathon Training Facebook group. It saved me in so many ways. It was here that I've gained a family and most of all, my very best friend (Twinarella). We clicked instantly and are two peas in a pod. Don't mess with the bad ass unicorn twins.

Training is training. It was tough training in the winter in eastern NY, so I'll spare you that. As race day approached, what to wear? I obviously underdressed for the occasion. I toed the line and took off. A sheet of rain hit me in the first mile and I was instantly soaked to the bone. I yelled out every obscenity and was miserable. With every step I took, I got colder and colder. My hands were so cold I couldn't eat, my teeth chattered uncontrollably, I couldn't stop them. I finally gave up on eating and drinking. My friends and family surprised me along the course and held me, I sobbed. At each warming/medical tent, I thought, "You can toss in the towel right now." But then I thought, "You can't quit. You're stronger than that. You have people here, you have people cheering you on at home, tuck this shit in and run." I don't remember most of the race at all, I blocked it out. At mile 13, I got sick and didn't want to come out of the lovely port o john, it was warm in there! I kept going. I saw the CITGO sign. Finally! I crossed the finish line, sobbing, with teeth chattering and there stood a medic. He handed me a generic mylar blanket. I walked forward to get my medal, which

I still don't really know what it looks like (it sits in a plastic bag in my basket full of medals). I walked forward for the heavier mylar blanket, they were directing us to move forward. A woman saw me and said, "Oh, dear you need one now, let me get you one. Do you need medical?" I replied, "Yes." She wrapped me in the blanket, held me, and called for medical, and told me everything is going to be ok. A wheelchair arrived, and I was taken to medical where I was stripped down and given the best care. I'm so grateful for all of the volunteers. I sat next to a woman who asked me to take a picture of her and send it to her husband, I gladly did.

After leaving medical, I found my family and friends. I arrived at my hotel to find them waiting for me. They drew a shower for me, had a beer waiting for me, and we celebrated. When returning home, I had a really difficult time talking about this race for a few weeks. I buried so many emotions and was angry- angry about my time, the experience, etc. I finally pulled myself together and ran Buffalo a few weeks later and re-qualified for 2019. I want to run Boston again for a new, positive, and fresh experience. An experience I'll remember- for the good! The Boston Marathon Training Facebook group helped me pull myself together. I want to thank every single one of you. You truly are an inspiration and a wonderful family.

Katie MacKenzie, Bib 12117

Newstead, AUS, 40, 3:41:59

Whilst a bit dramatic, this is exactly how Boston Marathon played out. No one walks up to the start line of a marathon without training. Boston Marathon especially. We had all BQ'd, which means we did at least another marathon first, to get the required qualifying time to run Boston. The girl I met at the start line had worked for 3 years to get her BQ time. This was all reduced to one cold, rainy opportunity, when our time came around to finally RUN BOSTON.

As per my previous post, my BQ time at Gold Coast Airport Marathon in 2017 was 3:21, well under the required 3:45 and this landed me in wave 2, corral 5. In a race as big as Boston (30,000 runners), there are 4 waves, each with 8 corrals. We were given color coded bibs and loaded into buses in the center of Boston, at 7am to be bused out to Hopkinton High School, aka Athletes Village.

Athlete's Village, on this particular day, was lined with snow and mud. We had all crazily built the most weatherproof outfits we could find, stripping the shelves of the local pharmacies, discount stores and running shops in the lead up. It was freezing out there, but spirits were still high. The rain poured down, but we tiptoed politely around the bodies huddling in heat-sheets and ponchos under the tents, waiting for our turn.

Finally, it was wave 2's turn. The "white bibs". We all walked the half mile or so to the start, chatting eagerly about our run. It was still freezing but no one was going to let that stop them at this point!

And off we went! Cheering, clapping, running into the horizontal rain. All rugged up and wrapped in plastic ponchos, each person wearing their best last-minute outfit. I had opted for tights I had never run in, and 3 shirts, under 2 jumpers and a jacket….and a poncho. This does not happen, ever. I always plan outfits, test them during my training runs, discard anything that rubs or doesn't work. I did this. I had an outfit. It just did not suit the conditions. I had to improvise massively.

By 5km, I was ditching the 2 jumpers. I never stop in races, ever. But had to pull over and gave a local Police Officer my 2 "throw away" jumpers and continue on. I think that cost me 50 seconds. The first 10km or so is downhill, so we had jogged out the first 5 km and I was able to pick up the pace over the next 5. Everyone had told me to take the first bit easy as the downhill was a trick. Too tempting to go out hard as it feels ok, but it was near impossible to execute any type of race plan in the monsoonal conditions. I ran as well as I could, checking splits every 5km.

By half-way, I had warmed up a little, so I ditched my outer layer and poncho. That took about 4 mins due to my cold hands, double gloves, zips on jackets, port-a-loo space constraints and everything else. I really cooled down during this break. A lot. Enough to make me realize that further stops were not really an option. The only way to survive this was to keep running. I also instantly regretted ditching my poncho and spent the next 2 km looking for a spare one. Luckily, I found a better poncho than my original and I managed to pick it up and put it on without breaking step! It might not be clear from our pictures and posts already, I must stress, it did not stop raining on us for the entire 42.2km. Further to this, the temp did not get higher than 4 degrees Celsius. Many of the runners who succumbed to hypothermia did so after half-way. This was really a battle of sensibility.

From half-way, my hands were too cold to undo my zip to access my gels, so I used the provided gels at the aid stations. Luckily they were the same brand I have trained with, but it meant I needed to grab a couple when they were offered and hold onto them until I was due to take them. At this point, I literally needed to look at my hands to visually check I hadn't dropped the gels. My hands were frozen.

During the hills, which felt good compared to the weather, I stopped working in kilometers and began to count the race down mentally in blocks of 3 miles. 15, 18 (gel), Heartbreak Hill, 21(gel), 24 (gel) then it was 25, 26 and we were turning into Boylston St for home. It was literally left, right, left for ages until then. Head down to protect the eyes from the rain and keep thinking of the end. Body scanning, checking in, making sure I felt ok to keep going. Pace didn't matter. Hills didn't matter. My watch wouldn't work through my gloves. I had no idea of my time. I just wanted to finish.

As I now realize, everyone including me, ditched the poncho on the final turn into Boylston. I placed mine near the fence line, however, apparently tons of runners just threw theirs into the middle of the road, making the finishing straight a landmine for those following. Lesson for all - please think of those behind you. We were all lacking awareness at this point, but it made it even harder for the later runners.

The finishing straight at Boston is what they come for. The energy, screams, cheers. Running up that road, I was actually overwhelmed by the intensity. The weather, energy, support. I had seen the commemorative wreaths the day before (marking the spot of the 2013 bombings) and had thought of this every time I felt like it was a tough day out there. There were snipers on course. I was finishing this race safely, when others had not. It really was too much to absorb.

Getting closer to the finish, I started to slow down (more). I hadn't seen my family. It was pouring as we ran up the straight. I didn't want my family to get wet in this cold, but I didn't want to miss them either. Then I saw hubby waving. I ran over for a high 5. He told me the kids were back in the hotel lobby and would see me after. Perfect. Well done to my support crew. I didn't need to worry at all.

Crossing the line, it all hit me. 2 years in the making. I had finished this thing. It had been the worst possible conditions for me to run in. I hate wind and cold and being wet. I had endured a marathon in these conditions. But it was over. So was the prep, the planning, the thinking. The "suffering". I shed a few tears with the other runners around me. We got our medals and our heat sheets. The volunteers were amazing. Stopping us to fix up our heat sheets so we could stay warm, handing us bags of food.

The baggage collection area was too crowded. I got way too cold in the congested line and left without my stuff. It wasn't ideal. Others suffered longer as they had to. I had other clothes back at the hotel and I knew it would be dangerous to stand outside for much longer.

I returned to the hotel and was greeted again by huge cheers from everyone in the lobby. I have never made an entrance like that and it instantly lifted me. It was all sinking in that this was a great thing. We had done the hardest thing. We had accomplished something amazing.

Once I was showered, dressed and warm, I could think again. I returned to the gear tent and grabbed my stuff. I cheered for those still finishing. I helped people get warm and back to their hotels. Many were in quite a state by then. Hypothermia was common, and the medical tents were busy. The volunteers and staff here were amazing. Such a great event, a marathon on steroids, with years of evolution and improvement, it runs like a well-oiled (huge) machine.

I listed 3 learnings from this race on Instagram recently. In brief, they were: Do your prep properly - train so your body is ready, the mind does the rest. Train in all weather, so you can cope with whatever race day brings. Be flexible mentally. The general theme seems to be that anyone who let their "A" goal go, and slowed down, finished. Some did not let their pace slide and ended up in the medical tent. It really was a matter of finishing, not perishing. Most of us ran approximately 20 mins slower than our "usual" marathon time but running under so many layers of soaked clothing and plastic ponchos is bound to hold you back. And finally, use external motivation when you need it. The crowd, my family, the thoughts of the previous devastation at this event, kept me from getting too caught up in my own situation and kept me focused on the bigger picture. The Boston community makes this race a world-class event. They still came out in the rain. The volunteers handed us cups of water for hours, standing in the rain. So much bigger than a "fun run".

Such a memorable event was made unforgettable by the conditions. A once in a lifetime. Although I managed to BQ (by only 4 mins, in a time of 3:41) for next year, I don't think I will be back there. There are many other races to try and I want that memory of Boston to last. I am not sure a "normal' marathon will ever be quite the same.

Elizabeth Clor, Bib 12394

Chantilly, VA, 39, 3:26:53

The 2018 Boston Marathon brought an entirely new meaning to the expression "soaking it all in." The trifecta of cold temperatures (upper 30s), a strong sustained headwind (25 mph) with heavier gusts, and pouring rain made the experience simultaneously miserable and thrilling.

After writing and publishing the book Boston Bound in 2016 (which mainly focused on my journey to qualify), I was ready for another story.

The big topic for discussion over the weekend was wardrobe. When I finalized my packing on Friday morning, the forecast was calling for temperatures in the high 40's to low 50's. I had a pretty good idea of what I was going to wear, and I wasn't stressing about it. But as the weekend progressed, the forecast became more severe. Every time I opened my  weather app, the temperature had dropped a few degrees, the rainfall totals increased, and the headwind became stronger.

Everyone was scrambling to purchase extra "supplies" for Athlete's village and modifying their originally planned race attire.

For better or worse, I have experience in running in similar conditions, so I was able to rely on that to inform my decisions. I suffered from hypothermia back in 2009 when I ran a marathon in pouring rain. It was in the high 40's that day, but I was wearing a tank top, a skirt, and no gloves or arm warmers. I was rushed to the medical tent by finish line staff and I had no clue what was going on. It was a scary experience. I decided that less was not more; more was more:

- Smart Wool socks with lots of body glide on the feet
- Nike LunarGlide shoes
- Lightweight capri tights, which I purchased at the expo
- Sports bra
- Tight fitting, long singlet
- Short sleeve shirt
- Thick arm warmers made of a wool-like material
- Very thin/light water-repelling rain jacket
- Mizuno Breath Thermo gloves
- Convertible mittens over the gloves
- One pair of hand warmers in each mitten (front and back of fingers)
- Shower cap
- Hat
- Vaseline on my face to keep the water off and protect against the wind
- Waist pack to hold my Generation UCAN gel
- Over-layers for Athlete's Village: Mid-weight rain jacket, Poncho, Sweatpants, Throwaway socks, Throwaway shoes with toe warmers inside

I wrapped my race shoes in shower caps and tied them around my waist and kept them under my poncho until it was time to walk to the start line.

My friend Lisa met me at my hotel and then we went to meet some of my other friends to all board the bus together. There were 9 of us total. It was already raining steadily as we approached the buses and the gusts were blowing my poncho around like crazy. My husband, Greg, was there to see me off and I gave him my final wet hug. We decided that it would be best for him to simply track me from the comfort of the hotel room instead of getting drenched himself. Last time, he went to mile 20 and I didn't even see him. Our plan this year was to meet at a spot shortly after the finish line chute.

Once we boarded the bus, I got hot and didn't want to sweat, so I undid my layers to the best of my ability. The bus ride took about 50 minutes (longer than I remember it taking two years ago) and I ate a bagel with peanut butter on the ride while chatting away with Lisa.

Another challenge that this weather presented was that I wouldn't be able to carry a water bottle. Typically, I carry a bottle for the first 15 miles of a marathon, so I can drink enough water when I want it. However, I suffer from Reynaud's syndrome and so my hands were a huge concern. Carrying something cold and wet would not be ideal, so I decided to drink water from the aid stations.

We were not surprised that Athlete's village was a mud pit. The mud was thick, cold and slippery and every step was more unpleasant than the one before it. My toe warmers were my savior, as well as the fact that I would be changing my shoes before the race. We waited in line for the porta-potties as ice pellets fell steadily upon us. There was slush on the ground in some places, and I witnessed several people slip and fall. Once inside the porta-potty, I had to remove my glove/mitten/hand-warmer ensemble and then wade through all of the aforementioned layers to be able to go to the bathroom. I likened it to being a bride and having to use the bathroom in my wedding dress.

Afterwards, Lisa and I approached the tented area, and it was jam-packed full of runners. I found a small corner to stand in and decided I did not want to sit on the muddy ground. If you add the walk to the porta-potty, the wait to use it, standing in the tent, and then walking to the start, I was on my feet for over an hour before I started running. Not ideal, but that's Boston for you. It's a logistical challenge even in the best of weather conditions.

When they called wave 2, I exited the tent and headed for the corral. There was a little hill to climb up before exiting the grassy area, and it was so muddy and slippery that I couldn't get up it without falling. The fall caused my gloves and the plastic bag I was carrying to get muddy and it was not pleasant, but I cleaned it off quickly.

The next step would be to find a good area to change my shoes. As I walked toward the corral, there was a group of three runners standing in a covered alcove of a building entrance. I asked them if I could duck in to change my shoes. And these three people were so remarkably helpful. One of them held my bag, another one held my gloves, and another one helped me keep my balance as I made the switch. I had to un-tie the shoes from around my waist and then take them out of their shower caps to put on my feet. I use Yankz laces, so thankfully I didn't have to worry about lacing the shoes— I just put my foot in and I was set.

The walk to the corral felt long and by the time I got into my assigned corral #5, there was only 10 minutes until race start. In 2016, people were offering sunscreen and cold towels along the walk. Yesterday they offered Vaseline. Same event, but under entirely different circumstances from the heat wave of two years ago.

I knew I was really prepared to run 26.2 miles physically, so I didn't worry about my fitness level. Instead, I focused on staying positive, "soaking it all in," and sticking to my race plan. My goal was to finish strong and to NOT regret my starting pace. I knew that if I bonked like I did in Indianapolis, my chances of hypothermia would increase significantly and the fastest way to warmth was to run the whole way. The idea of feeling like crap physically while also having to endure the punishing winds and rain was so unappealing that I decided to start conservatively, about 20-25 seconds per mile slower than the "marathon pace" I used in training.

In 2016 I underestimated the impact the heat would have on my race and I didn't want to make the same mistake again. Particularly not at Boston. The goal was to have a strong Boston. My #1 goal was a safe, strong finish and that meant a ridiculously easy feeling start.

Miles 1-4: Hopkinton and Ashland: I ditched my poncho and mid-weight raincoat about 100 feet before the start line and it felt amazing to finally be running. Athlete's village was the worst part of the day and as we started running, one guy even said to me, "if we got through Athlete's Village, we can get through this." He was right. Running and doing what I love most was so easy compared to standing in that wet mud in 5 layers of clothing.

I qualified last spring with a time of 3:21:54, which is a pace of about 7:40. The runners in my corral all qualified within a few minutes of that time, but most of them shot out so fast and I was getting passed like crazy. But I remembered what Greg McMillan had said: let everyone pass you at first, and then you pass them later in the race.

It was raining steadily during these miles, but it wasn't long before I got into a groove, my feet became un-numb, and I settled into the reality of a very wet, cold and windy journey into Boston.

Mile 1: 8:07 (-108 ft)
Mile 2: 7:47 (-52 ft)

Mile 3: 7:44 (-55 ft)
Mile 4: 7:43 (-66 ft)

Miles 5-8: Framingham: It was during the 5th mile that I realized my hand warmers were soaked through and no longer providing warmth. Instead, they were like heavy bricks inside my mittens over my wool gloves. I debated tossing them, but I am glad I did not. Even though they weren't providing warmth, it was an extra layer of insulation. My hands went numb very quickly, and I decided to simply ignore it because there was nothing I could do to change it.

At mile 5, I grabbed a cup of water with two hands from a volunteer, jogged to the side of the course, stopped and drank. Since I wouldn't be drinking often, I figured I should make sure I got enough water when I did drink instead of running with it and spilling it all over my face. My hands were numb, so I had to be careful about it, and I figured it was worth the 10-second stop to get proper hydration.

Everyone was in good spirits and the runners seemed to be helping each other out more than usual. We were all in it together and shared an unspoken bond that made us all a little nicer and more compassionate.

Mile 5: 7:46 (+15 ft)
Mile 6: 7:35 (-18 ft)
Mile 7: 7:39 (-12 ft)
Mile 8: 7:38 (+1 ft)

Miles 9-12: Natick: These miles flew by and it was more of the same. Portions of the course were completely puddle-ridden and there was no avoiding getting my feet completely soaked. My socks did an excellent job of not holding the moisture, so I became comfortably with puddle running, knowing that my shoes wouldn't feel soaked for longer than a few minutes post-puddle. The pack of runners was just as thick as it had been at the beginning and I was grateful that I was mostly shielded from the headwind.

My plan was to take my UCAN Gel at mile marker 11 and then drink water at the station located shortly after. I could not unzip the waist pouch because my hands were numb. After multiple attempts to unzip the pouch, I used my teeth, which worked. The gel itself was easy to open after I got it out of the waist pocket, and thankfully it went down well without being accompanied by the usual water. I finished it just in time for 11.2 where I stopped and had a cup of water. After that, I threw the waist pouch off of my body as it had been annoying me for 11 miles and interfering with my bib.

By mile 12 I began to wonder if I had sold myself short. I felt like I was out for an easy run. I didn't feel like I was exerting marathon pace effort. I wasn't straining, and I was very relaxed. I felt my way through the course by cruising, but also keeping my pace in check. Up until this point, I didn't want to go below 7:35, but I started to wonder if I should up the effort a bit.

Mile 9: 7:35 (-16 ft)
Mile 10: 7:35 (+19 ft)
Mile 11: 7:44 (+26 ft)
Mile 12: 7:37 (-52 ft)

Miles 13-16: Wellesley: The Wellesley scream tunnel was just as loud as I remembered, only the woman who was essentially naked last time wearing only a sign wasn't there. I usually don't care all that much about crowd support in races and sometimes prefer less noise, so I can focus. But in this case, I fed off of the energy of the crowd. I needed as much positivity as possible.

At the halfway point, I wondered if I could negative split. I had never felt so great at the halfway point in marathon in all the 22 I have run. I still felt like I was out for an easy run! I allowed myself to speed up a little bit, but once again, I made sure I wasn't straining into the wind.

For the majority of the race, the rain was a steady pour, but there were a few times when it came down in buckets. When that happened people would clap and relish in it. What else could you do? The roads were getting flooded and I was now accustomed to running in water and having other runners kick water onto me.

Mile 13: 7:31 (0 ft)
Mile 14: 7:37 (-6 ft)
Mile 15: 7:36 (+25 ft)
Mile 16: 7:30 (-121 ft)

Miles 17-21: Newton Hills: My general strategy for hills is to focus on my form, and to not look up to the top of the hill, but rather about 25 feet ahead, get to that point, and then look another 25 feet ahead, so I am doing it in manageable chunks. I also remembered all the hills I had run on my long runs and got a nice boost of confidence. I ran over the first 3 without too much strain. After the first hill, I was at mile 18 and I told myself I had three hard miles ahead and one easy (19 is downhill). And I that's all I had to do, and I would be done with the hills.

This mental approach worked and finally I came upon Heartbreak Hill. If I could get to the top in one piece the rest of the race I would simply fly home. Heartbreak Hill felt very, very long. But I was determined to run up it at a good clip. I knew I had gas left in the tank and I used it here.

Mile 17: 7:44 (+74 ft)
Mile 18: 7:38 (+50 ft)
Mile 19: 7:29 (-34 ft)
Mile 20: 7:42 (+ 22 ft)
Mile 21: 8:07 (+86 ft)

Miles 22-25: Brookline and Boston: I was elated to be in the home stretch and still feeling strong. I knew that it was technically time to take my chews, but my hands were completely useless, so I wasn't able to get to them in my pocket. In hindsight, I should have waited a little longer to take my UCAN gel because that would have helped me more in the later miles without the additional chews. Mile 22 was a downhill breeze and I remembered how much pain I had been in two year ago during this section. It felt great to fly down the hill and be so close to finishing.

Mile 23 also felt strong, but I noticed my pace started to slip. The field of runners was spreading out across the wider course and the wind seemed to be picking up. I was still able to power through it feeling good, so I didn't concern myself with my pace too much. Plus, I was passing a lot of people. I was loving the fact that I felt so strong this late in the race and was still energized enough to be passing through the crowd of runners.

That didn't last long; mile 24 was the first mile that felt hard. My quads were aching, and the pain was getting difficult to ignore. The wind was whipping around in all directions and water was splashing into my face. I was also annoyed at any uphill I came upon. The last 5 miles are supposed to be "all downhill" but there are a few pesky uphill portions that slowed me down. I realized I would not be negative splitting, but that I could still run a really respectable time.

In the 25th mile, I felt that familiar marathon pain. I was now working as hard as I could, and I was tired. I wished I had taken my chews, but I still couldn't get them, and it was too late now. I was running out of steam and I lacked the energy to push against the strengthening headwind. In many ways, this was a good thing. If I felt like a million dollars crossing the finish line, then I would have regretted not running harder. But given the way I felt during mile 25, I knew I had run my best possible race because I was quickly fading. Throughout all of this, I always remembered to soak it all in and have fun. I worked hard to be here and had spent loads of time preparing. This was my moment!

I realized that I should be seeing a Citgo sign and looked up and made out a faint image of the sign in the distance. The air was so cloudy and rainy that the sign wasn't very visible. In fact, if I hadn't made it a point to look, I probably wouldn't have seen it until I was practically at the sign.

Mile 22: 7:36 (-72)
Mile 23: 7:57 (-55)
Mile 24: 8:10 (-45)
Mile 25: 8:29 (-41)

Mile 26 and the Finish: Hereford and Boylston: Before making the final turn onto Boylston, I noticed the road was littered with ponchos and jackets. I later realized that people were shedding their outer layers for good finish line photos. It felt like this mile went on and on. Of course, I ended up running about 26.5 miles according to my Garmin due to not running the tangents and trying to draft off of various runners. I wasn't surprised by this and my focus yesterday wasn't running the tangents, it was running where I was most protected from the wind.

Shortly after making the final turn onto Boylston I looked at the total elapsed time on my watch, which I hadn't done in several miles. I often do this at the end of races to motivate myself to get under the next minute. I saw that I could still get a 3:26:xx if I ran fast so I mustered every bit of energy I had to get myself to the finish line. That run down Boylston is so exhilarating that it's easy to find the power.

I crossed the finish line in 3:26:53 and was so elated to be done. But before getting too excited, I knew that I needed to quickly exit the finish line chute, get to my husband, Greg, and then walk to the hotel. Even though I was exhausted I forced myself to walk quickly through the chute and I was pleasantly surprised at how well I was moving, as compared to how I typically feel post-marathon.

Mile 26: 9:05
Last 0.48 on Garmin: 8:14 pace

I made my way to Greg relatively easily and quickly. I had been concerned about that walk over the weekend because hypothermia can set in quickly once you stop moving. I was so relieved to see him and that Epsom salt bath at the hotel was like heaven.

Later that evening, I met up with my friends Lisa and Jenna for dinner. I was walking around quite well and in much better shape than I was in 2016, when I ended up in the medical tent. I'm so happy that I executed well on a difficult course in challenging conditions, and that's more important than getting a PR in my eyes.

Final Thoughts and Takeaways. I had a great day in Boston and I think the crappy weather may have been a blessing in disguise. I didn't go into this cycle seeking a PR in Boston; I went in to build myself up as an athlete. Success on a day like yesterday was dependent on staying warm with the right wardrobe strategy before and during the race, running conservatively, and keeping a positive outlook on the situation.

This was a character-building experience and now that I know I can run well in these conditions, it will make most all other weather feel easy. Even though the headwind was a force to be reckoned with and the conditions were far from "comfortable" I honestly believe I would have done worse in the heat. I overheat easily when I run, so I tend to be more successful in the cold, even if it means putting up with downpours, puddles, numb hands, muddy falls, ice pellets and the rest of it.

Keeana Saxon, Bib 26788

Roslindale, MA, 40, 6:54:48

I have basked in the glow of the glory since April 16th. I am so proud of myself for finishing the 2018 Boston Marathon. I am also proud of the 163 donors who helped me raise $8,581.20 for the Boston Children's Museum in just three months! As I look back to the tail end of 2017, I marvel at my progress and growth.

I was raised in Newton, Massachusetts and I once lived on a part of the course. As a child, I watched the runners go by on Washington Street in Newton Lower Falls and marveled at their athleticism. At the time, I had no idea that runners who aren't considered elite could also be in this race. I now live in Boston and serve as a Commissioner for the Boston Liquor Licensing Board. As a former classical pianist and former attorney, my lifestyle was rather sedentary. For years, if not decades, I tried to cajole, persuade, convince, and incentivize myself to exercise more. I would start running for a spurt and then I would peter out. When I turned 40 in August 2017, I knew I needed to make a dramatic shift. My husband and I committed to getting back in shape. My goal before the new year arrived was to complete the MuTu program, a 12-week workout program for diastis recti (abdominal separation, often due to pregnancy). It had been more than a year post-partum and my core was still not as strong as it needed to be for proper function. The workout program also required me to walk every day.

The key ingredient that I was missing during all of those unfruitful years of trying to be fit was to have accountability partners. This time, I found friends who had the same abdominal issue and who were following the same workout program. We checked in with each other to make sure we were staying on track. Then we increased our respective goals to walking more, jogging, or signing up for a short race. Then, one of them said, "let's do the Boston Marathon." Wait, wuh?? Na-uh. Nope. Can't do it. I'm not ready. I mean, I want to, I've always wanted to, but what if I get injured? What if I fail? I tried track in junior high school and I failed epically. I can't experience that again.

We worked through a number of issues—the pain, embarrassment, fears, and doubts. We were each other's therapists and clients all at the same time. Once I allowed myself to say yes, once I gave myself permission to imagine myself completing this race, once I sent in my first application for a bib, my life took a course I would not have otherwise taken on my own.

My first application was not accepted, but I somehow received an email from the Boston Children's Museum asking me to apply. Since I was a past patron and donor, the choice to apply was easy. With that, I plunged headfirst into tackling two fears at once: doing something athletic in public and fundraising. I approached both fears in the same way: little by little. As I asked each of my friends and family members, one by one (in private emails, texts, phone calls and in person), I so began my training mile by mile. Though I dreaded the feeling of rejection upon asking someone for money, I felt more prepared and a tad more at ease with approaching friends and family after my training with Emerge MA, a program that prepares Democratic women to run for public office. Though my fundraising strategy never changed, right through to the end, my training got hit with curveballs, forcing me to change my strategy dramatically.

At the end of November 2017, I began with Rick Muhr's 20-week training schedule. I didn't initially buy running shoes. Upon the advice of the MuTu System instructor, I wore shoes with zero incline in the heel. Inclines in the heel cause my body to lean forward, putting pressure on my separated core. Once I was several weeks into running, I bought a pair of ON running shoes. Love them. Because of a basic lack of fitness, bad habits and genetic gifts, I have several vulnerabilities: weak core, hyper-mobile knees, tight and narrow hips, an even narrower walk/run, flat feet, over pronating steps, and tight ankles.

Physical trainers helped me work through some of those issues, but ultimately my left knee couldn't sustain the mileage. I ran with pain for weeks until at the end of February, I was finally forced to rest. I couldn't put any more weight on my left knee after a 17.5-mile run. After an MRI and a visit with an orthopedic specialist, I was diagnosed with a stress reaction and bursitis in my left knee. I then had to change my training strategy. No more pavement. For over a month, I aqua jogged and used an adaptive motion trainer. I had run only 14 miles between the date of the injury and Marathon Day. Side note: who knew all of that aqua jogging was a harbinger of the marathon aqua jog to come??

In March, I also changed my fueling strategy. Gu, gels, and chews all made my stomach feel icky and heavy. I settled on Tailwind and I am happy with it for now. My cross training was in constant flux. I did gym workouts, Bikram yoga, CrossFit and just about anything else Groupon had to offer. On the one hand, I wasn't bored. On the other hand, I probably could have benefited from consistency.

Finally, I reevaluated my performance expectations. I originally wanted to run the entire distance. The Galloway Method, as recommended by a friend and fellow runner, proved to suit me. Then during my recovery/rest period after my injury, I made peace with the fact that I might not be able to run the entire course at all but walk it I would! At the beginning of my training, I remember incredulously staring at the later weeks of the training schedule. Training allowed me to break through those mental obstacles. Training allowed me to smash the fallacious notion that I couldn't go the distance. I cherish those mental milestones. I also cherished the friendships I developed with two women I met during my Emerge MA training. We were all training for our first Boston Marathon. I can't imagine going through the training without them. Though I missed them terribly during my recovery, they never stopped encouraging me and staying in touch.

As Marathon Day approached, I was beginning to question whether it was worth putting myself through all of this. After numerous visits with physical therapists, an orthopedic specialist, an acupuncturist, and a muscular therapist—after many trips to the pool and the gym—after hiking, walking, running, stretching—after yoga, meditating, listening to music, playing music, creating my play list, fellowshipping with friends, and praying—what would be my reward if I can't run the entire course? Then the Boston Children's Museum sent me the singlet I was to wear on Marathon Day. With this shirt, I was reminded of why I agreed to join this marathon. It was for the kids. Children have always held a special place in my heart. Teaching kids, helping them learn, and encouraging their talents and abilities have always been sources of inspiration. I decided that each mile I walked or ran would be dedicated to a child. Each mile for a child who deserved a fair shake at living a phenomenal life, full of learning. This was all for them. I was excited, elated, nervous, calm, hopeful, doubtful, all of the above and all at the same time. Was I going to be ready? Maybe not, but whether I was or not, I would run/walk the Boston Marathon anyway!!

In the few days leading up to Marathon Day, I had gotten cleared to run by ortho, had my last PT appointment and had my third acupuncture session. By Sunday, my left knee was taped up, hydration belt was packed, and my clothes were laid out. My obsession with what I was going to wear in that cold rainy weather worked to my advantage. I did not get hypothermia! I wore essentially the same outfit I wore on a 10-mile run I did in the rain: an L.L. Bean rain jacket and Olympia ski pants, spandex shorts, compression sleeves for my legs, Feeture socks and lots of body glide on my feet (I now wish I used more body glide under my sports bra). The one major difference was that this time I wore a Boston Children's Museum singlet underneath (which never saw the light of day, smh).

I woke up in darkness that morning. My husband made me oatmeal while I showered and dressed. I gave myself a pep talk while getting ready: don't go out too fast, as soon as you start to limp, stop running, don't make your injury worse! Have fun, smile and have no fear. While my mind attempted to be calm, my stomach began doing back flips and somersaults. I ended up in the bathroom way more times than I had anticipated. And with that, I missed a 7am chartered bus to Hopkinton. My husband dropped me off at we thought was the right location and he then left to drop my bag off at the gear check. The bus I thought was my bus ended up being a different bus. I then walked to Boston Common to catch one of the B.A.A. buses. I ended up on a bus full of runners who qualified for this race (talk about feeling out of place, whoa!) The bus driver got lost and had to drop us off a mile away from Athlete's Village. Despite the snafus, I was able to meet some really beautiful people. For instance, I met a young woman from Mexico, who is an experienced marathoner, but first-time Boston Marathoner. She gave me tips on how to qualify for a race, how to train, how to fuel and what places to visit in Mexico.

While walking to Athlete's Village, I was able to catch the wheelchair racers whizz by. At the starting line, I saw the hand cyclists take off and then the elite women walk toward the line. If I saw Desiree Linden, I would not have known that a history-maker just walked by me. As I continued on to Athlete's Village, I decided to veer off toward a line of port o potties and ended up hanging out in the archway of a CVS store. I was lured in by the chance for cover from the elements. While huddled like sardines with a group of shivering runners, I met someone who helped me duct tape my shoes (btw, that duct tape flapped in the wind and let buckets of water into my shoes by mile 10). I also met a 65-year-old man who was about to run his 29th Boston and 73rd marathon! He said he wanted to run a marathon in all 50 states, but wasn't sure he would make it before he died because he had been in an accident last year and tore his meniscus. He had already completed marathons in 32 states. I also met an older woman from London who was running her 123rd marathon. Amazing people!

By the time I got to the starting line, my socks were already damp and cold, and my clothes were heavier with rain. Once the gun went off, it felt like a stampede. Runners ran passed me in a frenzied state. The excitement and the nerves were palpable. I felt myself going faster than my planned pace, but I couldn't help it. I tried to stay on the left side so I wouldn't get mowed down, but then switched to the right; from driving, I have been conditioned to consider the right lane a slow lane. I searched for my friends, but I didn't see any of them.

The first ten or so miles were pretty easy and they went by quickly for me. I didn't feel tired and I was keeping up with a pair of walkers (yes, they were walking just as fast as my walk/run). Somewhere in Framingham, I saw a friendly face from my church, awesome! Hugs! Pic! Off I went! At Lake Cochituate in

Natick, I recalled my last long run, which began there. I was comforted by the fact that I knew the rest of the route. I can do this, I thought. The Wellesley scream tunnel around mile 13 wasn't as loud as I thought it would be, but all of those friendly faces were energizing. Between miles 15 and 16, my phone died. It took me several minutes to get it back online with my Mophie case. Music had kept me going since the beginning and I was starting to depend on it more and more by then. I was listening to a wide range of music, from Moana songs, to gospel, to R&B, to jazz—

anything upbeat or inspiring. I'll be listening to that playlist for my future runs. During my fiddling, I lost site of the walkers.

I saw my family, my husband, daughter and parents around mile 17 in Newton and that put a huge smile on my face for a while. My heart warmed when I saw them. There they were. Cold. Wet. And waiting for slow me to come to them. I love them so much! Hugs! Pic! Off I went!

Shortly after mile 18, the mental and physical obstacles began. I began to think about all the weekly long runs I had missed: the 18 miler, the 19 miler, the 20 miler, the 21 miler, I had missed them all. I had also missed all the daily shorter runs recommended on the training program during those recovery weeks. My pace slowed, weighed down by my fearful thoughts. I didn't doubt that I would make it, but I did doubt whether I could keep my pace up without further injuring my knee. I got a cramp in my right thigh, above my knee. Tiger balm helped, but only temporarily. I also began to "feel" my left knee, the injured knee. My legs began to die. In the midst of my pity party, I saw one of my husband's former co-workers! She walked with me until I felt I could pick up the pace a little. Hugs! Pic! Off I went! I mostly walked up Heartbreak Hill (mile 20). My walk/run intervals included more walking and less running. By mile 23, my legs died a second death. I had rubbed my wet legs twice more tiger balm, but it wasn't working. I couldn't even walk as fast. More runners passed by me and I winced at the reminder of my fear of failure and being compared to others.

Thank goodness I didn't stay in that mood for long because, more friends! My daughter's God-parents! They walked with me the rest of the way, all the way to the finish line. I saw two more friends on Beacon Street! Hugs and smiles all around! No pic (our phones were too wet or dead). I received a cheery-you-can-do-this call from my Pastors and I was able to read text messages from several other friends. The amount of encouragement I received during those last three miles will stay with me for a while. I tried to look at each of the cheering spectators in the eye. They gave me energy I didn't have. When I turned left onto Boylston, a wave of relief and triumph overtook me. I had enough energy for a limpy jog to the finish line. Between the tears in my eyes and the rain on my glasses, I couldn't see much, but I could barely make out another friend (a two-time Boston marathoner!) and an acquaintance (another two-time Boston Marathoner!) on Boylston Street. No pic (I couldn't stop, too tired). I could hear their voices of encouragement. I was so overwhelmed with appreciation. As I approached the finish line, I heard my husband encouraging me and cheering me on. I saw him and my daughter in his arms. Then I saw my parents beaming with pride. I had done it. I had really done it. I GOT MY MEDAL!! I was afraid that I was too late to receive it.

Thanks to a friend, I was able to clean up, change, eat, and get a massage at a luxury property on Exeter Street. That was a treat! I received a yes-you-can text from my two Emerge friends who had finished the marathon earlier. They're awesome! I felt their presence with me during my journey. The most-oft said words out of my mouth on Monday were "thank you." I kept on saying it and I am still saying it. Thank you to the volunteers who gave me water, Gatorade and paper towels, thank you to the police officers, thank you to the cheering spectators, thank you to friends and family, especially to my parents who took such good care of my daughter while I was training and who took such good care of me when I couldn't even walk, thank you to my supporters, thank you to the Boston Children's Museum. THANK YOU!

Sleep didn't come easily that night. I was tired and wired, hyped up on triumph and Tailwind. I spent the entire next day relaxing and limping around the house. Every time I caught myself in the mirror, I beamed. It was automatic. My decision to do this marathon took courage. The training took commitment. Persevering through my knee injury took faith. Deciding to do the marathon even though I wasn't 100% recovered took dedication (okay and perhaps a little insanity as well ;-)). Taking 6 hours, 54 minutes and 48 seconds to complete the marathon in a relentlessly cold monsoon took sheer grit and endurance.

What's next? After a relaxing vacation in Haiti with my husband and daughter, I need to start training for the B.A.A. 10K in June. My husband and I are doing it together, along with several other friends. Did my knee hold up? Yes, I am able to walk! A little PT and a lot of exercise should have me up and running again soon enough. Will I run another marathon? Absolutely. Just not in the rain. Bump that.

Kelley Batton Duell, Bib 22468

Windermere, FL, 47, 3:52:05

This is the letter Kelley wrote to the two Red Cross volunteers that helped her in her time of need after the race.

Dear Rob and Rocco,

The two things I remember most about you both are your smiles and your shoes. After these last few weeks of searching for you, those two things have stood out the most- but both mean so much more than what one may think.

My Boston race was awful. I switched into survival mode in Athlete's Village and remember next to nothing about the run. I was cold and wet and completely miserable. The sights and sounds of this iconic race that I have dreamed of running for so long were blacked out- replaced by freezing rain and wind gusts and a mantra of "just get through". I felt cheated out of the "Boston Experience". By the time I finished I felt flat and distant. I didn't feel the joy I had visualized for over a year, I was unable to run the race I had trained for- I knew if I "bonked" and had to stop, I would never finish due to my muscles cramping and the hypothermia that was setting in. I had to slow down just to get through.

As I crossed the finish line, the race director came on and asked us to take a moment of silence. I was so confused at this point, I thought they were stopping the race due to weather. (Only now do I know I crossed the finish line at the same time the bombs went off in 2013.)

Somehow I managed to walk down and get my medal and a heat poncho. Those heat ponchos are awesome and one of the things I wanted most from this race. I dreamed about taking a photo in that poncho, just my head poking out, looking like a victorious E.T. With a wide grin and my medal by my cheek, but I was just too cold to even try. After I was wrapped in my poncho, I was told to keep walking forward-so I did. My husband texted me and told me they were waiting in front of Old South Church. I was so clueless as to where I was, I began asking and kept being told to move forward. I ended up at the end of bag check but did not have a bag- my husband had all my dry clothes. So I asked again and was pointed in a different direction. I walked to a church I was told to go to, but it was the wrong church. I asked again and was told to go yet again in a different direction. I really don't know how long I was walking around but to me it seemed like forever. I was lost.

Then I saw a Big Red Cross and these two amazing smiles. I'm not sure what I said or did when I met you, it seems so foggy. I do know that The Red Cross and those two smiles meant "safe" and that's what I felt. I felt safe. I know one of you asked me if I was okay as the other held me steady. I know you both had umbrellas and you covered my soaking wet body and not your own as you took me to get help. I remember uttering the word sorry and one of you asking me why I was saying it- I was saying sorry because I couldn't pick my head up and I noticed you both had on such nice shoes and they were getting ruined as were the rest of your clothes because neither of you would leave my side in that pouring rain. I remember one of you getting loud and demanding someone help me. You were both so protective of me, this total stranger that looked less like a marathon runner and more like a drowned rat. Honestly, I don't know what would have happened to me if it weren't for you. My husband's phone stopped working because it was soaked, and he could only text- but I was unable to text back because my hands were so cold and stopped functioning. I was still 1.6 miles from where I was supposed to meet him, and I would have never made it. You two could have made the choice to tell me I was not in the right place. You could have opened the door and told me to keep going with a "congratulations" and a pat on the back. Instead you made a quick decision to help a complete stranger and quite possibly saved me from being hospitalized.

I was suffering from hypothermia and fading very fast. I spent over an hour in the med tent trying to get my temp back up. Rob and Rocco- You two ARE my Boston. You were the race I visualized and the sense of joy I thought I would feel running down Boylston. My Boston Experience came in the form of compassion and humanity, it came through in your selflessness and warmth. I can't tell you what Newton looks like or how I felt when I saw the Citco Sign, but I will never forget your smiles, the fact that you refused to leave me, and how you shielded me from the pouring rain with no regard to your own well-being. Thank you for saving me that day. Thank you for restoring my faith in humanity. Thank you for being my protective angels. I may be one of many you helped that day, but you two will forever be my happy ending to a very intense experience. I don't know if you will recognize this gift initially, but this is a piece of my heat poncho from that day. I didn't get my cheesy E.T. picture but I did get something a lot more meaningful. I hope you both can hang this someplace to remind yourselves that you two are what is good in this world. I owe you one.

Andrew Watson, Bib 2398

London, Great Britain, 42, 2:59:21

My experience of Boston was a simple one. That should not preclude the possibility of it being profound. A couple of months after I ran my hometown race: the London marathon (2017) it was time to sign up for 2018. I had qualified with my 2017 time. "Good for age", they call it in England. At the time of sign up I had taken all social media apps off my phone as I wanted as few distractions as possible. My wife was having an operation for her second bout with cancer. If I couldn't be with her because I had to work, or if I was with her and my daughter, I wanted to be as present as possible. The day I did finally looked at Facebook, I saw the reminder about it being the last day to sign up for "good for age" in the 2018 London marathon. The post was a day old. I had missed the deadline.

I wasn't planning to run any other races that year or in the near future. I called the London marathon organizers to plead with them and to point out that I understood that I had missed the deadline but "this is ME we are talking about". Apparently, my being "me" was of little concern to those people. I sat and made no attempt to quiet my vocalizing how angry and disappointed I was at myself. That was going to be MY race. I had run it two years previously and loved it and got a PR/PB each time. I usually excel at profanities, but I truly outdid myself on this occasion. As marathon runners, we compete against ourselves, try to better ourselves push and sometimes punish ourselves. But much like when I would discover a new and crucial part of training, I realized that I had to do things differently. My usual ways and instincts were not working. I remained hopelessly unorganized and had paid the price. That's when it hit me; "I'll run Boston!"

I had qualified, registration had yet to open. I would be adventurous and bold and different. Yes, it would be expensive, but worth it! I had to run a truly epic race at that precise time. I just had to, goddammit!! I had been accepted into Boston for 2014 after qualifying at the Indianapolis monumental marathon in the fall of 2012 (I used to live in the States). But by 2014 I had moved my American family back to London to be nearer my mother, father and sister after being away for 15 years. Before we made it back, my father (an ex marathoner and triathlete) died. But back we were, and I couldn't afford to fly to and stay in Boston. So, not really knowing what I was missing, how could I? I ran the Brighton marathon on the south coast of England at almost the same time as London and Boston. A nice race. A bit hilly to be a real fast BQ-er but fun and the people there seemed to understand the spirit of the thing. Yes, it's true, I am wandering off topic, perhaps even rambling. Never mind - fast forward; welcome to April 16, 2018. I, as an English person (half Irish for what it's worth), completely forgot what rain was. I frequently tell newcomers to London, during the spring, that are surprised by how bad the weather is, it's springtime in the British Isles, that means we are going to get pissed on, for months. But today I had realized that I couldn't do much about the wind, dressed for a cold day but dressed as though I was impervious to freezing rain. Every day since, I have wished that I put on the celebration jacket instead of putting it in my gear check bag. Damn!

The bus journey to Hopkinton was quite fun. I got to catch up with my friend Robert S. Warden. We had gotten pretty wet while waiting for the bus though. My throw away fleece and (allegedly) rain resistant throw away jacket were useless. Being slightly damp on the bus was ok but when we got off the bus, it was miserable. The driving rain meant that we were not going to dry off but perhaps, we thought, we might get warmer in the athletes' village. We wouldn't. There was no relief from the wind. A kindly gent took pity on me and gave me some toe warmers and they almost worked. Robert and I sat back to back in order to try and keep one side of us, relatively, warm. This worked to a point. While it was a relatively good idea, in theory to have some throw-away socks and shoes, they were still very wet and made my feet very cold. Plastic bags between the socks and shoes would've been the way to go. Fortunately, I realized how saturated my beanie was going to be and used a spare plastic bag from Robert as a hat/shower cap.

On the way to the start from the village, the consistently unrelenting rain became annoying. I drink a lot of water on any given day so not drinking as much on race morning as I might have done, meant that I wasn't going to the toilet as much as (pre-race) usual. This was a positive to hang on to. I was half way through Deena Kastor's book, which spoke of the importance of finding and using any and all positive thoughts. That was one, YAY!

Being in the corral knowing that we were close to the gun was another story. This is when I truly got my first unadulterated taste of the raw and powerful chemistry and energy of the Boston Marathon. The electricity was palpable. It sounds naff but is totally true. Perhaps it was the weather, but we were a very still bunch, considering what was about to be underway. Although I got the feeling that many a muscle was engaged in anticipatory twitching. Maybe we just didn't dare risk getting colder or expend any more energy than was necessary for the compulsory shivering.

The anthem is always poignant. It always was for me. Despite being English I am an American citizen. This is the land where I went to college, met my wife, bought a house became a parent and generally lived a happy 15-year segment of my life. Imagine my surprise when someone (mid anthem) turns to me and says, "Are you from the U.K.?" - "Errr, yeah..". What had happened? Was I paying silent respect for the people of the nation in the wrong way? I knew I wasn't wearing an enormous "Union Jack". Wait, let me check....no just the usual silly running gear (I don't manage to "style it out" the way some runners can). "I recognize your energy gels. I get the same ones shipped from the UK." "Oh", I said. "I notice that you don't have nine of them strapped to your belly like I do."

We rapidly approached the time of the gun. I tossed aside my throw away fleece and jacket, leaving me wearing a relatively normal running outfit with the addition of a beanie and a long-sleeved thermal shirt. Again: NOT rain appropriate. I also left my sunglasses on the top of my head. I thought that they might become useful later on to stop the rain from being blown into my eyes. I thought wrong. Just seconds away from the gun you could hear the murmur of numerous people saying things like "alright guys" or "let's do this", as a general address to people in their vicinity whom they mostly did not know. It didn't matter. While we may well have all been thinking different things, I suspect that there were only a few simple and immensely strong feelings that were being shared by all of us.

As the starter pistol shot it's round into the freezing wet sky, it also shot thousands of people across a, suddenly tangible, threshold between being someone that was going to run the Boston Marathon and someone that was actually doing it. Ah, the sweet relief. Followed by the light relief of taking a minute to actually cross the start line. Later I would be so grateful for that minute. I will attempt to avoid recapping the specific weather activity as we were all there and remember it all too well.

The first few miles were typically crowded and nervy. I had vowed that I would find strength in positivity, just like Deena had told me too and I would run this race intelligently. The circumstances seemed to require that. This means, as we all know, that many runners will pass you at the beginning of the race. Being a few seconds off my average pace, for the race as a whole and given the prevalence of going out too quickly amongst a lot of runners, I felt as though I was walking. "No no", stay on a sensible pace. The watch doesn't lie. Unless it's like last year in London when it told me that I was keeping pace with the world record holders. Lying bloody junk watch!

It wasn't long before I saw people on the side of the road having dropped out. I wasn't surprised by this so much as I was surprised by how soon it happened and how bad those guys looked. No need to worry, as it turned out, I would have my turn to look that bad, later on. It would even be pointed out to me. Oh good. I had listened to a number of different opinions and pieces of advice regarding the tactics to employ or avoid for Boston. Ultimately, I was concerned, by the fact that no one runs uphill as fast as they do downhill. Normally I would say that aiming for a negative split would be the way to go. In Boston however, I was skeptical about my ability to run a second half that contained the Newton hills, faster than running the first half that contained so much downhill. My tactic was to run a little faster on the downhill than the flat, without using any extra energy if possible and then slow down as little as possible on the hills. I would have to be honest with myself about my rate of perceived exertion. Something that I've never found easy.

Within the first five miles, while bowing my head to shield my eyes from the rain, I saw an intensely large amount of foam and suds coming out of the top of my shoes. I thought that this was weird and didn't seem to be happening to anyone else. I felt the urge to ask someone, "What the hell is going on with my shoes." Then I thought better of that kind of oxygen use and of bothering someone else just because there were still some traces of antibacterial sanitizer in my shoes.

Not long after this I noticed that I was drawing level with my cool-dressed English gel using friend from the corral. From what he had told me at the start about his time goals, I might be able to use him as a visual pace indicator. I have heard many stories of people running long sections of a race with runners that happened to be of a similar pace. So far it has never happened to me. After a couple of more miles of him not noticing, or not acknowledging me (sensible, thought I, no point in wasting that energy), matey-boy took a sharp turn off the course into a group of "porta-potties." I tried not to take it personally. I hoped that his toilet break went well and never saw him again.

I don't remember where, exactly, but at some point, two saint-like individuals had taken it upon themselves to hand out vinyl food service gloves. I heard the shout, from what I assumed was a volunteer, of "gloves." I'm sure that my hands have been colder than they were at that moment, at some time in my life but I really can't remember when. I was having a lot of trouble getting the gels from my gel belt (every 20 minutes). I made a viciously efficient bee line for the gloves and practically fell upon the poor woman that held the box of gloves. I didn't stop running and kept a decent pace for what felt like an eternity while I struggled to get the vinyl gloves over my wet hands. They ended up being what allowed me to remain freezing cold but without getting hypothermia.

I noticed the big party at mile 5, of course. The support was great. Everyone says so, amazing. The volunteers were some of the most positive people that I've ever met. They weren't just doing it selflessly for the runners. Those people seemed to be taking huge pride in "their marathon", their hometown race and their own personal connection to a sporting event that is not only historic, relevant and important but also ABSOLUTELY HUGE!!! They do all this for no money, very little appreciation and over a long period of time. I sincerely hope that they get at least a fraction of the joy and fulfilment that they give the runners. I wondered, briefly, if the Wellesley girls would be out in force as usual. I swore that I could hear them over the rain from mile 12 or wherever I was. They were there, alright. I couldn't pay them much mind as I was trying to take advantage of the hill/gravity combination. Or was I? I was definitely cold. Too cold, like collapse-type of cold.

As a freshman Bostonian you dread the Newton hills. I was determined to save some energy for them (to not walk on them). After all there would be 5.2 miles left to go AFTER the hills. I had this sense of foreboding that something terrible would happen by the time I got to Newton. Either I would fall, exhausted and be unable to get up or the cold and wet would become too much to bear and I would "DNF"! I knew that my wife, daughter and mother would all be waiting, cold and soaking wet, to cheer me on at the bottom of "heartbreak" somewhere near the 20-mile mark. They would all be happy for me to stop, if I needed to, all things considered. But they also knew that doing this would make me unhappy for a looooong time.

Alright hills, "come, an' 'ave it!" (London for; "give me your best shot"). Perhaps channeling some kind soccer hooliganism would aid in strength or "grit"! I was more trying to fortify myself than I was daring the hills to not be pansies. I meant no disrespect to the topography. That would be a fatal mistake, for sure. Seeing the family and hearing their cheers is always brilliant. I told myself that I had enough time to slow a little for the hills. Who doesn't have to, when it comes to Newton? I didn't think that I could feel a lot worse than I already did and I was coping so that's what you were talking about, right Deena?

I didn't expect the downhill after the hills to be so hard. Not that it was hard so much as it was hard for me to go downhill QUICKLY! It was about this time that I noticed how close I would be on time. Ok-time, everybody's favorite abstract concept. It didn't matter what the watch said (the watch that didn't say I was running any faster, no matter how hard I tried). There was no arguing with the time of day. But the downhill, on the other hand, was just NOT HAVIN' IT! At this point I should mention that my time goal was under 3 hours. I should have perhaps had a gold, silver and bronze series of goals but I didn't. I harbored a secret desire to get close to my PR/PB of 2:54:47 but that wasn't likely. But longer than 3 hours and I would've allowed that to tarnish my enjoyment of the whole event/trip. That is sad and disrespectful, I know, I know. I'm a bad and sad person. Sorry. Sincerely.

Around the 23-mile mark with my time window dwindling and the required arithmetic becoming very simple, I reached for the last volunteers cup at a water station. Yes, that's right I missed it completely, wasn't even close. I didn't stop, as usual. As we all know, people like Bill Rogers could stop and drink water and then run on and win. Needless to say, I could not. There was also a strong likelihood that I would seize up and be unable to ambulate any further at all.

Immediately after muttering whatever it was that I muttered having missed the water, I felt a nudge at the back of my shoulder. Turning, I saw dude of about 6'4" wearing shorts and sunglasses and compression sleeves and nothing else, holding a nice pre-squished cup of Massachusetts purest and coldest. I took it and tried to yell, "Thanks, you're awesome". Whatever it was that I did actually say he replied, "That's alright, bro, we're all out here for each other." Then he tried to, I presume, pat me on the back. Due to the discrepancies in our dimensions, he somewhat clotheslined me from the rear as he passed me. Never had such a nice gesture been such a cruel blow. But, honestly, I was helped greatly by that camaraderie far more than I was wrestlemania'd.

The Citgo sign was nice to see but I remember it being on a bit of a hill and from what I could tell from the numbers on my watch glowing dimly through the vinyl glove, I only had time to run a 3-hour marathon not a SUB 3 one. DAMN! Seeing the "Boston Strong" sign on the bridge was a welcome sight despite thinking of the hill immediately after it. I couldn't read the street sign for Hereford until I was right by it and had already said to myself "please say, Hereford. Please say, Hereford. Please say, Hereford!" It did! Knowing full well that Boylston was at least .3 of a mile, I didn't dare get too excited. That's when I found out that the slight incline in Hereford just before Boylston had turned into "Mount Hereford!" I pleaded, "Enough with the hills, please!" As I got to the turn I leaned slightly to the left as if I were an Olympic level 200-meter runner, hitting the track bend. A woman in the crowd met eyes with me briefly and recoiled away from me, much like one might do from a leper. I hadn't had that look from a spectator since mile 23 of a marathon in 2015. I knew I was in bad shape then and I knew it now. But it's always nice to get strong visual cues from the crowd. Boylston was hard. Epic, yes, but haaard. I tried to turn on the after burners, hit "turbo boost" and pull myself along by grabbing handfuls of fat raindrops. That didn't work, needless to say. Did all other things just "fall away" as I stiffened and shivered and burned while kinda sprinting? No. A few thoughts passed through my mind. Thoughts like "no excuses"; I'd missed a week of training, 3 weeks before the race with a back injury. 2 weeks after that, I missed 5 days training from the flu. I was going to spank it and crank it despite these setbacks. I could see the official race clock go over 3 hours. My watch suggested that I would make it under 3 hours by 20-30 seconds. At this time and place, I can unequivocally say that if I had any more to give then whatever it was, it was hiding perfectly from me. I crossed the line in 2:59:21 to the sound of almighty squeaking. I wept uncontrollably but had so little energy and was so wet that it just looked as though I was grimacing somewhat.

I shook violently while getting my medal and a bottle of water. I dropped the cap from my water bottle (I was raised to not litter) and bent down to pick it up. The volunteer that gave me the water laughed at the spectacle, warmly.

She said "don't pick that up. We'll get it. Just leave it down". She smiled broadly at me. That's Boston volunteers for ya, classy affection all the way. Bless 'em. Really truly. Another runner that finished with me put an arm around me, pressing the wet clothes against me and making me even colder, if that was possible and said, "Are you ok? You're shivering a lot". This account is quite lengthy so you're probably having a hard time thinking of me as speechless. But that I was. Now I was in a wheelchair. What sounded like a young lady, was wheeling me down the street at tremendous speeds. Now I was in what must have been the medical tent. For some reason I couldn't look up. I saw the knees of a medical professional? "ARE YOU IN NEED OF ANY MEDICAL ASSISTANCE TODAY, SIR?" My jaw had locked up and I managed to spit the words, "Just. Really. Cold" "OK, TAKE HIM TO THE WARMING TENT!" Back out into the cold. NOOOOO!!! The wheelchair's front wheels got stuck in a manhole cover or something. I couldn't help the young lady move me. In my peripheral vision she looked to be about 80-90 pounds, soaking wet. And we were all soaking wet.

The warming room was in the basement of a building. I'd been wheeled to the top of two flights of stairs. I didn't understand. But I was warming up and I wasn't going back out there to freeze. I'd run the race I could do 2 flights. At the bottom of the stairs I joined a long line of people that were being told about the chicken stock and massages that awaited us once we'd made it to the front of the line. To my left I could see exactly those things through a door. They weren't lying. It was clear that I would be there in a couple of hours time. I couldn't wait for that. My wife would be worried about me. She'd been in this weather, seen me looking bad at mile 20 and I was now away from my phone and unable to reassure her of my relative wellness. I went back upstairs. There were no more charming and urgent ladies with wheelchairs. My legs were too cold to get to gear check. I rummaged in and around some kind of lectern, podium thing and found an unused garbage bag. I made 2-foot holes in the bottom and I was off to gear check. Wait. Where was I? My eyes were closed on the way to this place. I held my space blanket closed with one hand. The garbage bag didn't come with a belt, so I held that with the other and shuffled in wet confused rectangles until I found the purveyors of many plastic bags who claimed to have my clothes. I messaged my wife "I'm ok" and then dressed. Having changed I was instantly transported back to the land of the living. I could even walk almost normally. So I almost normally walked, rather indirectly, to my hotel. Yes, I should have worn the rain jacket. Yes, I should have gone straight to gear check after finishing. But I'll be damned if it wasn't just perfectly awesomely epic!! This last paragraph will serve as the short version of my account of the day. Will I be back in 2019? Ha-ha, I wouldn't miss it.

Stephanie Virding, Bib 23463

Las Vegas, NV, 50, 5:10:38

It has taken me a couple of days to figure out the words to sum up running the 2018 Boston Marathon - the 122nd running of the race. My heart is forever full, and I am forever grateful for the experience. I am so grateful for all of my friends out there on the course and for those who spectated in crazy weather!!

So here it is - the Tale of Running Inside a Washing Machine or Boston, Brent, and the Battle...Grab a sammich, sit back, it's a bit of a long story...

A few days out, I started watching the weather a little more seriously. Spring in New England is fickle and can change in the blink of an eye. I kept hope, but race morning would reveal that running conditions were

going to be awful. I put together the best outfit I could think of with help from friends and the Boston Marathon Training group (#BostonBuddies) - the information and ideas in this group became invaluable.

Luckily, I had secured a nice cushy coach bus ride with bathroom on board for the drive out to the start line. As we neared Hopkinton, I noticed the snow on the ground and kept thinking, "It's just going to be really cold". I was also thinking, "It's a LONG way back to Boston". The BAA had been sending out information on hypothermia and what to watch for. Since I don't usually run in driving rains, with high winds and low temps, this was my fear, as I readied myself for the race. Once in Hopkinton, I just had to make my way to Outside Interactive at the start line, where I had a warm, dry office spot to hang before the start of the race. It was a mile walk to the office and I was soaked by the time I got there - even with a rain poncho. Luckily, I had a change of clothes & sneakers and everything I needed for the start was dry. During the walk there, I was instructed to go through Athletes Village. I was SO relieved to not have to be waiting there. It was an absolute mud and water pit, with nowhere dry or warm to be. I know this had to be so hard for runners that had to wait it out there.

Once at the office, I got ready for the race and watched the first two waves take off. It was such a unique and cool opportunity to be able to share this time with some amazing runners with significant running histories. And I was dry.

I headed out to the start corral - about a 5 min walk. Once in the coral, I realized my feet were soaked already and getting cold. The wind whipped, and the rain flew. I knew I was in for a hard run, but it's BOSTON!!! I had decided at the last second to keep my throw away pants on and this decision saved me, I didn't stop to take them off until mile 24.

The first three miles went as good as possible. I heeded the sage advice of not going out too fast. I tried to check my watch, but the water was so thick, I was having a hard time reading it. So by feel, I held back on pace and was feeling ok. My heel pain kicked in fiercely with the cold and every step felt like a driving nail going up into my foot. By mile four, I was walking a little bit to try to shake the heel pain and my hamstrings seized up with the cold. My right hamstring decided we were not going to run this race. Several other people were walking due to seizing muscles and we just continued to check in on each other.

I had several moments of "holy crap...really??? How am I going to make it to the finish line?" The pain was fierce, but so was my New England spirit. Being New England born and bred, we are made of a grit and determination that doesn't allow for stopping something once you have started. And after all, it was BOSTON. If I needed to crawl to the finish line, I would. Nothing was going to stop me. Luckily, I was able to maintain an ok pace run/walking.

I needed to make a bathroom stop a handful of miles in. Shifting soaking wet clothing around your body to do your business was a feat. That stop cost me a lot of time, but it had to be done.

At some point, I met up with a guy named Brent. He was struggling with injuries and ready to call it and bail on the race. We got to chatting and I decided that helping each other was the best way to get us both to the finish line. We took turns picking spots to run to - the next light, or pole, or umbrella...when one of us needed to walk, we walked. I had no time goal, so this worked well. With about 11 miles left, my new fueling plan kicked in well and I found a renewed energy. Brent told me to go on, but that wasn't going to happen. We were in it together! Unless you are shooting for a specific time goal, this race is all about helping each other out. I could have easily at that point gone ahead and probably finished closer 4:30, but there was a more important task at hand. Brent struggled more with his pain, and I felt better and better, but we hung in it together. I took his lead on what he could do - when he could run and when he needed to walk. Really, we saved each other out there at certain points.

Around mile 24, I ditched my throw away pants - I swear they weighed 10 pounds soaking wet! I couldn't even get them off - Brent had to help me. Then I decided to ditch my trusty trash bag, that didn't really keep me dry, but it kept me a little warmer. I knew photo ops were coming and I was going to at least salvage that part of the race!

When we made the turn onto Hereford, I started scanning the crowd looking for my husband and my friends. No husband (he had already made his way to the finish area, afraid I would need immediate assistance with the conditions). But I did see Barb & Jenn right away! I had warned Brent that we would need to stop for a photo - I wanted to make sure I remembered the person who got me through a few tough miles!

The run down Boylston to the finish was a dream. I can't even put into words what I was feeling and what that experience was like. I want to live in that moment forever!

The weather for this race was like running inside of a washing machine during the heavy spin cycle - constant heavy rain, with crazy downpours every couple of miles. The start temp was 30, with a real feel of 17. We finished with a temp of 38 and real feel of 24. There was a headwind the whole way at around 35 mph and reported gusts up to 50 mph. At some point, I didn't feel the wind or the cold. Just the constant pelting of the rain. And then the pinging sting of hail as it hit my face. My shoes were constantly filled with water and I contemplated how bad my toes were going to be when I finally finished. You couldn't avoid puddles, because the entire course was puddles or rivers of water. It was a true weather shit show. This was not about embracing the suck, it was about getting very intimate with it - for 26.2 miles. Coldest temps for the Boston Marathon since 1970 and some of the worse weather conditions for the race on record. The beautiful medal at the end was truly earned.

I can't say enough about the volunteers, police officers, and spectators along the course. The spectators were handing out everything from beers & Jell-O shots, to orange wedges, bananas, pretzels, cookies. Many were offering up hand warmers to stick inside our gloves. About halfway through the course, a couple of ladies had plastic bins full of dry socks we could change into. A good thought for a minute, then I realized the dry socks would last about 30 seconds. Still, it was so incredibly thoughtful. We stopped briefly to have some spectators help put hand warmers inside our gloves. They offered us warm tea. As good as it sounded, we had to keep going. The energy of the spectators was unlike anything I have ever experienced in a race. Although the crowds were reportedly thinner because of the weather, there were still thousands of people out and they were EXCITED!!! SO much screaming and yelling. They wanted you to do well and they let us know it! And they stayed out there in those same conditions that we were running in. Perseverance became the name of the game for runners AND spectators. New England grit and sprit - alive and well with all of the spectators. I am forever grateful for all of them!!

Regardless of the obstacles and the weather...my running journey has come full circle - in the town that has my heart, running the race that started it all! Five years later, I will never forget, and I am forever changed and grateful...

I am a Boston Marathoner!

Kelly Putnam Necioglu, Bib 13555

Macungie, PA, 34, 3:24:39

In the week leading up to the Boston Marathon, I started hearing rumblings about rain. I checked my weather app: it would happen later in the day, they said. It would be 50 degrees. At the last minute I threw in my waterproof running jacket, but never thought I'd actually wear it. By the time we got to Boston 3 days before the race, it was clear it would be much colder and that the rain was starting earlier. By the next day it became clear that the conditions would be difficult, with a strong headwind to top it off. I agonized over my outfit for the day, finally made a decision, and got some sleep.

I woke before my alarm clock Monday and got ready. I met a friend downstairs and walked to the buses that would take us to the start. The bus ride to the athletes' village took over 45 minutes. I was happy to be dry and inside, but the long drive was intimidating. When we arrived in Hopkinton, it looked like a disaster area. Anything loose was whipping in the wind and of the two tents I saw, one was 50% full of ankle-deep mud to the point that nobody could stand in it (except for the brilliant lady standing all alone in an upside-down umbrella). The second tent was so packed that we were smashed against each other, clutching our gear bags to our chests. The weather had officially become all anyone could think about and the inability to prepare as planned in the hour before the race gave me anxiety.

It was so cold out that the "rain" falling from the sky was forming into piles of sleet/snow on the ground by the port-a-potties. I was so scared to get my hands wet and cold that I resisted the urge to record the scene, other than a quick video in the tent, which I couldn't even upload. I wore an old throw away pair of sneakers and socks to the athletes' village and we found a covered area closer to the start where we could change into our dry shoes and socks. Right before we left, an older man came up and asked us if we'd seen any shoes. There were hundreds of pairs of discarded shoes around us! He explained that he'd accidentally left his bag with his good shoes somewhere I felt terrible for him and can't imagine he ever found them. I keep thinking about that poor guy and wondering how he made out. What an unlucky mistake to make!

I ended up late for my start because I used the bathroom one last time. I thought I had a great plan to simply tear off my poncho and throw-away fleece and go, but realized at the last minute that I had accidentally put my fleece under my waterproof jacket. I had to step aside to pull the jacket off in the downpour, then put it back right-side out and zip it back on. The inside got wet in the process and I was terrified that I'd made a bad mistake that would come back to haunt me, but all I could do was start to run.

Aside from the weather, my first impression of Boston was that it was so crowded! I tried to be patient, but people around me were running a full minute slower than my goal pace. I got frustrated and started weaving around people even though I know it wastes a lot of energy. I ended up on the right side of the road, which was less crowded – I think partly because the headwind seemed to be coming on an angle from that direction and partly because there were lots of puddles and drains to dodge. At mile 6, I spotted my brother and his girlfriend – and then again at mile 8! The fans in the early miles were awesome. I mostly remember people hanging out of apartment windows cheering and people standing in their front yards.

Around mile 10, I finally felt like I had a little more space. By mile 13 I could mostly relax, but I still stuck to the right side. Someone just ahead of me discarded their poncho into my face. At some point I noticed that my right calf and left hip were affected by the slope of the road. I moved to the middle, but it was still too crowded, so I shrugged it off and drifted back to the right, hoping neither would become an injury.

My brother and his girlfriend popped back up at mile 13 and totally lifted my spirits – my brother even ran with me for a bit. My pace dropped to 7:15 when he ran with me, so I think I owe my 5 second PR to him! At mile 16 the rain increased to an absolute deluge of water and people went nuts. I think I actually laughed out loud. What else could you do? We were all whooping and throwing our hands out to our sides. It was surreal. The crowds were amazing! It was also around then that I marveled at a guy in bare feet wearing thin running sandals. Eventually I got a little too warm and unzipped my jacket and took my buff off of my neck. This resulted in gnarly cuts at my collarbone post-race thanks to the exposed zipper, but I never felt a thing. I contemplated ditching my bright orange kitchen gloves, but thought I might not survive post-race without them. At mile 18, the wind really picked up and I felt ice cold again. A middle-aged man and an older man collided and fell hard to the ground. They both popped up and I did see the older guy running, but I never saw the middle-aged guy again.

At mile 20, the cold really started getting to me. It felt like my legs were turning into blocks of ice. My quads were numb. I went into survival mode and stopped looking at my watch. My pace slowed by several seconds. I was surprised that I started passing a lot of people – all I could think is that they must have been even more worse off by that point than I was. I made it up heartbreak hill, never out of breath, but felt like I was dragging my numb legs behind me. It was my slowest mile, but again – I passed so many people on the way up. We were all struggling in the conditions. I wasn't even sure it was heartbreak hill until I got to the top and saw it on a sign. The crowds picked up and I did constant pace and time calculations in my mind to distract myself. I was getting colder by the minute. I was in awe of the crowds, undoubtedly even colder than I was and so enthusiastic!

By the time I hit the last mile, I was out of competitive juice. Usually I'm laser focused and pushing myself hard in the last few miles, but after doing that for over 3 hours thanks to the weather, my competitive drive was dulled. I knew I should try to run faster, but I had no intensity left. It was my second slowest mile. I admired the crowds, got choked up as I passed the site of the bombing, and finally dug deep and pushed through the finish to miraculously get my personal record and qualify for next year's Boston Marathon by over 15 minutes.

After crossing the finish line, my hip locked up. My calf was in a knot and I swung my leg to walk, painfully slowly, to get my medal and post-race food. I felt like a walking ice statue. By the time I saw my brother and his girlfriend, I was starting to shake. By the time we got the hotel, I was shaking uncontrollably and starting to feel nauseous from the cold. I took a 30 minute, scalding hot shower and was still shivering. I got out and put on as many layers of clothes as I could before joining my family and drinking hot chocolate. Finally warm and dry, I climbed into bed to watch the rest of the race on TV, track all of my friends, and reflect on the day. It was

nothing I had expected and yet exceeded my every expectation. It was the hardest race I've ever run and the most rewarding. It was a once in a lifetime kind of race.

Thank you, Boston, for the opportunity to truly test my will, my strength, my commitment, and my training. Thank you for creating a race so hallowed and so prestigious that it gave this stay-at-home mom a new sense of purpose. Thank you for presenting a challenge that I could only overcome by setting aside my do-it-all-myself "supermom" cape and allowing my family to help me achieve it. For every mile, for every raindrop, for every gust of wind that tore at my jacket and tried to hold me back. Thank you. You were worth the battle and all of the sacrifice.

243

Kurt Kovanen, Bib 19021

Hot Springs Village, AR, 57, 4:04:59

"2018: A Cold Run to Boston"
The morning regimen hinted of the day
ahead.
Puddles on the way to gear check,
slipping on mud near buses to Hopkinton.
Riding warm and dry, and then, a soft
surprise,
"Is that snow?"
The sullen mood at Athlete's Village.
Words heard between runners…
"Good luck."
"Be careful out there."
"Let's finish this thing."
Already soaked in the corral, the shivers
uncontrollable.
Five more minutes 'til start, then two,
then…
it begins.
Moving forward, thousands of feet
tingling numb slap the road.
A historic unforgiving road washed clean
of sentimentality.
Well-trained athletes, biting lip, seek a
stride.
The blur of town and people collide.
Is this Framingham? Or Natick?

Each has helpful and wet volunteers and soaked spectators.
Hearts swell with thankfulness at their remarkable presence.
Half-way already? Pace seems too fast.
Irrationality says, "The sooner the better."
We all trudge on, ponchos billow, gloves discarded.
Heartbreak Hill didn't seem that tough,
"Wait, there it is…"
Legs stiff, body sluggish.
"What just happened?"
Someone pulled a plug, and all went swirling down a drain.
The rigor sets in.
"Where am I?"
The Citgo sign finally appears in the misty fog.
Tell yourself,
"This is the Boston Marathon."
Back to basics, one step in front of the other.
A hearty and hoarse cheer echoes,
"Boston Strong."
You can do it.
Be careful out there.
Let's finish this thing.

Lynn Kearman Nill, Bib 29680

Salem, NH, 65, 5:51:04

My thoughts two days before the Boston Marathon went something like this: The weather sounds pretty bad. But it's not heat, thank God. It's rain, wind and chilly temps. I've run in the rain many times, even races, but never an entire marathon. I have enough experience to know I must make sure I stay warm, and relatively dry before the race. I have enough experience to know the wind will slow me down, but the rain probably will not. Much of my race plan can stay in place, try to maintain my pace, walk the hills, keep on top of nutrition and hydration. But I really have no idea how a driving rainstorm and a headwind will affect me over the course of 26 miles.

I went to the expo on Saturday. I was generally purposeful, got my bib, got my T-shirt, which is very cool. It has the names of all the towns you pass through on the back. Got my celebration jacket, a little stuffed unicorn named Spike (the symbol of the Boston marathon), a marathon commemorative pin. Then I walked up and down the rows, trying various products, looking for free stuff. I bought some water-resistant gloves and that was about it.

And then it was Marathon Monday:

I woke up at 4:30 am. Usually I can't sleep the night before a big race but last night I slept like a rock. No getting around it, the weather will be terrible. Lee took me to the Boston Express bus station in Salem New Hampshire at 6 AM and before too long we were heading into Boston. Everyone on the bus wished me good luck! From South Station I took the T. Red line to Park, switch to Green line, Green line to Arlington, where dozens of marathoners huddled in the station staying warm and dry and using the bathrooms there. Me too. Eventually I put my plastic bags over my shoes, donned my plastic rain poncho and marched with the other runners to the bus pickup to Hopkinton.

That's a long bus ride, but at least during it we could stay dry and warm. Hopkinton's Athlete's Village is in the field behind their school, which had turned into a sea of mud. Even with my plastic bags my Brooks Run Wicked Run Happy Lobstah Launch 5 shoes got muddy, and it was so wet that before too long my plastic bags were full of water, so I just got rid of them. If I ever try that again I'll have to refine my technique!

The walk to the starting line was exciting, even in the pouring rain. I stopped at the bathrooms at CVS (dry parking lot and no waiting, thanks Robert Wang!), shed my rain poncho and heavy sweatshirt at the last minute. Many, many people ran in their rain ponchos, but I thought I would be ok in my water-resistant jacket. Who would have ever thought I would have been better off running in my water proof jacket? I was so worried about being hot, and that was never the issue!

Instead of making us get into corrals the race officials told wave 4 runners to just go ahead and GO. This made for a lot of people passing me in the first mile as we got ourselves sorted out and I settled into my 30/30 run/walk intervals. In fact, sometime during the first mile a girl lost her footing and fell, almost knocking me over. She was okay, but I was a bit unnerved. The last thing I needed was for my race to be over before it even began! I've been telling myself for weeks that this was a race with a bunch of BQ's (Boston Qualifiers), the best runners for each age group in the world, so there was no need to even begin to compare myself to anyone else. I later found out that there were 112 finishers in the women 65-69 age group. Most of those women were much, much faster than me. But there were around 10 DNF's in my age group too. And there were lots of charity and invitational runners back with me. I never felt out of my league, OR alone.

The first 12 miles of Boston are very enjoyable. They don't get talked about as much as Newton and the infamous hills, but it's really nice going from one little town to another, with enthusiastic crowds in each downtown. I'm sure the crowds were much thinner than usual but there were lots of people cheering us on, especially considering the weather.

After mile 2 I changed to a 45/30 run/walk and that's what I did for the remainder of the race. I realized pretty quickly that between my hood, my cap, the crowd, and rain and wind noise, I couldn't hear or feel my watch when the timer went off to change from running to walking and back. So I scrolled to the view that showed me whether I should be running or walking, and how many seconds were left in each interval. Every once in while I scrolled back to see how my pace and progress were going. I wasn't setting any records, but I was doing okay and with the conditions I didn't want to push myself too much, so it was probably just as well that I was mostly running by feel.

At mile 13 we entered the town of Wellesley. The famous scream tunnel at Wellesley College could be heard from far, far away. It was SO MUCH FUN! I must have high fived 50 screaming, enthusiastic, cute little college girls. It was invigorating and joy-producing. It buoyed me on for several miles after that!

My hands were wet and cold very soon after the start of the race. After the first gel I had to ask unsuspecting bystanders to open the zipper in my SPI belt and get a gel out for me. Same with my phone; I got it out, realized I couldn't use it because my hands were so wet, and had to ask someone to help me put it away. I worried about finding my friends in Newton and Lee at the finish line since I couldn't contact them.

After Wellesley came a quiet portion, reservoirs and pockets of population. We descended to the lower Newton Falls and then turned right at the Newton Fire station. I have the strangest concept of the overall elevation changes in the marathon. The first 16 miles are a net elevation change that is downhill, but I noticed plenty of uphills in this portion. And the 4 Newton hills, including Heartbreak? Well I noticed two of them. I'm not sure I would have even known it was Heartbreak Hill except that the crowds were screaming that it was. There were two long hills and neither one was very steep. I really don't know what all the fuss is about!

My strategy all along had been to walk the hills but with Boston I think I should have modified this a bit. There are plenty of hills, but they are long and not nearly as steep as the ones in the Manchester City Marathon that I ran last fall. So I think I could have run more of them. I'll think about this for Twin Cities in the fall, because it's not very hilly but it does have some long moderate hills at the end.

As we entered Newton I started looking for my friends. I think they saw me before I saw them. I knew the streets leading to my cousin Mark's neighborhood so as each of those streets passed I scanned the thin crowds for the sight of them. They were at the bottom of Heartbreak Hill, at the Johnny Kelly statue. They had beautiful signs and the sight of them made me cry. I hugged them all, kissed my cousin and told them to go get warm. It made me SO happy to see them!

Although the weather was so insane, just buckets of pelting rain that actually HURT at some points, giant puddles and impromptu streams mid-street that were impossible to avoid, gusts of wind that made it flat out stupid to try to run, and cold temps that gradually crept deep into my bones, I didn't start to really suffer until around mile 22, after the Newton Hills. I never hit the wall, I was always able to keep running, and although I slowed down, I stayed under 14 minutes per mile the entire way. But the cold….my leg and arm muscles hurt, my hips hurt. My teeth would start to chatter, and I would force myself to relax and stop. After the Newton Hills there is a whole lot of downhill, and THAT hurt. It was very, very hard.

Most of the race went by very quickly. I was almost always surprised when we came to a mile marker, that we were already to 8, 12, 14 miles. But after mile 22 time stopped. I'd been warned about seeing the famous Citgo sign from far away. I don't remember where the Citgo sign is on the course exactly, but I think it's close to either mile 25 or the "one mile to go" sign. I did see the sign far off in the distance, shrouded in fog. At the time I was so confused about how far we had left to go that I thought the sign was at least a couple miles away. I was pretty surprised when we ran right by it not too much after that. By then I was so tired and cold. I longed for the "right on Hereford, left on Boylston" that marks the last half mile of the race.

But of course, eventually I got there. Turning right on Hereford we ran into a veritable sea of discarded rain ponchos. I guess lots of runners wanted to look good for their finish line photo!! But it was dangerous. Here come a bunch of exhausted runners and now we have to dodge mounds of plastic and try not to slip and fall. But at least when we turned on to Boylston anything that was going to be discarded had been lost and the road was basically clear.

I knew Lee was going to try to see me at the finish line. I scanned the crowds for him. I think I even heard his piercing whistle but didn't see him. I tried to smile and hold my head up at the finish. I ran all of the last half mile too. Boy I was tired, in pain, and freezing. A volunteer gave me a water bottle, but it was too cold to hold, and I put it down. Someone draped a medal across my neck and said "Congratulations! You just ran the Boston Marathon!" They put fleece lined heat ponchos around us and that helped a little. Very little.

I limped to the gear check tent and got my dry clothes and went into the women's changing tent with a bunch of other freezing, moaning women. It was hard, but I took off all my wet clothes except for my compression socks. I didn't think I could get the socks off and I was too tired to try. I put on dry shoes, but they were quickly wet again. I put on dry pants (that also got wet quickly), a turtleneck, a fleece, my BOSTON MARATHON CELEBRATION JACKET, and the poncho and went out to find my husband.

I slowly made my way to the family meeting area. When I got to the "N" sign at first I didn't recognize Lee in his bright yellow rain jacket. Besides he was with two other people, Paula and Steph!! I couldn't believe they made their way from Newton to the finish line too! God what wonderful people....

We found some building with a lobby where I could sit for a few minutes and try to get warm. Lee had my warm rain coat and that helped, and dry gloves and a hat. When we entered the building suddenly I couldn't breathe, I was actually wheezing. I was a bit like what happened in Duluth, but I just calmed myself and it gradually went away. I think I might be developing a bit of exercise (or maybe just marathon) induced asthma. We walked a bit more and stopped into a smoothie shop. My stomach was in revolt and I didn't really want to eat or drink anything until someone mentioned hot tea…that tea was so wonderful. Finally I began to warm up.

I was just too cold and tired to try to make it to the North End to eat. But I suggested going to Tbones in Salem and everyone was up for that, so that's what we did. Amy and Amy and Bill joined us too. Lee went home to feed the dogs and let them go potty.

Boston is an interesting course. I can see why people come back and run it year after year. It's different, so historic, the subtle and not so subtle changes in elevation, the little towns, the massive collection of very good runners. I'd love to run it in a good year and see what it was like with more crowds, but it will probably never happen. It was hard enough to get a bib this time, I'll never qualify and there are still lots of other marathons on my list. I'm so glad I got to run it though. And yeah, this year will go down in the history books. Probably one of the very toughest Bostons in its 122-year history. And I did it, finished and smiled at the end. EPIC!

Melissa Troisi, Bib 29661

Peabody, MA, 35, 4:07:04

In March, on a pouring day I jokingly texted my boss, a local meteorologist, "if you could use your connections to the weather gods, and make sure it's not like this on Marathon Monday I would be happy". Two weeks leading up to the marathon I kept asking what's the weather going to be? At one point it was going to be rain in the early morning with a wind over my left shoulder; It could not be better than that! Leading up to marathon day the report kept getting worse and worse. They had to be wrong. On the morning of the marathon, my boss texted "it's really cold". The news kept saying this is going to be the worst weather conditions the marathon has had. (One marathon was even close to being called off).

My dad picked me up. I had a throw away coat and he said, "please bring my rain coat/ windbreaker with you" To which I replied, "if you are ok with it being thrown away I am ok with bringing it", This will prove to be the smartest thing I did! I will wear it for all 26.2 miles. I had received text after text saying, "Enjoy today." "You don't have to prove anything today." "This is your victory lap not your marathon." These comments stuck with me, but I am stubborn. I had trained for months. I had given up too much morning sleep, alcohol, and certain foods to not give this my best effort. My dad's last words were, "No one is going to PR (personal record) today." I said, "Well at least one will!" (I was thinking there was no way in heck that was happening but wasn't knocking myself out of the game yet)

I got onto our team van. Looking around I felt like I wasn't worthy to be on this bus. These girls are true running girls. There were women that had BQed (Boston Qualified), one who was also pregnant and had BQed. A woman that ran two marathons within weeks of each other, the coach of a private school's long-distance running team, and soccer stars. Despite the feeling I did not belong, I was so thankful for the ride and warm place to hang out for hours. I was supposed to meet up with my two bosses, my charity team of three girls and my run team but all plans were kicked to the side because of the weather.

Half of the girls got off the bus and got ready to run. The rest of us still had a half hour of waiting. The anxiety level was growing. It was finally time to go. We walked about a half mile, maybe more, to the corrals and starting line. I had watched videos of this and these corrals were filled with people ready to cheer you on. There were a few there but not a lot. I had on a few pairs of gloves that were already soaking at this point. I had on a long sleeve shirt, a singlet, the jacket my dad gave me, a dollar store poncho, a buff, a hat and shower cap. As we were waiting for the porta potties I could feel my Reynolds phenomenon, a condition that causes some areas of the body, particularly the fingers and toes, feel numb in response to cold or stress, starting to go into full force. I had a run where I cried the whole time this training session because of it and no way was I letting that happen again. I also told myself if I get to my family (mom, dad, Meg, Chad and Charlie) at mile 10 and still feel this way no one will blame me for stopping.

Mile one through five were slow going. I knew they would be and should be, that this would keep me on track which needed to happen. I had a pace watch and voices in my ear saying, "Don't go off too fast; it is not worth it." The team's running coach had told me the faster you run in those first miles the more time you lose in the end. The first miles were close to my goal time according to my pace bracelet but a little off. I told myself I can't worry about that now. The miles were easy and downhill, I can easily see where you would lose yourself in this run. The crowds were not as much as I had heard before, but they were still out there. My Raynaud's was also really bothering me but had been since we got out of the van.

Five through ten were a little more challenging but I knew at ten my parents were waiting. I was still running in all the layers I had told myself I could throw off. I knew when I reached my parents if I wanted to call it quits I could, and I had a ride home. There was always next year. I got to my parents, and instead of stopping they gave me the drive to run faster!

Miles ten through fifteen was through Wellesley college and the scream tunnel. The girls came out with their "kiss me" signs and I slapped their hands and blew kisses but kept running. All these people out in the pouring rain just to cheer us on kept me going! The elites had already won. At mile fifteen Nicole, Steph, Madi and Mason were there. Five years earlier I was with Mason at the finish line during the attacks and I told him I would run the Boston Marathon someday. We had a good laugh at the impossibility of that idea. To get a huge hug from a thirteen-year old boy means a lot, that hug along with all the others were as valuable as the fuel.

Mile fifteen thru twenty was the part of the course I had been dreading. It was downhill at first, so I told myself not to get too carried away. At mile eighteen, the Newton Firehouse, my dear friends Jenna and Robert were there along with the surprise of Aunt Marge from California! This would prove to be so valuable. Their support would get me over the hills even Heartbreak Hill. I personally believe Heartbreak is not as bad as the first hill and thought the same when I trained on this hill. A guy I was running next to said, "Just make it to the lights, that's your first goal." A bunch of us chanted, "Lights!" At this point, I was seeing signs that Des had won. What an amazing thing to see! The knowledge that an American woman had won for the first time in thirty-five years was an unbelievable motivation for me! I thought "if she can do it, so can I!"

At mile twenty to twenty-three, I was still a few minutes off of my lofty goal which was fifteen minutes faster than my PR. However, I still thought there was a chance I may PR. I just needed to work so hard. Mile twenty-two was my own personal scream tunnel. Our team was volunteering at this station and everyone was cheering me on. I felt pretty important.

At miles twenty-three to twenty-five I thought, "there was no way I'm not doing it now!" My body had other thoughts, I had a huge cramp coming on. I ran over to a police officer asking him to open my hot shot. He offered to either help me with the cramp or call medics. I didn't want either I wanted my hot shot open. It was a rookie mistake not having them ready to open already.

Miles twenty-five to twenty-six point two - The home stretch! I told myself if I made it to this point I was crawling through the puddles if I had to. There was no DNF (did not finish) after all this work. The crowd support was huge at this point. All these people were standing outside in the rain. The right onto Hannaford left into Boylston is what everyone says it is - absolutely crazy! At this point I ran past Carlos the cowboy who had saved Jeff Bauman's leg five years ago! I also saw a few friends!

I crossed the finish line having PR'ed by eight minutes! All the training had paid off. I found my kids, Abby and Max, and my husband, Mike. They were soaking wet waiting for me! That was the best hug I ever got from all three of them. I was so cold! The kids and I jumped on the warming bus. The three of us took up one seat so more runners could get on.

The shower at my in-law's house could not have felt any better! I had hot chocolate which warmed me up. Mike and my father-in-law threw me a huge celebratory birthday dinner!

I absolutely will run again someday but probably not for a while. This memory of Boston and running in a poncho will stick with me for a long time!

Sarah Foley, Bib 15004

Old Lyme, CT, 44, 3:26:56

I've run 4 marathons in my life: NYC '99, San Diego Rock N' Roll '01, Hartford '16, Boston '18. I finished the first two marathons in approximately 4:05 and the second two in 3:27 and 3:26, respectively. The interesting observation here is why, after a hiatus of 15+ years, did my performance improve so significantly?

The key factors that I believe contribute the most are:

1) Diet (Let's face it, in my mid-twenties living in NYC, I wasn't exactly on a "wellness kick." It was all about happy hours, eating out, staying up late, etc. These days, I make green juice daily and try to eat whole, nutrient dense foods)

2) Training (Unlike most runners, I don't follow a traditional training program. I've never done a timed interval or speed workout in my life. Instead, I supplement my running with daily spin classes and strength training on my Peloton bike.)

3) Fire in the Belly (You have to want it bad, enough that you can endure suffering and grind through even the toughest circumstances. There's a quote I read on the Boston Buddies page that stuck with me, which is "Your MIND is

the athlete." You have to believe to achieve! I wanted to make my children proud, and come hell or high water, I was determined.)

As a single mom raising three kids and juggling two jobs, it's challenging finding the time to fit in sufficient training, particularly in the cold, dark winter months. The Peloton bike has been the solution to all of that. Now, there are no excuses. I can get a powerful cardio workout and instruction from the best fitness coaches from the comfort of my own home whenever I want. It has been a total game-changer in my life. I am not only competing with myself, but with other riders from all over the world. And it's not only about staying fit, it's my anti-depressant. It keeps me happy, motivated and productive in all aspects of my life.

Looking back on my running performance on April 16th, I'm proud that I was able to power through the brutal weather conditions and pull off a PR (by one minute). Boston is a race that I've always dreamed of doing, but never thought I would. As a student at Boston College in the early 1990's, I watched the runners go by every year and watched in awe. Having now achieved that goal, I thought I would feel a sense of closure. And in a way, I do. But there's still a fire in my belly and an inner voice calling out to me: "What if the conditions were better? Could I have run the marathon in 3:15? Or even faster?" There's only one way to find out. Keep showing up.

Myla Green, Bib 26767

Jamaica Plain, MA, 34, 5:46:59

I am honored to have run the 2018 Boston Marathon with team Fenway! I raised $13,000 for Fenway Health through my fundraising efforts.

Growing up in Ashland at mile 2, I used to go to the start line and cheer for the runners. I would marvel that these people were actually *choosing* to run 26.2 miles and would try to imagine them running all the way to Boston without stopping.

As an adult, after many years of doing almost no exercise and being fat-shamed by two different doctors, I discovered running and found that I enjoyed it. I loved that I could just put on my sneakers and go outside for a run, and that I could explore the surrounding area on foot no matter where I was. I worked up from walk-running to running two miles every other day over several years. Then right after my 30th birthday, I ran my first race with a few friends, and was hooked. I went from my first 5k race to 5 miles to a 10k to running a half marathon in just over a year. I was astounded that my body was able to keep doing these incredible feats and keep going mile after mile. I was slowly beginning to conceptualize that I was a real runner!

When I was preparing to train for my first marathon, I talked to my doctor at Fenway Health about it. As I told her my plan, I cringed - I was afraid she would say I was too heavy to run a marathon or make some thinly-veiled judgy comment about the health of my knees. Instead, she put down her pen, looked right at me and exclaimed, "That's amazing! All of us should exercise that much." I have run two marathons in the last two years, both of which were incredibly powerful and humbling experiences. I pushed myself beyond what I thought I could do, and then kept going.

The Boston Marathon is not only the marathon I grew up watching wistfully; it's also perhaps the most famous marathon among runners world-wide. If a marathon is the ultimate running achievement, Boston is the ultimate marathon. For me, the opportunity to run the Boston Marathon is a dream - that I almost didn't allow myself to dream - come true! I can hardly believe that I'll get to run through familiar towns and see familiar faces on the world-famous course, all the while supporting a wonderful and worthy organization.

The mission of Fenway Health is to enhance the wellbeing of the lesbian, gay, bisexual and transgender community and all people in our neighborhoods and beyond through access to the highest quality health care, education, research and advocacy. They are a fantastic organization known for inclusivity and cutting-edge work, and are where me, and many queer, trans, and straight Bostonians get our health care. I am proud to be a large woman marathoner and am so glad to have a doctor who is supportive of my passion for running.

Monday was an amazing day. I am honored by the incredible outpouring of support - so many texts, posts, calls, people following me on the live tracking, complete strangers through the "fatgirlrunning" fb group making signs for me on the course, and the spectators - much fewer than usual but so vocal and supportive! I am so grateful to my dad for making the "I'm From Ashland!" sign which I ran with through my hometown, to the delight of locals. I think I got more cheers in Ashland than anyone! Totally great way to begin the race.

If Wellesley College's "Scream Tunnel" was at all diminished from the weather, I couldn't tell - they were SO energetic and supportive. I was smiling for miles, and, as was promised, heard them from a half mile away before I got there. Thanks for the kiss, woman with the "kiss me I'm gay" sign!

I was able to accept the race for what it was at the beginning - a rainy, cold, windy mess. I stopped avoiding puddles early on because there was no point, no way my shoes could get any more soaked. Athlete's Village in Hopkinton looked like Woodstock - mud everywhere. I gave my glasses to my dad at mile 3 because I couldn't see through them. Check out my fashionable last-minute rain outfit in the attached photos! (Thanks mom for the help and dad for the drop cloth we turn into a poncho.) I was determined to enjoy this race and many spectators seemed happy to see me happy/giving them two thumbs up.

I had some hamstring pain and stopped to stretch a few times; stopped to pee twice; stopped to hug friends and family briefly; and slowed to futz with my rain gear multiple times. My headphones were taped shut for waterproofing, so I could listen to music but not call people (which was OK!) I didn't get too cold, which I am grateful for as many runners (about 2000) had to seek medical attention, mostly for hypothermia. My only "injury" is the chafing I got from my hoodie's zipper just below my collar bone.

I wanted to get through the hills and then run like hell. After a bit of pain post Heartbreak Hill, once I got to mile 23 I began to book it and increased my speed each mile. In my past marathons I was only able to speed up at mile 25, but this one I had a decent amount of energy left (probably because my waterlogged clothing plus sideways rain and puddles prevented me from going as fast as I would have liked). At mile 25, I shed my drop cloth poncho and ran even faster. My dear friend Charles showed up biked alongside me.

I cried as soon I saw the Hereford sign ahead of me and turned right onto Hereford and left onto Boylston Street simultaneously crying and grinning ecstatically. I missed achieving a personal best by 2 minutes, but I wouldn't trade the hugs and selfies and connection with all of you for anything. Also, this course is much harder than flat Philly (my current best marathon time), plus considering the absurd weather, my stomach issues the first two hours of the race, running in about 10 extra lbs. of waterlogged clothing (literally), and my hamstring suddenly acting up, I think I can declare this race a personal victory.

I'm completely pleased with the race, and also think I might have to run Boston again to have the full experience in better conditions. I'll give myself a few weeks to think about it.

Finally, I received donations from <u>178</u> of people(!!), and together we raised $12,586 for Fenway Health! I am so happy to support their groundbreaking work. Thank you for the many kinds of support that helped me get to this goal and through race.

Thanks everyone and much love,

Myla

PS - Huge thank you to everyone who braved the rain, wind, and cold to cheer for me and the other runners - especially Roger and Rachelle (who came all the way from New York to see me run), my dad and stepmother Chuck and Andrea (who met me on the course at mile 3 AND somewhere in

Newton/Brookline), my mom and stepdad Sharon and Allen (and my mom for calling me several times to check on me and sending me energy on Heartbreak Hill, plus live Facebooking all my progress), Eli at mile 23 (my marathon buddy!), Jessica, Ilana, and Emil at mile 20 with the great sign, Lilly at mile 25 with a sign for me, Gamal who I didn't know would be there and may not have been expecting to see me but gave a huge cheer when I passed, Amy, Cayla, and Hannah at mile 20.5, Carolyn and Bill at mile 22 I think? Malka and Aliza at mile 21 with oranges (and Aliza running alongside me for a few minutes), Neige for big hugs at mile 20, my trainer Kate at mile 18 and for inspiring me with her previous Boston Marathons (not to mention helping me get in shape for my marathons), Sarah, Joey, and Emily for the big November Project reception at mile 18 and Sarah for running me a few minutes down the street, Steve, Linda, and Sara for the hugs at Coolidge Corner, Charles for surprising me at mile 25 and biking alongside me, and MJ for meeting me with warm clothes at the finish after cheering me on super hard on Boylston Street as I ran towards the finish! Also, great to run into new marathon expo friend Lumina and run together for a few minutes during the race. Thanks Pella, and Nalasa for calling several times even though my mic wouldn't work.

Richard Brodsky, Bib 24241

Atlantic Beach, NY, 65, 4:48:09

My name is Richard Brodsky and I'm President of the Richard M. Brodsky Foundation. I'm HIV+ since 1997, a brain cancer survivor since 2002, and a marathon runner for life. At age 65, I finally qualified to run the 2018 Boston, Marathon.

Boston was my 58th marathon and it was very questionable that I would be able to run my first Boston Marathon. I took a bad fall at the end of December 2017, and my orthopedist said I did not need surgery, but my arm was placed in a soft sling for 8 weeks and I could not start running again until the end of February plus I needed extensive physical therapy. My doctor said it was questionable if I could ever lift my left arm above 90 degrees again. And now I only had 4 weeks in March + 2 weeks to taper to train for the Boston Marathon.

I pride myself as being a smart runner and I'm very much aware of how to run the shortest distance which is usually to hug the inside corners, but this was not possible because the torrential rain forced the runners to run closer to the middle of the road, so instead of running 26.2 miles, I ran 26.6 miles which added 5 minutes, so I finished in 04:48:09. I also took a bad fall after running just .3 miles. I was feeling good at the start and running a 9-minute mile and then started passing runners as I was running an 8.5-minute mile. But then I took a bad fall as I stepped on a plastic garbage bag which was on the soaked road and down I went. It took a full minute for me to get up and my knees were hurting a lot. But did I really come to Boston to run .3 miles and call it quits. My hotel was 4 miles down the course so if there was really a problem I could stop after 4 miles, so I knew I had to get up. I also realized I am running for everyone living with HIV and cancer because there are no other runners in the world who run marathons and are living with HIV and brain cancer, so I could not quit. Even though my time was slow, I was thrilled just to finish and could take solace in what race director Dave McGillivray wrote, "The athletes faced worse conditions than those on the ice sheets at the Antarctica Marathon which I (Dave) recently ran."

I had been taking my wife Jodi to the Boston Marathon, every year since 2012. It had been very frustrating for me being in Boston and not doing what I normally do: I run marathons and also organize marathons and 5K Events. I even have a pair of Bill Rodgers running shoes he trained in and a cap and shirt he wore. One day I hope to have a fundraiser for my Foundation where I can sell the shoes to raise money for my Foundation. Hmmmm… maybe that money should be returned to a Boston charity and I could run the 2019 Boston Marathon for a Boston charity as I have not qualified to run the 2019 Boston Marathon. I know I can sign up to raise money for an approved Boston Marathon charity but any donations I receive will cut into donations I need to raise for the 13th annual World AIDS Marathon in Kisumu, Kenya where we only charge Kenyans $1 and they can buy a t-shirt for another dollar.

A few paragraphs back I mentioned I was the only runner in the world who runs marathons and is living with HIV and brain cancer. I've been running marathons with both illnesses since 2002 and the only reason why I just found out I'm the only runner is because I had to change my anti-seizure medicine and that also meant I had to change my AIDS medicine. I was not sure if I should change the medicine before or after the Boston Marathon, so I did a search on the Internet for HIV+ brain cancer marathon runners. I wanted to write to someone who was living with both illnesses, but to my surprise there was no one else running marathons living with HIV and brain cancer. I started to wonder why and then I realized that many people who are living with HIV are depressed and people living with brain cancer do not live that long. It has always been important for me to remain upbeat, lead a healthy lifestyle, and being married to a marathon-running-loving wife helps a lot, too. Jodi and I both do our part to help eliminate the stigma of AIDS. I get so much positive feedback when I wear the shirt below.

I'm actually writing a movie script based on a book I wrote, Jodi, the Greatest Love Story Ever Told, and the work the Richard M. Brodsky Foundation does. The Foundation will be sponsoring its 13th annual World AIDS Marathon in Kisumu, Kenya and the 4 days leading up to the marathon we will be sponsoring 4 orphan dinner dances for 800 – 1,000 Kenyan orphans plus we provide medical care for 200+ orphans. If you are a doctor or nurse, not only do you get to examine and treat the orphans, you get to dine and dance with them plus they get to run with the Kenyans on World AIDS Day. And I do mean run with the Kenyans as the marathon course is four loops which means the Kenyans will more than likely lap you, unless you do a sub-three-hour marathon,

My wife Jodi and I stayed near the start of the Boston Marathon and we had to walk about a mile from where we were dropped off as we could not get any closer. It was cold and rainy and the buses traveling from Boston to the start splashed water on us. Thrilled to be at the start we had to negotiate walking through inches of mud to get underneath the tent. Then we had to run another mile to get to the start. I recall some runners discussing whether or not to wear racing flats or heavier waterproof shoes. It hardly mattered because everyone's shoes were waterlogged at the start or at least that was my experience from starting at about 11:20 am.

It was kind of like a Biblical experience and wondering why Noah's Ark could not have included my wife and me. Looking up at the sky I asked if I could ask God one question. When he didn't answer I asked, "Why me and why this year?" And then another bucket of rain dumped on me and another 30 – 35 mile per wind gust rustled by and I realized I'm still running, and you will not get me to quit even if I have to slow down. The funny thing was Heartbreak Hill was not as bad as I had heard. I followed another runner's advice and did not look up plus I knew the last 6 miles was almost all downhill.

It wasn't a pretty finish as I was exhausted. I managed to find a BAA official and asked him to take a photo, so I threw both arms up in the air and gave it all I had.

It does not look like I will be running the 2019 Boston Marathon but there is always 2020. One thing I will try and do at the 2019 Miami Marathon is finish with a few people living with HIV and or cancer to give hope to others living with HIV and cancer and their families and include this scene in the movie script.

263

Even though I will not be the actor, I think my wife and I running with others living with HIV and cancer could be an uplifting, final, feel-good scene.

To read more about the World AIDS Marathon in Kisumu, Kenya on World AIDS Day visit www.worldaidsmarathon.com.

Natalie Dorset, Bib 23377

New York, NY, 51, 4:24:09

It has been one week. One week since My First Boston Marathon. One Week since the skies opened up and unleashed a deluge that washed away my thoughts and reasoning. I have had such a hard time gathering my thoughts, because my thoughts have never been so all over the place, so fractures, so scattered. How can I be so fiercely proud of my accomplishment, and yet, so profoundly disappointed? How

can I think the "success" in getting to Hopkinton was shared among all my running women, and sisters, and friends, and yet, the "failure" of not meeting my time was singularly mine? How can I think it was the best running day of my life, and yet the worst? How can I be glad I soldiered on, yet think I should have stopped myself?

My journey to Hopkinton began right after my terrible New York City Marathon in 2016. I had stomach pains after poorly mixed sports drink and walked the second half and came in at 4:39 still a PR at the time. My Brother Irapaul told me not long after that he likely had a spot with Team For Kids for Boston 2018. We had been through so much together and shared so much of our running journey that I knew I had to get to Boston for 2018.

After almost 10 months of training (a treadmill injury made me miss my Spring attempt) I ran my BQ in Sept of 17 (dropping my time 44 mins 8 secs) and began my training for Boston in Dec. 16 months after I first started training to BQ, I'd get to run Boston on the 16th of April.

And then, the cold rains came.

I brought extra shoes, a poncho, shower cap, rain jacket, garbage bags, extra gloves, only the extra shoes helped. Within 4 minutes of being in Athletes' Village, my feet went ankle deep in an icy mud puddle and it took 5 people to pull me out. I changed shoes, and then they called my wave. As wave 3 was still struggling to get out of Athletes' Village, and make it to our start corrals, they announced "oh what the heck, wave 4, you go too." It was mass confusion.

I managed to run into my friend Jan, and I thought we each had to go to our separate corrals, and then hundreds of people just mushed together and shoved forward. I was glad to find Jan again, and I ran with her a little and then I had to use the Porta Potty. I almost caught back up to her when I had to go again, I got a little annoyed with myself, why was I being so weak willed? I'd run the first 21 miles of the course before, so, I knew not to fall in to the fast pacing trap. Let Jan go, run your own race.

I was very cold, and felt a lot of discomfort, but I decided I was going to smile and enjoy myself, despite the circumstances, I worked too hard to get here, I was NOT going to be miserable. Unexpectedly I saw some Certified Running Nut friends at mile six, and I was happy to hear one of them say "here she comes, oh look, she's smiling". When I see their pic of me at mile six, I look pretty happy, I also see that I already don't have my poncho, big mistake. (By mile 4, the winds were so strong, they kept ripping my raincoat hood, and the hood of the poncho off my head. My hands were already frozen, so I had to ask spectators to put my hood back on, tighten it down etc. One gust of wind was so strong, it was blowing the tied poncho hood back on my throat so tightly I felt like I was choking. I freaked out and ripped the poncho off).

After I saw my friends I told myself I at least had to make it half way. By mile 13, the smile was plastered on my face, but I felt worse than I have felt ever on a run. I had never been so cold, my hands were useless, and I had used the porta potty three times, but, I was still under two hours, so, I could make my goal, I pressed on. At this point, my thinking was like this. "I have never felt so cold in my life, there is something wrong with my body, it's never done this before, I've never had to keep going to the bathroom. If I smile, it'll trigger endorphins and my muscles won't hurt so much, so, I'll keep going and I'll keep smiling"

The spectators (God Bless them for being out there) liked that there was a happy runner, and, I got a lot of support, and spectators chatting with me. I hardly noticed when my thinking switched to this "I feel terrible, now I have a migraine too, and I can't see out of my left eye properly, but, I'll keep smiling. I should probably go to medical, but, I feel like I'm going to die, and I shouldn't take up their time and space. If I'm out here smiling, when I die they can tell my Mother I died happy doing what I love"

The muscle spasms started around mile 17, and then I thought "I just have to make it to mile 18 ½ cause TFK is expecting me" then I had to get to Dan at mile 24 "my phone isn't working, I can't call him, he won't find me" and my Sister and Brother in Law at mile 25 ½. It wasn't until I turned that famous corner on to Boylston Street, and, with the finish in sight, I had to stop and hold on to a police officer until I got my balance, that I really knew that I was in bad shape and should have stopped ages ago. I had wandered by the medical tent at mile eighteen, and vaguely pointed out my jumping muscles before running off saying I'd find medical at the finish.

When I look at my Sister's video of me near the finish, I know she sees me happy and smiling. I think I look demented. I know how much I hurt at that point, and I was trying so hard to mask it. The painful, medieval experience in the medical tent is a whole other story. The next day, hearing about everybody else's experiences and doing some research confirmed it was hypothermia. Apparently, Cold Diuresis is when your body is trying to protect itself from hypothermia, and it forces all the "extra" liquid out of your body to focus on pumping blood, well, that explains the porta potty stops. Still disappointed though.

Checking in on the Boston Marathon Training Page, I learn that because of the torrential downpours, some people skipped the porta potties and just let Mother Nature wash things away. Is that what I should have done? Did I waste time by stopping, especially since my hands weren't working? Was I wussing out when I stopped because it was "dry" in there? I trained so hard for so long, surely I hadn't failed at my goal because I was weak willed? Could it be? I thought I had learned about myself and the effects of hypothermia until someone asked me "knowing the symptoms as you do now, would you stop yourself next time?" I paused, and, I had to admit, I didn't know. Maybe the drive to finish what I started would prove once again to be greater than the drive to take care of myself. Not good.

I took a little break, I had a great running weekend, complete with PRs and AG awards a week and a half later. I don't like when it rains, I take a raincoat everywhere, but, it has now been three weeks since My First Boston Marathon. Three weeks since the skies opened up and ripped me apart emotionally, and I am starting to heal.

Sheri Martin Lubniewski, Bib 17667

Geneva, IL, 37, 3:42:15

Well I started on my quest to Boston back in 2015. I ran the Fox Valley marathon in 3:39:01 which was barely a BQ (my age group I need 3:40 to qualify). I submitted my application (because you never know) and got rejected. I wasn't shocked but knew I could do better.

3 months later I signed up for the Kiawah marathon and ran a 3:37:53. It was another hot and humid marathon but a much better shot at getting in. But I signed up for the BQ.2 marathon in Geneva for the fall of 2016 just to best that time. I figured in 9 months I would have plenty of time to get faster.

During a tempo run early in the morning in June 2016 I sprained my ankle. It was a bad sprain too. It was so stupid because I tripped on the sidewalk! That took me out for 2.5 months of no running. I was doing everything in my power to stay fit though (lots of swimming and biking and rock climbing). But needless to say, running the BQ.2 marathon was out of the question because I was not given the go ahead to run outside until the last week in August (the BQ marathon is the 1st week in September). I decided to train for the Indy marathon in November (with 9 weeks to train) and submit my Kiawah marathon time for Boston.

One of the worst days of my life came when I got my second rejection letter from Boston. But this time I missed by 1 second. Yes, that was not a typo. 1 second!

I was beside myself. I was recovering from injury, missing my goal marathon and not getting to run Boston, again! With 9 weeks to go I knew I had to lay it all out there at Indy. I went to Indy with that 1 second rejection letter in my suit case to remind me what I was fighting for. And I did it. I got a 3:32:07 at Indy which put me almost 8 minutes under the qualifying time. I was so emotional that day and for days after because I knew that finally I was not going to see another rejection letter.

Training for this 2018 Boston was going really well. I was crushing my times until another freak injury almost took me out 6 weeks before Boston. I had a very bad sprain of my Tibialis Anterior in which I couldn't run for 3 weeks. I was beside myself. How could I come so far and not run the race I've been working so hard for? I decided whatever happened I would run or walk it either way. I wasn't going to sit it out. Luckily, I recovered enough to get a few miles in before the marathon. I knew I had lost fitness and in no condition to PR, but I was so grateful to have the opportunity to just run Boston vs walking it.

And I guess it worked out to my advantage because there was no way I was going to PR in those conditions! But I made the most of the weekend. Enjoyed doing a lot of things around town and obsessing over what I was going to wear for the craziest ride of my life.

Some people asked if I was upset that I got such bad weather. And I tell them that the race was definitely a different experience for sure. Was it fun running in 38 degrees, soaking wet with a strong head wind? No! Was wearing 2 ponchos and 4 layers annoying? Yes! At various points did I want to cry because I was so wet and cold? Absolutely? But I made a point to remind myself at every single mile that I was so blessed to have this opportunity and that it is only fitting that such a tough journey would end with another tough test of my determination and quest to become a Boston marathon finisher. I think I would have been disappointed if I got a perfect weather day. It just wouldn't be the same. I hope to one day come back and run Boston in better conditions. However, for my first Boston, the conditions were just right!

Sarah Bachand, Bib 11139

Lachine, CAN, 41, 3:19:19

Apparently, a movie came out a few years ago called "Sarah loves running". I've never seen it but I'm sure I'd love it. I've been running since I was a little girl, but my passion for running bloomed once I started running after my kids. The little one was two years old. I was running after time, so I decided to run a little more. I can look excessive for those who run less than me, but I work hard to maintain balance and harmony between family, work, friends and laundry. No more than two marathons a year plus a few other races.

Being a full-time single mom, I am blessed to have very independent kids and to live near work which allows me to mix in my training and run to work. This way, my kids don't have to suffer from their mom's passion. I think my Strava has more mileage than my car.

Why do I love running so much? Maybe because I was lost in my twenties and everyone I knew seemed to walk proudly toward their diplomas. Maybe running gives the sense of direction that once felt so inaccessible. Maybe running makes me feel invincible and strong. It might allow me to meditate and take me far away from daily worries such as bickering children and lost bus passes. It takes me far away from the powerless feeling I get when I try to help my daughter figure out why a shop owner buys 120 boxes of 6 granola bars. He later sells 520 bars and we have to figure out how many are left.

Every morning at 6am, I wake my daughters. Their breakfasts are ready and lunch boxes lay near the door. Mom takes off greeted by the many surprises mother nature has to offer. There's no such thing as bad weather. It's all a matter of clothing! April 16th, 2018 was the day of the mythical Boston marathon, it's 122nd edition. It was my fourth Boston. With an average of 100 km a week since the beginning of the year and several hilly long runs with solid runners, I was ready to face that journey that still intimidates me the fourth time around.

Monday morning, it's 6 am and I haven't left my hotel room, but I can clearly hear the whistling sound of the wind outside. Rain fogs up my windows and the view of a somber wet Boston. I feel like I'm going to the slaughter house on my way to the school bus that will drive us 42 km away from my cozy hotel room. I can't see the rowers this year as the bus windows are covered with humidity. I wait one and a half hours in the big white tent that will greet 27 000 runners on a muddy slippery ground. After 15 minutes of walking in the rain and cold towards my corral, everything happened fast. All I know is that I went for a long run with thousands of passionate runners.

Two days before running this marathon, there was a sense of deception of having done all this preparation and having to show what we got in this awful weather. Once we crossed the finish line, the feeling shifts to pride for having completed the 2018 Boston marathon in that crazy weather. For my part, not only did I PR but I ranked 7th among Quebec women.

After being greeted by my loving partners arms and having changed in dry clothes, my trembling hands tried to turn my phone on. I was swept with emotion watching a congratulations video my colleagues sent me which then plunged my thoughts to Nicole a life marathoner that left us 2 months ago. She was always the first to congratulate me on Facebook.

The 2018 Boston marathon is my biggest sports achievement. It's a challenge that I chose to do knowing full well the preparation it takes, the course, the distance and a finish line after 42 km.

My dear Nicole had to face her challenge without all this preparation, not knowing if there was a finish line. In fact, this challenge, she did not choose.

Fortunately, her family was as powerful and supportive as the volunteers and 500 000 spectators I saw on Monday.

Maybe I like running cause it gives me a sense of direction and maybe it is because it gives me time for me. It also may be because I have great admiration for Nicole and others that face big challenges that they did not chose. So maybe it's to push my limits and convince myself that I might be strong in a future life challenge bigger than my control. Maybe it's not important to know why I love running. All I know is that Monday morning, when I crossed that finish line on Boylston street in Boston, I had never felt so alive. I will therefore try to keep doing it a little more while I can.

Wendy Tocha, Bib 17606

St Petersburg, FL, 41, 3:34:23

I am 41 years old and have been running for 30 years. I have completed 14 marathons, 9 Ironmans, 6 Half Ironmans, many half marathons, 5K'sm 10K's, triathlons, duathlons, and etc. I started running when I was 11 years old. After watching my dad do races I decided I wanted to participate too. So from then on I just kept running. Ran in middle school, high school, and college. In college I noticed just running was taking a toll on my body and I was always intrigued by triathlons. So cross training began, and I got hooked on multi-sport events.

I was born and raised in Buffalo, NY. Never thought I would leave until I met some people from Florida who invited me down a few times to train. I loved the idea of training all year round outside!! So 6 months later I moved to St. Petersburg, FL in 2003. Two weeks after I moved, I was hit by a car doing a holiday training ride. 14 of us got hit. Two surgeries and 16 months of physical therapy resulting in permanent nerve damage in right shoulder/arm. Long story short I did a marathon the following year keeping my arm secured in a gait belt while I ran.

That same year I completed Ironman Florida swimming with one arm and running with my arm tucked in the gait belt again. From that I learned to appreciate physical therapy, physical challenges, injuries on all different levels. So I ended up going back to school for physical therapy and have been doing it since 2010. I continued to stay focused and kept doing races.

I met a coach by the name of Joe Burgasser (Florida Forerunners) in Florida in 2013. I always thought how cool it would be to qualify for Boston but didn't know how realistic it would be anytime soon. With Joe's coaching and amazing running buddies in 2014 I qualified at the Lehigh Valley Marathon for Boston 2015. Since then I have done Boston 2015, 2016, 2017, 2018, and qualified for 2019. My goal is to stay strong and continue qualifying for Boston as many years in a row as I can. The running community near me and abroad are so motivating and encouraging. They are some of the nicest people I've ever met my life. From my past experiences and what I've learned around me from different stories and people I've met. Never give up. Stay focused and go after your dreams. I hope by sharing my story it helps others and inspires others just like many stories have inspired me.

Nicki Houston Cave, Bib 18301

Sachse, TX, 44, 3:57:31

Several days have passed since the 122nd Boston Marathon and I've enjoyed reading all of the inspiring stories that came out of a race that has been described as "perfect chaos" and "epic misery." While my story may not be out of the ordinary, I believe it captures the struggle many of us faced along with the mental toughness and perseverance we needed to cross the finish line that day given all the elements that were against us. The whole Boston Marathon weekend experience was amazing…well, all except for the race part.

I'm normally a pretty positive person. Even when we left the hotel in the pouring rain and I was juggling my gear, my extra pair of running shoes, a blanket, several layers of extra clothes, and grasping tightly on to my umbrella while speed walking to keep up with my friends to reach the check-in tent—I was in good spirits. It wasn't until we got off the bus in athletes' village that my spirit was crushed. I died a little inside with each step toward the start. When we stepped off the bus into 30 mph wind with the rain hitting my face. When we arrived at the tent with two feet of water where the runners had to wait. When I opened the port-a-potty door and thought someone pooped on the floor and I had to stand in it until my friend, Melissa, told me it was mud. After falling several times; sliding in the mud; dodging flying umbrellas; and taking the longest, coldest walk of my life to the start line.

My only saving grace was the umbrella, being wrapped up with Melissa's body heat in her table cloth and laughing hysterically together in disbelief along the way. We thought about quitting then but we had already bought our Boston gear (and who could reach us to pick us up).

I thought well at least the worst part was over. Somehow, we were late to the starting line and ended up in coral seven. We finally started running. The first few miles were miserable but tolerable and I felt like we had a good pace going. Seeing Melissa's family at mile six really boosted our spirits. Even with all that I had no idea what the Boston sky had in store. My mom always said if you don't have anything nice to say then don't say anything at all. I don't think I said one word the whole race. Out of my 8 marathons, this was the quietest race from the participants that I've ever experienced.

I kept thinking it couldn't get any worse and then it did. Over and over again. We stopped around mile 7 to use the restroom and I had a medic help me get my energy gel out of my back pocket because I couldn't feel my hands. About mile 10, I couldn't feel my feet and I could feel my legs increasingly getting worse with pain. We stopped again around mile 21 to use the restroom and to try to take another energy gel. We spent what felt to be about 5 minutes trying to get it out of my pocket. We never could get it out. I felt bad that I was holding Melissa back. I still thought it couldn't get worse. But it did.

The rain poured down sideways. The winds seemed to be worse. My legs were in excruciating pain. And I broke. I was crying so hard I was hyperventilating. Then I realized I need to breathe so I could run. I tried to get control so Melissa wouldn't see me. She kept looking back and I told her that her finger pointing would not work today, and that she should run ahead. She tried so hard to keep me with her, I just couldn't mentally and physically push past the misery.

At mile 22, I was looking for "heartbreak hill" and then realized we must have passed it. At mile 24, I tried to hide behind people so she would run ahead. I knew she could run faster and warm up. I wanted to walk so badly given the pain in my legs but knew my body temperature would get too low, so I went as fast as I physically could get my legs to move. I thought just push through for 16 more minutes. Then I realized it would be closer to 20 minutes and right at that moment, it started pouring even harder. I cried again.

I don't remember hearing the crowds on Boylston. I just remember thinking I have to get to the finish line. I felt such relief when I crossed that line. Then I was panicking looking for a blanket. I walked what seemed like forever for my medal. I walked what felt like another mile and saw bananas. I saw people taking pictures and thought, *how are they functioning right now and where are the blankets?!!!!* I finally got to the blankets and the lady asked if I was ok. I told her I wasn't sure and started to sob again. She called for the paramedic. He wheeled me back to the start line where the medic tent was which seemed like an eternity.

They got me back to a bed and my temp was low (93 degrees). I'm not sure how long I was in there. I was laying there shaking uncontrollably thinking, *now what?* I'm never going out there again. I still had to make my way a few blocks to get my warm clothes. The wonderful medic let me borrow their phone so my friends knew I was ok. They got my temp back up to 96 degrees and I somehow made it to gear check and to a building to get my warm clothes on and had my phone. Melissa and her husband, Gage, were amazing! They found me and helped me back to the hotel.

The 2018 Boston Marathon is by far the hardest thing I've ever done—and I've given birth to four kids. The only thing that kept me going was that I already spent the money on my Boston gear (I wouldn't feel right wearing it unless I crossed that finish line) and I wanted that medal. It really put things into perspective when I passed a handicap runner and realized how tough they were and how lucky I am to be healthy and able to do what I do.

On a more positive note, Boston treats all their runners like celebrities and has wonderful people. That city generates amazing positive energy despite the miserable weather.

After my mom read this she said, "Oh honey, you didn't have to do all that for a t-shirt." I replied, "Mom, it was for a jacket. A really cool jacket." Some may wonder why? Why put yourself through that much misery for a jacket or a medal? For me it's about what the Boston Marathon finisher's medal represents. It's about the blood, sweat and tears put toward reaching a goal. It's all the sacrifices it took to get there. It's the 55 to 65 miles each week, the 4 a.m. alarm clocks, the painful track workouts, the hill workouts, and the 20-mile runs. It's about making sure it was worth killing myself in the qualifying marathon that got me there. But most of all, it's about the incredible opportunity to run on the exact same course and to cross the same finish line as the world's best elite runners. What other sport can you do that?

As my friend said, we will cherish that medal as a reminder of the day, the entire weekend, and how much fun we had, how our abs hurt from all the laughing, the friendly Boston people including the incredibly kind woman who bought us a round of drinks at the airport just to celebrate us. We celebrate the hard earned physical and mental battle fought through every step along that journey.

It's easy to keep going when things are in your favor. It's the challenging times that shows us who we really are. This is when we find the strength within us (that sometimes we didn't even know we had) to get to where we want to be.

Carlos Soto Tock, Bib 9467

Quetzaltenango, GUA, 50, 3:18:38

Running the Boston Marathon in 2015 didn't seem like a good idea the night before, at least not for me. Conditions were similar to 2018 except it was a little warmer. Rain was predicted to pound the runners the entire race. One week before my doctor still hadn't cleared me to run. I had been so sick, so energy depleted, so bad, that it seemed unlikely that I was going to be able to finish. Early that night April 19th I decided not to do it, later that same night I decided I didn't want to live without trying my hardest to reach my goal. It took me 8 years to BQ, so I was not going to leave Boston without crossing that finish line. It was a crazy cold rainy day, too much for this old man born and raised in mild temperatures. I hurt so bad that I  decided to quit several times during the course without actually doing it. After I finished, I ended up in the medical tent, hypothermic and in the worst shape ever possible, but maybe the worst part were the hallucinations I had while I was running. It was madness out there for my family when they weren't able to find me, I gave them a real scary time. They made me promise not to do such a stupid thing again and I did, gladly.

It took me almost a year to be able to recover physically and mentally. For months I broke into tears when I commented about my hallucinations and the fear of being out in the rain. But I became a runner that day when I crossed that finish line. There's nothing they can throw at me that I cannot handle. You see it's because of that that I found 2018 not to be so bad, I was there in worst conditions and overcame it.

I remember a message from a guy who saw one of my comments in the BAA Facebook page and asked me if I wanted to join a group to be formed. I am glad I said yes and became one of the first members, and you know what? It would have been so much easier on that day April 20, 2015 if the Boston Buddies would have been there watching my back. We are in this together, like.... Forever.

John Hadcock

Dedham, MA

As I stood at Heartbreak Hill cheering on my friends at Boston this year, I could not help but feel a sense of dread for coming thousands of miles and training for hours on end. I arrived at Heartbreak about 10:30. I never imagined that we would have weather worse than the forecast. Despite the weather I knew my friends, many who I never met would persevere, dig deep and fight tooth and nail from start to finish. All I could think that two days before I was competing in the BAA 5K in perfect conditions and wishing I could trade weather condition for my Boston Buddies.

While Marathon Monday was the end of the chapter, my beginning was in November 2016 when I was invited to join a Boston Marathon Training Facebook Page. I think I was number 5. We now have over 3000! Along the way I have met so many great people, not because they are great runners (many are) but because we care so much about each other. There is incredible support for all!

Even though I did not run Boston this year, my favorite runs were Fred Lebow ½, the March 24 Hopkinton to BC run, the BAA 5K, Cheers, and, of course the Boston Buddies Shakeout run the day before the big day. I had the honor of organizing the Boston Buddies Shakeout run, in my adopted city of Boston. We even got a pic with Bill Rodgers!

I am so thankful to be part of this group. You are a second family and am excited to be lining up in 2019!

Some race day tips, mostly for first timers:

- Stay to the left when going through the water stops. The left-side water stops are after the right-side water stops. Most runners go to the first one they see. The left side is always less crowded than the right.

- There are water/Gatorade stops every mile. I prefer Gatorade because it gets me everything, hydration, carbs and electrolytes. Plus, I cannot do Gu so I rely on the Gatorade.

- Like most other big marathons, you will be out there a long time prior to the race. The school buses drop you off. Make sure you dress appropriately. I always go to a Salvation Army to pick up a zippered sweatshirt that are easy to dispose of.

- For the first timers I am sure you have heard about the up hills and down hills. Respect the downhill at the start of the race. Going out too hard can wreck your race. Once you hit the top of Heartbreak you have a long downhill. If your quads are wrecked, you will find out quickly. Hence the need to train on down hills and up hills. When I train for Boston I have a 1.5-2 mile uphill and downhill on Beacon Street to train on. it is hugely helpful.

- Don't fight the crowds at the start. It takes at least 2 miles to get breathing room, sometimes longer.

Dan Clemo, Bib 5349

Calgary, AB, 36, 2:52:57

As new parents, my wife and I were like ships passing in the night. The only time we spent together was when we attempted to catch a few fleeting moments of sanity in front of the TV, typically scarfing down whatever fast food we gathered on the ride home. As you can imagine this was a recipe for disaster, and when my wife proposed joining a local running program to get in shape and spend a little more constructive time together I first thought, 'The sleep deprivation has clearly gotten to her, but I could set aside my complete and utter distain for running to support my wife.'

Our first run was a 2-mile lap around our local lake. That day I recall my wife moving like a graceful gazelle galloping down the trail with rays of sunshine defining her silhouette as she elegantly floated across the freshly paved pathway. Me on the other hand, I looked like a wounded elephant, slapping my feet against the pavement gasping for air until I abruptly veered to the left to expel whatever McMeal I had just recently eaten.

While this was a less than an ideal introduction to any sport, it was the running community that day which instantly grabbed me. Everyone from young to old, slow to fast, had the same desire to compete. Not with one another, but to be better today than they were yesterday. Within that first year I completed two half marathons and my first marathon. With every race I was able to breakdown mental barriers to what I thought was possible, and then a magical unicorn came into my life. One that put this crazy aspiration to run a marathon greater than 30 minutes faster than what I could currently do. That day I looked up what my goal marathon pace would be, and I eagerly set out on a run to see how long I could maintain that pace. The answer was a grossly disappointing 1 mile. What the hell was I going to do for the other 25.2!

After three years of dedication and multiple near miss marathons, I finally qualified at the Edmonton Marathon in 2017, and 9 months later my wife and I were at 30,000 feet preparing to descend on the mecca of running for the very first time. It was absolutely everything I had imagined. The sun was shining, the old-world charm of Boston was at its apex and runners weren't just the odd occupant on the sidewalk but rather blanketing the streets in herds. But the honeymoon was not destined to last. As the rain and winds picked up, my plans and goals seemed to fade along with the dreams of a sunny run.

While historically I had been incredibly disciplined in my pre-race dinner, this night was different. The bottle of wine we shared over a decadent dinner seemed like a logical consolation to what inevitably was going to be a harsh, grueling and unforgiving journey from Hopkinton to Boston the next day. Race morning, I woke up eager to open the blinds in my hotel room to see a calm New England spring, but instead I saw an apocalyptic scene that I will never forget. I am certain that at one point I saw penguins at home in the cold walking down Boylston, and cows violently tossed across Boston Common by the wind. Mind you this was pre-coffee so trust what you may. As I dressed, adding layer over layer over layer, I can see that my wife is searching for those perfect words. That phrase that is going to motivate me to tackle what is going to be the most memorable and iconic day of my running "career". As I reached for the hotel handle, my wife spoke up. "You're crazy! Good luck!". Not exactly a Kennedy speech, but it seemed to do the trick. At least she didn't tell me to climb back into bed, because with the sounds of rain punishing the window and the wind hallowing against the hotel, I would have taken that offer in a heartbeat.

The marathon itself was by far the worst and best experience of my life. The wind was relentless, the rain was constant and the cold just amplified it all. As I splashed from puddle to puddle, looking down to find my next dry foothold, I was lost in self-interest. It wasn't until around mile 2 when I lifted my head to see the amazing spectators enduring the same conditions. Men, women, boys, girls and dogs were dressed for the elements and cheering so passionately for absolute strangers. It was so emotional and beautiful. It was Boston. As the race neared to an end, the adrenaline of the upcoming iconic "Right on Hereford, left on Boylston" pushed me beyond. As I rounded onto Boylston I could see fellow runners struggling against hypothermia and yet driving for those last few hundred meters. It was then when I heard my wife shout my name. In that moment a flash of my journey flooded my mind. The sacrifices that my wife had made so that I could train, the number of spaghetti dinners my kids were forced to have so that I could fuel for the long runs the next day, even the numerous non-eventful training runs flashed across my eyes. This is it, it all came to this last push. As I crossed the finish line I looked up to find that I had set a personal best, finishing almost 5,000 spots up from my initial seeding.

But the joy quickly turned to distress. Runners were crossing the finish line and dropping from the conditions. I tried to help some to the tents, but I quickly realized I wasn't much help and needed to get out of the cold myself. I can honestly say, the three blocks back to the hotel was more difficult than the initial 26.2 miles. At one point, the wind gusted a deathly cold burst of air and I thought "this is the end", and I'm Canadian so you can only imagine how cold that had to be! When I entered the hotel lobby I realized that my hands were so cold that I couldn't reach the room key that was in my shorts. As embarrassing as it was I asked the hotel clerk to assist me. In hindsight he probably could have just given me a new key, but instead he willingly came over and sifted my rain/sweat soaked pockets to pull out my waterlogged access card. I awkwardly thanked him and started the slow journey to my room. Once there I tried to remove my freezing clothes, but to no avail. When my wife finally made it back to the room, she opened the door to find her near hypothermic husband chattering in the shower, fully clothed and murmuring, "next year can't be like this, next year can't be like this". It was then, that it truly hit me that I'm not just a Boston Marathoner now, but a 2018 survivor!

Ron Joseph, Bib 963

Rockaway Park, NY, 34, 3:04:19

So, let me tell you about my sub 3:05:00 which was the best experience ever. Stayed in the village to stay warm. I missed my wave. I ended up starting in wave 2, corral 1. Meb comes along and I'm like "hey you, come here and take this picture." He gladly obliged. Now, the gun goes off and I'm running 6 flat with my thin poncho on. I am in the lead by 1/2 a mile. I dumped it by mile 1 (huge mistake). What made the wave 2 start great was...I HAD MY OWN POLICE BIKE ESCORT AND I WAS ALL ALONE FOR THE FIRST 10 MILES!!!!! Everybody was going crazy for #963! I had to poop at mile 10. Not cool when your hands are frozen. My shoe became untied around mile 3. I pulled over to the curb and had a guy tie it fast and double knot it. I was also running low carbs from Friday afternoon until the race. It caught up to me after I got out of the bathroom.

I started to feel off after I got out if the bathroom. I was ready to drop out shortly had I not found a poncho!! Just past mile 11 I look to the right and a thick yellow poncho was sitting on a guard rail!!! I ran past it and then ran back to grab it. I was saved!!!! I ran with the poncho for about a minute when I realized it had snaps on the side. I pulled over to the curb and had a woman do the snaps on both sides for me. Started consuming oranges and bananas to keep my already fatigued quads from dying completely like they did in NYC.

I was just cruising along around a 7:30-7:45 pace just trying to finish in one piece and never stopping to walk. Got to mile 24 and changed the screen on my watch to show my overall time and distance (I usually use a 1-mile lap counter). I saw I was going to be close to a 3:02:00. I started to pick it up to 7 flat with no regards for my quads. Guess I stopped my watch during the race b/c I finished just under 3:05:00. The carnage from mile 18 on was rough. I'm totally okay with my performance today. BQ'd here today and almost had a 55-minute Boston PR. TOTALLY STARTING IN WAVE 2, CORRAL 1 NEXT YEAR AGAIN!! THAT EXPERIENCE WILL STICK WITH ME FOREVER!

I know I am born and raised here in NYC, but the NYC marathon just does not compare to this. The sleeping on the floor in trash bags, under a tent, in close quarters with your fellow man knowing how hard he had to work to be in this same spot as you is just absolutely priceless. The stories you share under that tent with each other!!! Proud to be a part of this prestigious fraternity of runners. The guides out there in the pouring rain and wind leading their deaf and sometimes blind runners along was an amazing site. Starting from wave 2 I got to see it all, including people pushing disabled people in that 3 wheeled contraption. If I had any race to choose to run it would be this. I could know it would 6 inches of snow going in with crazy winds and I still would choose this race over another race with ideal conditions.

Sandra Heriot, Bib 24178

Rozelle, AUS, 57, 3:57:55

Over the last 18 months, my mother kept saying, take care Sandra you're not getting younger. Well, I guess she's right, at 57, I'm not getting any younger, but I am getting fitter and stronger and feel like a better runner. In August 2016, I got a stress fracture – I think it came from falling over running fast downhill. I ran the Sydney ½ marathon without quite realizing that was what I had done but when I finished that race I surely realized something was not right. I had been training for Melbourne marathon but that had to go. I got lots of support and held onto Vlad's words "stay strong and positive and use the opportunity" and I did. I couldn't run for 3 months but I could do lots of gym work and even one-legged push-ups! The return to running was a wonderful experience but so much harder than I imagined. I decided to set my sights on a long-term goal so that I could really run again and decided on getting back to Boston. I did a half marathon in February and trained slowly to get a qualifying time in Brisbane, a good enough time to get me in for Boston. Hooray I was on my way.

My running fitness has always been a bit like a rubber band – it stretches out to meet the race and then sort of springs back to where it started. This time I decided to give training a real go. So I signed up for everything that was going with Runlab and tried to put myself out of my comfort zone. Summer sessions, done, UTA run camp in January, done, MyRungroup, done, Runstrong done, run program done, UTA 1-day session, done. Loved all of it and loved feeling stronger over time. If it was on my program I just did it – Runstrong class Thursday followed by either a hill session or tempo run on the same day. 2-day camp Saturday & Sunday followed by MyRungroup (note there were hills that night!). 36km run in high humidity, oh well, I sweated a lot. Wear compression tights, get those good socks, do it all!

When I did the camp, I took advantage of the sweat test which confirmed I am above average but unfortunately in the 'wrong' direction – above average sweating and well above average sodium loss for females. I got nutritional advice on how to manage these things, especially for long runs and also dietary advice. So six weeks of sticking to an eating plan and changing what and how much I ate made a huge difference to how I felt. I got used to drinking 750ml electrolytes (65g carbs) each hour for two hours in long runs and managed to run 36-38kms without stopping and still feeling good.

I always get a bit nervous about those 3km time trials, always want to run faster than the time before but never quite make it but this year I got a PB first time trial and then another PB at the end of the term – so happy and so thankful for the training and coaching. I have felt like I've been surrounded by wonderful people. One of the people in my Rungroup, Jo, was also running Boston and what an inspiration she was to me, what courage and attitude she has – a real fighter. And of course people like Vlad kept winning races or achieving tremendous results and all the other runlabbers and coaches, like Pete, I trained and ran with were so positive and encouraging to be around. It's just been months of fun!

After a wonderful relaxing taper week in sunny warm Miami, off I go to Boston. Enjoyed watching my husband run Boston 5Km on Saturday morning (4th in his age group…) and had fun at the expo, of course, I needed all that extra running gear!

I was feeling great, had a couple of nice shake-out runs and looking forward to running a PB. Of course, who knew what the day would hold – weather in New England is unpredictable and there's no use looking at 3 or 5- or 10-day forecasts because it can all change. But certainly, the closer it got the worse the predictions for rain, cold and wind. And sure enough, the day arrives and it's about 1 degree Celsius. It's ok, I have my whole outfit worked out (after changing it about 3 or 4 times), partly thanks to the Boston Marathon training FB group which I joined several months ago- mostly Americans and a few international folks but some fantastic runners and full of positive support and useful ideas and training tips – wear disposable surgical gloves over your gloves to keep them dry, buy a Houdini jacket from Patagonia clothing. So I'm bundled up in running singlet, tech long sleeve top, newly purchased wind jacket, disposable raincoat, Runlab buff, cap, gloves, disposable gloves, decided on shorts because if it was going to rain as hard as predicted then I'd just have wet cold tights for 42 kms. Good decision, plus some throw away clothing to wear to get to the athletes' village - top, long fleece pants and another poncho.

On marathon morning, I just read a BM training FB post - it could be really gnarly out there, so just chill the dickens out, put on some Lonely Island or Spice Girls, make it to the line smiling, and be proud to run like an animal with 30,000 of your newest friends – well ok, I will then.

I was in the last wave so didn't need to get to the buses early – they have fleets of those yellow American school buses to take you to the athletes' village. Climbed on board and the guy next to me didn't say a word – kind of pleased so I listened to my music and chilled out, spying sprinklings of snow along the road on the near on hour ride out to Hopkinton, the start of the marathon.

When I arrived, it was chaos – there was a huge line of people (blue wave) weaving its way out of the village to get to the road to walk to the start line. Short toilet queues, down to 1 or 2 in a line, mainly because it was a mud bath out there. Strangest sight I have seen at a marathon was a Japanese guy smoking a cigarette while waiting his turn! Another guy was changing out of his old running shoes and putting on beautiful new orange ones...what a waste because within five minutes they would have been soaked and muddy.

So I go to the toilet and then decided to make my way to the start. Oh I feel the need to go again, and having run in 2015 and having to stop two times I decide to use the toilets near the start, great, so I head to the start line but where's corral 1? Or any corral? No, they've dispensed with all of that, just start running, when you cross the 'start line' you've started...oh well, may as well get going! It was crowded and had to weave around loads of people and puddles and flooded roads, but quickly gave up on the watery roads and just ran. What a relief to be moving. After a few minutes I couldn't feel my feet, so cold, and never felt them again until well after I was finished. The rain was pelting down, and it rained the whole time I was on the course, light rain to squally torrential rain, cold the whole way and windy gusts at times, mostly head winds with a bit of relief now and again.

Get to about 10 kms and what, I need to pee, seriously what is this, oh well, I lose some time but feel relieved. Run on and get to 18 km and what? I need to pee again, oh seriously, I reckon when it's hot I sweat buckets and when it's cold, well you know, buckets too! So I felt minutes slip away spent in a nice warm, quiet sheltered port-a-loo. My PB was literally going down the toilet. Both times I came out and couldn't feel my legs, in fact they felt like I had plastic wrapped round them and took several kms to thaw again. On I run, feeling good, oh no 24 kms and what, I need to pee – no I'm not stopping again, push on Sandra! It was the strangest conditions to run in because the usual body signals weren't getting through due to the cold. I had to consciously check my running style and posture, consider how my legs felt but it was also quite good feeling slightly numb.

I was running thinking of all these people out there in terrible conditions, all running for their own reasons, many charity runners, people running to say they'd run Boston and yes that was going to be me too- never crossed my mind to stop, ran the entire course (minus port-a-loo stops), and felt positive the entire time, even if I thought it was ridiculous from time to time. More amazing were all the volunteers and spectators. Reports said there were fewer spectators than in previous years, but honestly there were crowds and crowds, all cheering so loud, calling out people's names, calling out support, smiling and laughing and clapping and dancing, blowing kisses, handing out paper towels to wipe your face, or fruits and snacks, even hand warmers – it was so uplifting.

So we get to the start of the Newton Hills, renowned for making Boston tough – a set of 4 hills – what makes them tough is that they start around the 16-mile (26km) mark and finish 4 miles later (~32km mark). But you know, I actually 'enjoyed' them. Having a change of pace and a little more effort going uphill warmed me up and the hills seemed smaller and shorter than I had remembered or imagined, nothing worse than running up Victoria Road, near where I live and nothing on the Blue Mountains! All that hill training and cross country running paid off. Yes CBD hill training up and over and over and over again worked a treat.

As I got to 38km mark, I was nearly there – just a few more kms than my longest long run. I got to 40kms and started to feel really happy (really, really happy). See the 25-mile marker and just 1 mile to go – hey, we ran 1-milers in CBD training, easy! The joy I started to feel was just overwhelming. Sure, I always feel a blast of happiness at the end of a marathon, but this was just wild. I ripped off my poncho and surgical gloves (photo op approaching) and ran for my life, wild and free, tears welling up and crowds just cheering down the boulevard and over to the finish line, yes I did it, I finished, and it was over. Hardest run I've ever done, most tremendous feeling I've ever had. No not a PB (3:57:55) but never felt so happy with myself and so grateful to be getting older and better! (top 18% in age group). Got a qualifying time for Boston 2019 but hey, think I need something more challenging now.

It's day two post Boston – too soon to go for a run? Feel so good, still happy and can't wait to get back and train up a storm. Thank you so much coaches and runlabbers – a great supportive group, helping each other achieve our own impossible.

Never been one for mantras or sayings but I did read a Salomon quote (not a paid insert!) 'embrace the unexpected' – yep, embracing it!

Rosemarie Simone, Bib 21911

Richmond Hill, ON, 48, 4:08:24

2018 was my first Boston and I'm still on a runner's high. I travelled to Boston from Richmond Hill, Ontario Canada with my husband and our 25-year-old daughter. My sister and her husband drove from Burlington Ontario. My 2 nieces and one of their boyfriends drove from Richmond Hill, Ontario, and finally my sister flew to Boston from Port Aux Basques, Newfoundland Canada.

I basically had an entourage. I was overwhelmed with so much support and my birthday was April 15 so there was celebrations for that as well. I come from a small town in Newfoundland and now live in Ontario. Once word got out that I was running The Boston Marathon, I had numerous Facebook messages before and after the race. It was truly overwhelming.

Additionally, all of my running friends that I trained with for the last few years were also sounding me wishes before and during the race. Obviously, no matter the conditions, I was going to finish that race! It wasn't just about me anymore, I had so many people involved and tracking me that I couldn't let them down and just knowing that they were all out there in cyberspace with me definitely kept me running.

Anyway, the support of family and friends add to the experience and I am truly blessed.

Sheryl Preston, Bib 12844

St. Catharines, ON, 42, 3:24:59

When we set out for the Boston Marathon, a race now 122 years old, challenging point to point route held in early spring on the Atlantic East coast, we know we are certainly signing up for something epic. The heart and spirit of this event with the immense community of volunteers, spectators, and Boston Strong-Bostonians never subsides. Being a part of this event is something never forgotten once experienced. The 2018 Boston Marathon 2 days ago, was my third Boston Marathon, certainly my most memorable, and definitely not my last.

I and 26,000 other runners set out on Monday April 16th. on to the start line of the 122nd Boston Marathon. The weather forecast consistently predicted a bad-ass, monsoonal, Bostomania of a storm on this Boston Marathon Monday. Meteorologists had predicted 60-80km head winds and 60+mm of rain to the hour and Mother Nature certainly delivered. It was one of those days when the wind gusts blasted so hard and rain pelted down so relentlessly that umbrellas proved to be dysfunctional. It was one of those days that getting from the grocery store to the car soaks you to the core, let alone running a 42.2 km into it.

With the forecasted storm, I had no race goal time expectations whatsoever, but I decided to approach it with a smiling (actually laughing) face. Thankfully, my 20 years of rowing, and now coaching, early in the morning in every kind of weather and often before sunrise, along with the 17 other 42.2km (plus) marathons and ultramarathons I have run in a variety of conditions, helped me devise my very simple race plan for the day.

"Don't think. RUN."

Athletes Village was beyond comical. Just imagine a mud-fest with 30,000 runners all dressed in ponchos, garbage bags, and plastic bags tied over our feet to attempt to keep the mud and rain out of our shoes. I had 2 jackets, a poncho and a garbage bag on, 3 pairs of pants, and a white army navy plastic bags tied over my shoes with an attempt to keep the mud out.

With seconds to spare I got to my start position of Wave 2 coral 5. I quickly stripped my multiple layers of warm up clothes (that the race organizers then donate to charity) and set on my soaking wet way running for my life from Hopkinton to Boston along this historic route.

As the miles went on, I was utterly water-logged as the rain pelted into my every crevice, the head-wind was moving my body however it wanted, my legs were partially numb, and the water was pooled in my shoes. When the passing monsoonal waves of rain flooded, I raised my arms out, looked up at the sky and laughed, then kept on my merry way. I realized that my core temperature was to remain okay if I just kept running as fast as I could.

I passed many shivering runners in shorts and singlets. My ticket to some degree of comfort was my surgical gloves overtop my $5 Army and Navy wool gloves, smart wool running socks, capris and a running jacket. The only thing I was missing was a shower cap!

What is tear-jerkingly unbelievable is the Boston spirit that relentlessly remained. This horrific weather did not stop the millions of spectators who were still screaming and encouraging us at the top of their lungs through the entire 42.2 km route, as they themselves soaked to the core. The 2018 Boston Marathon was a 100% heartfelt effort from every single person out there including myself, spectators, family members, volunteers, and the race organizers.

The second I started the 2018 Boston Marathon, I did not think, I just ran. I ran marinated with rain, and cold-pressed by traditional Massachusetts Nor'easter head winds for a heartfelt time of 3:24:59 and not a second to spare.

Within minutes of finishing I had put on my post-race poncho and met my husband at a local pub near the finish line with a "recovery" drink in hand, and warm clothes to change into.

Will I do this again? Of course, without a doubt. I have goosebumps just thinking about it.

Dan O'Neill, Bib 14368

Bel Air, MD, 59, 4:02:44

I started running when I didn't really have to back in January of 1978. I had graduated from the 3,000+ student strong Bel Air High School in 1976, where I got really good grades and played baseball (against Cal Ripken BTW) and soccer - and I hated the obligatory 3 mile in 20 minutes run (in soccer cleats) that started each practice. I was normally about 7th or 8th from the front of the pack. Anyway, during my college sophomore "winter term", I evaded the 4 x per week commute to Loyola in Baltimore by getting the high school track coach to sponsor me in "Independent Study in Running." I went to the track 5 days a week for a month, and the main thing I recall is

timing myself in a mile run one day (5:15 in "Thom McAn Jox" on the Timex, if you're curious). I actually began to enjoy it, or at least how good I felt afterwards, and running slowly became a thing. I also liked that it kept the weight off - I was 6', 200+ pounds entering 9th grade; now I'm 5'9+ (thanks, bad back) and weigh 160 (at least at the end of training cycles!). I do have to point out, though, that as a kid/teen I was a dang fast runner - even at my size, I won the 8th grade 100-yard dash, and the gym teacher thought he was sending the next

Jim Brown on to high school. He begged me to play football. Someday I'd like to be able to run fast like that again, but Father Time and Mother Nature are mean parents (unless your name is Gene Dykes).

I kept running after college. I always ran outside ("jogging" back then), and for 15 years or so I rarely encountered another soul running. I joined the first of several gyms when I graduated, but it did not have a treadmill, nor did the multi-million-dollar Bel Air Athletic Club until maybe 20 years ago. Pretty amazing, right? It's been fascinating to see running evolve the last 40 years. Also, even though the tales of Bill Rogers, "Pre", Jim Fixx, K. Switzer, and Eamonn Coghlan (mandatory plug for the Irishman!) were interesting, I never got the bug to try to run a race. There was a Maryland Marathon, which became the Baltimore marathon, but I was too busy doing other things (slo-pitch softball addict) and too cheap (paying $20 to run in a race when I could run the same distance myself for free made no sense) to take a crack at it. Many thousands of pain-free miles wasted competing against myself! Of course, that's kind of what we all do anyway, right?

My first "race" was the Bel Air Town run in the early 2000s. I remember getting outkicked by two 12-year-olds (a boy and a girl) the last 50 yards - which actually gave me a cold slap of determination that I've never let go of. I ran the race a couple more times. I had siblings that ran the Baltimore Marathon, and I gradually started to enter more races (running the Army Ten Miler 4 times and the Baltimore half twice). Finally, I decided it was time to take a crack at 26.2. As luck would have it, I ran my first in Rehoboth Beach in December of 2013, on my 55th birthday. The race director gave me bib number 55. I stood in the corral at the start with my sister and sister-in-law, who somewhat dismissively asked if I was going to try to BQ. I did - just under the wire, the last 4-5 miles being the second worst I've ever felt running. That got me to Hopkinton in 2015, for the most amazing running event I could ever imagine. I'll never forget the elation of that weekend and Patriots Day.

I began to train more (instead of just going out running), trying to follow the Hanson's plan, slowly getting less slow. Last year (December 2017) for the 3rd year in a row I ran 3:26 in Rehoboth, putting me at an old guy BQ-29. Training is tough - I mentioned the bad back above. I have 3 bad discs and chronic back pain, am out of alignment, with one leg longer than the other, and have a broken toe on one foot that I've had fixed twice only to have it break again. It seems like something new usually begins hurting as I kick up the mileage. I am always sore during the cycle, and I never come close to hitting the speed goals I should be capable of during training.

Anyway, going into Boston 2018, I was in great albeit sore shape, and decided to run (for the second time) a local hilly and muddy 50K trail run called the HAT Run in March. Cool swag but a bad move. My already tight hamstrings basically got shredded that day - I was much slower than I thought I would be. Nothing was good about this 3 weeks out from Boston.

Boston 2018? Miserable. Actually, that's not even the right word. The worst I've ever felt before, during, and after running. Honestly, it was the first time in 40 years and many thousands of miles of running that I was actually miserable. Part of it, I know, was trepidation that the wheels might fail me. On top of that, I didn't really prepare for the cold and rain, as the forecast got worse in the last 2-3 days. Travel to Boston meant no expo until Sunday, and I couldn't find a pair of gloves in Boston. That morning, I didn't want to get overheated - so I left my water-repellent winter wear Under Armor hoodie at home. Bad move. It poured - no, it snowed - on the bus to Hopkinton, which was an almost comical, cold, and rainy version of a massive Yellowstone mud pot. It looked and felt otherworldly. The closest I'll ever come to what it must have felt like in December on the Eastern front in WWII - without the bullets of course. There was no non-paved surface without standing water and mud - the kind that pulled your shoes right off. Literally. There was no dry space anywhere. Just sheer physical misery, and numbness, and the cold and the rain and tightness in my hamstrings weighed on me.

My friend Chris and I got to the corral late. As usual. I don't think the buses are timed correctly. We get there, get in the bathroom line, and are already being called. Anyway, my hammies started hurting 3 miles in. My shorts kept sliding down, as I never got them tight after the bathroom stop, and I couldn't do anything during the race due to numb fingers, which even made it hard to pull them up. Finally, I got a volunteer (female, about my age) to tie them - we had a good laugh about it. I think it was the only time I smiled all day. My Garmin wasn't working the first 1.5 miles. I think it was my poor eyesight and frozen fingers. I had on an Under Armor short sleeve t-shirt, covered with a worn-out all-cotton top I was going to toss at the beginning or right after. Chris warned me at mile 5 or so that chucking it might just bring me hypothermia, so I kept it and the 5 or 6 pounds of water weight with me. My strides per mile - thanks hammies - increased by 20% by mile 9. I was pretty much done then - in survival mode. Just an awful day. I saw the Angel of Death a couple of times. People were passing me left and right by mile 15 or so. Not to brag, but I'm a closer, and I hardly ever get passed that late. My amazing daughter met me just past Fenway and encouraged me - she actually ran on the sidewalk in boots and a coat for a 1/4 mile. She was faster than I was. Rounding the bend - or I should say "Right on Hereford" - I entered the "don't trip on any of these things" mode. I don't understand why some people feel it's okay to throw your garbage bag or poncho in the middle of a crowded pack of other runners. Nor do I get wearing something for 25+ miles and then throwing it off to have your picture taken. I expected more from serious runners. And these were the fast people, the first few thousand of them being really top notch. I guess it's the Catholic guilt thing in me too.

I finally crossed the line in 4:02 - 36 minutes slower than Rehoboth 4 months before. I waited at the end line to meet my family for about 45 minutes, but we never connected. Mercifully, I was able to use the Prudential Center (heated!) for a chunk of the Frankenstein shuffle back. I temporarily forgot my sore legs as my left groin felt like it had taken a musket ball. Even the Sam Adams 26.2 afterwards was disappointing. Of course, a better performance would have had me feeling better. I was embarrassed by my time - something really stupid, and something only other runners will understand. Only Chris even knows my time. And I worried about what I had done to myself by running a 31-miler and a 26-miler with really bad wheels. I've been trying to recover from the hamstring issues since then BTW. PT and rest failed. I continue to work on "butt strength" and just started with a chiropractor who does ART, so I'm hoping to get back running one of these days. Three races before Boston 2019 now look like no-shows for me. Still hoping to get to the line in Beantown in 2019. For what it's worth - looking back - I am glad I stuck it out - even if that means I ran myself out of some upcoming races.

That's enough about me. I told you it wasn't really interesting. However, going off script, I have to say a few things about Boston Buddies. First - thanks Vince - the Boss - what a stroke of genius! I remember getting the invitation from my running buddy "Santa" - aka Duane Watts - to join this group right after it started. I hemmed and hawed, not needing to spend any more time on Facebook, but I finally gave it a shot. What a good move it was. It has helped me not just become a better runner with some great technical advice, but it has motivated me to train harder, while at the same time helping me to put running in the right perspective (it's not really all that important). I've seen posts by a legally blind woman, a sister of a marathon bombing survivor, cancer survivors, and fantastic runners who've had their careers and the happiness running brings derailed by injuries that always seem random. All of them help me to quit feeling sorry for myself that I can't do what I did when I was younger.

There are also some real characters here - and some great stories! Besides Vince and Duane, I haven't met any of them, but here goes. Somehow we have both of the 2018 Boston champs here - amazing! They seem no nice and normal. And a bunch of past champs who just seem like regular guys and gals - running for fun with the mortals. And Katharine Switzer. I've seen her a few times, and always notice how friendly and elegant she is. She seems to just float through a crowd. I have to remind myself that she is a runner.

In 2017 I passed a guy on crutches. Yup - that guy. He was fast pre-crutches as he started ahead of me. Of course, that was the king of BB videographers, Timothy Moley. What a hoot he is. I have to meet him. Then, there's people like John Hadcock and Jim Chaves. I'm so impressed by their friendly natures, and the love of family I see in them. And they're fast. Lori Ann Fromlak. I've never known of anyone that trains so freaking hard. Queen of the 5AM long runs. She amazes me. Lori Eidson-Riggles. Literally "trucked" while running and has made an amazing comeback. The Man in Black - Rob Fried. He's off Facebook for a while, but pretty much every post is either him whipping a bunch of young guys in a 5K / 10K, or grainy pictures from his 1980s Boston days. With spelling that looks like he was typing with swim goggles on. Just poking him on that! But the guy knows running for sure. "Run fast until you have to throw up" is his unpleasant but valuable training mantra. Then there are the fast as heck younger guys. Chris Battoo and Ronald Joseph and "Coach" Brendon O'Leary. Red bibs and low numbers every year for these guys. And Gene Dykes, mentioned earlier. Holy freaking cow. World class. Very friendly and just an astonishing ability to run far and fast and often without ever getting hurt. And Tony Garcia. The running poet. That guy can really write! Marty Clark. Somehow he can smile and look good after 20 milers with his patented slice and dice selfie skills.

There are more. So many role models. I know there are some I've just forgotten to mention. We're in the thousands of people and, as far as I've experienced, there's never been an angry online exchange. Pretty astounding really. I can't wait to sit down and read what Vince has collected! Way to go Boston Buddies!

Stacy Endres, Bib 22079

Hastings, MN, 45, 3:48:45

You all better settle in with a good cup of coffee because this has turned into a small novel. I mean how can I put my first Boston experience, and one that will go down in the record books for weather, into one short page or two? Not possible! I just hope I don't bore you all too much as I carry on. What a trip it was! One I will NEVER forget.

Cailie and I flew out on Friday. Lexie and Kristin arrived that afternoon as well. We went to lunch and they had lobster grilled cheese and I filled up on 2 cups of lettuce with a side of artichoke. Yep, that's how I roll. We had a fun afternoon with lots of laughter. I think most of the laughter came from them making fun of me, but I'm used to it! They even let me get a sneak peek of the expo before Cailie and I had to head back and get ready for the Red Sox game. Our game seats were in the 2nd row from the top. Way to pick them Mom! The lovely gentleman greeter noticed my marathon sweatshirt and gave us the royal treatment. He told us to come back at 8:30 and he would put us in better seats. Sure enough, he sat us about 10 rows up from the field. He and I had multiple conversations about the marathon and he kept saying how excited he was that it was my first one and welcomed us to Boston. What a way to start off our trip!

Saturday was expo day!!! It's like Christmas for me. We walked into the conference room where I picked up my bib and that's all it took. I started to cry. I was so overwhelmed with emotion. We got in line and I cried some more. The woman who handed me my bib was so kind and told me how excited she was for me. She said it was ok to cry but I needed to get my picture taken with my bib. Cailie tried her best to get some decent shots but I didn't make it easy for her as I, yep, was still crying. What a sap!

The expo was incredible but oh so packed full of people. Cailie and I were walking by the Cliff booth and I saw Scott Jurek. I forgot he was going to be there signing his new book *North* which I had just ordered on Thursday. For those of you who don't know Scott Jurek, he happens to be one of the most dominant ultramarathon runners in the world. He is also a New York Times bestselling author and his books are phenomenal. I think this is the first time I have ever been star struck. So much so that I didn't even realize there was a line of people waiting to get an autographed copy of his new book. I just went on over like no big deal and handed the gentlemen behind the booth my credit card and he asked what it was for. I told him to buy the book. He smiled and said I didn't need to buy the book. They were free. Score! He asked my name and at that moment I couldn't even remember how to spell my name. Geez, get it together, Endres. Then I hear this voice behind me say, "What we don't have a line anymore?" I turned around to see the long line that I totally cut in front of and turned bright red. Oops, sorry! Scott was ready for me and saved me from the mad Cliff bar guy! We chatted, he signed my book and Cailie snapped a picture and we got out of there! We laughed and laughed realizing that I was THAT woman!

That afternoon Eric and Justin arrived. We met them for dinner and enjoyed our time together. The last time I was with them was Chicago 2016 and that's actually when we first met. We've become family since then. I have adopted them as my additional sons and I am honored they call me their ACS Mom. What a treat to have such a wonderful support crew. I do not take for granted the sacrifices they made to be in Boston with me. Lexie renting a car completely saved our sanity even if we were on opposite ends of the city.

Sunday was laying low and getting ready for the big day. Running errands and trying to figure out what to buy and wear to stay dry. If only any of it would have worked. I didn't sleep well that night but that's pretty normal for marathon night and I was having reservations about the weather. We were being told by the B.A.A (Boston Athletic Assc.) how truly awful the weather was going to be and come prepared. I am sure most of you know by now they were spot on.

Rise and shine, it's Marathon Monday!!! My stomach was so nervous, yet I felt like I was handling it all pretty well considering I was about to run the Boston Marathon in a freezing monsoon. I mean how bad could it be, right? The minute we walked out the door to the car, I was sick to my stomach realizing how bad it really was. Getting into the city was a bit challenging with road closures and traffic but made it to baggage check in plenty of time. From there I headed to the Ritz Carlton to meet some of my Boston Buddies that I had met online through my training group. I can now say I peed in a Ritz Carlton. Probably the only thing I will ever do there. Holy fancy and $$$. By the time I got there, I was already soaked. The shower caps duct taped over my shoes didn't hold and I was already sloshing when I walked after just a few minutes of being outside. We headed to the bus to get loaded and stood in line to become even more drenched. The wind was blowing so badly that my umbrella was useless.

The bus ride seemed to take forever but at least we were warm and starting to dry a bit. Just in time to get off the bus into athletes' village which we have all renamed the mud pit. 4-6 inches of mud everywhere! Once we got into the village, we realized that's when survival mode would begin. People everywhere, mud everywhere, total chaos, couldn't get to any food because of the conditions of the village. It was intense and stressful. I lost my plastic shower cap I had over my shoe on the way to the potties but my new Boston Buddy, Denise, went back through the mud, grabbed it and put it back on my shoe. That gesture alone made me realize we would be friends for life. Runners are amazing. However, it didn't hold. As we made it over to the potties, previous runners had dropped their heat blankets and I grabbed two of them and wrapped them tight around my shoes and legs to prevent anymore mud and water getting in. I only wish my fingers wouldn't have been so frozen at that point, so I could have taken a picture of how ridiculous it was just trying to survive in the village. We were in line for the potties and they called our wave a half hour early. We figured they were trying to get runners out onto the course as fast as they could considering we were already soaking wet and freezing. They realized we were all in for a very long day.

Trying to get my soaking wet layers off to go to the bathroom and then back on was a marathon in itself. The lines were taking forever because of this. We got to our corral and they let us keep our throw away clothes on as long as we could. We entered another portion of the village and got in line for the potties again. It's what you do before a race, especially a marathon. You go as much as possible in hopes that you don't have to go during the race. Denise and I were late getting into our corral but at that time the volunteer said just go wherever you can because there isn't really a rhyme or reason right now. Just go! We dropped our throw away clothes and took off. It really was so unofficial for the start of the Boston Marathon all due to the weather. I noticed right away the sound we were making with all our ponchos. Swish, swish went the plastic and I could also hear the sloshing of all our wet shoes. One of the runners from Boston yelled out Welcome to Boston. It's a fantastic city with fantastic people. A little rain and wind isn't going to stop us. Who's gonna have fun today? We all cheered, and it definitely lifted our spirits.

Denise and I stayed together up until I saw my crew at mile 4 and had to hand off my ear buds. I ended up with them and their case in my bag somehow. I never run marathons with them and it was bulky on top of all the wet layers so getting rid of them was a must and they were too expensive to toss. My hands were already so frozen at mile 4 that I couldn't get the zipper down on my rain jacket or I got the zipper stuck, who knows. It was also cumbersome. I just told my crew to rip it if you have to, I gotta get going!!! That's when I lost Denise as I told her not to wait for me. We all run our own race; however, I was a bit sad that I had lost my new friend so early on in the marathon. It was such a comfort having the support of another during such a crazy ordeal. So there I was, on my own. I decided it was time to get busy. I told myself that I was in this for the next 4 hours or so - DEEP BREATH - I had to suck it up and accept how miserable the weather was. I could let it bring me down or make the best of it. I decided on the latter. One of the things I like most about marathons is the comradery between runners. Due to the weather, there wasn't much. We all had our heads down fighting against the weather, focusing on getting through and making it to the finish. It's sad in a way yet it was also pretty amazing to see what we were all trying to accomplish with such odds against us.

I do remember at some point my body starting to warm up a bit and it almost felt tolerable for a while. Too bad so much was such a blur due to just trying to survive. I saw the real Santa in the first few miles telling us all Merry Marathon and some amazing parties taking place with the spectators. I ran by people grilling food and thought really, in weather like this? That's pretty amazing in itself. We were being offered beer right in the beginning as well, but the runners were playing it smart and not taking any.

At the half way point is the scream tunnel where the Wellesley girls line up to get kisses from the runners. This has been a long-standing tradition. They were amazing. You could hear them screaming a half mile away. I wasn't going to kiss the girls. I mean how weird is that, right?!? Well as I got down to the end of the line I panicked and thought this may be my only chance to take part in this tradition. So I grabbed a girl and I almost pulled her over the railing and out onto the course. I guess I was a bit too aggressive. Oops. I did kiss her though and then I was off like a shot again. I saw my crew again at mile 14. They told me prior to the race they would always be on the left. Imagine my surprise when they were on the right! I ran across all the runners and yelled to them, "You said the left!" I was so perplexed. It didn't take much at that point. Kristin handed me my fuel and I took off. I had bad sportsmanship and didn't say thank you. I have been reminded of this a few times in fun. Kristin – Thank you!

A couple miles down the road I stepped in a pot hole full of water that went up to my ankle. The shock and jolt of this caused me to swear out loud. One of the spectators asked if I was ok, and I waved and kept on going. It was a small miracle I landed straight into the hole and came back out without twisting my ankle. I mean it is me we are talking about. My angels were on full alert. What I remember most is the amazing crowd support, especially when we came to each town we ran through. Absolutely mind blowing how many people were out in that weather supporting us and acting like it wasn't even raining. The more it rained and the more the wind picked up, the louder they were. I had my name on the front of my singlet, but it was hard to see through my poncho. I still heard my name being yelled repeatedly though and I smiled and waved every time. I saw the man trying to make the Guinness Book of World Records by running backwards. He didn't make it, but he did attempt this for the Epilepsy Foundation. He was running down the yellow line with a guide and I gave him a high five. I also saw at least 4 blind runners with their guides. I told each one of them what an amazing job they were doing and to keep getting after it. These are the people that deserve the recognition. I am so honored to have shared the course with them.

My running watch is synced with my phone and my watch vibrated and buzzed at me nonstop during the entire marathon! Especially after a mile marker where you all received updates. I can't even tell you how much that meant to me. It helped me get through the tough moments and I can't thank you all enough for what you did for me on Monday. My sister, Sara, sent me messages and just seeing her name "Sara my favorite sissy" on my watch brought me to tears. Then I remembered what she had messaged me the day before, "One breath and one step at a time." I held onto that the rest of the way, especially when it got really tough through the last 6 miles.

I had been dreading the hills that I had heard so much about. It's not the severity of the hills necessarily but where they land in the marathon. They start around mile 19/20 and that's when we usually hit our wall and start to struggle. That combined with the 30-40 mph winds and rain we were running dead into; well it wasn't my favorite part of the run. After our first hill, I was ok. I trudged up it pretty aggressively with my up an over motto. I tend to be a strong hill runner. However, I avoided hills during my condensed training cycle because they caused my injuries to flare. Well that definitely happened during these hills. Remember, we had zero time or a place to stretch out or warm up in the village due to the conditions so that didn't help. At one point after one of the hills, us runners came around a corner and the wind and rain (which was almost sleet at this point) hit us so hard if felt like we all stopped dead in our tracks. It was at that point that I had enough of the weather. It got to me. I was so frozen. I couldn't feel my legs, my feet, my hands, my face . . . I was done. At least that's what I told myself. I usually don't walk in marathons but at that point I told myself, if you want to reach this finish line you better take it easy and catch your breath. The wind was literally taking my breath away. I slowed to a walk and was upset for allowing it to happen, but this was Boston and I wanted my finish line. I could maybe feel some hypothermia setting in and I got a bit scared that a lot could go wrong in the next 6 miles and I need to play it safe. I started having some pain in my diaphragm and this was also causing some concern.

I hadn't been walking longer than a few seconds and I looked off to my right and there was the first amputee that I saw on the course. He was walking with a guide on each side. He had a prosthetic to his knee on his left leg and a prosthetic up above his knee on his right. I said to myself, I have two good legs so what's your excuse? There wasn't one, so I got my butt moving. There's a lot of self-tough love out on the course. I won't repeat some of the other pleasantries I said to myself that day, especially in those last 6 miles. Kristin found her name on my ACS bib that morning and she pointed to it and said, "Do you feel this? It's almost right by your heart. When you need me, I'll be right here." I needed her, and she was there. She was not only on the course cheering me on in some pretty awful weather that makes her symptoms worse, but she was right there poking at my heart from the back telling me to look alive Endres!

I lost count of my hydration almost from the get-go. Boston has water and Gatorade at every mile and on both sides of the road. Well take a girl like me in those conditions and you expect me to keep that all straight when I am used to every 2 miles and always on the right. Nope, not going to happen. A lot of us would just open our mouths and look up when we needed some water, but it really wasn't the same. That and not being able to get my fuel out because my fingers were so frozen caused some problems. I was getting a terrible blister on my right arch due to my wet feet. I stopped two times to try and adjust my shoe. One time a spectator asked if I was ok and if I needed any help. These people are the best! I did have to walk a couple more times toward the end when I needed to get at my fuel. I just couldn't run and try and tell my frozen fingers what to do. I heard from a lot of my friends in my online training group that the spectators helped them get out their fuel, tie their hoods and numerous other things they needed and couldn't do on their own. I believe they said the temp never got above 37 but with the 30-40 mph winds our temps felt like 20-24 and soaking wet to boot.

Those last few miles were tough. I know I slowed way down and felt like I was running or almost walking at that point through sludge. I was moving so slowly against that wind and I just couldn't will anymore strength than I already had. I thought of all our loved ones on my bib and asked them to keep me moving forward. Please just let me keep moving forward. I saw runners being hauled off in gurneys or being escorted off the course by EMT's. I saw multiple runners heading into the med tents and running sideways and really struggling to fight the elements. I saw runners that shouldn't have been on the course anymore for their own safety. It's was alarming wondering if I was next and thinking Is the weather going to take my finish line away? I knew if I could just make it to mile 24 I would be ok. At least that's what I told myself and it seemed to work. Just keep moving forward. I could feel when I was getting closer to the city not only because the weather was intensifying but the crowd was changing. It was getting loud, really loud, and there were so many people! This is why I missed Eric and Justin right around this time; still so bummed over that. I knew that when I reached the famous Citgo sign I had one more mile to go. That sign was so damn beautiful. ONE more mile to go.

And there it was, the famous, "Right on Hereford St, left on Boylston St." Only a HALF mile to go. I saw all the ponchos lying in the streets and felt the need to rip mine off as well. It was so freeing realizing I made it. Letting that poncho go was a symbol of what I had been through. Unfortunately, I didn't realize how slippery all those ponchos were for other runners and there were many falls due to this. I didn't even think about it and felt awful that I had thrown mine as well after finding this out after the fact. At that moment, I wasn't thinking clearly, and I know I was experiencing some symptoms of hypothermia. I remember the crowds, the cheers and feeling like a celebrity. I remember they all got louder as the rain and wind intensified. I came around the corner and saw Boston Strong painted under the passageway. This is when it got real and I lost it. At that moment I was hit with all sorts of emotions. All I had been through in the past years and months to get here. How hard I worked and fought for my Boston finish line. How I thought in December and again in March I wouldn't make it to Boston. I NEVER GAVE UP. I kept getting back up and fighting for what I wanted every time I got knocked down. How I fought like hell not only for me but for our loved ones. I wanted so badly for so long to give our loved ones that Boston finish line. I was going to make that dream come true finally. Then I thought about the bombings in 2013 and what those people went through for the sport so many of us love. Lives lost, people mutilated and traumatized for a lifetime, families changed forever. I missed qualifying that year by a little over 2 minutes. I would have been finishing right around the time those bombs went off at the finish line. I will never forget. BOSTON STRONG.

Running is truly incredible to me. It brings people together from all over, different ages, different sizes, and different nationalities and for the most part we are always supporting each other. Complete strangers coming together with the same goal no matter how individual our goals are. We run. Yes, that was a lot to think about in a very short time, but it flooded in. I can't even explain to you how loud the crowd was. Ten people deep everywhere you looked, and they were all screaming and cheering. It was an out of this world moment. I was .2 from the finish line and for some reason I turned and looked behind me to my right. I can't explain why but to know that some higher power was in charge. There was Cailie. She was looking down the course behind me still waiting for me. She had missed me because I guess I was faster than my tracking all day and they were having a hard time keeping up with me. I like the sound of that! I yelled Cailie and she turned and saw me. I ran over to her waving my hands in the air and she yelled, "Momma, goooooo!!!" All the people around her were cheering for me too. I ran to the finish, held my hands high and crossed the

Boston Marathon finish line. The clock off to the right said 4:20. It didn't matter. I was so happy to get my finish line and be done with that awful weather. I made it and I never gave up. However, the emotions came flooding in again and I cried. I cried hard. I was covering my mouth and the volunteers said it's ok and congratulations, you did it! Like that didn't make me cry more. I walked to get my heat blanket and the older gentlemen that put it on me was so sweet. I told him I loved him more than any man in my life at that moment. He laughed and said, "I've been getting that a lot today." I laughed and thanked him and moved on. Next up - my medal! Damn we had to walk a lot in-between. Was it just because I had run a marathon or because I was so cold? I saw this sweet older woman and I was drawn to her. She put my medal around my neck and I cried some more. She told me to cry all I want as I deserved every bit of what I was feeling. I asked her if I could give her a hug and she embraced me. Yep, I cried some more. Wow no medal has ever felt like that good around my neck.

I walked some more and finally made it to the food. All kinds of goodies and then it was time for a picture. Oh why not now that my mouth and teeth are full of a frozen Cliff bar. That was a struggle, but we finally got a halfway decent picture. Walked some more and I reached baggage claim. I couldn't wait to get to my dry clothes. The woman couldn't find my bag. While she was looking, I was at the edge of the tent where all the water was dripping off. I couldn't move as so many runners were behind me and I was pushed up against a table. That's when something changed. I didn't feel so well. I couldn't feel my fingers and I couldn't really make my body move at that point. I got my bag and trudged into the herd of runners trying to exit the finish area. I could barely walk, I couldn't feel anything, and I started to shake so bad that I was having a hard time holding onto my stuff. I could feel my lips turning purple and my teeth were chattering uncontrollably. It was tough going. I started to panic a bit but thought just make it to the church steps where I am meeting my crew. I somehow made it, but they weren't there. I panicked again. I stood under the awning and finally was out of the rain. It took me awhile for any common sense to set in considering my condition. I remembered I had my phone. The trick was getting it out and trying to use it. Thank God for voice prompts. I called Cailie, but we couldn't hear each other. Those poor people standing next to me as I was screaming into my phone. I then sent Kristin a text letting her know I was at the church. There was a gentleman next to me and he was concerned about my condition. He asked if there was anything he could do for me. I told him I had a bag of dry clothes to change into but didn't know where I could change. He asked if I minded changing right there if they blocked me. I had my heat blanket on, so I could make it work. I mean at that point why not get butt naked on the steps of some famous church in downtown Boston with a million people around? I'm sure I have done worse things?! It took forever to try and get off my wet pants and get on my dry ones especially while trying not to drop my dry clothes on the wet steps. Oh that is what heaven feels like. Those dry pants were so amazing; however, I couldn't get my body to move the right way to get my jacket (zipper) and my shirts off. I was starting to tear up out of total frustration. At that moment I heard Cailie say Mom! I turned around and saw the prettiest face ever. She was there, and I was going to be ok. She started to help me with my shirts. I couldn't talk, and I was shaking pretty badly. I was making noises but no words. Then I heard Lexie say Stacy! There she was on my other side. Cailie told her they needed to help me get my wet clothes off and dry clothes on. I can't tell you at that moment how grateful I was for the help of strangers and the help of my loved ones. Lexie gave me her long winter coat. They both gathered my belongings and we were off down the steps to the car where Kristin was warming up.

We crossed the street and Cailie was holding me and helping me walk while trying to warm me up. She said, Mom, do you know what time you got? I said, I think it was 4:20. That's what the clock said when I finished. My watch wasn't set right when I started. I somehow had it on lap time instead of overall time even though I was getting my mile splits. I really had no idea what my time was. It was unfortunate but there was nothing I could do about it once I started. Cailie said, Mom, you got 3:48! I know I looked at her like she was crazy. Ummm, no I did not. She said, YES you did! You got 3:48! Mom, you qualified again! I told her that wasn't possible because I walked a few times, fixed my shoe twice, ran back to them a few different times and the weather . . . have I mentioned the weather? I mean I really only had two good months of training and even that was limited at times. I hadn't run from August to January due to injury and when I started it was a walk/run combo for a good three weeks. There was no way. Cailie said, Mom, would I kid you about this? You qualified again, and you are coming back next year! I think I collapsed a bit at that point and Cailie held onto me. I must have made her repeat herself a half dozen times because I just couldn't believe it. I still can't. I admit I have checked my official time on the B.A.A website a few times making sure it really says 3:48:45. I don't know how this happened except to say our loved ones were working overtime Monday AND all your support and love!!!!

313

I am still processing what took place that day. It was the craziest ride I have ever been on. I still don't know how I survived that weather and pulled off qualifying again with beating my Chicago time by 2 seconds. I also received my stats and I finished 392 out of 1664 in my female age group 45-49. I made the top fourth in my age group and almost fell off my chair. Unreal. I am still flying high and I hope this feeling doesn't end for a very long time. It's like when I had my wisdom teeth removed without being put under, or when I gave birth to my first born, or when I ran my first marathon and thought, if I can do this, what else can I do? Well if I can run the Boston Marathon in those conditions with all the stops I made and still qualify, what else can I do? I had a fire burning inside me before, but it's gone from a small bonfire to a massive forest fire.

I mean if I can do this and in the end it all started by helping others, what can you do? I challenge all of you to just start with one small thing to help someone else and make this world a better place for them. I can't even begin to tell you how incredible it makes you feel when you know you are making a difference in the lives of others.

You know what else; together we have raised $4,360 this year alone!! I am not sure what that puts our total at since we started but it's well over $30,000.

THANK YOU! THANK YOU! THANK YOU!

You all are just amazing. You support me every single year not only with donations but your unconditional love and kind words. You push me to be better and do more. You allow me to keep going and fighting for a cause I am passionate about. You allow me to continue to honor my Dad and all our loved ones. I owe this journey to so many of you. I owe my gratitude to all our loved ones who have battled this awful illness and continue to do so. Thank you for allowing me to fight for you. It's my absolute honor.

This has all just been so incredible. I can't even tell you the number of messages I received on Monday and leading up to Monday. I couldn't keep up between texts, Facebook and messenger. It was insane. I felt your love and your support and even though I haven't been able to get back to everyone, please know that I appreciate what you did for me. My heart has been smiling ever since. I don't see it stopping anytime soon either. I go to bed at night and fall asleep with a smile on my face. That's because of all of you. You all made me feel like a Rockstar on Monday and I can't thank you enough for giving me that day. It was definitely the most challenging thing I have ever done but also the most rewarding.

Thank you for a great Boston!!! I'll be back next year!!

Stephanie Dyer, Bib 22963

St Petersburg, FL, 48, 3:46:04

I am from St. Petersburg Florida. I am a Boston College alum and our daughter is there now as a freshman. My best friend from college still lives in the area so it is dear to me! Boston is my favorite race and one of my favorite cities. This was my 20th marathon and 12th Boston. One that will be in my memory, always. I have never used a coach till this year and trained harder than ever. I anticipated a 3:25 but ended up with a 3:45 (happy with that, given the circumstances!)

When I was on the bus looking at people walking to athlete village, this Florida girl just wanted it to be over! Everyone I've met or spoken to agree there is definitely a bond for 2018 runners! Things that stuck with me:

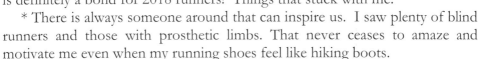

* There is always someone around that can inspire us. I saw plenty of blind runners and those with prosthetic limbs. That never ceases to amaze and motivate me even when my running shoes feel like hiking boots.

*The mind is a powerful thing. You can be in amazing shape physically, have excellent prep but your mind can take you on a downward spiral in a second. It can also take you to places you never thought was possible which is what happened on Monday. I personally believe there's a spiritual component to that. Your mind and your spirit are constantly in a dance together. Your mind is what tells you to have faith in what God can do (which is absolutely anything if He wants to). Your mind self-talks and you know the importance of that. I firmly believe that never ever giving up hope in the impossible no matter what has happened leading up to that. Be the unrelenting MASTER of your MIND.

•Perspective is so very important. As you know I was nervous leading up to Monday, what do I wear, such uncharted waters, a bit of frustration knowing that I had to adjust my expectations and be at peace with whatever happens, but I have never worked so hard. Six months of full on training. Race morning I was in an outright in a state of dread. An hour before the race we watched people outside of the bus walking into the wind with hats blowing off and rain coming at them- But whenever I would feel that way (dread, anxiety, fear) I would make myself stop and say, NO. Not today. Not after everything I put into it. Whatever happens happens, but I am going to leave everything on the race course. I will choose not to let the elements get to me for one second. I went into all-business mode.

I think God wanted me to know just how important it is to lean on him because that was basically all I had. Some said just find the biggest widest tallest guy and run behind him. Draft. I never did find one person to run behind! I chose confidence. I chose belief. Yes, I worked my booty off and I have never been stronger, but my mind and my faith were the strongest. Together. They danced well in perfect tandem. I never let either one slip out of the state of strength. That was the secret sauce. That IS the secret sauce.

Churchill was right. Never ever give up. My friend Ellen who is a stronger faster runner than I and trained so incredibly hard for this race as well, just couldn't stay warm and had true hypothermia. She had to drop out at mile 15 after going to the medical tent. She truly never gave up in her spirit and mind. She gave it her all. It just wasn't her day that day and sometimes we just have to fold given the circumstances. (As I told my son: Just like some days the putter just doesn't work). We are human. Then you put it behind you and you keep going. I spoke to her in the airport and she can't wait to have a great race in Utah in June and she was encouraging those of us who had a great race. She will rest her body, give her mind a break for a week or two, and she's jumping right back into training just like she did for Boston. I love that spirit! We all got stronger on Monday regardless of the array of outcomes. Just like our life experiences. They make a stronger, better, and more equipped for the next challenge and I think equally as important, we then have something to pull from when people around us need encouragement. We all have so much to learn from one another.

Look for angels around you. They are there. Open yourself to see. I always have a race angel. My daughter, Allison is a Boston College freshman. She and her boyfriend ran a few minutes alongside of me on heartbreak hill and it was so sweet and made my heart so happy! She said to me the night before, "I can't wait to see who you're race angel will be tomorrow, mom!" Well, I was in a sea of people walking a mile through the mud and pouring down rain to the start. Not much chatting. I missed my start time by 10 minutes due to the crowded mess and I was just by myself. But I really wasn't. I took off my poncho, 2 layers, sweatpants, and wet throwaway shoes and I laced up my race shoes (which I knew would very soon feel like hiking boots). I looked down at that Philippians 4:13 verse and said OK I'm truly standing on your word, God. It's fricking cold and pouring down rain and miserably windy but let's just do this. Game on. Just me and Him. The ultimate "race angel".

Since it was a milestone race, I ran for the Red Cross (wonderful experience top to bottom) and they had a HQ for us at Webster bank after the race with massage, changing rooms, coffee beer and it was heavenly! Then we celebrated my daughter's boyfriend's 21st birthday at Stephanie's on Newberry. Champagne and a burger never tasted so good!

My last sweet thought is my 10-year-old Sophia who always prepares my running shoes. That helped so much!

2018 was memorable indeed! We are all stronger mentally and physically.

Tricia Cecil, Bib 19221

Elkridge, MD, 35, 4:07:29

I first heard about the Boston Marathon when I was visiting law schools in Boston. It seemed cool but something so out of reach it wasn't worth pursuing. I did my first marathon during my second year at Baltimore in 4:45. Then almost broke four hours at Marine Corps the following year. Turns out dropping 40 minutes between marathons doesn't happen after your first. I broke 4:00, ran some low 3:50s, had a couple babies, DNFd a couple marathons. Then the Boston Athletic Association dropped five minutes from each age group and got rid of the 59 second cushion. And the popularity of the race led to a cut off system -- there were more qualifiers than spots, so qualifying wasn't enough, you needed to run faster than your BQ time (how much faster, no way to know until registration closes). I needed a 3:40 but really 3:3? to get into the race. I missed 3:40 at Steamtown in 2016 by 46 seconds. I DNFd at Shamrock the following spring because of the high winds and hail. I qualified the next month at Coastal Delaware but "only" by about 90 seconds. Then I had a "stars aligned day" at Erie last September and ran a 3:35:56, a BQ by four minutes four seconds. I worked so hard for the right to be here. Double digits before work, tempos at paces I didn't believe I could sustain, mile repeats at 5k pace, long runs with marathon pace work. Tomorrow the weather will be ridiculous, and it will be epic. I will turn right on Hereford and left on Boylston and I will cross the finish line at the Boston Marathon.

Wayne Shuttleworth, Bib 9157

Rock View County, AB, 58, 3:49:21

I started running in July 2011 while I was on a two-month work assignment overseas. My family was back in Canada, and I wasn't interested in TV, sports bars or anything like that, but I did feel that I should do something along the line of cardio health, and running was the obvious choice as I could do it alone, and when it fit my schedule. I had run in high school, but at 52 that was many years ago. So off I went, with this thought in my head – "my Dad was a non-smoker, non-drinker, quite thin, and did a lot of physical work, but he still had a heart attack requiring by-pass surgery, and I don't want that to happen to me". Maybe just maybe I could stave off a genetic predisposition to heart trouble by starting a new habit while I was living alone on this assignment.

That first evening I could not run the length of a city block (from one set of lights to the other) before being completely winded. Bent over hands on knees gasping for air. I took this as a bad sign and decided to run the next night and the next until I could at least get from my apartment to the beach walk a kilometer away. It seemed so far. Not long into it though and I was able to do this and even more. I kept at it and was even asked by one of my foreign co-workers if I would be interested in running a 10-k race with him. I did that and enjoyed it so, that I did another one two weeks later.

To back up a bit I am also a cancer survivor. Four years earlier I went for prostate cancer surgery, so after feeling invincible health wise when I was younger I realized that wasn't reality and I had better not take anything for granted anymore.

I did another 10-k when I returned to Canada and was challenged by my son to participate in a Spartan Race. I was hooked on running.

Then in 2015 during a routine Dr's visit I was diagnosed with COPD (Chronic Obstructive Pulmonary Disease). I had asthma my entire life, and as a non-smoker it was either just genetics, or from years of not properly taking care of my asthma. I don't know which, but this was very shocking and hard to take, because I knew this was one disease that is progressive and can't be beaten. My Doctor recommended that I should quit running because the limited oxygen flow could be hard on my heart. My Doctor then sent me to a respirologist to see where I was at with respect to my lung capacity. My respirologist was very encouraging about running and encouraged me to continue. He even said to run a marathon if I wanted because if I started to run out of air I would just be forced to stop, but I wouldn't die or anything like that. He said that I would not regain any lost lung volume, but what I had I would make more efficient by running.

So I kept running, and as quite a few runners know, you have to have help along the way, and I was no exception. I had help along the way, and lots of it from family and new running friends I met on my journey from a 10-k newbie thinking that I was really doing it, to successfully running marathon races. This didn't happen overnight, and my wife became a marathon-training widow for many months. However, she was always very supportive, even going on running shoe buying trips with me. She even bought me a registration to the Calgary Marathon and the Stampede Half-marathon as Christmas gifts. So with my new marathon gift I went to the Running Room and registered in their marathon training program. This was the best decision I made because up until then I just self-trained for the 10 k races I had participated in, but I knew a marathon was a completely different thing and I didn't want to try to self-train for marathon distances. The Running Room provided a great program and running environment, plus it was also the new community of very helpful and supportive runners that I met and trained with which made the whole thing such a great experience.

So in May of 2016, at 57, and after almost 6 months of hard training I ran a Boston Qualifying time in the Calgary Marathon – a city with an elevation of 3600 ft, and a course that has about a 400 ft uphill climb in it to boot. On this run I didn't just get a Boston Qualifying time, I was under it by 22 minutes. Then in April 2017 I ran my first ever Boston Marathon, achieving a personal best by shaving another 4 minutes from my previous time, and attaining that elusive negative split. I did this at 58, as a cancer survivor, lifelong asthma sufferer, and with COPD. I had something to prove, and now I have the running world's most coveted marathon medal to show for not giving up.

At home none of my family, including me to a lesser extent was all that much into athletics – I always thought it would be nice to do if I had any athletic skills, but I didn't think I had any, other people did but not me was how I felt. And my family was even further away from an athletic mindset. My wife hated everything about sports, she absolutely hated anything that would make her breath hard or sweat. My daughter wasn't too far behind my wife on that account and my son was athletic playing men's rec soccer, and swimming, but he wasn't living at home anymore and so wasn't tickling anyone's athletic funny bone here. That changed for me when I was working overseas as I had mentioned earlier, but a funny thing happened to my wife and daughter's attitude when they were watching and cheering my son and myself on during a race. My wife said that all she wanted to do when she saw me coming was to hop over the fence and start participating as well. Now we are a running family. My wife has completed a number of 10 k events and now she is ready to take on her second half marathon, and my daughter is training super hard for the Calgary Marathon to achieve the very difficult Boston Marathon Qualifying time. This is her first marathon, but then I did that on my first as well, and during a recent Calgary Marathon 30 k tune-up race she has kicked my butt. So good to see!

It didn't end there for my family either as my Mom at 82 is entering her second 5 k event. She will be walking it, she is a fast walker, but that doesn't really matter because she is 82 and just seeing her out there participating – standing up to the starting line with runners a fraction of her age is just so inspiring which is the great irony of it all because she became inspired to try her hand at athletics while cheering me on at one of my races.

The most recent exciting development to come from my running came through a work colleague. He is younger than me and from quite a different cultural background from myself as he immigrated to Canada when he was an adult to start a new life in a new country. He was in athletics in his native India but dropped it to get established with his family here in Canada and as time went on he felt that his athletic days had passed him by, until he saw me, the old guy in the office don running gear and go for lunchtime, or after work runs. His interest in me was really piqued when I successfully ran a Boston Qualifying time and then was actually able to have a successful run in Boston. He said my running got him back into athletics. Then, and this is the cool part, he asked if he could pass my name and number to a friend of his who is the President of the Calgary Indo-Canadian Cultural Association. This person is also the one organizing the Canadian National Indo-Canadian Master Games this being held this summer in Calgary, and they asked me to be their poster person. I am so flattered to be asked to be part of this event.

So far in 2018, I have been awarded a certificate of appreciation from the City of Calgary Councilor for the ward where these games are being held, I have been interviewed by two of Calgary's main multicultural radio stations, and with another group I was asked to be a guide for a runner who was running blindfolded to raise money for the National Brail Press, which interestingly enough is in Boston and is one of Boston Marathon's sponsored charities. For this last event my picture appeared on both of Calgary's major newspapers.

Running has introduced me to new communities, many new close friendships, and a great many more wonderful people. And it started during our goal setting meeting at my very first Running Room training clinic when I decided a good goal would be to work towards running in the Boston Marathon. Now I look back at how that simple personal challenge has changed my life, my family's, and friends' lives as well as a community of people around me. That is what to me is so special about running – what started out as a person health endeavor has grown to be much more than I could have ever imagined, . . . it is much more than just putting one foot in front of the other over and over again for 26.2 miles, it is the pull of something bigger. It must be something bigger because there is no motivation from seeing a 58-year-old guy with a runny nose, covered in sweat run by. To me it has to be partly the running, but more than that it must be the Boston Marathon as the most storied marathon race in the world as the one big event which has helped make all these wonderful and positive events and life changes come to my family and myself in such a short amount of time.

Tatum O'Sullivan, Bib 27528

Haverhill, MA, 43, 5:56:24

Adapted from an article about Tatum from the Eagle Tribune

I ran the Boston Marathon in my dad's honor. He was long-time track and cross-country coach Pete O'Sullivan, who died in 2006 at the age of 56. He passed away after having just gotten home from a run. He was my hero, it was devastating for all of us. He had an amazing effect on a lot of people, as we found out at the wake and funeral. It was tough on all of us. After being a smoker, he quit and took up running as an adult, including qualifying and running in five Boston Marathons. He fell in love with running and being healthy, I was never a runner. Neither were my sisters. He loved it. He had to run every Christmas Day, no matter what the weather was. It was his passion.

After he passed, I tried on a few occasions to run on a daily basis. In 2009, I ran for almost a year. Then a few years later, I started running again, but stopped. In 2016, I started again, but this time I stuck with it. I started running in a few races, and eventually did seven half-marathons in a year. I ran my first marathon in Pittsfield, Mass. My goal was five hours but I ran a 5:19. As a penalty I ran a pair of half-marathons a month later on back-to-back weekends in

Peabody and Newburyport, with the express goal of combining the two races and beating the five hours. I did and it was inspiring.

The Boston Marathon, my dad's all-time favorite event, was up for consideration. The only drawback was I'd have to get a number through a charity, which meant raising more than $10,000. I applied to 12 different charities, but my biggest concern was being on the hook to raise so much money. I finally got a phone interview with the Boston Medical Center. I just said, "I'll do it. I'll raise the money." I hosted a painting party, sold Super Bowl squares, and two friends gave me front row balcony tickets to the Bruins-Leafs game to raffle off.

Then I posted my story on Facebook, about running in my dad's memory, and many of his former students and athletes started donating money. Unbelievable, I was in awe. The way people came through for my dad was amazing.

Before the weather report, I was hoping for five hours. But that was obviously out the window. At mile six it was pouring. At mile 11 it was coming down harder and I said, "Maybe it will let up." Well, it never let up. Then there was the crying. I broke down about eight times during the race. My mind would wander, and I realized why I was doing it. A few times I wondered if I'd make it. Then I'd tell myself, "Suck it up! Remember why you're doing this!" I had pinned my name to my shirt and the words "First Boston for Dad." There were a few times when I was struggling, and I'd hear someone say my name. It was amazing how much it helped me.

Once I got over Heartbreak Hill, at Boston College, I realized I would be able to finish the last six miles. I looked over at BC and saw a sign that read, "Heartbreak Stops Here!" Plus the fact my dad went to BC. That's all I needed.

It was the hardest thing I've ever done in my life. I finished in 5:56. My feet were squishy the entire way. The wind was in my face and I was cold. I still can't believe I had the strength to finish. But in some way, I'm glad it was so difficult because it made me stay focused. This was very important to me. It was for my dad. And he was there the entire way.

Patrick Hamilton Hutton, Bib 1812

Encinitas, CA, 25

I could be like other guys and say I ran and qualified but I'm not. It goes like this. In 2011 I dropped out of college mentally and physically started abusing myself. I had non-passing grades and my life was heading in the direction of rehab or death, I was being a college kid drinking past noon, skipping class, and having fun instead of investing my time in school. My parents wanted me to, ya know, do what every college kid does, learn to grow, I was going opposite the direction. I

In 2012 I moved home from Montana, I became depressed and began to go to school at a community college here, I had no confidence, had a baby face from the alcohol use, and weighed about 175. My parents and brother were determined to have an intervention with me they wanted me to go to rehab for a lifestyle change, stop the partying and the alcohol drink nights. I decided I didn't want to do what they wanted me to do obviously, so I blurted out loud, I want to go back to school in Montana, and re-start, so I re-applied. My academic advisor at the time in Montana had still not given up on me however, I walked out of my dad's office crying because I had realized I lost myself.

I had no idea who I really was. I was lost in the bottle and lost in my youth 21 years old at the time. When 2013 rolls around I find a roommate in Montana and start showing up to classes stopped drinking for a whole month and picked up marijuana use to replace the need to have a beer or whatever. I got right, I started making grades in 2013 I was so happy to show my family I could do it. I kept going. I got a job at the YMCA helping kids, and every night after shift I'd go run a mile or so on the treadmill. I began playing pick-up basketball but was never good enough to make the shot to get in the pick-up game, so I simply ran the track surrounding the basketball stadium upstairs until the next opportunity to shoot, however I'd miss. And run more. The YMCA hosts a river bank 10k, 5k, and 1 mile and a gentleman at the Y told me all about it early 2014 and said your pretty good at that running thing. I kind of was like whatever about it. I was healthy though. I ran that race, my first 10 k in 39 minutes ripping away all the bad things that had happened to me in my life. I got 5th place in my first try. I saw a path right away. A path that to this day I am still on. I took my life at a young age and said look I either die or go make life for myself. I graduated college in 2017 I got my degree. I met a buddy in 2015, Jacob Verrue, who helped me stay straight. He's ten years older then I, he told me about Boston all of it. I do drink beer now like a normal person. I do not smoke marijuana, but it did help a period of my life. I was able to say I'm going to take all my emotions out and just put them in running.

Rosemary Spraker, Bib 21084

Lorton, VA, 54, 4:54:23

My life-changing Boston Marathon 2018 story with #261Fearless.

Thanks so much to all who have donated to my charity fundraising campaign for 261 Fearless, the organization that empowers women through local running clubs connected through global communications, events, and training programs! It was so great to see Kathrine Switzer, Jacqueline Hansen, Pete Thalmann, Thom Gilligan Angela Kwong and all my friends from Hawaii, previous Boston Marathons and 261 Fearless. I kept the memory of my mom, Shirley Whipple in my heart the entire way.

I feel like I finally came up for air after I ran (dare I say swam) the Boston Marathon on April 16, 2018 with 46 other charity runners from around the world. Together we battled the elements with icy wind gusts and pouring rain with a wind chill of 23 degrees F. I ran the entire race with a GoPro on a selfie stick capturing the 45 women and two men on our team to share on our 261 Fearless Facebook, Twitter, and Instagram pages and with the media.

Within the first mile, I caught up with Demi Knight Clark from North Carolina who was pacing Sophie Tedmanson from Australia. Sophie had an injury and appreciated her new friend Demi's support. Demi had experienced PTSD as one of the last few marathoners to cross the finish line during the 2013 bombings and appreciated Sophie's support. Before long, we were all best friends as I decided to stick with them to provide support for both of them which ultimately resulted in my life-changing experience. We all had five layers of clothing on including rain ponchos which we only peeled off for the celebratory run down the Boylston Street homestretch to the finish line. At one point during the first big hill at mile 17, Demi and I locked hands, and I literally and psychologically pulled her up the

hill. Running is a team sport! The experience was about women supporting women which is what 261 Fearless is all about!

The three of us crossed the finish line together just like I did with Kathrine Switzer Marathon Woman during her 50th anniversary run last year. We melted into a group hug followed by medals and high fives!

Joy Donohue, Bib 28182

Hopkinton, MA, 56, 4:50:22

To me, running feels great and is energizing for everything else I do in my life – not to mention a perfect excuse to listen to great music on Spotify during valuable time alone. It's almost like a mini-vacation of sorts. Additionally, I love the challenge of strength training and pushing myself a bit further each time I run to achieve goals. It's a feeling of strength and power no matter what level you train on – and is specifically tied in with my life motto, "It CAN be done!"

I am also equally passionate about giving back to the community and have done so in various sports capacities for many years. I live in Hopkinton, Mass. a mere mile away from the start line of the Boston Marathon and fortunately, I am able to be inspired by that every time I run by throughout the year.

Combining my passion for running and fundraising, I have participated in many charity running events including those in my hometown such as the Live4Evan and Sharon Timlin Memorial road races, as well as others in NYC including the More Magazine half marathon and the YAI Seeing beyond

Disability 5K. I also have run in many Boston Athletic Association events -- which I consider the top of all running experiences.

Living in Hopkinton, I was fortunate enough to receive a fundraising bib for two years in a row thus far, allowing me to test my running skills as well as raise money for two local non-profits – the new public library and relatively new Hopkinton Center for the Arts. I am extremely grateful for BOTH opportunities and found the entire experience life changing and hugely rewarding on every level imaginable.

Most memorable was the 2018 Boston Marathon due of course to the historic weather conditions including torrential rains, winds and freezing temperatures. Since I live so close to the start line, I also had the pleasure this year of hosting the Newton-Wellesley Hospital Boston Marathon running team – a group of 25 runners who all bonded together at my house hours before the race as we anticipated vastly challenging conditions waiting for our time to line up.

From start to finish – it was EPIC, and I actually improved my time by 10 minutes (4:50:22) from the year before. Below is my firsthand account of the day as posted on social media. In both cases, I also doubled my donation minimum requirements and was able to donate a total of more than $20,000 thanks to extremely supportive and generous friends and family.

"Torrential rain, huge puddles, windy, little to no fans, hamstring tight from cold miles 1-20, sneakers soaked, then — unexpectedly gain second wind at mile 22 Heartbreak Hill, break loose, do sideline dance for BC fans while running, spot Citgo sign, 2 miles left, shed poncho, nearing finish line, run as fast as I can down Boylston Street while freezing cold, beat last year's time — help HCA. Yay! A dream day. Thank you so much for all support/opportunity to help others through running. So truly grateful. Final Stats: At 04:07 PM: Athlete Alert. Joy Donohue Finish. Time 4:50:22, Pace 11:04."

Violet Rucci, Bib 20333

Chicago, IL, 40, 3:33:15

My running journey has been one of perseverance and redemption. After my father lost his battle with cancer, I found myself trying to overcome gut wrenching grief and regret. I battled with depression, and the only thing that made me feel better was liquor, it was my numbing comfort. I was plunging headfirst into a dark hole and I didn't see a way out. I was overweight, unhappy, and not at my healthiest. I was going through the motions and that was no way to live. I knew I had to make a change because I had the power to become the healthiest and happiest version of myself. I owed it to my father, who was not ready to go at the young age of 55. Through running, I found a way to focus on a healthier lifestyle, which my body and mind both benefitted from. I became the best version of myself and found solace in  the time I spent logging miles. There was a time when I wished to just be normal. I'm almost there and it feels good. The girl who had taken a downward spiral into darkness had found her light.

When I signed up for my first marathon, I had no idea what I was getting myself into. At the time, the longest run I had under my belt was three miles. I use the term "run" loosely, as it involved more walking than anything. I was determined to cross that finish line, so I armed myself with a plan. I didn't have much time to train and had no running base, but I believed I had a chance. That confidence is a gift my father gave me. Growing up, he always told me I could do anything I set my mind to.

One of my favorite authors, Paulo Coelho wrote, "an awareness of death encourages us to live more intensely." When I read that, it rang so true. Running gave me a new outlook on life and filled me with a new passion I desperately needed. I trained for the 2009 Chicago marathon and dealt with all of the aches and pains an unprepared newbie experiences. I had it all – shin splints, knee bursitis, back pains.

I crossed the finish line in 6:03:06 and it was beyond exhilarating. I cried as I received my medal. I was in pain, but I had done it. My father was with me the whole way. I could hear his voice in my ear, "mind over matter, your mind is tougher than your body." That was his approach to his decade long battle with cancer. As I stood still, listening to the crowd, I whispered to myself "vini, vidi, vici". It was his motto. I believed in myself and I didn't give up, even when I was weary. When I felt I couldn't take another step, I continued on as my father had. He fought until the end in his battle with cancer.

I loved the structure running gave my life. It helped me become better in every aspect: as a mother, a partner, a daughter, a sister, at work, etc. I continued running marathons for fun; I even did a couple of ultras, because I loved testing my limits. I never really cared too much about my finish times, until I broke my toe eight weeks before a race. It was a devastating time but it taught me much about patience and resilience. I worked hard in order to maintain my fitness and sanity. I spent many hours in the pool, swimming and aqua jogging. When I received clearance to run, I left the doctor's office and went straight to one of my favorite running locations. I started running and tears of gratitude streamed down my face. I was so happy. What surprised me was how fast I ran given so much time off. I didn't want to push myself, but I felt amazing. I had also lost some weight.

I signed up for a marathon and had four weeks to train. It was an aggressive plan, but one that I evaluated on a weekly basis to ensure I wouldn't cause any damage. I ran hard, smart, and determined. I stuck to my plan and ran that marathon with such a passion; the time flew by rather swiftly. I PR'd, coming in at 4:28:37. What an amazing feeling, to be able to finish so strong, never having hit the wall or feeling too tired to go on. My splits were pretty even and my body felt so strong. Overall, I think I can now say that breaking my toe was the best thing that happened to me. At the time, I had blogged, "I've got Boston on my mind and while I have a long way to go, the dream of achieving that goal is much more of a reality now than ever before. I may just do it by the time I turn 40!" I was 39 years old. That was the first time I had spoken my dream of running Boston into the universe. I armed myself with the "Run Less, Run Faster" book, and got to work. I did the work, tweaked my plan here and there and did some serious racing in 2016. I had begun training with the Nike Run Club and learned so much from the coaches and pacers. I was doing speedwork, tempos, and killing it in my long runs.

I ran four more marathons in 2016. Two of them were only a week apart. I had spent so much time researching whether one could run two marathons at hard pace within a week. I finally decided that the only way to answer the question was to try it, so I did.

February LA Marathon 4:05:18
May Wisconsin Marathon 3:53:51 (upper 50's, 30 mph wind gusts)
May Chicagoland Spring Marathon 3:41:45
September Last Chance BQ Grand Rapids 3:51:13
October Chicago Marathon 3:40:04

I had done it; I had accomplished what I set out to do. I qualified at my hometown race with a 4:56 cushion. The emotion was so overwhelming, I burst into tears as my friend, a race photographer hugged me. I couldn't talk, and she was barely able to make out what I kept repeating, "I did it, I did it!" I was so happy. The key words from this particular training cycle had been adjust, perspective, humility, and faith. I had to really focus on my own ability and progress. When I stopped measuring against what I thought I should be doing and started measuring based on what I could do, it all started falling into place. Celebrating the good even when missing a big goal, believing in myself even when I didn't feel or "look" like a faster runner. This had been a truly introspective cycle full of self-discovery and growth.

My family and friends were beyond supportive, and I believe they contributed heavily towards my success. For that, I'm forever grateful. The moment I submitted my application for Boston 2018 was monumental. I remember thinking of every single moment leading up to that point and every person who encouraged me to chase my dream. I waited patiently for my confirmation. I stressed, I refreshed my email. I tried to focus on other things. The day came, I received the coveted email. I was in!

I ran Boston with a grateful heart, and that is how I finished so strongly, with a PR and almost 12-minute buffer for 2019. I never imagined that I would even be able to qualify, let alone be accepted to one of the most prestigious races in the world. The whole journey to fulfill my Boston Bound dreams was magical, and one I will forever remember. I logged the most mileage of my life in my Boston training cycle. I trained in strong winds, snow storms, and subzero weather. I was prepared for Boston, until I hurt my hamstring two weeks out. The workout was Yasso 800's. On my 6th rep, I felt a burning sensation on the back of my leg and I shouted out in pain as I struggled to finish the last 100 meters. I cried as I lay down on the turf while one of my run mates massaged my hamstring. I immediately feared the worst and continued to cry the whole way home. I stopped at the drug store for pain relief and ointments. I looked up remedies, exercises, and recovery times. The next morning, a friend was able to get me into his PT for an assessment. She gave me some exercises and soothed my frazzled nerves with positive talk. She said if I followed her instructions to a tee, I would run Boston. I rested as much as I could, did my exercises, and took every supplement I could find that was recommended for muscle recovery. I tried a couple of test runs when approved. Some were ok and some were scary. I went to my chiropractor, who said I would get to the start line but had to listen to my body and assess how I felt as I continued into the hills. He used ART (active release therapy) then Graston on my last session. I woke up the next day very bruised. I was four days out from the big day. I stayed calm and just iced and focused on mental training. I knew that there was a chance I would struggle to cross the finish line, but I was going to give it my all because I had worked so hard for this moment.

We arrived into Boston, and the whirlwind of activity made me wish I could slow time down so that I could savor each and every moment. Receiving my bib was beyond emotional. Here I was, me - that girl who struggled to run a full mile without huffing and puffing, that girl who wondered if she would ever lose her back fat and associated pain (from all the extra pounds). I was among the fastest people in the world, and I was running the same race as them! The day before the race, I went for a shakeout run. As I approached the legendary Boston Marathon finish line, I was overcome with so many emotions. I looked around at all of the other smiling faces and felt a sense of comradery. I was headed to the runners' mass and noticed the makeshift memorial for the victims of the 2013 bombing. I reflected for a moment and thought of them as I headed to mass. It was a beautiful ceremony, and I loved seeing all of the Boston jackets in the crowds. I sat next to someone who quietly sobbed as I did. We hugged each other and instantly became friends. We cheered loudly as Carlos walked out holding the Boston Strong flag. On my way out, I ran into Meb and Bill. I took these all as great signs that I would have a perfect race. As I got ready for dinner, my friends stopped by and they all bustled about to set up a quick video they wanted to watch. I had no idea that they had conspired with all of my loved ones to make a video full of encouraging message from everyone. I bawled, laughed, clapped, and waved at the screen. It was too much, and I felt so loved. It helped tremendously. Right after, I met up with my run group and we enjoyed each other's company over the yummy pasta dinner hosted by the marathon.

Marathon morning, I woke up. The sound of the winds was loud. I looked out the window and saw people walking with umbrellas. I knew that the weather would be bad and was not the least bit preoccupied. I was so happy that the day had finally come. I made my coffee and started to get ready. My husband had left a ton of inspirational messages in the bathroom mirror. They made me smile and cry, even though he had used my good lipstick! I slathered on the Vaseline to protect myself against the elements and layered up with throwaway clothes. He woke up and asked me if I needed anything. I told him everything was set. He teared up and hugged me goodbye as I left the hotel room. I felt like a kid heading to her first day of school. I headed to gear check and then lined up for the buses. I met a girl in line and we chatted. We were both first timers. I asked if I could sit with her on the bus, she said of course. We finally boarded the bus and were on our way to Hopkinton. We talked about our goals and our lives, and discovered we were both in the Boston Marathon group. We were meant to sit together. We helped calm each other's nerves. She was pregnant, and I was worried about my hamstring. Just before our exit, our bus driver slammed on his brakes to avoid hitting a vehicle that had stopped suddenly. I'm so grateful for his quick thinking. I reached out to protect the girl sitting next to me and breathed a sigh of relief when we arrived safely at Athlete's Village. In conversation, we realized we were both part of the Boston Buddies Facebook group! It was such an amazing discovery.

The rain was not stopping. There was mud everywhere. People took cover wherever they were able, others just sat in the pouring rain, waiting. There were runners falling in the mud, and so many looks of concern and fear. I had arrived as the blue wave was starting. There was a bottleneck and I worried I would miss my start. I clutched my little gallon bag full of nutrition to my chest and decided not to fret, but to take in all the excitement. I tied bags to my feet so my shoes would not get wet. Water still seeped in and I giggled. I searched through the discarded items from the previous wave and grabbed two more bags to tie on so that I wouldn't be super muddy. I skidded through the mud and pushed my way past the crowd that seemed to be frozen in place. I then broke out into a light jog until I saw the corral fences. I realized people had already started running so I quickly shed my outer layers and realized I didn't have time to warm up. I reached for my Chipotle beanie and watched with dismay as it landed in a mud puddle. I quickly concentrated on putting my hood on and tying the strings securely (as best I could with limited dexterity) and I hit start on my watch as I passed the start line. It was go time.

I was immediately bowled over by the crowd support. The cold and rain did not keep them from showing up. They smiled and encouraged us, cheering and clapping. One woman had a bin full of new socks, ready to help anyone who needed it. I remember seeing a dog with the Boston Strong flags in his mouth. I kept running, and just took in as much as I could to distract me from the numbing cold. I ran in shorts, a tank, arm warmers, and a light windbreaker - a last minute purchase. I had cotton gloves on my hands, with surgical gloves stretched over them. I had a neck gaiter on as well, and it helped protect against the elements. I remember when I stopped avoiding the puddles then happily splashed through them in my Nike 4%'s. It started to feel good in a strangely comforting way.

I thought about all of my loved ones and felt my father's presence. The night before, I had seen a Pi sign, which was his favorite formula. I even saw a cardinal, which I always see when I send out the "dad, I need you" vibes. I thought of all of the advice I had gleaned from the Boston Buddies page. The most memorable was:

"2007 the Nor'easter Heavy Rain; winds gusting 25–30 mph; temperatures in the mid 40s. It was tough but nobody thought we had signed up to play checkers." Gary Allen, Boston Buddies

"Gloves and a hat and less clothes to soak up water. Our skin is the best raincoat of all." Gary Allen, Boston Buddies

Boston Buddies

I never really felt cold, and honestly, I'm sure it was thanks to that extra little layer of body fat I am still trying to lose. I remember the sound of the girls. I knew I was about to approach them before I saw them. They were amazing and hilarious! As I continued on, I remember seeing people looking into the crowds earnestly as they tried to spot their loved ones. It made me so happy! I ran alone but never felt lonely. I fed off the energy on that course, and the history that was made there. I was getting tired and felt myself slow down. I pumped myself up by thinking that I had gotten to this point, I would not let some rough conditions slow me down. I said, "you don't stop, you keep pumping those legs. This is what you came to do, now get it done!" I began to pray when my pace dropped a little. I was able to say the Our Father but had to try the Hail Mary a couple of times before I finally got it right, in Spanish. I still felt strong, but the hills were leaving me a little breathless due to the increasing winds and rain. I looked down and saw my legs were bright red. I wasn't shivering, I wasn't tired. I kept going. Fear has always held me back, but that day, I believed I was capable of anything. I missed the landmark signs: Hereford and Boylston, and the Citgo sign itself. Because at that point, the sky opened up and it felt like buckets of water were being poured on us. There was unanimous laugh from the runners around me. We all looked up and I wonder if they thought what I did, "hey Big Guy, is that all you've got?" We were strong, Boston strong. All of those men and women out there running were connected by hope – the bloodline in our special family. That day, I had 45,000 brothers and sisters. We absorbed strength from each other and used it to push forward relentlessly.

I saw my running group cheering near mile 23 and felt an instant urge of energy when I heard one of them shout my name. I kept looking for my husband and friends, but I never saw them. Little did I know that they were by the finish line, desperately looking for me. My husband had set up his phone to record and as we reviewed the video later, we found the moment I ran past. It was hilarious. When I crossed that finish line, I had to pump my fist in celebration. I smiled, laughed, and made it to the volunteer who was waiting for me with a warming blanket. I lost it when she patted it closed and said, "there, snug as a bug in a rug." When my medal was placed over my head, I closed my eyes and whispered, "Thank you." I felt like it was a statement of gratitude to the universe in general. I proceeded to grab my gear and just changed there, not wanting to wait in another line. At that point, many of the runners were doing the same. We didn't care about flashing a butt cheek or a boob, we had just completed the FREAKING Boston Marathon! Together, we did it, and that was all that mattered in that moment.

Laura Stellato, Bib 18725

Arnprior, ON, 36

I remember the first time I went for a jog other than in gym class. I was in Grade 10, it was my first year wrestling and the coach suggested running for fitness. I'm not going to lie, I hated it. I was slow and struggled with mild asthma. However, I loved wrestling and would do anything to get better and so when my coach said "Run", I ran. Our coach also suggested us join cross country and track and field teams to keep up our cross training. Which I obediently did, but I remember coming in last in track meets and cross country wasn't much better. So once I graduated and stopped wrestling, the running stopped as well.

Years later in 2009, my company sponsored the Ottawa Race Weekend 10km run and I was encouraged to participate. I didn't train properly, I ran 10km on a treadmill one morning thought "ok, I can do this" and signed up. I was busy with Judo and in decent shape so I thought "This will be fun!" in reality, only part of it was. It was intimidating at first, lining up with eight thousand other runners many of whom had raced before. But when the gun went off, the nerves went away and I ran. I loved the cheering of the crowds, the feeling of running with a large group all working towards the same goal. There were also times of pain and questioning what I was doing running when it hurt so much. Just when I thought it would never end, I realized I was in the finishing chute and something incredible happened. The cheering crowd gave me a final burst of energy and sprinted over the finish line. A feeling of accomplishment flooded over me and I was hooked! I apparently blocked the painful kms out of my memory and I quickly signed up for another 10km. This time I actually trained a bit and started running more regularly.

Thinking back to running back in high school, I realized that something had happened…those feelings of dread I used to feel when running were gone. What I had found was the feeling of freedom when I ran, the quiet and stillness of the road, the rhythmic sounds of my feet and my breathing. It was almost meditative. Running became my form of stress relief and kept my anxiety at manageable levels. And the races were FUN! I loved the feeling of crossing the finish line, earning a new personal best time and sometimes even placing well in my age category.

Over the next 9 years from my first road race, I continued to run, train and race with only a few months off when I had my son. With actual training, my times quickly dropped and I took 10 minutes off that first 10km race time. Having mostly run 5km or 10km races, I had never thought I could train for a full marathon. I didn't have the time to put in the training. I worked full time, had a young son and also had other commitments to a masters swim team.

Then my mentality shifted. My boyfriend and I kept reading all these incredible inspirational stories of people who had been through so much, cancer, heart transplants, and yet they were doing something incredible and running marathons. We realized we had no excuse to not try. So we found a low mileage training plan that I could work around my schedule and we signed up for the Ottawa Marathon. There was a lot to learn; types of runs, how to hydrate, how to fuel, how to analyze running form…the list goes on. My training runs went well and I started to estimate a finishing time. I realized that it might be possible to make a Boston Qualifying time. So I used that as a goal to train towards. The training was hard, those first 30km training runs were brutal and it took a lot of will to push through them.

After 5 months of training through the winter, we lined up at our first marathon on one of the hottest marathon Sundays in Ottawa history. The people of Ottawa were incredible! So many people had their sprinklers and hoses out, were handing out water bottles and ice or spraying us with water guns! The first ¾ of the race were incredible! I felt strong despite the heat. Then the last ¼ of the race came. Having only ran to 35km during training, I had no idea how hard those last kilometers can be. I remember trying to run up an overpass thinking it was the biggest hill in the world and I had thought the course was flat. At km 38 a spectator was trying to cheer me on and yelled "Keep going, you're looking good!" and it took a lot to not yell back "No, I'm not!"

I persevered and although I felt awful, I kept pushing to the finish. And that feeling of crossing a finish line? It was incredible for a couple seconds and then my calves started to cramp, and I didn't know if I should stop or keep running. However, the feeling of accomplishment was 10 times more than any race I had done until that point. I then looked at my finishing time 3:34:43! I had done it, I had made a Boston Qualifying time by over 5 minutes in my first marathon!

I'd love to say Shawn also ran a BQ, or even had a good race, but unfortunately, we learned how unforgiving the marathon can be. The heat and the grueling distance got to him and he had to walk. He did still finish however, which is an accomplishment in itself. He is a great runner though, and I know he will try again.

The next several months I mainly focused on shorter races and then applied to run the 2017 Boston Marathon. I got the email confirmation about a week later, I was in! It was time to plan out my training plan. Not being very experienced in running marathons I was constantly searching for information and advice. Then one day in early January of 2017 I came across a Facebook group for Boston Marathon Training and quickly requested to be added in. Little did I know what a great source of information, motivation, inspiration and friendship I would find in that group. The group helped me get through my training and on April 16th, I toed the line of the 2017 Boston Marathon. Once again it was warm, but I didn't let that bother me too much. I hydrated, dumped water on my head, took ice from spectators and ran the incredible 42.2km from Hopkinton to Boston. Words can't describe the feeling of being part of such an iconic event. There are times when all you can hear is the sound of the feet runners around you hitting the road. Then there are times when you can only hear the cheering of spectators or the blasting of motivational music.

Shawn, my sister Tara, brother-in-law Terry, Uncle Victor and Cousin Michael drove from point to point on the course and were able to see me at 3 different points along the run. Knowing they would be just up ahead gave me strength and energy to get to them. Gradually, I made my way through the 8 cities and towns of the marathon and somehow I eventually was making that glorious left-hand turn onto Boylston Street. I was hot and tired but there was the finish line! The street was lined with thousands of people all cheering for us to finish! And so I ran to the finish line and completed my first Boston in a time of 3:34:45! Another BQ!

Over that next year, I ran a couple more races, including an incredible Trail Relay race with Boston Buddies; Vince, Kristen, Kevin, Duane and Mary-Jo. It was comforting to have a bond with them over a common love of running and we had a great time.

Although I was unsure I wanted to run another marathon, or at least Boston, because I had requalified, I felt I needed to. I had been so set on proving my abilities in 2017 that I wanted another Boston to enjoy it. So I applied for 2018. And once again, I was in!

I trained in much the same way, lucky to only have minor injuries and was able to complete my training plan feeling good. My training runs hadn't been as fast, but I was uninjured and happy to be going to Boston with a new attitude this year. This year I would have even more of a support system. My Mom, Dad, Aunt Norma and Cousin Ryan joined the previous year's cheering team and came down to support me. Most of them also participated in the weekend by running the 5km race on the Saturday. I was so proud to see them training and working towards a goal. We had a great weekend, my family made red shirts with funny sayings on the back and we got a lot of attention wearing them! But my excitement was a bit overshadowed by the looming weather for Monday. I had looked at the forecast and it wasn't pretty. My family lovingly went to a department store and found me an extra sweater to toss at the start, a blanket and shoes for afterwards and a pair of ridiculous bright red rubber boots that had a small heel and a bow to wear in the athlete's village. When the morning came, I donned about 5 layers of clothes and ponchos and my fancy rubber boots and boarded a bus with my running shoes safe and dry in a plastic bag. Man was I happy for those boots; the athlete's village was a mud pit! But it was raining so much that it was hard to keep dry regardless of what you were wearing. I changed into my running shoes and took off a few extra layers right before starting the race but I was chilled and wet already when the gun went off. I did warm up quickly though and peeled off the remaining extra layers which were getting wet anyways.

My first 10km was amazing; I felt strong and fast and greeted my family with smiles and happiness. But then the first sign of trouble at km 12, my hands started to go numb. Having Raynaud's Phenomenon, this is nothing new, but my body can usually cope once I am warmed up from running. I kept running with my hands tucked in my gloves to try to keep them from getting worse. When I saw my family again at 22km I was uncomfortable, I hadn't completely felt my hands in an hour and my body was starting to chill. Last in line was Shawn and he knew something was wrong. "I'm cold" was all I could say. He gave me mitts for my gloves knowing they would get wet but needing the respite of warm hands for a few minutes. Not long after that, I started to shiver as I ran. Something I had never experienced before. I could no longer focus on running, all I could think about was how cold I was. Around 26km I ducked into a porta-potty and the reprieve from the wind was incredible. I stopped shivering and ran back out on to the course with new found vigor. It didn't last long. Only a few minutes later my shivering had started again so I ran to the next porta-potty. I willed my shivering to stop, but it wouldn't. The protection from the elements no longer allowed my body to warm up. I cried because I was cold and frustrated. Then I got out of the porta-potty and kept running. Every time I passed a Medical Tent, I thought I should stop and get help. I eventually did stop at one and they gave me a reflective blanket and tied it around me. I kept going but I was in pain, my leg muscles were sizing up and I was losing touch with where I was. I had no idea what hill I was on until someone yelled that I had made it to the top of Heartbreak Hill. I no longer thought about finishing, all I could think about was that it would be a pain for my family to find me if I stopped at a Medical Tent. So I kept going, knowing they were at km 34. Finally, my mom and my boyfriend came into sight and I started crying because I was so cold and scared. My boyfriend didn't say anything, he just pulled me off the course and held me while I cried. There was no discussion, my race was done. They took me to my sister's car, gave me hot chocolate, wrapped me in blankets and turned up the heat. It was still over an hour and a hot bath later before the shivering subsided. And that's when I cried because I hadn't finished.

I turned to my faithful Boston Buddies training group for support. Although most of them had finished and some even had great races, they were there for me with encouraging words and concern for my health.

I'm not going to lie, I cried on and off for a week. The pain of not completing the marathon ate away at me and I kept thinking about what I could have done differently. Then I pulled myself together and decided to put all that training to use. I signed up for the Mississauga marathon 3 weeks after Boston. I lucked out, the weather was perfect, the course was nice and the run was amazing. My parents and Shawn came to watch and cheer me on and I ran. And for my first time ever in a marathon I sprinted at the finish passing 2 other runners and smiling as I crossed. I also achieved a Boston Qualifying time by just over 4 minutes. It may not make the cutoff as the times keep getting faster every year. But I'm proud of my accomplishment, not because I re-qualified but because I got back into my running shoes and finished a race when I felt discouraged. And most importantly, it made me fall in love with running all over again.

Linnae Satterlee, Bib 24507

Grand Rapids, MI, 57, 4:18:18

Boston was supposed to be a one and done for me. I came to distance running later in life and was fortunate enough to qualify for Boston at my second marathon. I had a little over a minute cushion, and I made it in with 2 seconds to spare. My husband kept reminding me we were only doing this once, and I was fine with that. I was thrilled that I even earned the opportunity to run Boston at all!

That was 2012. And as many of you know, 2012 turned out to be one of the hottest Bostons in history. The forecast kept getting hotter and hotter, and the BAA sent out dire warnings, offering the option to defer, and strongly advising that only the most fit of runners participate. It was 89 degrees out on the course that day, and it was brutal. I was determined to finish, and I simply willed myself from one mile to the next, promising myself a stop at every water station. The last 6 miles felt like a death march, alternating walking with running, along with everyone around me. I finished with a PW, relieved to be done and so happy that I made it across that iconic finish line, considering many didn't make it due to heat stroke and dehydration. Later that day, my husband said to me, "You know you have to come back and run Boston again." He was right. I needed the opportunity to experience the Boston Marathon without extreme weather conditions. So much for the one and done.

Fast forward to 2018, and I am training for my 6th Boston. My plan is for this to be my last Boston. This will be my 5th Boston in a row. My body is tired, and the years of winter training have taken a toll on me, both mentally and physically. I need a break. My hope is for a beautiful day in Boston to run well, enjoy the course, and go out on a high note. Little did I know what was in store for me.

As Marathon Weekend approached, and the usual nerves and jitters set in, I began obsessively tracking the weather. 10 days out, rain forecasted, but it will change, right? Five days out, same. At the least the temps looked mild. Some rain with decent temps- it could be worse!

We arrived in Boston for the weekend to chilly but dry weather. Race day forecast was now more rain but reasonable temps. The day after the marathon looked beautiful, of course. At the expo on Saturday there was a lot of talk about Monday's weather and what to wear, but people were in good spirits. Jackets, hats and gloves were selling briskly.

Sunday afternoon the conditions began to really deteriorate for Monday. I was becoming increasingly concerned, and really rethinking my clothing choices. The predictions now called for heavy rain, strong winds, and cold temperatures. I was not looking forward to this at all at this point, especially since I tend to run cold. My husband and I went to a thrift store where I purchased a heavy Sherpa-lined men's flannel shirt for race morning. I also had a disposable rain poncho that I had brought from home, as well as old wind pants. I only had one pair of thin gloves, so I bought a second thin pair and figured I would be fine.

Sunday night I nervously laid out my race clothes and extra layers, preparing for the worst but hoping for the best. Wishing that somehow, miraculously, the forecast would change overnight. I could take the cold, I was just hoping for less rain. I ran in 2015 when it was cold with light rain, and actually had a great race that day. We had gone out for a simple Italian dinner and a glass of wine, hoping that would help to ease my nerves. I settled into bed, praying for some solid sleep, but of course that didn't happen. Throughout the night I heard intermittent wind and rain, and I steeled myself for what the morning would bring.

Race day morning came and I gloomily began preparing for the day. Coffee and the little bit of breakfast I could choke down. Started getting dressed. Short sleeve shirt with arm sleeves, compression capris that I wished were long pants, thin jacket, hat, headband, socks, shoes, thin gloves, poncho, and finally some warm throwaways. I had purchased a waterproof waist belt for my phone and nutrition, and a belt for my bib so I could easily move it between layers if need be. Having driven from Michigan to Boston, we had our car, so we loaded up and began the trek to Hopkinton. As we travelled the miles, the rain came down, and my anxiety went up. My husband dropped me off for the final bus to Athlete's Village and promised me he would see me along the course.

I arrived at the high school, bags tied around my feet, latex gloves given to me by someone on the bus in my pocket, and joined the other athletes as we trudged into the staging area. What I encountered was far worse than anything I expected. The entire field was a mud pit, with debris everywhere, and runners dressed in varying degrees of strange protective layers, doing everything they could to seek shelter from the elements. It was a bit like a war zone. Because I had not arrived any too early, (what was the point?), I went under a tent for a brief period, then realized I needed to make my way over to the start corral. The line was moving slowly, and my panic level began to rise, as I realized I was not going to make it to my start corral in time. I had arranged to meet a friend and we were going to try and run together, but I had been unable to reach her by phone and confirm her location. As I neared the final turn to the start, I heard the announcers telling everyone to get to the start line and just go. They were not starting the groups in waves or corrals, it was every man for himself. No celebratory announcements and fanfare, just hunker down and go. I tried to peel out of my heavy layers, and tried to start my music, but it was raining so hard and everything was getting so wet that I finally just gave up. Wearing my dollar store poncho that I was sure would only last a few miles, I crossed the start line with a dismal attitude and realized it was time to dig in and get this thing done.

It was cold. I mean REALLY cold. And raining. Raining HARD. Also extremely windy. I started running, hoping to just tick off the miles and power through. As usual, adrenaline and the long downhill start caused me to run the first few miles much faster than I should. But that was the best I would feel for the entire race. It didn't take long to realize that despite my best attempts to protect myself, I was going to be wet. Very wet. My hat shielded my eyes, and the poncho was doing a remarkable job of keeping my upper body dry, but my hands and feet were quickly soaked. And I didn't expect the poncho to last.

Around mile 4 I encountered my husband and got a quick pep talk. "You've got this", he said, "just keep going". I had him try and help me get my music started, but it wouldn't connect, so I gave up and soldiered on. I continued ticking off the miles, focusing on the road in front of me and trying to avoid the rivers of water streaming across. There was no joy on the course. Everyone plodded on, trying to stay ahead of their own personal misery.

The next "pit stop" with my husband was around mile 10. My hands were frozen and shaking, so I needed him to dig into the belt that I had unfortunately worn under my jacket (so sure that I would be shedding it at some point!) and dig out a gel for me. I couldn't even open it myself, because I couldn't feel my fingers. He again encouraged me and told me he would see me at Heartbreak Hill. I numbly carried on, moving through towns, past Wellesley and the scream tunnel, oblivious to most of the goings on around me. The rain continued to pour, the temperature dropped, and the winds howled. When I thought it couldn't possibly get any worse, and I said to myself "Come on, Mother Nature, is this the best you've got?", it actually rained harder. Torrential downpour were the words that came to mind. I was wet, downtrodden and cold, although remarkably the poncho was still intact and offering at least some protection. I wondered to myself what I had done with the latex gloves and wished I could find them, but it seemed like way too much effort, and my brain wasn't working very well at this point.

Finally I made it to the hills. The long downhill stretch after the overpass is typically one of my favorite parts. I usually feel like I am flying at this point. Despite the downpour, I did get minimal enjoyment from that stretch. I began the ascent into Newton and was happy to have a reason for my physical discomfort that was not merely associated with cold and rain. Just before Heartbreak, as promised, my husband was on the course. Teeth chattering, numb and exhausted, I told him I didn't know if I could continue. He reminded me that after Heartbreak I was in the home stretch and promised to be on the course for me once more, around mile 22. I cannot tell you how much that meant to me. I literally willed myself along the course, counting down the miles until the next time I would see my husband.

I proceeded on, crested Heartbreak, and began the descent into the city. As I approached Boston College, feeling cold, wet, and battered, I began to feel like I was having an out of body experience. It was as though I was floating above, watching myself struggle with the elements and push on. Later I would realize that this had happened to me multiple times along the course, something I had never before experienced. It was as though my body's defense mechanism kicked in, protecting my brain from the trauma it was experiencing.

The Citgo sign gloriously appeared, and I began checking off the last turns and landmarks. My husband appeared as promised and told me he would see me after the finish line! I felt a strength and resolve I didn't know I had, and though I felt battered and broken, I was not beaten. I would finish this race, come hell or high water.

At the mile 25 mark, I decided it was time to shed the poncho that had become my best friend. As much as that poncho had protected me, I didn't want it on for my finish line photos. With a little over a mile to go, I bravely ripped it off and discarded it. Feeling a new freedom and knowing I really couldn't get any wetter than I already was, I found a final burst of energy to carry me toward the finish. I made that right turn onto Hereford, through a sea of discarded ponchos, (everyone else had the same idea as me, just not as soon!), and made that final turn onto Boylston. My tears of joy mixed with the rain hitting my face as I ran that last stretch toward the finish line, trying to soak it all in, the misery I had felt and now the glory that I was experiencing. Crossing that finish line, cold, numb, and soaked to the skin, I was elated knowing that I could finally get out of the rain, but more importantly, that I had survived and endured.

I trudged through the finisher's chute, collecting my heat sheet and medal, posing for the obligatory photo (I needed to forever remember this moment), moving through the water and food, none of which I wanted, and I finally spilled out of the chute, huddled under a roofline, and dug out my phone. I called my husband, delirious from cold and exhaustion, unable to find him. "I'm right across the street from you!" he yelled. I walked unsteadily towards him, hugged him with relief, and we started towards the car. "I'm so proud of you" he said. He knew what I had gone through to get to that point. Almost as if to taunt me, the rain again increased in intensity. I was shaking uncontrollably at this point, wondering what kind of insanity leads a person to do what I had just done. We got back to our condo and my husband started a hot shower for me. I was still shaking so badly that I couldn't get my rain-soaked clothing off, and he had to peel them off for me. After a long and gloriously hot shower, dressed in warm clothing, we headed out for food and drinks to celebrate. As exhausted as I was, I knew if I sat down I wouldn't get back up, and I needed to celebrate what I had just survived. Grit and determination carried me through. It wasn't a BQ that day but it also wasn't a PW, and after learning how many people had to drop out, I felt grateful (and badass) that I was able to finish!

Takeaways and final thoughts:

The human body is remarkably resilient, and you are able to endure far more than you think you are capable of.

Running a marathon is no joke, especially in those conditions, and the mental fortitude you glean from that experience will carry you far in every aspect of your life.

Never underestimate the value of a dollar store poncho. Sometimes it's the little things that are lifesavers.

I truly do not know what I would have done without my husband. He isn't a runner, but his unwavering support means the world to me. He is my cheerleader and greatest fan. Having that person out there for you makes all the difference.

The Boston Marathon is, hands down, the greatest race in the world. Despite the insane conditions, the spectators and volunteers were incredible and amazing. I thank them from the bottom of my heart; I don't know what I would have done without them.

Yes, I know I am crazy.

Yes, there WILL be another Boston. Even if it takes me a few years to get back. Although it may seem fitting that my proposed last Boston was the polar opposite of my first, going from extreme heat to torrential rain, brutal cold and headwinds, this will NOT be my Swan Song. Having also run Boston in perfect conditions as well, I need one more shot to redeem myself and create a new last memory.

Mark Johnson, Bib 17645

Sayre, PA, 56, 4:11:34

I didn't want to run just any marathon, I wanted to run the Boston Marathon. My wife and I were eating dinner at the restaurant we got married at. You can't just tell your spouse you want to run a marathon in casual conversation. There is a time and a place to break that kind of news. I would classify her reaction as supportive, but not enthusiastic.

It's January 2016 and my journey was underway. I'm registered. Training. And injured. Well that didn't take long. After a few months of PT, and a bit of knowledge gained, training for Wineglass 2016 begins. Wineglass finishes in Corning, NY. About 40 minutes from my house making race day logistics simple while allowing for tremendous support from family and friends. After following Boston marathon training plan, what else would a novice follow other than the plan for the race they want to be in, I was ready.

Race weekend arrived. While attending my running club's social event we were all discussing race goals. I naively thought being a 55-year-old first time marathoner and running a BQ was entirely reasonable. Based on the reaction of my Facebook running group in attendance that day, it wasn't. Three hours and 32 minutes after the start I crossed the finish line with my BQ goal met. Now I merely had to wait a full year and a half to realize my Boston dream.

Along comes September 2017. I'm agonizing over registering. In the past year I have learned a tremendous lesson about the value of a Boston bib. Runners have dedicated years of training to get one. If I register and can't run I can't give it back. Someone else, who probably worked harder than me to get one is left at home. Friends told me it's my bib, I earned it and should use it even if I have to walk. I had just been cleared to run after my second heart attack of the summer. I didn't know if I would be able to run again, let alone train for Boston. That registration confirmation made it all seem so real.

We all have our reasons for running. I wish I wasn't one. I wish I didn't have the opportunity to make the promise I made on that cold December night. For reasons I'll never understand I was in a situation where continuing the strides my 14-year-old son used to take. My promise was to run a 5K for Chase. Since that day my running has always been to honor my son. Training for the race went great. I stumbled on the Boston Marathon Training group and that enhanced my training experience and helped me prepare for the whole weekend.

Race weekend was a wonderful experience. I was amazed at the warm welcome the people of Boston gave to the runners. From the Expo to watching the 5K to attending the Sunday morning service at Old South Church to walking around the finish line area all activities just heightened the expectation for Monday morning. Race Day clearly added to my long list of memories. I felt tremendous compassion for the volunteers, spectators, and fellow runners. It wasn't a good day for me and I was initially quite disappointed. I felt I had let everyone down by my race performance. And in the end, it was quite the opposite. I am beyond words appreciative of the support from family, friends, and the running community I received. Several months have passed since race day. After processing everything I registered for Wineglass 2018. I hope to earn another BQ and get to participate at Boston again. Either way, I recognize how truly fortunate I was to be a part of the 2018 version of The Marathon.

Amber Crowley, Bib 24193

Naples, FL, 60, 4:20:53

I'm a late bloomer runner. At age 60 I ran Boston for the first time, under historically adverse conditions in 2018. I am so much stronger of a person for having faced that challenge. I learned to dig deep and draw on all my physical, mental and spiritual resources. As a physician I run for stress reduction and wellness. I love the comradery of other runners and treasure the shared miles. I hope to keep running for many years to come. Thank God for the strength to run, the heart to love and the spirit to dream." Thank you, Vince, for writing the stories of the Boston Buddies.

Uma Staehler, Bib 26254

Cambridge, MA, 48, 5:13:05

Originally from Indianapolis, IN, I moved to Boston in May 2017 after 3 years in Shanghai. I have been running most of my life, after running as a kid, I came back to it after college after seeing my hometown Indy 500 half marathon for the first time. After many years of running that annually, I added a fall half to do twice a year. Training for a marathon seemed overwhelming, but after a life altering personal/professional experience, I needed to do something for myself to remind me of what I'm capable of.

I ran the Indy Monumental Marathon, and the next few years I would do several halves a year and one full (Chicago, Shanghai, Great Wall). I looked for a running group when we moved to Shanghai as a way to meet people, and the group became my tribe (expats need a lot of support!) allowing for several running vacations with people I know will remain lifelong friends. When we learned we were moving to Boston, running the Boston Marathon was quickly identified as my bucket list item. Not knowing how long we'd be here, I decided to sign up as a charity runner for the Red Cross. The marathon journey was more than I could have ever imagined; training runs along the course with race size groups and support, and marathon weekend with all its festivities was AMAZING (busier than when I go to a conference!) with packet pickup, expo volunteering, events, movie, shakeout runs, etc.

I had a fair bit of fundraising to do as well; my husband was onboard with us footing the bill if needed, but local businesses were so supportive allowing me to create a few raffles for generous friends and family and my company did a match lightening the load. Marathon Monday will remain a milestone event for me -- the volunteers and spectators (thank you sock ladies for helping my fingers stay warm, first time for having friends make signs for me), my husband surprising me with a kiss at mile 23, turning right on Hereford and playing hopscotch over the shed raingear, and left on Boylston with teary eyes that blended in with the rain to finish something that seemed so unattainable a few years ago.

Boston Buddies has been a great gift to me—not just helping me prepare for the marathon but seeing the hard work and sacrifices that runners put in to have strong finishes. It helped me realize how inconsistent I was, reflected in my time and stamina. It's almost 6 months later, and I've almost worked thru my tendonitis, more consistent and focused, and got my eyes set on a 2020 BQ. I'm excited to be a volunteer in 2019 and see the race from a different perspective, and cheer many of you on!

I will forever be grateful for the vulnerability and candidness that Boston Buddies share about things going thru my head. I would be unfriended if I shared/discussed so much running in my regular social media feed!! I know I'm not alone and that together we are stronger! Boston Strong.

Brian Siddons, Bib 20941

Andover, MN, 60, 4:04:53

My 10-year journey to Boston began in typical crash-and-burn style at the 2008 Medtronic Twin Cities Marathon. After an encouraging 20-mile race three weeks before, and a 5k tune up the weekend before, I felt ready. Unfortunately, I was totally unprepared to execute a smart race. Picture a glazed-eyed, frantic looking runner holding the drawstring of his shorts out so the five gel packs that were pinned to his waistband wouldn't pull said shorts down to his ankles! Starting out too fast and hitting the wall at 20 miles kept me well off the 3:35.59 finishing time I needed. My finishing time of 3:42.08 didn't totally destroy my confidence, but I felt that such a disaster would never be repeated.

Fast forward to the same race in 2011. My good friend, "Fly Bry", would be running with me to keep me going, especially during the hills from 20 to 23. We had also lined up to run with the 3:40 pace team, as I was now shooting for a new age group time. Just before five miles the group had come together and we were in a nice groove. That is until the pace leader said he had to stop for a potty break. We never saw him again and the group began to break up soon after. So did my race. Erratic pacing, no pace bands, no GPS. I didn't realize all the things that could still go awry. Finishing in 3:42.18 was tougher this time and I vowed to be fully prepared for my next attempt.

The target for 2012 was Grandma's Marathon in Duluth, MN. My friend, Dave, who had run his first marathon in 2011 in just under four hours, had come into his own and had caught up to my pace. At 20 years my junior he was already pulling me through some solid training efforts. We were confident the 8:21 pace was doable. We were primed, as were my wife, Jeanette, and the final of our foursome, Stan. Unfortunately, the weather was also primed; 70' temp and 70% humidity at the start. It was a brutal day and by the 8 mile point we were sweating way too much. We gave it a go, but to no avail. Dave and I battled to the finish and crossed in 3:44.40. We were in too good of shape to let it go to waste.

We all signed up for a fall marathon within a couple of weeks. Dave and Stan chose Twin Cities, and they both did very well. Stan set a course PR for himself in 3:55.57, and Dave busted through our target with a 3:39.53, showing me our training was on target and the goal time was within reach! Jeanette and I picked Whistle Stop in Ashland, Wisconsin although she got sick just before the race and wasn't able to run. It's a small, well run trail race, and the flat course in normally mild temps draws a number of runners looking to BQ. It didn't disappoint! It was a cool day with enough runners to key on that kept me in the race and on pace. At 21 miles a guy in the small group I was running with started to pull away. I was tempted to go with him but after three fails I kept on my target pace, knowing I was under goal by more than a minute. Struggling through the last three miles I lost a bit of time, but still finished 1:28 under my BQ with a time of 3:38.32!

The joy of sharing that accomplishment with family and friends who had supported my journey was priceless. I'll never forget how fun it was to talk with everyone on the ride home! My time was not only 1:28 under my BQ, but also under the recent changes of dropping 5 minutes off, plus the 59 seconds. I felt pretty confident I'd make the cut for 2014. Then things changed forever at the 2013 Boston Marathon, and everyone wanted to run in 2014. Totally understandable, totally Boston Strong! I missed the BQ cut by just six seconds for 2014. It was tough to take, but I had hit my goal of earning a BQ and I'd always have that day.

It took a couple of years, but I was back at it in 2016, aiming for a new age group BQ. With a number of changes in our training, we used Grandma's 2016 as a test marathon. Even being another hot and humid June day, I had a solid training race and finished the last 8 miles in good shape, closing with a 7:42 last mile, and a finish time of 3:44.51. We picked Twin Cities for our BQ attempt, as I knew even with the hills I'd be well under the 3:55 BQ for 2018. Jeanette would also run, and her streak of BQ's was pretty much assured to continue - she's amazing! Twin Cities was another beautiful fall day. I had a great run, although I was not in the shape I had hoped I'd be in. Dave crushed the course with a 3:30.02, nearly a half-hour faster than his first marathon in 2011. Stan hit a solid 4:00.39 after battling injuries for a month before the race. Jeanette earned a -17:03 BQ with a 3:52.57, and I crossed in a -11:52 BQ at 3:43.08, exactly one minute slower than my first attempt in 2008.

I knew we'd make the cut for Boston 2018, so I was very happy with the race, but not satisfied. I was still hungry for a faster time. With the high cost of getting to Boston, Jeanette and I decided we'd pass on running the race. As crazy as that sounds now, it seemed okay at the time. With that decision made, Stan and I decided we would run the Fargo Marathon in May of 2018 and do our best to run a fast time. Not long after we signed up, the reality of earning a BQ in the same year hit Jeanette and I. With some additional prodding from family and friends we signed up to run Boston 2018 and would make it a celebration run. We'd enjoy the trip, run the race at a respectable pace and check it off our bucket list.

I now had a few things on my running calendar I had never done before. Boston Marathon, of course, was the big highlight, however my race goal of breaking 3:40 at Fargo was a keen focus for my personal improvement. Now I'd have a 26.2-mile training run just five weeks before Fargo, something I'd never done before. The incredible day that was Boston in 2018 will forever be remembered for the wild weather, and for me it will also be a day that paid big dividends five weeks later. Running at a pace that made it a long training run on my schedule, Jeanette and I finished in 4:04.53. I was able to recover in a couple of weeks and then ramp up for Fargo. Boston was everything we thought it would be, and more, and yet Fargo was the time goal I had been working on for years.

There's something the Boston class of 2018 will be able to carry into any future race, and that's the knowledge we can finish a race in any weather. The morning of Fargo, winds were blowing with gusts nearing 30 mph, and an air temp in the low 40's that felt much colder. I had to laugh, because it was too cruel to cry about. My big attempt was not going to get ruined because of some wind and cold. I dressed for success and set off not letting the weather get the best of me. It worked, and I have Boston to thank for two key parts of my success at Fargo. The ability to run the Boston Marathon five weeks earlier gave me a solid long run base, even though it beat me up a bit more physically than I had expected, it gave me a huge mental boost. Second, the weather didn't get me down at Fargo. Sure, we had some tough winds, but I kept focused and told myself I'd handled worse, with driving rain! Crossing the finish line in 3:35.42, a -19:18 BQ, at the Fargo Marathon was as big a day as my first BQ. Not only was it nearly three minutes faster than I ran that BQ in 2012, and a revenge BQ of -4:18 in that age group, I have a higher value on what it takes to BQ.

It also adds emphasis to how lucky I am to be able to hit the time I did. Yes, there was plenty of hard work, especially during the winter months in Minnesota, but I still feel blessed to be running faster at age 60 than I was six years ago. The biggest thing I've learned through all of this is how much family and friends (including my Boston Buddies) enjoy seeing me succeed. They want me to do well, and they are so kind and supportive along the running journey. I dedicate my success to each and every one of them. It makes the tough days easier to get through, and the good days that much sweeter!

Carol Sexton, Bib 17313

Woodinville, WA, 60

"We can plan all we want for an event - clothing, nutrition, mindset and training - but when it all comes down to it, unexpected things happen. Regardless of yesterday's result, very proud of this lady and can't wait to see her take on the next marathon! Don't worry Boston, she'll be back!"

This message was sent by my daughter who lives in Boston. She has steadfastly watched me in each of my Boston marathons (five completed, one DNF - Boston 2018!). I loved her message, which pretty much sums it up. She got me started running when I was in my mid-50's. All my marathons have been a BQ. I never thought I'd ever not finish a marathon.

Oh how I pondered the weather on that day in 2018 with the worst weather on race record and a DNF. I was humbled. Six days later I ran London in the hottest weather they had seen, my 25th completed marathon. How poetic? What doesn't kill you makes you stronger, hey?

I will always remember that race day in April 2018. When I did decide to stop at mile 8.5, I was humbled walking into the medical tent. There were others, many who had stopped but it didn't make it easier to swallow. The medical staff and volunteers were so kind. With my hands blue they gently said: 'I don't think you should resume the race, you'll likely have to stop later'.

The rest of my body was relatively fine but obviously cold. I was tragically underdressed for this race. I always loved running in cold and wet - these had been my best race times. However, I was lined up to run London six days later and I didn't want to risk missing out on my 6-star medal.

Would I end up in the hospital? So much hinged on this decision. You only know that feeling when you're in pursuit of something grand. It took them three hours to get us to the finish line via bus. We had to transfer buses because there were so many DNFs.

I remember hearing someone say: 'We have three elites here, 10 pickups there.' It went on and on. Oh my goodness. The medical staff was incredible. Offering water, food - even their phones so we could call our families.

'Awesome job', I was thinking, I could have walked there in this time and gotten my medal. Ugh. Things happen for a reason. I'll be ready for anything next time. Thank, you Boston.

Michael Gannon, Bib 28100

Waltham, MA, 57

I grew up in Watertown, MA when it was an ordinary place. I now live in Waltham, MA with my wife Bonnie, and have never lived far from the course. My love for the Boston Marathon started when I was age 9. My parents started taking us to Cleveland Circle, and I was hooked. I have been a spectator, volunteer, or runner in each one except 1 Boston since then.

At age 19 I finally started running to become a better basketball player. I then got addicted to it, read all I could, and a year later ran a 40:30 10k, still my fastest race. 26.2 was never a realistic goal until someone in grad school talked about how possible finishing was via training. Another friend and I kept that in mind when our respective kids (Jake and Mia) were a little older.

We completed the Cape Cod Marathon in October 1999 (4:30) and set our sights on Boston 2000 which we ran unofficially. Not getting a medal for all that hard work, was enough to deter from me ever doing that again without a number. We ran the Cape again that October (4:14) but had already started looking into officially running Boston.

I joined the Greater Framingham Running Club (GFRC) and was able to win a Boston 2001 # in our lottery. I ended up getting shin splints, and a bad sinus infection during my taper. I was told by a physician not to run which I ignored. This was back in the days of being told to drink fluids often which I did to excess (1 water, plus 1 Gatorade each mile) but finished. Later I was taken to Mass General where I had seizures, and later diagnosed with hyponatremia.

In total I have run 11 marathons so far. 6 Bostons, 2 Cape, 2 Baystate, and 1 in Saint John, NB Canada which was my mom's hometown, and a bucket list item when I ran 4:53 in 2015. I started Boston 2018, but had stomach problems early and couldn't run after mile 3 so bailed at 13 when I still couldn't fix it. My last Boston finish was 2014 when I ran 4:59 which I was so thrilled to be part of.

In addition to always wanting to be part of the Boston Marathon, I'm also a big fan of the elites. I have been able to meet 58 of them who signed 2 posters. My biggest get was Alberto Salazar in 2012 my very first favorite elite, and just recently met Des Linden for the 3rd time.

Lori Ann Fromlak, Bib 16733

Valencia, PA, 37, 3:59:49

Three years ago I couldn't even run half a minute without stopping. And when I ran that 30 seconds I was winded. But I was out there, eager to make a change. In 2014 I weighed 200 pounds and had been a regular smoker since my teens. My sister-in-law and I made a pact to lose weight together, and we began using MyFitnessPal and following a couch-to-5K program to get healthy. And soon, we were dropping weight.

It wasn't easy, but the results came. I started running and tracking my food on MyFitnessPal that June, knowing the progress might come slowly. But it did come. By the time I ran my first 5K that Thanksgiving, I was already down to 163 pounds. By my second 5K in the spring, I was 145 pounds. But I didn't stop there. It turned out I wasn't just using running to lose weight — I was a pretty good runner, too. My training partner, Scott Wardle says "There are people who run and there are runners. Lori is a runner." From the very first time I ran with him, he knew I "had it." Soon, I was racing and qualifying for the Boston Marathon, which requires roughly 8-minute miles from its participants.

The beginning of my journey was the hardest. The extra weight and smoking made it hard just to break into a run. A marathon was the furthest thing from my mind. It's tough, the more weight you're carrying, the slower you're going to go. When I started, 11-minute miles were a very modest, reasonable goal. But I kept at it, alternating walking and jogging. I also began keeping a food diary on MyFitnessPal, which I still does to this day to help me train. Slowly, the weight started to come off and, bit by bit, I got a little faster. Soon, I met My goal: run a 5K in less than a half-hour. That's when I started thinking about longer races.

Running and keeping track of what I was eating were two important steps in my transformation. They got me moving in the right direction, but the last step was the hardest: quitting smoking. I knew it was bad for me, but it's not easy to break a habit you've carried for 20 years. It finally came down to my then 7-year-old daughter. I saw the disappointment in her face every time I'd light a cigarette. It wasn't until I finally reached a point when I was training for my first half-marathon in May 2015 that I knew I couldn't keep it up. I had to pick, did I want to keep running or did I want to smoke?

As a full-time nurse, I work two eight-hour shifts and two 12-hour shifts each week. Most days, I wake up around 3:45 a.m., run, then wake up my kids and take them to school. If I have to get in a long run on the weekends, I wake up early so I won't be out too late after the kids are awake.

I had to run a sub-3:40 marathon to qualify for 2018. I didn't quite get there during my first two marathons. The training and stress of trying to hit that goal led to injuries and disappointment. So, instead, I took a little break, regrouped and then ran the Philadelphia Marathon without putting as much pressure on myself. That's when it all came together: I crossed the finish line in 3:30. A spot in Boston was mine.

Brian Towler, Bib 24039

Taringa, AUS, 67, 5:19:15

I previously ran the Boston Marathon in 2016. However, just three months after my Boston debut, I was diagnosed with blocked coronary arteries and consequently, in August 2016, I underwent a quadruple bypass operation. I recovered from that and began running again in November 2016 and in July 2017 I ran the Gold Coast Marathon (Gold Coast, Australia) finishing in 3:58:06. This qualified me to enter and run the 2018 Boston Marathon (I am 67 years old). After I began my marathon training in November 2016 I noticed that I was having problems, which I attributed to the statin drug (to lower my cholesterol) that I was taking (20mg of Rosuvastatin). I decided that statins were incompatible with running training, and I discontinued the statin and put myself on a plant-based diet instead. That is a whole other story in itself!

I also ran the 2018 Tokyo Marathon in February 2018. However, training for Boston and Tokyo marathons also proved problematic. Firstly, training for them was in the heat of a Brisbane summer, which is quite hot and humid. Secondly, I noticed my running times in the weekly Park Run 5km races were degrading quite rapidly. I have still yet to determine the exact cause of my current problems. I ran a disappointing 4:29:19 in Tokyo. After returning from

Tokyo I arranged for blood tests and stress tests on my heart, because I was sure that something was physically wrong with me, but I was given a clean bill of health.

I arrived at the start line of Boston under trained and lacking any confidence. The conditions were atrocious, pouring rain, near freezing temperature, and a fierce headwind. When I was walking the 2km from my hotel, east to Boston Common to catch the bus, the wind was so strong I had to take shelter at times. When we got to the Athlete's Village in Hopkinton the sporting field where we were supposed to congregate was a sea of mud.

I tried to wrap my shoes in plastic bags to get across to the tent and the port-a-loos, but by the time I reached there, the plastic bags were long gone, and my shoes and socks were soaked and caked in mud. I was wearing a hat that covered my ears, gloves and layers of clothing, but none of these were water-proof. I did have a plastic poncho and suede leather jacket, which kept me reasonably warm until the start line. However, you can't run in those and I ditched them soon after the start!

I decided early on not to worry about my time, just run to get to Boston. The goal was to take home a finisher's medal, and they give you one of those no matter what time you run. I ran the first half in 2:02:30, which, in the circumstances, is a decent time for me or even someone my age. In the second half the lactic acid was building up and causing me a lot of pain. I powered up the Newton Hills, giving it all I had. But by the 35K mark I had hit the wall. I had no energy left and I was in severe pain.

By the 37km mark I was staggering, not thinking clearly and in serious trouble. I decided to walk it in – yet still focused on getting my medal. When I reached the medical tent just before the 40km mark, one of the medical officials said to me, "Are you ok?" Well I wasn't ok, I was in severe pain, I had no glycogen in my muscles, I was shivering, and I was just trying to finish. But if this guy standing on the side of the road could tell I was having trouble, I thought it must be obvious. So I decided to enter the medical tent. They put a blanket around me, put me in front of a heater and gave me some hot vegetable broth.

Meanwhile, back in Australia, my family had been following my progress online and had seen me pass the 35km mark in reasonable time. But then I disappeared off the radar and they were freaking out, fearing the worst, because I had told them about the tough conditions that had descended on Boston, prior to leaving my hotel.

After about 40 minutes in the medical tent I decided that I had recovered enough, and I told them I wanted to finish the race. They understood enough to not try and stop me, and I staggered out into the cold and got running again and forged forward to the finish line. I finished in 5:19:15 - my worst marathon time, but I don't blame the tough conditions for that. I should be able to run a marathon in under 4 hours. The tough conditions at Boston 2018 might add 5% to your time, so 4:10:00 would have been a reasonable time for me. The rest I attribute to a lack of proper preparation. I can do better, and I hope to be back there one day.

Karen Selby, Bib 21402

Leicestershire, GBR, 47, 3:59:09

My road to Boston took 8 years. It all started back in 2009, when my teenage cousin was diagnosed with Hodgkins. Being a close-knit family we were all devastated to say the least. We watched in despair as she went through grueling chemotherapy, standing back and watching as the brilliant doctors and nurses looked after her. She never complained once and just seemed to get on with it. I wanted so much to do something to help.

It was going to be my 40th birthday soon so I decided I was going to run London Marathon for the children's cancer charity, Children with Leukemia, to help raise funds. I'd never ran any farther than 5 miles before so it certainly was going to be a huge challenge. I got in touch with the charity and they gave me a place straight away once I told them why I would love to run for them. Not knowing anything about how to run a marathon, I looked around the internet and found a very basic training plan. It was the hardest thing I'd ever done; the training was hard for me but I found a lot of support from family and friends I'd made on social media (whilst looking for tips on Marathon running!)

I ran the London Marathon (for the 1st time) in 2010. It was so hard, and I hit the wall around mile 17. I just wanted to give up, but then I thought of my little cousin and all she'd had to endure without a word of complaint. There were also thousands of people supporting me at the side of the road, willing me on every time I stopped to have a walk when I felt I couldn't go on. I had to keep going. By the time I reached the finish line hours I swore that was my first and last marathon I'd ever run. However, I did feel an amazing sense of achievement that I'd actually crossed that line. That was where I'd caught the running bug.

I joined a local running club and I loved it. Running became my passion, I ran another 2 marathons the following year, then in 2012 I ran London marathon again. I had my own entry, but I ran for another cancer charity raising funds as a very close family member had been diagnosed with breast cancer for the 2nd time. It was a terrible marathon for me as both my aunt & uncle had lost their battles to the terrible illness 2 months (six weeks within each other) before the race. Every step I took was so emotional, I was a wreck. But I finished and had raised well over £15,000 for the charity's running those marathons.

Every year I kept entering New York City Marathon but was never successful in getting through the lottery. It took 3 years before I finally got through in 2014. I was ecstatic. I'd watched NYC marathon on the TV every year and now I was finally going to be part of it. All was going well through training until the last 5 weeks when suddenly out on one of my training runs I felt this searing pain on the outside of my ankle. I stopped and walked, was fine - no pain so began to run. Nope as soon as I started the searing pain was there again. I didn't know what was wrong. I walked home, got some ice on it but not overly worried, thought it would be ok next day. It wasn't, same pain again when I tried to run. I saw a Physio who said after examining it he was 95% sure I'd fractured my fibula but wouldn't know unless I had an MRI scan to be sure. WTF! I hadn't tripped or slipped. How could this be? I decided I didn't want to know if it was - he was a runner and knew how much this meant to me so he advised me to get a floatation belt, get in the pool and do some pool running, which I did every day until a week before flying to NY. I then did a very wary, slowly 10 mile run to see how the ankle was. No pain so I made the decision to go to NY and run the marathon but put no pressure on self to get any kind of time just go to enjoy it & take it all in.

I was blown away by the whole NY experience. I'd never experienced a marathon like it, so many runners, everyone hyped up, making new friends from across the globe. One of my friends from London was also running it so we travelled to the start together. I loved it from start to finish, I'd never experienced a race quite like it. I loved running through all the different boroughs, I ran with a few of the NYCPD runners, they were great. As was everyone, the supporters were fantastic. The ankle held up with the help of a shed load of painkillers & tape - I even managed a PB of over 23 mins. I was ecstatic. The medal was huge - much bigger than the British ones. It's still one of my favorites. It was a really special marathon. This is where I really started to LOVE marathon running.

Next up I entered the Chicago Marathon and got through the ballot and should have ran it in 2015 but ended up with a hip injury so I had to defer until 2016. I trained really hard for this one. It was at this point I'd heard about the Abbott World Marathon Majors Series, I'd already ran London & NYC with Chicago being next. Nearly half way there, I thought I'd love to do this, I'd seen the huge medal at the expos, and I wanted it, it was a bit of an elite club, being a six-star finisher, only a few thousand people in the world had done it. It ignited a spark in me, something that grew and grew and took over. It was all I could think about. I knew Boston was always going to be the one that was going to be the hardest one to get into. To me it was the most special one of them all. The one which every marathoner wants. I wanted to run it, but knew I had to really push myself together a qualifying time. I'd heard so much about it from other runners who'd ran it. They made it sound so fantastic, I could see the twinkle in their eyes when they spoke of Boston. I never ever thought I'd actually qualify to ever be part of it. It was a dream. A dream at that point which felt a little out of reach.

So into Chicago I went. There's something really special about the American marathons, I love them. I walked to the start line with my friend, she wasn't running, she'd came with me to Chicago - girl trip:) to support me, we had a great time whilst there. It's strange as I didn't have any pre-race nerves, this was the 1st time I never suffered from it. I was really calm, when I hugged her and left her as I made my way through the security checks and off I went to baggage area.

I watched the sun come up. Made new friends at the start line and then we were off. I knew I had to push myself in this one, I was hoping to bag a BQ time, not really knowing if I'd get it. The first few miles my Garmin was all over the place as we ran through the huge sky scrapers, just run I said to myself, forget the watch and just run, bit silly I know. I never really took a lot of the sights in as I raced my heart out, Boston BQ time on my mind throughout, not really paying attention to my Garmin just knowing I had to give it my all if I was to try and bag a place for Boston. I pushed myself so much, when I crossed that finish line I nearly threw up, and nearly fell over. Looked at my time, thought I'd missed it by a couple of minutes as I knew I had to have a buffer.45 seconds over :(

I was so upset, felt drained, not just physically but mentally. I shed a few tears, I'm glad I had my sunnies on to hide the tears of disappointment. Everything hurt, I felt terrible with having pushed myself so hard, I PB'ed by roughly 14 mins and I should have been ecstatic, but all I could think of was Boston, and that I'd have to push myself even harder again in my next marathon to try and BQ.

It was then my husband text me to say he was so proud of me, that I'd done it and had a buffer of 9 mins for Boston. WTF! Had he gone mad, did he not see my finish time correctly? Then he rang me, he double checked on the site with the times for my age that I needed, and YES I had done it, I'd actually BOSTON QUALIFIED by over 9 minutes. My tears of sorrow had now turned to tears of joy within minutes. OMG I couldn't take it in, I'd actually done it. I couldn't stop crying. It meant the world to me. Here I was, on my road to Boston, I'd done it. I was actually going to get to run in the world's most prestigious marathon on my own merit. There was a bit of celebrating in Chicago that night despite feeling a tad achy.

I came back from Chicago a few days later on a total high. A bit of planning came next as I knew I wanted to finish the Majors in Boston. I knew it was going to be special, running that marathon itself sent shivers down my spine but to receive my 6-star finishers medal in Boston, the holy grail of marathons, would be the icing on the cake.

I entered the lottery for Tokyo but was unsuccessful so approached Sports Tours to see if I could get a package. They were all sold out but I went on the reserve list. A couple of weeks later a place became available, a female had cancelled. Yes, it was all coming together.

Tokyo was an amazing experience and until Boston was my favorite marathon. The night before the race though, I became so close to pulling out as I had developed a bad chest cold days before, it was getting worse. I was awake most of the night and felt so bad. But then when awakening on race morning I pulled the curtains back and there in the morning sunshine was Mt Fuji. Something inside me changed, I was so excited to get ready and get to the start line.

It was chaos as soon as we got out the hotel, met a few friends to wish each other good luck then it was off to our gates and pens. I ran with my roommate to start, I want to take it easy with having this chest cold, but after a few miles I was feeling strong so decided to pick up my pace a bit. Wow the local people were amazing, clapping non-stop, the biggest of smiles, willing you on. I loved every step of that marathon, and it was all down to the people. The course wasn't great but I enjoyed it just the same. Never saw a lot of international runners at all and that seemed nice, also think I was the only one with blonde hair. I somehow managed to finish that one 5 mins off my PB. Crazy happy I was. No 4 done and dusted.

Next up Berlin, I wasn't successful in that ballot either, but they released a further 1000 charity places at an extra cost, as the extra fee was going to a local charity, I managed to get one of those places. My least favorite of the majors. I wouldn't have chosen it if it hadn't been part of the series. I had ongoing issues with my Achilles since coming back from Tokyo, and to be honest wasn't really looking forward to it. Training hadn't gone as well as before, sprained the same ankle a few weeks into training, so was back in the pool for a couple of weeks aqua running. The time soon came around though.

Berlin expo was pure madness, too many folks in a too small a building, and the only one I've ever been where everyone was queuing around the building. There were a few friends I'd made along my journey there so we all hung out together which was great fun. The weekend turned out to be fab! The race went better than I expected it too and I ended up knocking about 20 seconds off my PB- not much but with all the Achilles trouble I was pleased. I ran with a local friend for the first 18 miles and we kept each other going with chatting. After the race a group of us met up at an Irish bar and had the best night ever dancing and singing. I made so many new friends that night, I love this aspect of running, we all have the same thing in common, share a passion, some on the same journey, I love the new friendships that have been made through running.

There's a few of us that have stayed really good friends. It's great to meet up with them at the same events. Ok, so Berlin done, it was back to the UK and get planning for Boston. In a few months it would be time for the biggie.

I became obsessed with Boston. I wanted to know everything about it, for me it was like all my dreams came true the day I qualified but things moved up a notch now that it was getting nearer the big day. A friend told me about Boston Marathon training Facebook page also known as Boston Buddies. It's a great group of folks all obsessed as each other - that's what I love about it, though I can't keep up with the amount of posts, but really helpful with advice on everything about Boston. They're fab!!

When I wasn't training I was non-stop talking about it to everyone, I'm sure my non-runner friends were pretty fed up listening to me. Also, my runner friends who weren't running Boston, ha I'm sure they were pretty fed up too, listening to me going on and on about it. I was so stoked about it, eat, breathe, sleep Boston Marathon.

Training was now done, it was time to go, I was super excited boarding the plane, I'd even had my nails painted with the legendary blue and yellow 26.2. There were a group of us running it, some I knew, some only on social media. It was super exciting to be meeting up with them all in Boston. When we finally arrived, I was blown away right from the start. Never have I seen a whole city get behind a marathon like Boston does. It's like the whole city has marathon fever, blue and yellow colors everywhere, whether it's flags, flowerpots every single person is geared up for it. The atmosphere is electric.

My husband and I had pre-booked to go along to the Boston marathon documentary screening with Dave McGillivray & Amby Burfoot, wow what an evening. I was getting more inspired by the minute. Then there was the blessing of the athletes in the church that touched my heart so much I had to wipe a few tears away. I'd recommend everyone goes to this. We had so much fun doing the Boston 5k too. I knew it was going to feel even more amazing when I was actually running the course. Every single thing about Boston was just awesome. The Runners World pop up store had all the big Boston marathon names doing chats about their experience when running Boston. They all hung about afterwards for a meet n greet - all free events. I can't tell you how I felt when I met the legendary Katherine Switzer, Deena Kastor, & Bobbi Gibb, running heroines. Such special ladies.

Even free medal engraving was going to take place, I couldn't explain it, still can't, it simply put, was just a mind-blowing experience, all of it, and that was before I'd even took part in the race itself.

The weather took a turn for the worse - it was so cold and the wind had started up, it was raining then snowing - weather forecasts on tv were turning it into a horror story, heavy rain was predicted, minus freezing conditions along with gusty winds. Oh well nothing we could do about the weather. After all this was Boston Marathon, NOTHING could dampen my spirits. We'd been out for dinner with friends, the evening before the race, friends from all over the globe, and it was a great night. The running community is the best. everyone was so excited. After dinner it was back to the Bostonian to go through the pre-race ritual of sorting race kit and then bed. I never sleep the night before; this night was no exception. I had butterflies all night.

Waking up on race morning, the weather was the worst yet. It was pouring and the wind was starting to pick up. The excitement was building and by the time I'd hit Boston Common to catch those legendary yellow school buses out to Hopkinton, I was as nervous as hell in a good way. The number of runners with plastic bags on their feet to keep their running shoes dry was hilarious. I wished I'd thought of that as my feet were soaked before I even got on the bus. But still, my spirits weren't dampened. Quick loo stop and FaceTime with my mum back in Scotland, quick hug & kiss to hubby then I was off on the bus. A gent sat next to me, we got talking, he was a journalist and running his 10th consecutive Boston Marathon. Wow talk about inspirational! I was fascinated with his stories. He had run the year of the bombing, as he told me his story my heart strings tugged. You actually feel more in touch with what happened when you are there in Boston, I know when I saw it on tv, I watched in horror, but when you're actually there in Boston it touches you even more so.

We were nearly there and there was actually snow on the ground. Apparently the worst weather Boston had ever seen for marathon day. As I stepped off the bus, I felt overwhelmed. I was actually here at the start about to run the most special race in history. The most iconic race in the world-the holy grail for all marathon runners, and little old me was here. I managed to squeeze under the open sided marquee to get out of the cold and rain, there wasn't much room, hundreds of runners everywhere trying take cover, the floor already muddy and squelchy, but somehow, I managed to bag a spot to get my yoga mat down and sit down and wait. The nerves were starting to build again. The girls I'd sat huddled with just happened to be in

the same starting wave as myself so we chatted, shivering away waiting for our wave to be called. We didn't have to wait long before it was called, time to leave the little shelter and brave the horrendous elements. I was surprised, even in this weather how organized it all was, and how happy everyone was. Not a miserable face in sight. It's true what they say about the spirit of The Boston marathon, we were all soaking wet and cold but we were excited and actually very happy and lucky to be here. Walking to that start line I'll never forget the rows of US uniforms wishing us good luck, they had stood there in this weather for hours and soaked right through but still they smiled and encouraged us. They were fantastic. I felt so lucky and privileged to be here.

I barely had time to get the layers off and we were off. OMG! I was actually running Boston Marathon. My dream for so long was now a reality. I loved the course, with the ups and downs, the rain hadn't let up but I was loving it. The supporters and volunteers were amazing- roaring their hearts out for each and every one of us, the time seemed to pass so quickly. Heartbreak Hill was nowhere near as bad as I thought it was going to be. I saw my husband in the crowd a long way off, I ran over for a quick hug and a kiss and obviously to tell him this was the best race ever. And then, it was nearly over, I could tell I was nearly at the finish when I could hear the deafening roars of crowd support, OMG! Boylston Street was something else, I had tears in my eyes, I had goosebumps all over, from the yelling, the screaming roar of the supporters, encouraging us, so happy for us, willing us on to the finish line. I'll never ever forget it. Special, special memories made right there that day.

I crossed that finish line and it felt almost euphoric. I took a minute and then burst into tears, I'd done it, I'd actually ran the Boston Marathon, it had meant more to me than any other race I've ever ran. A volunteer lady came running up to me, put my medal around my neck, congratulated me and hugged me for what seems ages. All the volunteers that were on the course had been amazing. Actually, everybody had been amazing.

So, after I finally stopped blubbering it was on to the Abbott's tent to receive the medal I'd waited years so to get. I was grinning like a madwoman. I didn't care that I was near frozen to death, I just felt so pumped. I was overcome with emotion; my majors journey had come to a close and what better way to complete it than finishing here in Boston. I couldn't have felt any happier than I did that day. That evening was fantastic, celebrating with so many friends, 8 of us who'd received our six-star medal that day and a whole lot more with the Boston one. Great night.

In the beginning I'd dreamt big, dared to believe, and now here I was in the city of Boston. I'd done it. I'd ran the Boston Marathon, and I'd achieved my dream of being an Abbotts World Majors Marathon Six Star Finisher. I followed my dream and caught it with both hands. If you work hard, it pays off, I was proof of that.

I was disappointed I never met my Boston Buddies from the Boston Marathon Training Facebook group in Cheers after the race, I had to do a toast to all us Boston Buddies, it was just too cold and wet to hang about. I aim to fix that in 2019. I'm coming back. I'm in. I qualified in Berlin in 2017. See you next year!

James Chaves, Bib 10619

Somerset, MA, 47, 3:17:39

4:30 am: My gear bag had been set out the night before. I had to be extra quiet, as to not wake him. When he wakes up it's "Go time." Like many races before, I would be going alone. Christian doesn't tolerate long waits, and this would be the longest! I wanted my wife sleeping. God knows she worked just as hard for this as I did. All the sacrifices she made watching him and keeping him entertained while I logged the miles. Not an easy task for a 17-year-old boy with Down Syndrome and Autism. But my brother had flown in from Alaska and that would have to do.

7:00 am: The atmosphere was both surreal and somber. Was this really happening? It's dark, it's raining, it's damn cold! But yes, after four attempts and a missed entry by 9 seconds I was boarding the bus to Hopkinton to run the Boston Marathon.

It's "La Palozza" all over again. Mud pits, discarded clothes and a sea of humanity. Damn, I should have stayed home and made him breakfast. But no, I decided to chase unicorns!

10:20 am: Screw it, it's just rain. We always walk in the rain. I started thinking if my wife was already walking in the rain. He loves finding street drains and listening to the rain fall. Something unique to Autism. Damn it's going to be a long day with him. No school, crappie weather and no help. Daddy is running "again".

I'm doing it. This is it. All those miles of missed family time had finally led to this and it's fantastic! Everything I imagined. The crowds, the adrenaline. I was in the Boston freaking Marathon. Bring on the cold, rain, wind and hills. I'm going to make them proud and finish this bitch.

1:15 am: The only time I became emotional was at mile 22. I saw my brother standing in the rain. Cold and wet, screaming, "You're doing great! You're on pace!" I practically lost it. I missed my wife. I missed my special boy. Nothing was going to stop me now.

The last two miles threw everything at me. The heavens opened, and buckets of rain fell, followed by wind and all I could think of was how was he behaving for Mom? He's a daddy's boy and by now he was surly ornery. Waiting and wanting me home.

Soon after crossing the finish line, I Facetimed them to share in the joy and to assured him I would be home soon with a surprise and a bed time story.

Boston 2018 was more than a Marathon to me. The journey had serviced as therapy. The sacrifices had paid off. He would earn his medal!

Lori Warwick, Bib 24621

Nanaimo, CAN, 60, 4:06:51

My journey to Boston started four years ago when I realized that I might actually be able to make the qualifying time if I could just get a teeny bit faster. It took three marathons and lots of hard work before I finally got the time I needed. I know some will see me as one of those runners who aged into their qualifying time. And maybe to some extent it is true. On the other hand, it takes a lot of training and perseverance to get faster as we age. I've been running since I was in my thirties, but I didn't do a structured training program until I was in my early fifties. Who knew there was such a thing as hill repeats! I'm 60 now and Boston 2018 was a PR for me. I know I am lucky. I have enjoyed good health; I have a great family; and I have been blessed with a great group of supportive running friends who believed that I could do it. For this I am grateful. I am also grateful to have found the Boston Marathon Training group. Thank you, Vince Varallo, and thank you for giving us this opportunity to share our stories.

Looking back on that day on April 16, 2018, I realize that I had the opportunity to experience something so incredibly amazing. Yes, the weather was terrible, but it was also a real test of physical and mental strength. We faced the storm and rose to the challenge, which just made crossing the finish that much more rewarding. The hardest part was making my way around the sea of mud at Athletes Village, while trying to stay warm. I don't think I've ever been so happy to start a race so that I could get warmed up!

Even though the temperature and wind that day could chill a person to the bone, the memories will always warm my heart--seeing the crowds and hearing the loud cheers, almost deafening at times, running on roads and streets that I had only seen on TV, high fiving spectators, especially the children, hearing "Go Canada!" shouted from the sidelines (so glad I wore my Canada shirt). And then there it was, the turn onto Hereford Street. I will never forget the sea of ponchos on the ground when I came around the corner onto Hereford Street. At first, I thought it was a funny sight, then it quickly became an interesting feat of navigation as we had to make our way through the obstacle course. When I

came around the corner onto Boylston Street, with that famous finish line in front of me, I was hit with the realization that I was about to finish the Boston Marathon. I knew my husband was somewhere in the crowd, but there were so many people. Knowing he was with me was enough. The roar of the crowd and the sight of the finish carried me those last few hundred meters. Even if I run it again, I don't think I will ever have that same feeling that comes with the first time. It was unlike anything I had ever experienced before.

Although there was a lot of anxiety about the weather leading up to race day, I gleaned some great race day tips from the Boston Buddies. The two that really helped me were to coat myself in Vaseline (sounds gross, but it helped to keep me warm) and to wear latex gloves over my running gloves, which kept my hands warm (they still got wet, but they stayed warm). The whole experience was amazing. We enjoyed the city so much. The people were so friendly. I can't say how many times someone apologized to me for the weather. I'm so glad we took the extra time to do some touristy things. If I had to pass on any other advice, it would be to soak it all up. Make an effort to meet fellow Boston

Buddies. Their stories were a great source of inspiration. Go to the speaker events, go to the book signings, wear the jacket, buy souvenirs, and go to the beer tasting! One of my most memorable moments was meeting Kathrine Switzer.

Boston is an amazing place, and it truly is Boston Strong. I honestly don't think I would change a thing. I look back on this now, and I still have to pinch myself. This journey has taken me to a new level as a runner and as a person. Thank you to everyone for the support along the way.

Blake Crossley, Bib 30370

Fort McMurray, AB, 43, 5:18:46

My name is Blake Crossley and I am from Fort McMurray, Alberta Canada. I was fortunate enough to have been selected as a charity runner by Running For Rare/National Organization for Rare Disorders to run the 2018 Boston Marathon. Having multiple heart issues that requires medication and a pacemaker, I am unable to meet the required time to qualify. So when one cannot qualify one must do what it takes to make it to Boston.

Being a bean town fan (Bruins, Celtics and Red Sox), I always wanted to visit Boston. I've always imagined seeing my idol Larry Bird at the Garden, David Ortiz (Big Papi) at Fenway and even Zdeno Chara on the ice (which came true in the playoffs!). Boston has always had a special connection to me ever since I was a kid.

But anyway, as a charity runner I had

to raise money. It is part of the deal when it comes to running as a charity runner, but one that I don't mind doing. Why? Because the community partner or person(s) you are running for, like your family and friends, you are representing are your biggest cheer leaders and elevate you when the days are doubtful, and the path seems impossible. It rekindled a friendship to someone whom I hadn't seen in over 20 years. Tracy Caines Tanner and I were classmates (well she was a year ahead) but we hung out with the same people and both were involved in sports. When I got word about Boston she also got an invite. So we trained with each other and decided to run together. Ah the beauty of sport and virtual training.

I spent many months training in the cold Canadian winter, some days reaching -40 below with 2-3 hours of training. Maybe that's why the day of the race was a treat for me. Take the worst weather possible and stick it over Boston. Heavy Rain, sleet, hail, sun, and wind. A typical Canadian Day! So that was Boston's way of saying, "Welcome Blake!"

I remember the day well, I had to meet my ride to our team's HQ at the Plaza at 6:30am. After saying good-bye to my wife who would meet me at the finish line and posting on Facebook so that people can follow me using the Boston Marathon App (which is amazing btw). I hailed a cab to meet Ross at this infamous hotel. Holy Smokes what a crowd, the energy and vibe. THE CHAOS! So amazing!

We made our way over to our team's HQ and enjoyed each other's company, some fuel and photos before getting on the shuttle that would take us to the outskirts of Hopkinton. I remember talking to my race teammates and just enjoying the moment. Well like Forrest Gump I enjoyed the moment too much and had to use the bathroom. Imagine asking the driver of the shuttle to slow down while I ran outside in the rain using the washroom. Imagine that!

Anyway, when we made our way to the school bus that would take us to the high school, I never experienced a crowd like this. Everyone had the same face (wide eyed and ready to go). Once at the school I became part of the crew on what was the biggest mud bath. Luckily, I remembered to take an extra pair of sneakers, my fuel belt and a few snacks. Thank god the Boston Marathon committee decided to allow an extra bag.

Once there, I trudged through the mud bath and got in line to use the washroom. The sea of people and port-a-potties was pretty cool. We were all like Cheerios floating in a bowl of cereal except it was mud. Picture that! Anyway, I had an hour before my run, so I went to the tents and found a yoga mat that was there by someone who was in an earlier coral/wave. I then texted Tracy and told her where I was and where we would meet. After I went to the use the washroom the weather got worse, I stayed in the port-a-potty until it was time for me to run.

That may sound gross to you but I carefully calculated my make shift change room so I can fuel up, get some energy, slap on some Penaten crap and change sneakers. Once my corral was called I made my way to the start line a half mile from the school and met Tracy. I did notice along the way that the freezing rain/snow had hit and the run off from the tents caused a few snow piles at Athlete's village. A welcoming gift from the running gods to the "ymmtinman", aka me. Thanks! But anyway, water logged but with smiles we began our journey to Bolyston street. HERE WE GO!

Along the 26.2 miles myself and Tracy enjoyed some great conversation, multiple pee breaks, refueling and the best crowd you can imagine. I remember Tracy always saying, "We got this, we got this." I said it earlier that if it wasn't for her, I wouldn't have made it. You see, Boston was my first official marathon. Yup, you would think that a runner of 20 years would at least have done an official 26.2er, nope. I mean I have done the training before and ran over 40km before but that was during the Fort Chipewyan: Dare to Dream quest in 2009/2010. I'll save that for another day.

They say you should be ready for the elements, well I was (5 top layers – 5 bottom layers including 2 ponchos and accidently a bag. You see during all the excitement I forgot to ditch my clear bag with fuel in it. So for 25.2 miles yes 25.2 before ditching the bag I lugged an extra pair of socks, fuel, chews, medical supplies from the start to just outside Herford street. Not bad eh?

Despite the crap weather, the spectators were amazing. I mean I heard "GO CANADA GO", got a few kisses from the girls at Wellesley who can be heard 2 miles up to the ground. Tracy was like do you hear that, I asked what? Then suddenly, I heard this roar, I'm like ohhhhhhh! Anyway, these girls are awesome and more importantly they must have some stock of lip balm. Ah to be a runner enjoying these perks.

Making our way through the course we experienced the 4 seasons and then some. I remember pointing up to a building and seeing a military officer who was positioned on a roof. I muttered sniper? Nervously I waved, and he waved back while giving a nod. Tracy and I both said, "Wow." I believe we saw a few snipers on the route that day. Which was an amazing thing. Why? Because of what happened in 2013 and that they didn't let a senseless act define the race. So I felt like I was being a part of something bigger that day. I have a lot of respect for people who enlist in the armed forces and are the reasons why we have our freedom today.

The crowd, oh how I loved the crowd. There were people handing out towels, fruit, hydration, places to warm up. You name it! They say Seattle has the 12th man in football, well Boston's is the Boston Marathon crowd who get you across the line. Mine was my running partner Tracy.

As we made our way to the finish I had to stop at our team's tent, say hi, refuel and grab a fresh pair of sneakers, hydration and most importantly see the community partners. A 4-minute break from the rain was time enough to sit down, change and be on my way. It felt very much like a pitstop and Team Rare/NORD was my pit crew. So much fun!

I remember entering the Newton Hills and then asking a spectator a little while later, is this Heartbreak Hill? The spectator replied do you want it to be? I had no idea if we were on it or not, I guess being in the zone and facing these brutal elements probably had something to do with it. I was just focusing on not stopping because if I did this day I probably would be walking. That wasn't an option. I do believe though that Heartbreak Hill was where "Whole Lotta Love" by Zepplin came on and then when we went under the bridge Stone Cold Steve Austin's WWE theme hit. Yes, my play list is something else (named after Tessa – the little one I've been running for since 2016) is quite a variety. There is anything from instrumental, to folksy, to rock, to rap. Why be normal? Embrace your inner weirdo.

Anyway with a few miles to go I remember glancing over and seeing Fenway Park, which I still can't believe I was in, and the infamous CITGO sign which meant the finish line is close. I remember taking that infamous "right on Hereford / Left on Bolyston" and thinking I did it! I remember the cheers, the love and seeing my wife just before the finish line. Holy crap what a moment. Hand in hand, friend to friend we finished what we started. Tracy went off to get her medal with her team and I walked 3 blocks and realized CRAP I need to get my medal

– I walked right past where you got the medals and managed to end up where the medical tents were. Excited much?

Anyway, the whole day, despite the weather was fantastic. It challenged all of us, the true running spirit and brought many of us to our limits. 3000+ didn't start that day, 26 of them being pros and I am proud to have finished in less than 5 ½ hours. Not bad for a tinman, a guy whose running days at one time were over.

I texted my wife, called my mom, shot photos and made sure Tessa was on my phone. Proud is an understatement. But when you have the support of your hometown, country, your family, friends, donors, sponsors and ones who believe in your cause and follow your journey you can do anything. XO see you in 2019.

Lisa Newman, Bib 24128

Philadelphia, PA, 58, 4:02:15

This was my fourth Boston marathon and by far the worst weather conditions I had encountered so far - in any marathon. It was not my worst Boston marathon experience, however. I suffered from the cold much more in 2015 because I did not dress correctly and the heat in 2017 almost destroyed me, until a little boy on top of Heartbreak Hill gave me a bottle of ice-cold water - but that's another story.

I'm going to skip over describing transportation to Boston and my accommodations. I just want to say that I am so grateful to Vince Varallo for helping me out and for including me in his great Boston Buddies group.

The night before the race, while I was relaxing in the hotel room, I remembered getting really depressed about the forecasted weather conditions. I called my husband and he reassured me, more or less, that it would be ok. I don't remember his exact words, but I did feel better after our conversation. This was my 13th marathon so I'd been through pre-race anxiety before but not this kind of dread. Anyway, on race morning, after thinking and rethinking what I was going to wear, I ended up making what turned out to be the perfect choice in race clothing. I only had one pair of shoes and didn't bring anything to change into at Athletes' village. I had on a throwaway shirt under a throw away sweatshirt under a clear plastic rain cape. I had three layers of gloves on my hands, thin base layer, plastic, throw away cotton. Sounds like a lot of stuff but I figured some I could just toss if I warmed up.

My shoes were completely soaked just walking to gear check before boarding the bus to Hopkinton. And I started getting cold waiting to get on the bus. We all got pretty cold on the bus ride, too, because some windows were stuck open and the heat wasn't working. Athletes' village was a nightmare. I never saw so much mud and so much debris everywhere. That's all part of the experience for us fourth wave people unfortunately. I waited in the mud for the port-a-potties then stood on someone else's cast off clothing in a tent surrounded by mud and very cold people. I was already shivering, and my toes were numb. Wave three was called and the rest of us waited and waited. We then realized that the pa system had completely disappeared. We still waited a while, but our start time had come and gone and still nobody was calling us up to the start. I just decided to head over to the corrals anyway and see what was happening. My feet were still numb and my shoes were caked with mud during the walk but by the time I made it to the port-a-potties near the start my shoes were clean. I decided to toss my sweatshirt at that point and keep the rain poncho on, which took some doing in the wind and pouring rain.

At the start, there were no corrals, no announcements, no national anthem, no cheering crowds. It was very weird but the volunteers just motioned us to start running, so I did. I was glad I had experienced the real normal race start in previous years.

My memory of the next 21 miles or so is a little vague. These are the things I remember. My wet feet warmed up after the first mile and I never thought about them again. I decided to get rid of another throw away shirt about mile 6 which was a challenge, see above! I also decided to run with my arms and hands inside the poncho to keep my hands a little dryer. When I got too warm, I would just put my arms through the arm holes outside until I got cold again. It worked pretty well.

On the course I noticed how quiet the runners were compared to previous years. People were running with their heads down and the rain and wind were really loud. I tried to run behind groups of people to get some relief from the wind but it didn't work very well. I had a lot of slower charity runners around me so I found myself wasting energy getting around them.

I remember seeing runners stopping a lot and I felt some envy for spectators and volunteers who could just bundle up as much as they wanted and stand under an umbrella! I felt a little irritated when the spectators would cheer louder for every fresh outburst of rain.

Somewhere during the miles leading up to Heartbreak I remember giving up on my BQ goal. My brain gave up, but my body trudged on. I figured I just had to keep moving to get to the finish where my stuff was, and my ride back to the hotel. I was warm enough and nothing hurt so I didn't have a good excuse to DNF.

Heartbreak Hill was exhausting and challenging like it always is. I probably walked some of it. I had been trying to speed up when the wind was calmer and during down hills and slow down uphill against the wind. It probably wasn't even a conscious pacing strategy at that point. There also seemed to be far fewer spectators cheering and much less fanfare then I'd remembered. I wasn't sure if I was actually on the Hill, or over it, or where it was, because it was so hard to see through the rain.

Then I started to speed up. It seems to be what I always do in this race. Five or so miles to the finish, mostly downhill, lots of cheering, Boston sights, I don't know what it is. Here I remember flying! I realized somewhere that a BQ might be possible. The wind was still blowing and the rain was coming down in buckets and the course was flooded and spectators were getting louder. I remember how loud it was. I was so tired at this point. So very tired of fighting that wind.

I finally made it to Hereford and saw the sea of discarded rain ponchos. That was quite a sight. I had to slow down and very carefully make my way up the street because it was very slippery. I stopped briefly to add my poncho to the pile. I apologize to those who came after me on that small stretch of road but one more wasn't going to make a difference! Then it was just around the corner and all the long (long) way to the finish line with a 4:02:15 and a 7:45 cushion for next year. I was so exhausted and so relieved to have finished and qualified again. It's hard to describe the feeling.

I picked up my gear bag and got in line for the women's changing tent. We were standing there in the pouring rain congratulating each other waiting. The cold was just starting to set in by the time I got inside. The tent was crowded and dark with about three inches of standing water on top of more discarded clothing and stuff. I was lucky to get a chair to sit on. I changed into some dry layers and since my hands had stayed warm in three layers, I was able to help other women untie their bags. I gathered my stuff, wrapped myself back up in the finish line poncho and shuffled off across the Commons to Cheers. I stopped once to text my husband and check my phone because my run club friends were texting and messaging me. I was being tracked by a lot of people.

I gained a new feeling of self-confidence from this race and I proved to myself that I was a lot stronger than I thought. And I made some new friends with whom I was privileged to be able to share this experience with.

Vince Varallo, Bib 12992

Fort Washington, PA, 45, 3:20:57

The 2018 Boston Marathon was the eighth time I had lined up for this historic race. My first was in 2011 when conditions were perfect, and Geoffrey Mutai won the men's race in a then world marathon best time of 2:03:02. Yes, 2:03:02, that's an average of 4:41/mile, 2:54/km. On the women's side Caroline Kilel took first place in a time of 2:22:36 and American Desi Davila (Linden) took second place, only two seconds behind! I can remember watching the replay of her finish and thinking, "Wow, I just ran the same race these professional athlete's ran". I also remember being so impressed by Desi's performance that she became my favorite runner to root for. She was a huge underdog but on marathon day it doesn't matter what the pundits say, it's what you say to yourself.

In 2011, I did what a lot of first time Boston Marathoners do and went out way too fast. I was under 7-minute miles for the first 9 miles, with the fastest being mile 4 at 6:22 per mile. But mile 10 was a 7:03 and I never saw sub seven again. By mile 14 I was walking the water stops and as each mile ticked off I walked just a little bit more. Somewhere around mile 22, after I had unintentionally used the Galloway Method to get through the Newton Hills, I was walking again. But a woman came at me from the crowd and approached me saying, "Hey, you didn't come here to walk. Let's go, I'll run with you." I really didn't know how to respond. She started running next to me, so I started running. She kept encouraging me and reminding me that I'm in Boston and this is the greatest marathon in the world. I kept thinking, "Is this real? Did a complete stranger just come out of nowhere to become my personal running coach and cheerleader?" She ran with me for about a quarter mile and finally said, "You've got this, you don't need me anymore, go get your finisher's medal". And with that she disappeared back into the crowd as if she was one of the White Sox players disappearing into the corn fields in the film "Field of Dreams". I ended up finishing in 3:26:02, my worst marathon to date, but then again, it was only my third.

The experience of that first marathon and how that woman touched me by selflessly jumping on the course to get my motor running again will live with me forever and is one of the main reasons why I will try to get back every year. I would love to meet her one day!

Since then I've run every year. I crumbled in the heat in 2012. I finished in 2013 and luckily left the finish area 10 minutes before the bombs exploded. I came back in 2014 and set a personal best of 3:00:08. My goal that year was sub 3, and I know exactly on the course where I lost 9 seconds, Wellesley! 2015 was a year where I had to make some very risky decisions. My wife was due May 4 and couldn't make the drive up with me. She was sure she was going to go into labor that weekend. Literally the Friday before the race we went to her doctor and I flat out asked him if there was any chance she would go into labor in the next 3 days. He first asked me why, so I told him I was supposed to run the Boston Marathon. He looked at my wife and chuckled and said there was a very slim chance this was the weekend. That was good enough for me! I drove up from Philly to Boston Sunday afternoon, got my bib, woke up Monday, ran the race in pouring rain and absolutely miserable conditions, and hopped right back in my car and drove home. I was gone for a total of about 36 hours. And no, she didn't have the baby. 2016 was a bit of a hot year and I went into the race injured and only made it much worse. I finished but had to take the summer off. 2017 was another hot year but I was able to run a 3:21:58, three minutes and two seconds below my qualifying time needed for 2018.

I was counting on my 2017 Boston time to get me into 2018. With over a three-minute cushion I was worried but optimistic that I would get in. I can still remember sitting at work on that fateful day in September when I got the email.

"Sorry your application was not accepted...". The cutoff was 3:23 so I missed it by 21 seconds. This was devastating. My seven-year streak was over. Risking divorce in 2015 was all for naught. I am the administrator of the Boston Marathon Training Facebook group and I wasn't even going to run the race. I must admit, it took a few weeks for me to come to terms with this.

But qualifying wasn't the only way to get into the race. I could go the charity route. First, I emailed the BAA to ask if my streak would still count if I used a charity instead of a qualifier. They said it doesn't matter how you get there, as long as you finish, the streak is alive. Then I looked on the website looking for a charity and saw that most needed you to raise $7500 or more. Ugh, I am not one to ask people for money and I feared I would be on the hook for any monies not raised. And my wife was not having it if I had to shell out from our vacation fund for me to run a marathon! I pretty much gave up on getting in and figured I would just find a marathon in the spring, train real hard, and get back in the next year. October, November, and December rolled along, and I was watching all the posts in my Facebook group from the people starting to train or asking questions about the race. I couldn't help but feel inspired by the energy and excitement all these people exuded in their posts. January rolled around, and I was looking for my mojo. I hadn't really seriously started training for a spring marathon but in the back of my mind I kept contemplating a charity bib. I signed up to run the Utah Valley Marathon that takes place in June, to try to get me jump started and motivated. Finally, at the beginning of February, I started the Hanson's advanced marathon training plan.

Then I got a Facebook alert that John Hadcock mentioned me in a comment. Someone had posted in a trail and ultra-running group that they had a Boston charity bib still available and he was looking for a runner. I looked. I looked again. I did not call my wife. I couldn't resist. I replied back to the post and said I was interested. It was pretty late in the game, so they lowered the fundraising minimum to $5,000. I only had a couple of months to get my act together to raise the funds, train, as well as hold down a full-time job, and raise three kids. I figured at worst I would have to shell out $5,000 out of my own pocket and risk divorce again. "It's only money right, and you can't take it with you," said a voice inside my head.

I then spoke with Deborah Maini with the charity "The Second Step". I hadn't heard of it before and Deborah and I had a lengthy conversation about the cause, where the funds go, and how much the charity meant to her personally. The Second Step helps victims of domestic abuse get their lives back on track. They provide temporary housing for victims and their children. They offer help with legal services, safety planning, counseling, and other essential services. This conversation was a life changing event for me. I stepped back for a second and thought how silly I was because I was just trying to get into a marathon, while this organization is actually helping people who really need it. I wasn't so concerned about raising money anymore and wanted to figure out what I could do to help. The worry about running the marathon seemed quite trivial compared to the obstacles these people were facing. Every minute in America, 20 people are victims of physical violence by an intimate partner. 1 in 3 women and 1 in 4 men in the United States have experienced rape, physical violence, or stalking by an intimate partner in their lifetime. I was a bit shaken after this phone call.

I won't go into the details of how I raised the money, but I will say this, my Boston Buddies came through for me big time! The people in this group are so genuine and supportive and many of them are like family to me. Long story short, I was able to raise what was needed so I could lace up on marathon morning. It's funny when you see how people are concerned that they are a charity runner and aren't as fast as the qualifiers. They often are worried that they aren't worthy of running in the race. What people don't realize is that when the BAA enacted the qualifying standards it wasn't because they wanted the marathon to be limited to elites, it was because they didn't think the towns and the small roads would be able to handle such large crowds. I can tell you I've run this race as both a qualifier and a charity runner and both are equally as hard and anyone who has done either deserves to experience this race.

Sunday, April 15, the day before the marathon and Jon Dunham and Tom Derderian, who directed and produced the "Boston Marathon" documentary, were having a screening of their movie and helping me raise money for The Second Step. I attended the movie and my good friend John Hadcock was there supporting the cause. I distinctly remember a conversation in the hallway of the theater with John and Gene Dykes about John's first Boston Marathon in 2007. This was the monsoon year. Conditions were similar to what was being predicted for the next day. John ran a 3:15:41 and I remember thinking to myself "wow what a great time." I could either worry about the weather and make excuses for why I wouldn't do well, or I could put my big boy pants on, put my head down, and just power through whatever Boston was going to throw at me. I hadn't told John this, but that conversation changed my whole perspective on whether I would let the weather affect the outcome of my race. I made the decision to stick to my game plan and try to reach my goal of a BQ.

Race morning rolled around and I woke up early and immediately looked out the window. Ugh, rain was pelting at the window. I could hear the taps of ice scraping the window as I glared outside still hoping the weather forecasters were wrong. Oh well, there wasn't anything I could do about the weather, so I just needed to be prepared. I had on a long-sleeve Under Armor tech shirt, my Boston Buddies running shirt, a black throw away hoodie, running tights, shorts, a head-wrap to cover my ears, my 2009 Philadelphia Half Marathon running gloves (not waterproof!), and my 2013 Marine Corps Marathon hat. I remember getting hot in the room and asking my roomie, Lisa, if she thought I had too much on. I was actually worried I would get too hot out on the course. I wasn't planning on wearing a poncho or anything plastic as I knew that would overheat my body. I was concerned my legs would get hot. She asked a simple question, "Do your legs usually get cold?" I thought about it and knew if I was running a marathon my body would warm up, so I decided to ditch the running tights and just run in shorts. I put on a pair of throw away sweatpants, so I wouldn't freeze on the way to the start, an old pair of sneakers, and put my marathon shoes under my hoodie to keep them dry, and out the door I went.

Lisa and I drove to the start where we would catch the bus to Hopkinton. I just remember thinking, "What are we doing?" as we drove through pelting sleet and rain. We parked in a lot near Boston Common and I walked to the buses. Lisa stayed back in the car because she was in a later corral, so I was on my own now. I was walking as close to the buildings as possible to try to shelter myself from the rain. When I got to Boston Common there was no place to hide but the rain eased a bit. The mood was not the normal cheery party like atmosphere filled with smiling runners about to embark on their dream race. Instead it was a large mass of hooded strangers hustling to seek shelter in the first bus they could get on to. Once I boarded the bus I moved to the back near the heater. I remember thinking this felt like the yellow school bus I had to take after a white-water rafting trip where everyone was soaked, and everything just smelled damp. The bus finally left Boston Common for Hopkinton and I just stared out the window. I could feel the cold air coming off the window pane. We were driving through rain and passing small snow piles that still hadn't melted. I usually like to talk to the runners around me on the bus but not this time. The mood was really somber.

We finally arrived at Hopkinton Middle School and I couldn't believe my eyes. I've run this seven times before and I didn't recognize the place. I was used to a huge party with runners wrapped in last year's heat blanket. Volunteers handing out bananas, Gatorade, Gu, water, whatever you need. This year the field was nothing but mud. There didn't seem to be any grass on the field and the mud was deep. As I shuffled off the pavement into the field my shoes were sinking, and it felt like I was walking with suction cups on. I was lucky though; Gary McNamee from Outside Interactive had offered to have me and 12 runners join him at his headquarters on the start line of the marathon. However, I was in wave 2 and when I went to leave Athlete's Village the volunteers wouldn't let me leave because I didn't have a red bib. I didn't want to start an argument, so I ventured under the humungous white tent that seemed to be the only shelter for all the runners. I still had on my throw away clothes and wasn't cold, but I was wet. I was doing whatever I could to keep my running shoes dry hidden under my sweatshirt. Once they called for wave 2 I darted out of the tent and began my trek to the start line. I finally made my way to the Outside Interactive office with only about 15 minutes before my wave started. I joined my fellow Boston Buddies on the third-floor office and had a bird's eye view of all the runners in the corral. I was debating whether I would rush and run with wave 2 or wait it out and just run in wave 4. I took off my sweatshirt and sweatpants and changed my socks and shoes with the dry pair I had hidden under my sweatshirt. What a difference it made when I put my dry socks and shoes on. My buddy Carlos from Guatemala was with me and he was also set to start in Wave 2. I kind of got a second wind when I removed all the wet clothes and stood up to head to the start corral with Carlos. We both scurried along the outside of the gates around the start and headed to our respective corrals. I wished him good luck and I would see him at the finish. We both got into our corrals with only about a minute to spare before they sent us off.

My stretch goal was 3:10, my realistic goal was 3:20, my fall apart goal was just to finish. I started out feeling OK. My strategy was to stay in the middle of the road and take it easy for the first half of the marathon and then see how I felt and possibly negative split. I remember seeing Boston Race Director, Dave McGillivray's interview in the Boston Marathon documentary the night before saying, "If you run a smart race and leave something for after the Newton Hills you could pop a good time." Well that was my plan, conserve and turn it on after the hills. The rain really wasn't bothering me. There definitely were lulls in the rain but then there was also gusts of wind and periods of hard downpours too. But once I was wet it really didn't matter to me how much wetter I got. As long as I was warm I was fine. My head-wrap was keeping my ears warm and even though I was in shorts I wasn't cold. Whenever it got windy I would tuck behind other runners and I didn't care about pace, but when there was a break I would dart around the pack.

I started out with 8:13, 7:56, 8:03, 7:40, and 7:53. These were nice comfortable splits for me. I can usually tell within the first few miles of a marathon if I'm going to have a good race and I was feeling it today. I just wanted to control my urge to run faster and save it for the second half. I didn't want any mile faster than 7:30 or slower than 8:15. I almost broke that rule when I got to Wellesley. I love the girls at Wellesley. The crowd this year was a bit smaller than previous years but the people who were there were much rowdier. They were all soaking wet, the ink was running down on their signs as if they were crying. I wanted to give people an idea of what Wellesley is all about, so I actually whipped out my phone and went Facebook live! I ran on the right side of the road and must have kissed 18 girls as I was running by. It really rejuvenated me as it always does. I always enjoy Wellesley and it's something you just don't get in other marathons.

I made it past Wellesley with an 8:13 mile. No biggie. I was feeling good and trying to soak in the whole experience. I crossed the half way mark in 1:43:43. That's when runner math entered my head. I knew 3:10 was out of the question at this point, but 3:20 wasn't and I need a 3:25 to BQ for next year. I just needed to run a 1:37 for the second half and I'd have a fighting chance to get into Boston next year. I was feeling great actually. I wasn't cold, my energy was feeling good, and I actually thought the rain was helping me from overheating. I can remember running at one point when the rain let up and shouted out "this isn't so bad" and I thought the runners around me were going to kill me. Anyhow, I turned it up a bit on the second half. I had a 7:30, 7:27, 7:12, 7:36, and 7:31 to start the second half. If I could keep up this pace until after the hills I could turn it on for the last few miles and hit my goal. Heartbreak was my slowest mile on the back at a 7:50 pace, but I really felt good at the top of Heartbreak and then rattled off a 7:13, 7:11, 7:06, and 7:07 for the next four miles.

As I entered the city of Boston and passed the historic Citgo sign I distinctly remember the crowds. They were getting larger and larger and louder and louder. I couldn't believe these people had been standing in the cold, rain, and wind for hours and were still so electric. I high-fived as many of them as I could as to say, "Thank you." The fans of the Boston Marathon are what will keep me coming back as long as they'll have me.

At mile 26, I slowed down a bit as I ran down Boylston street to soak it all in. I crossed the finish line in 3:20:57. I did it! I actually had a 6-minute negative split in Boston on one of the toughest days possible. I was ecstatic when I crossed the finish line and the icing on the cake was I finished just behind my buddy Carlos and we met up as we were getting our heat blankets. We then ran into Eric Carpenter and Stefan Ljungberg from the Boston Buddies page. We were all within a few minutes of each other and somehow were able to spot each other in a sea of silver shiny blankets. I remember hugging Carlos and taking a selfie with him. It was great to celebrate with these guys who had trained with me for the previous 4 months.

I look back on the 2018 Boston Marathon and the amazing journey I had getting there. From missing the cut, to meeting the Second Step, to meeting so many new friends sharing the same goal. The weather was just one more obstacle I had to get past to get to the finish line. I wouldn't trade this experience for anything! In fact, I hope we do it again in 2019!

Made in the USA
Middletown, DE
20 November 2018